W9-AMT-631

Politics in the Rural States

Also of Interest

The Family in Rural Society, edited by Raymond T. Coward and William M. Smith

† *Education in Rural America: A Reassessment of Conventional Wisdom,* edited by Jonathan P. Sher

† *Poverty in Rural America: A Case Study,* Janet M. Fitchen

Rural Education in Urbanized Nations: Issues and Innovations, edited by Jonathan P. Sher

Rural Society: Research Issues for the 1980s, edited by Don A. Dillman and Daryl S. Hobbs

The Myth of the Family Farm: Agribusiness Dominance of U.S. Agriculture, Ingolf Vogeler

† Available in hardcover and paperback.

A Westview Special Study

Politics in the Rural States:
People, Parties, and Processes
Frank M. Bryan

As the states gain prominence in the political arena and rural areas increase in population, a new perception of the importance of rural state politics is called for. Frank M. Bryan investigates political processes in three rural states—Montana, Mississippi, and Vermont—representing the western, southern, and eastern regions of the United States. Using these states to note similarities and variations in the model, he describes how the political systems of rural states operate overall and then presents a detailed comparative analysis of the three states in terms of political participation, parties and elections, and legislative policymaking. In a final essay he identifies the kinds of political patterns that may be found in rural states in the future.

One major contribution of the book lies in its reliance on extensive data sets, used for the first time to provide in-depth comparative treatment of rural states.

Dr. Bryan, assistant professor of political science at the University of Vermont, is the author of *Yankee Politics in Rural Vermont.*

Politics in the Rural States: People, Parties, and Processes

Frank M. Bryan

Westview Press / Boulder, Colorado

A Westview Special Study

Copyright © 1981 by Westview Press, Inc.

Published in 1981 in the United States of America by
    Westview Press, Inc.
    5500 Central Avenue
    Boulder, Colorado 80301
    Frederick A. Praeger, Publisher

Library of Congress Cataloging in Publication Data
Bryan, Frank M
    Politics in the rural states.
    (Westview special study)
    Bibliography: p.
    Includes index.
    1. Local government—United States. 2. United States—Rural conditions. I. Title.
JS425.B79   1981   320.973   80-22998
ISBN 0-89158-561-3
ISBN 0-89158-984-8 (pbk.)

Printed and bound in the United States of America

To
Melissa Lee:
She fills up my senses

Contents

Tables and Figures

Acknowledgments

Certain people were of special help in the development of this book. At Montana State University in Bozeman, my secretary Cathy Johnson kept my life organized and my spirits up with her consistent pleasantness and optimism. Political scientists Jerry Calvert and Lauren McKinsey at MSU and Jim Lopach at the University of Montana helped me to better understand Montanan politics. Richard Roader and Mike Malone, historians of the land under the big sky, added perspective and insight to my efforts, and Pierce Mullin and John Jutila added enthusiasm. Jerry Gabris at Mississippi State and Jim Lowen of the University of Vermont filled in gaps in my understanding of Mississippi politics.

My colleagues in the Political Science Department at the University of Vermont, Garrison Nelson and Chuck Bann, were always willing to cock an ear in my direction if need be. Clark Bensen's insistence on precision at the Government Research Center was therapeutically helpful. Stan Staron worked hard to make the rigors of research in the context of a busy teaching schedule less painful. Barbara Noel and Ilene Barth were involved in many of the more technical aspects of book building, and their efforts are deeply appreciated. Several students made contributions, including Jim Gilbert, Matt Hayes, Janine Grewcock, and my graduate teaching assistant and sidekick Britta Anderson. Special thanks go to Karen McKnight who spent two summers over data sheets and in front of computer terminals on my behalf, brightening what were sullen tasks with her smile and good cheer.

To Fred Praeger goes a heartfelt thank you for his faith in me and in the subject matter. Miriam Gilbert at Westview Press has been patient and kind, and to Megan Schoeck, also at Westview, goes the credit for the final skillful polishing of the manuscript. Most of all I deeply appreciate the efforts of my wife, Lee, who recorded tens of thousands of roll call responses and infinite numbers of election results, suffered through the coding of thousands of biographical sketches of state legislators, typed the manuscript twice, and throughout the three years it took to complete the data base maintained her status as the sexiest wench in the galaxy.

F.M.B.

Politics in the Rural States

Introduction:
Country Songs for City Folks

Fifty degrees below zero was to him just precisely fifty degrees zero. . . .
It did not lead him to meditate upon his frailty as a creature of temperature
. . . and from there to the conjectural field of . . . man's place in the
universe.

— *Jack London,* "To Build A Fire"

Blind, jazz-soul musician Ray Charles is an urban black man. But
when he published the album Modern Sounds in Country and Western
Music, a decade before Watergate, he displayed a profound clarity of vi-
sion. The album's success forewarned a watershed of cultural values that
would broadcast a clear message to an urban nation: Come back to rural
America.

The Rebirth of the Rural Ethic

The message was heard. And it was heard first by the commercial
establishment. "A bottle of Coke" carried Americanism around the globe
in the 1960s but returned to the front porches of small midwestern farm-
steads and became, like the land around it, "the real thing"—akin to
dances on Saturday night and "the song that the bluebird sings." It was
possible to "take Salem out of the country" but impossible to "take the
country out of Salem." Luxury automobiles were driven from the city
and advertised in apple orchards; fried chicken was served up on the
lawn of the First Congregational Church; beer was alternately sipped and
guzzled in the shadows of tractors and combines; and meanwhile, out
West, the Marlboro Man rode lonely, his steel gray eyes peering into the
past reflecting the glint of rural virtues—hard work, pain, solitude; the
price one paid for clean air, pure water, real friends, and meaningful
relationships—the good life, the rural life.

The message was also heard by politicians. If his campaign in total was
a debacle (as many claim), George McGovern's campaign slogan was a

work of genius. Come Home America, it said. Come home from Southeast Asia? Yes. Neoisolationist? Perhaps. But the slogan's power was generated from a bond with the quickening heartbeat that was pulsing loud and clear from "the outback," a heartbeat that McGovern himself must have heard on the prairies of his South Dakota homeland. It is difficult to tell if the cry to Come home America packed any punch in the polling booth. But it is clear that it was linked to something very real indeed, something Barry Goldwater sensed was afoot only two campaigns earlier from his position on the far right of the Republican party. In your heart you know he's right, the campaign slogan said. Both Goldwater and McGovern were aware of this new romanticism flowing from the countryside. Both men sensed that urban rationalism was under attack, and both asked that we pay attention to the values of simplicity, straightforwardness, and morality—romantic values, rural values. Jimmy Carter ran for the presidency and won on those values. Ronald Reagan, for good or ill, used them to perfection in 1980.

The call was heard on the airwaves, where reflections of American culture are portrayed for all to see. Although the spotlights of popular music have shifted here and there during the decades since the end of World War II, there has been a steady increase in the popularity of "country" in the huge area of popular music where the records are sold. Country rock star Jerry Lee Lewis knew how to say it best: Country Songs for City Folks read the cover of his album. In the 1940s and 1950s when country-music singers lamented the loss of rural life, they sang to lost brethren who had been driven to the great cities by the Depression. They sang words like

> The world was dark and God made light
>   To brighten up the night.
> But the God above that made the stars
>   Didn't make those city lights.
> They're just a place for men to hide
>   When things don't turn out right.
> A masquerade for loneliness, behind those
>   City lights. [from "City Lights," by Bill Anderson]

But Hank Williams's generation sang to a minority. Seldom, if ever, did country music break onto the nationwide best-selling charts.

By 1970 the situation had changed radically. Now Johnny Cash was singing to the nation, and he performed on stages far away from Nashville, Tennessee. Welshman Tom Jones, one of the most popular male vocalists of the middle to late 1960s, sold millions of copies of the song "Green, Green Grass of Home" by Curly Putnam.

The old home place is still standing
  Though the paint is cracked and dried.
There's the old oak tree that I used to play on
. . . .
Yes they'll all come to meet me
  Arms reaching, smiling sweetly
It's good to see the green, green grass of home.

Jones sold these records to middle-class urban Americans. Glen Campbell replaced the urban wit of "The Smothers Brothers" with an hour of prime-time Arkansas "pickin' and singin'" on CBS. All the way from the mountains of rural West Virginia to the Rocky Mountains of the West, John Denver has pounded out a simplistic and recurring theme to a vast national audience. He sings of "country roads," "Rocky Mountain high," "a night in the forest," and "a truck out on the four-lane." He sings, "thank God, I'm a country boy" and "sometimes this old farm seems like a long, lost friend." Throughout the agonizing withdrawal from Vietnam and the long, debilitating struggle with Watergate, John Denver reminded Americans of the world out there past the traffic lights. By so doing he became one of the most popular male vocalists in the nation. The message of the 1940s and 1950s (the city is bad) was a cry of anguish sung for rural folks gone away. It has been replaced by a message of hope sung for urban people. The new words say simply, rural life is good. No longer negative and sung to displaced rural minorities, the songs now are majority songs, rural songs.

The generation that refused to go to war had no trouble hearing the message from rural America either. For the young who turned their backs on contemporary life-styles in the 1960s, a profoundly consistent magnetism lured them in similar directions. These directions pointed outward, back, away—away from the smog and congestion and crime of the cities; away from the stultification of life in the suburbs; away from the sterile classrooms of the city colleges; and away from the complications and contradictions of Vietnam and the bomb, the perceived hypocrisies of organizational life, and the mass denominator that seemed to insist on sanding down the face of American culture to a smooth, mirror-like polish. The directions pointed toward rural America. Charles Reich understood. He called his book *The Greening of America* and early on he says,

For one almost convinced that it was necessary to accept ugliness and evil, and that it was necessary to be a miser of dreams, it [the new consciousness] is an invitation to cry or laugh. For one who thought the world was inevitably encased in metal and plastic and sterile stone, it seems a veritable greening of America.[1]

Reich insists that the enemy is the "corporate state." But his language brings to mind the words of Thomas Jefferson, "those who labor in the earth are the chosen people of God. . . . The mobs of great cities add just so much to the support of pure government, as sores do to the strength of the human body."[2] Much of *The Greening of America* echoes this Jeffersonian ethic. Metal and plastic and stone, ugliness and evil, loneliness, emptiness, isolation — these are the catchwords of Jefferson's view of the city. And how is America to be saved? Reich tells us that America will become *green,* like "flowers pushing up through the concrete pavement." Although in retrospect one might wonder whatever became of the revolution that Reich claimed was "spreading with amazing rapidity," one thing is clear: Reich's Consciousness Three is more than a mere figment of an active imagination. And, in essence, this new level of consciousness is not so new at all. Indeed, John Denver described it in his hit record "Take Me Home, Country Roads." The consciousness is "older than the trees, younger than the mountains, growing like a breeze." It is a simplistic consciousness, a day-by-day consciousness, a romantic consciousness, a rural consciousness.

Finally, the message was also received by the new cadres who arose to fight the battle to save the American urban place. Urbanologists have had their ears cocked in the direction of rural America, and as a result their strategies include the notion of bringing rural America back to the cities. Greenbelts, urban open places, and rural corridors are the stuff of which urban plans are made. According to the huge majority of urban planners, architects, and managers, beauty does not mean cement, it means grass. It does not mean density, it means space. It does not mean people, it means wildlife, birds, and squirrels. It does not mean gray, it means green. Engineering ruralism into the city is a basic theme of one of the world's great scholars of urbanism, Lewis Mumford. "In the cities of the future, ribbons of green must run through every quarter, forming a continuous web of garden and mall, widening at the edge of the city into protective greenbelts, so that landscape and garden will become an integral part of urban *no less than rural life* (italics added)."[3]

At one point Mumford suggests that the back alleys of Philadelphia be plowed up and turned into green pedestrian malls "threading through the city, now widening into pools of open space surrounded by restaurants, cafes, or shops." In the spring of 1980 a group of urban designers planned a new pedestrian mall for tiny (population 38,000) Burlington, Vermont, the largest "city" in an ultra rural state. Controversy arose over the creation of a waterfall on the main street. Some questioned the wisdom of implanting a fake rural landscape in the middle of Vermont's primary urban center when the real thing dominates every horizon. Let the city be a city, said the protestors.

The extent to which the ruralization process permeated the ranks of urban planners can best be appreciated by assessing the reaction that greeted one scholar who suggested that destiny, diversity, a certain chaos, and, in short, "hustle-bustle" are germane to the city; that they are in fact the critical elements that have made cities great. Rather than bring the countryside into the city, Jane Jacobs (*The Death and Life of Great American Cities* and *The Economy of Cities*) said that what is needed is an intensification of density, diversification, and dynamic, random patterns of interpersonal relations. The city, as a city, said Jacobs, *thrives* on these qualities. To swap them for a transfusion of ruralism would ultimately destroy the urban essence that has spawned so much creativity and culture in America. Perhaps, this daughter of New York City suggested, by removing all the "tumors" associated with urbanism, we will destroy the body itself and the city will be gone.[4]

Professional urban scholars reacted with near-universal shock and dismay. Mumford himself led the attack in a scathing review in the *New Yorker,* which was reprinted as "Home Remedies for Urban Cancer" in his collection of essays, *The Urban Prospect.*[5] The urbanologists laid down a blanket gunfire, and when the smoke cleared, Jacobs's position had (at least in the short term) been overrun. The city of the future would be a place where order produced simplicity, where green replaced brick, where space dispersed "the lonely crowd." The modern American city must become a place of slow living, a place of neighborliness, and a place where birds sing and flowers bloom, where children romp and dig, where shaded and tranquil pathways are conducive to moments of solitude and contemplation—in short, a rural place.

The People Return to the Land

The message has not remained muffled in the ears of the people themselves. They are returning to the land. The great urban pendulum reached its apogee in the fifties, hovered nearly motionless in the sixties, and began to swing back in the seventies. It will take some time for this fact to be recognized, and the implications of the phenomenon will be resisted heartily. But the operative principle governing population movements in the United States is real: Americans are going back.

Some are inching away from the megalopolis into the hill country of northern New England, into the little towns and villages. In Vermont the newcomers from the cities are seeking out and resettling the rural areas. They are swelling the state's total population, and at the same time they are increasing the rural-to-urban ratio. Twenty-five hundred miles to the West others are returning to the towns of the Great Plains. In Montana, where the distance from New York City to Chicago marks the distance between the northwest and southeast corners of the state, the rush to the cities that typified the decade of the fifties had ground to a near halt by 1970. Below the Mason-Dixon line in Georgia and Louisiana and Mississippi, the counties of the rural hinterland are finding new life. Slowly, nighttime shows the blinking of house lights where there had been none before. Blacktop roads are winding back to where earlier there had been only solitude and dust. To a nation attuned to the word "urbanization," this new development has received little notice, perhaps because our attention has been concentrated for some time on the exodus of population from the core city to the suburbs. But behind the camouflage of suburbanization, a large portion of those leaving the cities have continued on past the labyrinth of suburban sprawl into rural America.

In the spring of 1975 the first annual National Conference on Rural America was held in Washington. At that conference an economist from the U.S. Department of Agriculture, Calvin Beale, presented a remarkably perceptive paper entitled "Where Are All the People Going?" Beale makes two basic points in his paper, and both are noteworthy. First, he shows that the urban tide has crested and is receding; second, that the end of urbanization involves more than a simple spillover into suburbia. Counties "well removed from metro influence" are greatly affected by the swing in migration patterns. Counties at the rural extreme (with no town of even 2,500 people) gained population between 1970 and 1973 in a manner that suggests suburbanization has given way to ruralization.[6]

The wisdom of the rural sociologists seeps ever so slowly into the founts of America's opinion. But in the spring of 1980, with the 1980 census impending, the *New York Times Magazine* took note of the ruralization process in a major cover story entitled "Suburbia: End of the Golden Age." Says author William Severini Kowinski, "But more and more Americans are choosing not to live in big cities or their suburbs, either. In what Dr. Peter A. Morrison of the RAND Corporation calls 'one of the most significant turnabouts in migration in the nation's history,' areas outside metropolitan boundaries are growing faster than either cities or suburbs."[7]

Of equal importance to the reversal of the tendency of intensely rural counties to lose population is the nature of the new population growth. Since these are areas where there is a scarcity of adults of child-rearing age, growth has come principally from immigration, not natural increase. People are moving back into these sparsely settled areas by choice.

This choice is reflected in the popular-opinion polls. In 1966 only 22 percent of Americans responded "city" when asked in a Gallup poll, "If you could live anywhere in the United States that you wanted to, would you prefer a city, a suburban area, small town, or farm?" Twenty-eight percent said suburban area, 31 percent said small town, and 18 percent said farm.[8] In the ensuing decade, the popularity of cities dropped still further, and by 1976 over half of all Americans were specifying rural areas as the place they would like most to live. In August 1977, a Harris poll recorded a whopping 73 percent saying they would rather live in open country than in a city.[9] Open country. The circle is complete. The frontier has been reopened.

In short, after two hundred years of national life, Americans are in the process of refilling the massive empty spaces that were left when the great rural exodus occurred. In doing so they have reversed a trend that has been dominant in America for a century and have ended a pattern that has riveted the attention of social scientists for the past twenty-five years. There will be totally new problems created, while analysis of the old pattern (urbanization) is still warm. The symptoms sketched above predicted the change. The facts bear it out.

Paying Attention to the Backbeyond

Even if there were no rebirth of the rural ethic and even if the people were not leaving the cities, it would still be time for a fresh look at the manner in which rural people govern themselves and are governed by others. In 1973 fully one-quarter of all Americans lived in non-metropolitan counties, and more than 27 million lived in nonsuburban, nonmetropolitan counties. These are the people that produce our food. These are the people that stand watch over our recreational areas. These are the people that mine our copper, produce our lumber and paper, and bring life and light to the pathways that link our great cities. Most critically, these are the people that live close to the energy resources that we have earmarked for national consumption.

Despite this pattern of population distribution and despite the fact that hundreds of books have been produced in recent years on urban politics and metropolitan problems, there has not been a single book published exclusively on rural politics in America for over two decades. It is as if the rural areas have been wiped from the consciousness of American political scientists. Indeed, nearly all the works that have considered rural areas have focused on the conflict between rural and urban, as if some mystic causation has perpetuated forever the tension that allegedly existed between the two in the past.

Academia has hardly abandoned the rural areas completely. Solid research continues to be done by sociologists, agricultural historians, and economists. But the same cannot be said for students of government, politics and public affairs, and policy. The reasons for this neglect are not hard to distinguish. First, the metro-bias in political science stems from the nature of the professionals in the discipline. Most political scientists are urban people, and they view the world in cosmopolitan terms. More than that, the cadre of political scientists that nurtured the behavioral approach to the science, with its spin-offs in quantitative lore and hard-core empiricism, have been even more urban than the professionals of the discipline as a whole. They have dominated the research on state and local politics that has appeared in the journals in the last twenty years, leaving what few rural political scientists there were in the backwash of methodological approaches and technical skills.

Next, an ideological component is involved. Rural areas have been traditionally viewed as bastions of conservatism, where "red-necks" and "Birchers" abound, where simpletons mired in the Protestant ethic sling darts at reform, where proposals for change are met with stoic and hostile negativism. This kind of view of the countryside has done little to magnetize the interest of political scientists. Finally, political scientists have been anchored to the metropolis because that is where the action has been. In the 1960s it seemed as if the life of the American city was in danger of being snuffed out, and this crisis produced lucrative opportunities for scholarship. Obtaining grants to study the political socialization of minority groups in the city was no difficult task during that period. It was a different matter to ask for funds to study the problem of the population drain on services in rural counties.

Perhaps this focus was as it should be. After all, it was hard to detect a pulse in rural America in the 1950s and 1960s, while the heartbeat of the city throbbed violently, painfully—leaving the entire nation gasping for breath. It seemed to matter little how the folks left back on the farm conducted their public affairs. Now, however, the situation has changed. If the city mouse could ignore the country mouse with impunity before, the city mouse now must pay attention to his cousin in the sticks. Now the city mouse wants things the country mouse has. He has clean air and water. He has a hold on the recreational areas, and he has the energy resources to heat homes and light offices. He has a rural life-style.

A poignant illustration of this shift is the bumper sticker that appeared on automobiles in the sparsely settled provinces of western Canada when residents there realized that the eastern provinces were very suddenly and uniquely dependent on the long-neglected rural West for energy supplies. Let the bastards freeze in the dark, it read. In America the newly important resources of the rural states provide compelling reasons for reflection on the part of those urbanologists who have for so long dismissed the rural-urban nexus as unworthy of serious study.

Take, for instance, the acute need for recreational space for city dwellers. Lying just to the north of America's East Coast megalopolis is the quiet, green state of Vermont. With a tiny population scattered over hundreds of square miles of forested granite, speckled with lakes and ribboned with rivers, this land of the Green Mountains was bypassed by the urban-industrial revolution and so remains a natural backyard playground for 50 million people. But Vermont has a mind of its own. It has proclaimed that it is "not for sale," passed tough land-use laws, discouraged the coming of more people from the cities, and in effect closed its borders to all but the very wealthy who can afford the price of Vermont real estate and land taxes. What happens in the town meetings of Vermont's local democracy has a profound bearing on whether or not in the future there will be a convenient safety valve to ease the pressure of hot summers in the cities of the East. We have heard much of the "leisure-time explosion." Why have we heard so little about rural politics?

Or, consider the example of Rosebud County, Montana. Situated just south of the Yellowstone River and just west of the Little Bighorn where Custer fell, Rosebud County contains over five thousand square miles of land, about six thousand people (a bit more than one per square mile), a portion of Custer National Forest, a Cheyenne Indian reservation, and one of the richest coal deposits in the United States. The largest town is Forsyth with 1,873 inhabitants. The farmers and ranchers of Rosebud County are worried about the impact that strip mining for coal will have on their lives. The nation needs Rosebud's coal. The cities of the North need it for heat in the winter; the cities of the South need it for cooling in the summer. The nation will probably have Rosebud's coal if it wants it. But one thing is clear. There will be a struggle, and the people of Rosebud, all six thousand of them — presiding over a territory bigger than Connecticut, outgunned and massively outnumbered like Custer himself — will not go down without a fight. When we go after their coal, as it seems we will surely do, might it not be wise to know something about their governance so that the bloodletting on both sides may be minimized? We have heard much about the energy crisis. Why have we heard so little about rural politics?

There are those who argue that the nation's new interest in rural America stems directly from the urban crisis of the 1960s. When migration of the rural poor to the cities was found to be a prime factor in the causal chains that lead to urban disaster, many prominent politicians in Washington began to voice the view that the best way to settle the problems of the cities was to shut off the faucets of migration from the countryside. To do this rural America had to be made attractive and refurbished with economic transfusions — in a word, developed. The symbols of a new generation of policy priorities began to crop up: A presidential task force on rural development was created, and a coalition for rural America was organized. Slowly, a policy began to emerge, culminating in the Rural Development Act of 1972. In a paper presented before a 1972 symposium on rural development that was sponsored by several rural interest groups, including the North Central Regional Center for Rural Development, Jerry Walters pinpointed the principal causative point in the creation of the new policy directives. "A number of congressmen began to propose that the economic development of our rural areas was one of the best ways to ease the burdens of the cities."[10] This is a selfish reason to be interested in the rural areas, perhaps, but nevertheless an interest has developed. We are hearing more and more about rural America from the policymakers of an urban nation. It is time we heard more about rural politics from the academics.

The Plan of the Book

The paucity of research on rural politics sets the direction of this volume in several ways. First, it demands that the methodological thrust be descriptive and analytical rather than theoretical. A descriptive analysis of what now exists must preface any responsible attempt to construct a theory or model of rural politics. We cannot hope to establish causal linkages before we clearly understand the constituent elements that might be formed into a predictive equation. Therefore, the great bulk of this volume seeks to describe in a meaningful way (or analyze) what goes on politically in rural systems.

Second, it is not possible to glean enough material from only secondary sources to even begin a descriptive, analytical treatment. Most books on urban politics, for instance, are constructed from material sprinkled throughout the literature. But in the field of rural politics, the shelf is remarkably bare, and it is necessary in large part to generate one's own data. This parameter also helps to set the tone of the book and guide its organization. Finally, since so little has been done, one must make difficult decisions about which items in the array of legitimate political concerns to focus on. One cannot hope to cover in a single volume a spectrum-wide number of political phenomena even though no book can be complete without such a range.

With these constraints in mind, I have developed the book in two parts. The first part treats the nation as a whole, and the first two chapters attempt to describe and analyze (1) the socioeconomic characteristics of those who populate the rural areas of America, with an eye cocked to some comparison with the same characteristics of urban dwellers; (2) the political views and behavior of rural dwellers in juxtaposition to their urban cousins (Chapter 1, "Country Mouse and City Mouse"); (3) the socioeconomic environment of rural as opposed to urban states; and (4) the elements of the political systems of the rural states, contrasting them with those of the urban states (Chapter 2, "Rural States in an Urban Nation: Patterns of Politics").

Two notions about the nature of the beast we are studying prescribed this particular organizational format of the first two chapters. One notion is that socioeconomic and political systems are helplessly entwined and that it is the former and not the latter that comes first in the causal order of things. This causal priority was utilized, not because the author necessarily accepts it or because a rigorous testing of the hypothesis is contemplated, but because it is the model subscribed to most often in the science, and it provides a good heuristic framework for analysis. The second notion is that it is useful (perhaps even necessary) to compare urban and rural peoples and systems in any analysis of rural politics. For urban politics this procedure is not necessarily useful. Setting out only the dimensions of city politics provides an understandable script for most Americans since most Americans are urbanites or in other ways linked to the urban experience. But to discuss rural politics in a vacuum is to deny most readers a very handy reference point – the dimensions of their own political systems. As a spin-off of this procedure, the stage is set for the analysis of particular cases in the second part.

The second part of the volume deals with a comparative treatment of three rural states: Mississippi, Montana, and Vermont. It is recognized in the field of state politics that we have wrung about as much conceptual clarity as is possible from the cross-state studies that use the fifty states as cases or "observations" in classic comparative inquiry. Again and again we hear calls for in-depth studies of individual states or groups of states. This volume responds to that particular demand, and the analysis of rural politics at the national level (Chapter 1) and the state level (Chapter 2) is designed in part to prepare the way for the treatment of ruralness in individual states in the remaining chapters.

Traditionally, groups of states are studied by regions with intraregional variables setting the analytical boundaries. Thus we have such classics as *Southern Politics in State and Nation,* by V. O. Key, Jr.,[11] and Duane Lockard's *New England State Politics.*[12] Other books in this genre include John Fenton's *Politics in the Border States* and *Midwest Politics.*[13] Volumes on politics within geographical regions have also appeared that are composed of studies of individual states, each penned by a different author. William Havard's *Changing Politics of the South*[14] and Frank Jonas's *Western Politics*[15] are examples. Snapping out of the regional mold is my intention. Admittedly, the regional bond is still strong, yet we must break what seems to have become an impasse in the development of the field. To do this a new conceptual adhesive is needed. I argue that ruralism is just such a concept and that examining three rural states, each representing a different region of the county, and taking careful stock of what we find will provide fresh insights and, with luck, offer avenues for future scholarship. Treading new ground is always risky, but the potentially positive outcomes seem to balance the odds. Vermont in the East, Montana in the West, and Mississippi in the South epitomize the qualities we are after and are used as units for comparative analysis in the second part.

A second break from the traditional format for the study of a limited number of states is also necessary. Instead of matching the states as states with each other, each with its own individual chapter, I deal with a single function or process in each chapter, plugging in the states as comparative cases. Thus the second part of the book consists of five chapters that treat the following subjects in the three regionally diverse rural states: political participation, political parties and elections, political elites, legislative politics, and patterns of policy formations. By taking this tack it will be easier to keep our eye on the ball, which is, of course, rural politics. Therefore readers who seek a complete treatment of politics and governance in Mississippi, Montana, and Vermont will be disappointed. I have used the states as foils to test specific notions about rural politics. It is the rural concept that assumes organizational precedence in this book—even more so, perhaps, than did the concepts "Southern," "Midwestern," and "New England" in the works of Key, Fenton, and Lockard.

Notes

1. Charles Reich, *The Greening of America* (New York: Random House, 1970), p. 6.
2. *The Writings of Thomas Jefferson,* ed. Albert Ellery Bergh, vol. 2 (Washington, D.C.: Thomas Jefferson Memorial Foundation, 1905), p. 229.
3. Lewis Mumford, *The Urban Prospect* (New York: Harcourt, Brace and World, 1968), p. 27.
4. Jane Jacobs, *The Death and Life of Great American Cities* (New York: Random House, 1961); and Jane Jacobs, *The Economy of Cities* (New York: Random House, 1969).

5. Mumford, *Urban Prospect,* pp. 182–207.

6. Calvin L. Beale, "Where Are All the People Going?" (Paper presented at the First National Conference on Rural America, Washington, D.C., April 14–17, 1975).

7. William Severini Kowinski, "Suburbia: End of the Golden Age," *New York Times Magazine,* March 16, 1980, pp. 16–19, 106–109.

8. George H. Gallup, *The Gallup Poll,* vol. 3 (New York: Random House, 1972), p. 1996.

9. Louis Harris, *Harris Report,* August 4, 1977.

10. Jerry B. Walters, "Scope and National Concern," in Larry R. Whiting, ed., *Rural Development Research Priorities* (Ames: Iowa State University Press, 1973), pp. 9–19.

11. V. O. Key, Jr., *Southern Politics in State and Nation* (New York: Alfred A. Knopf, 1949).

12. Duane Lockard, *New England State Politics* (Princeton: Princeton University Press, 1959).

13. John H. Fenton, *Midwest Politics* (New York: Holt, Rinehart and Winston, 1966); John H. Fenton, *Politics in the Border States* (New Orleans: Hauser Press, 1957).

14. William C. Havard, ed., *The Changing Politics of the South* (Baton Rouge: Louisiana State University Press, 1972).

15. Frank H. Jonas (ed.), *Western Politics* (Salt Lake City: University of Utah Press, 1969).

1
Country Mouse and City Mouse

Jimmy Carter, the country boy from
Plains, is learning big city ways.
— Jack Anderson

The stereotype is well known. Ruralites are portrayed as either very, very good or very, very bad. They are honest, God-fearing, hardworking, and courageous or shrewd, hypocritical, lazy, and cowardly. The varieties of the stereotype are confounding. It is said that the New England farmer is crafty but hardworking; the western cowboy is honest but lazy; the southern ruralite is both lazy and dishonest. Rural people are either saluting the flag, saying their prayers, or eating a hearty breakfast, or they are lurking behind billboards in unmarked sheriffs' cars. They are either offering cool drinks to weary travelers or ambushing weekend canoeists on whom they intend to bring down insidious perversions. They are either wiping sweat from their brows or sleeping under a haystack on a workday afternoon. The common denominator that links both aspects of the stereotype is parochialism or naiveté. Rural people are unable to cope with the complexity of urban life. They are more easily shocked by deviant behavior patterns, amazed by innovations in technology, and frightened by change.[1]

In reality, of course, the stereotype is far from accurate. Yet the gallons of ink expended by academicians in probing its dimensions testify to the potency of the notion that rural life-styles differ from urban life-styles in ways that are important. Any attempt to set down the elements of rural politics must come immediately to grips with the question, Are the kinds of people who live in rural America substantially different from the great majorities who inhabit the cities? The question is immediate because people are, after all, the core element in the political process.

Epigraph: Jack Anderson, "Carter Becoming Adept in Political Gamesmanship Tactics," Syndicated Column, March 28, 1978.

Unfortunately the literature generated by the question has failed to nail down an answer. It is still impossible to say with any degree of precision just what the rural-urban dichotomy is, much less to establish whether or not the rural condition itself is a causative force.[2] Varying threads of research are interwoven in a fabric that has grown steadily in size and complexity over the years, and trying to sort them out is a difficult business. The weight of opinion has shifted from a near-universal recognition that differences exist and are important (generally accepted prior to World War II) to the belief that the development of mass society is diminishing the differences between urban and rural and that those residues that do remain are not causally linked to behavior (generally held in the 1950s and early 1960s) to a reassessment of the revisionist school and a rebirth of the argument that rural-urban differences are real and do count.[3] In 1973, two decades past the time when the revisionist literature began to appear, Willits, Bealer and Crider contended:

> What can be said presently is that, mass society theorists notwithstanding, the leveling of residence differences was not found in the present data. On the contrary, residence appeared to be more useful in 1970 than it was 10 or 20 years earlier. . . . Rurality may continue to represent a useful tool for dealing with attitudinal, and possibly other, differences as in the past. It may currently be more useful.[4]

In a nutshell, the question is very much up in the air, and no single volume will answer it. Nor is it important that we attempt a definitive treatment here. Nevertheless, there are several reasons why it would not be wise to sidestep the issue completely. First, it is the premise of most political scientists that social systems do much more to establish the characteristics of political systems than vice versa. If this is true, then we must explore the differences in rural and urban social systems before we tackle the differences in urban and rural political systems.[5] Second, the general model has spawned more tightly drawn hypotheses, which are currently alive in political science. The relationships that have been uncovered are correlational rather than causative, but they do suggest a connection between the degree of rural-urban differentiation and variables such as ideological conservatism, political participation, and party competition. Unfortunately, however, the lack of agreement by scholars in the field has riled the waters, and they remain very cloudy.

Finally, since we must sketch a descriptive overview of the population with which we are concerned (rural dwellers), why not follow the lead of those who say that the characteristics of rural life are "most easily discerned by comparing them with those of urban life?"[6] This approach has theoretical usefulness as well as an analytical utility, and it also provides a pleasant release from the doldrums of simple description. Simply stated, we will look again at the country mouse and the city mouse to see how they match up in the postindustrial age.

Defining Ruralism

One of the outcomes that may be credited to our inability to agree on the nature of rural-urban differences is the contemporary difficulty in producing a usable definition of ruralism. In the past the problem was solved by defining "rural" not only in terms of the most obvious quality of rural life, low population density, but also in terms of the life-style, economic status, and attitudinal and behavioral qualities of the people who lived in the sparsely settled areas. Often the definition of rural became simply the opposite of the definition of urban. Combining personality traits and attitudinal structures to form a definition of ruralism has come to be known as the composite approach.[7] Another way to define ruralism lacks the conceptual sophistication of the composite method and asserts that the only quality of rural life we can be sure of is low population density. That assertion is, of course, a step backward. By admitting that all we know about rural people is that they live apart from one another is saying very little indeed. The failure of deductively anchored composite definitions to produce satisfactory empirical results, however, means that to accept a composite definition would be to build on shifting sands. The spatial approach seems much better suited to scientific investigation.[8]

The case for the simpler technique is strengthened when the purpose is to study politics. To graft political behavior onto the causal chain that stretches from density to life-style to attitudes to behavior requires still more theorization that is simply not available to us. In looking at the differences between rural and urban people, therefore, we will use the spatial method and focus on the differences between people who live in high-density areas and those who live in low-density areas, whether they be white or black, rich or poor, farmers, tradesmen, teachers, or lawyers. Indeed it is our first task to determine *if* and *to what degree* people in these two types of areas differ significantly.

The data used are provided by two of the nation's most prestigious survey-research institutions, the National Opinion Research Center (NORC) at the University of Chicago[9] and the Center for Political Studies (CPS) at the University of Michigan.[10] The tables are presented to emphasize the spatial differences between rural life and urban life by including those people who live at the extremes of the rural-urban "continuum."[11] In using the NORC data comparisons are made between those respondents who live in places with fewer than 2,500 people, or open country, and those persons living in central cities of more than 250,000 population. The CPS data match people living in one of the nation's twelve largest Standard Metropolitan Statistical Areas (SMSAs) with people living in "outlying areas," which means counties that are neither metropolitan nor suburban and not adjacent to suburban or metropolitan counties.

Socioeconomic Status

Pulling away from the last traffic light and traveling into the "backbeyond," where the one-fifth of the American population that is most rural lives (with no stops in the suburbs or "rururban" belts), ought to reveal differences directly connected to the spatial variable, if in fact they exist at all. Some do. Unless you are in certain areas of the South, you will see almost no blacks.[12] Over half of the people will point to ancestry in the Northern Hemisphere—the British Isles, Scandinavia, and northern Europe. Thirty percent will evoke no foreign ancestry at all. The latter is an important statistic since it speaks to the existence of the melting pot in rural America.[13] The religious sects will be Protestant for the most part; Catholics are scarce, and Jews are nowhere to be found.[14]

These items (race, ethnicity, and religion) are called "ascribed," or birth-to-death, variables since one acquires them at birth and (with the possible exception of religion) keeps them through life. Rural people differ more from urban people on these variables than they do on "achieved" variables such as income, education, and occupation.[15] As the data arrayed in Table 1.1 indicate, the rankings for income levels, educational attainment, and occupational categories of rural people do not deviate seriously from those of urban people. Differences exist, of course, and they are in the directions predicted in the literature. There are more "professionals" in the work force, more people who go to college,[16] and more people with higher incomes[17] in the city. Yet these differences are not great. One key to the similarity of rural and urban people is that only 6 percent of the rural respondents in the sample were engaged directly in farming as farm owners, managers, or workers. It seems clear that rural-urban differences do exist. What we have is a rural population with status markings that are dissimilar to city people's on those variables that endure—race, religion, and ethnic origin. On variables that may be achieved, however, and that are more immediately associated with economic status, the markings seem more blurred.

TABLE 1.1

SELECTED SOCIOECONOMIC CHARACTERISTICS
OF RURAL AND URBAN PEOPLE IN 1977 AND 1978

ASCRIBED CHARACTERISTICS	Rural*	Urban**
	N=636	N=533
Race		
White	93%	68%
Black	6%	29%
Others	0%	2%
Ethnicity		
Great Britain and Ireland	21%	17%
Southern Europe	4%	8%
Northern Europe and Scandinavia	30%	15%
Eastern Europe	5%	6%
Others	11%	33%
Could Not Identify	30%	21%
Religion		
Protestant	80%	56%
Catholic	14%	27%
Jewish	1%	5%
Others and None	5%	12%
ACHIEVED CHARACTERISTICS		
Income (Family)		
<$8,000	31%	30%
>$8,000 ≤$20,000	42%	38%
>$20,000	20%	21%
NA	7%	11%
Education		
Less than High School Diploma	47%	34%
High School Graduate	33%	33%
Attended College	20%	33%
Occupation		
Professionals	9%	14%
Managers, Administrators, Sales	11%	13%
Clerical Workers and Craftsmen	24%	30%
Operatives, Laborers and Service Workers	40%	34%
Farmers	6%	0%
Retired, Disabled, No Answer	10%	9%

* Rural = Open country, an incorporated area of less than 2,500 population not within an SMSA or an unincorporated area of 1,000 to 2,500
not within an SMSA.

**Urban = A central city of more than 250,000 population in an SMSA.

SOURCE: National Data Program for the Social Sciences, 1977 and 1978
         General Social Survey (University of Chicago, National Opinion
         Research Center).

Anomie, Happiness, Authoritarianism

Central to the "massification" view of rural life is the premise that communications technology has so blanketed the countryside that enclaves of people who are isolated from mass culture are difficult to find. The electronic media (especially television) is said to have socialized rural areas to national norms and values.[18] It is clear that rural and urban people share in the media overlay on American society. Whether it stands above the rooftop of a lonely rural farmhouse or is hidden in the maze of electronic hardware that covers our great cities, the antenna is everywhere. Rural and urban people answer similarly when asked in national polls how much they are exposed to both electronic and print media.[19] Given these findings, it is proper to ask if pockets of atypical social attitudes can exist coincidentally with the universalization of the mass media.

One of the most useful ways to view social attitudes is through the measurement of what David Riesman called social anomie in his classic, *The Lonely Crowd*.[20] The concept has been developed steadily from its early meaning of social maladjustment to refer to the urban people's need to remain estranged from the great proportion of their neighbors — a need based on a psychological incapacity to deal in a close, interpersonal manner with a wide spectrum of human relationships.[21] Thus the urban person appears aloof and distant, distrustful and cold. How do those people who are surrounded by the alleged crime, congestion, and dehumanizing influences of the great cities compare to those who live in an atmosphere of quiet Sunday afternoons, whippoorwills, and unlatched front-porch doors at night? Lewis Mumford puts it this way:

> Thomas Jefferson's fears for the physical and moral health of his country if its predominantly rural culture became urbanized and industrialized have long since been justified by irrefutable statistical evidence . . . the mere increase in urbanization has in fact automatically increased the incidence of pathological social phenomena, as compared with still rural areas. Today's manifestations of hatred, fear, despair, and malevolent violence among the depressed racial and cultural minorities only exhibit in more virulent form the normal pathology of everyday urban life.[22]

Could the hypothesis be better put? The urban condition spawns social pathology, says Mumford, and it is "everyday" behavior. In concrete terms, what if you asked a sample of rural and urban people questions such as Do you think most people would try to take advantage of you or would they try to be fair? Would the responses split sharply along urban and rural lines?

These and similar questions were posed by the National Opinion Research Center, and the answers are revealing (see Table 1.2). Despite the dire predictions of Mumford, despite the theoretical development of the "urbanism means anomie" hypothesis, and despite the fact that we have pitted the very rural against the very urban, no significant differences exist. Sixty-five percent of the rural people said people would "try to be fair"; 34 percent said "most people can be trusted"; and 58 percent said "most of the time people try to be helpful." If these figures are low, they are not very much lower in the city.

Yet in some sense, Mumford may be correct. Rural and urban people

TABLE 1.2

REFLECTIONS OF CULTURE: SENSE OF SOCIAL
WELL-BEING OF RURAL AND URBAN PEOPLE 1975 AND 1978

	Rural	Urban
	N=634	N=591
Do you think most people would try to take advantage of you if they got a chance, or would they try to be fair? (Percent answering "try to be fair")	65%	56%
Generally speaking, would you say that most people can be trusted or that you can't be too careful in dealing with people? (Percent answering "most people can be trusted")	34%	32%
Would you say that most of the time people try to be helpful, or that they are mostly just looking out for themselves? (Percent answering "try to be helpful")	58%	52%
Taking things all together, how would you say things are these days--would you say that you are very happy, pretty happy, or not too happy? (Percent answering "very happy")	38%	26%

SOURCE: National Data Program for the Social Sciences, 1975 and 1978 General Social Survey (University of Chicago, National Opinion Research Center).

may share a similar view of man, but they differ on their assessments of how happy they are. As Table 1.2 shows, only 26 percent of the urban people said they were "very happy," but 38 percent of the rural people were willing to make the claim that they were "very happy." It may be that although rural people share their urban cousins' view of mankind, they do not despair because it represents a condition they perceive to be foreign to their own experience.[23] Kojak found his way into the living rooms of Bozeman, Montana, and Jackson, Mississippi, but he dealt with the crime of the city.

Social scientists have long sought to use studies of personality to distinguish between sets of people in ways that have a bearing on social life and politics, and treatment of the authoritarian personality has been one of the most successful efforts in the field. It would seem that attributes of authoritarianism are more likely to be found in rural areas than in urban areas, and it can be demonstrated that conservatism and ruralism show evidence of linkage. Since authoritarianism and conservatism are related, it may be that personality is the connection between the two.

How one raises one's children is a highly personalized matter, and opinions on the subject are potent indicators of personality.[24] Some parents insist that their children exhibit strict habits of cleanliness, have good manners, be good students, try hard to succeed, and above all, obey their mother and father. Other parents are more concerned with whether or not their children get along well with other children and are curious about life, considerate of others, and honest.

The NORC surveyors asked rural and urban respondents to indicate from a list of thirteen qualities which one was "most desirable" for children to have. In 1975 and 1978 both groups listed "honesty" first and "good sense and sound judgment" and "obeying parents" second or third. A larger portion (42 percent) of rural people chose honesty than did urban people (34 percent), and a slightly smaller percentage (12 percent) of the rural group chose "good sense and sound judgment" than did the urban respondents (16 percent). Nevertheless, the overall picture is one of similarity, not difference, and there appears to be no evidence at all that rural parents are more "authoritarian" with their children than are urban parents.

Opinions on Social Issues and Support for Institutions

A well-documented entry in the catalog of rural-urban differences is that rural people feel differently about social issues — matters concerning religion, sex, marriage and the family, feminism, and so forth. Rural

America is the land of traditional values, the backbone of the nation where people hold out against the liberalizing effect of urban mores.

There still seems to be much truth in this idea. In the NORC samples of 1975 and 1977, half of the respondents living in the most rural sections of the country agreed with the statement, "Women should take care of running their homes and leave running the country up to men." Twenty-three percent would not give birth control information to teenagers, and 29 percent were against sex education in the public schools. A large majority of the rural people disapprove of the Supreme Court's ruling that bans prayers in the public schools, the legalization of marijuana, and the liberalization of the divorce laws (see Table 1.3). In all these matters rural people responded in a manner resistant to change and protective of the past. Urban respondents, on the other hand, are more willing to accept an expanded role for women,[25] sex education, the legalization of marijuana, and all the rest of the items in Table 1.3.

Much of the literature concerning rural-urban differences focuses on the ruralites' fear of the encroachment of urban-based institutions on rural society—the bank controlling farm mortgages, the scientists creating technological wizardry, the great companies and the unions locked in struggle in the streets of the cities—and especially of the media, which is the bearer of so much of the bad news. Much of this hostility to institutions has taken the form of rural radicalism and populism as farmers fought the banks in the Midwest, the railroads on the Great Plains, and lumber companies in the South.[26]

Given the current complexion of American society, if only 13 percent of our sample of ruralites say they have "a great deal of confidence" in the people running organized labor, for instance, will this figure be far different from the percentage of urban respondents who so rank labor leaders? The answer is no. Both groups rank labor at or near the bottom of the "confidence ratings" on ten major institutions in the United States. Only 17 percent of the urban people are willing to say they have great confidence in the leaders of organized labor.

In their support for the other nine social and economic institutions in America, rural and urban people show a remarkable similarity. Both rank medicine the highest. Both score organized religion, the press, major companies, and television almost the same. Support for "banks and financial institutions" is much stronger among ruralites than it is in the urban sample. But that category is the only exception. In short, the dissimilarity between rural and urban respondents on specific social issues is not reflected in their assessments of the major American institutions (see Table 1.4).

What emerges from this overview of characteristics, attitudes, and

TABLE 1.3

REFLECTIONS ON CULTURE: VIEWS ON MORALITY-LINKED
SOCIAL ISSUES OF RURAL AND URBAN PEOPLE, 1975 AND 1977

	Rural N=636	Urban N=580
Do you agree or disagree with this statement? Women should take care of running their homes and leave running the country up to men. (Percent answering "agree")	50%	37%
Do you think birth control information should be made available to teenagers who want it, or not? (Percent answering "should not")	23%	16%
Should it be possible for a pregnant woman to obtain a legal abortion if she is unmarried and doesn't want to get married? (Percent answering "no")	60%	45%
Would you be for or against sex education in the public schools? (Percent answering "against")	29%	22%
Should divorce in this country be made easier or more difficult to obtain than it is now? (Percent answering "more difficult")	60%	39%
Do you think marijuana should be made legal or not? (Percent answering "no")*	84%	65%
The United States Supreme Court has ruled that no state or local government may require the reading of the Lord's Prayer or Bible verses in public schools. Do you approve or disapprove of the Court's ruling? (Percent answering "disapprove")	69%	65%

* Uses 1975 and 1978 data: Ns = urban, 591; rural, 634.

SOURCE: National Data Program for the Social Sciences, 1975, 1977,
and 1978 General Social Survey (University of Chicago,
National Opinion Research Center).

TABLE 1.4

CONFIDENCE IN AMERICAN INSTITUTIONS AND ATTITUDES TOWARD CHILD REARING

QUESTION: As far as the people running these institutions are concerned,
would you say you have a great deal of confidence, only some
confidence, or hardly any confidence at all in them? (Percent
saying "a great deal of confidence") 1977 and 1978

	Rural	Urban
	N=636	N=533
Medicine	48%	46%
The Military	37%	33%
The Scientific Community	36%	42%
Banks and Financial Institutions	43%	31%
Education	36%	36%
Organized Religion	38%	36%
The Press	25%	22%
Major Companies	23%	23%
Television	16%	16%
Organized Labor	13%	17%

Top Five Qualities Chosen as Desirable for Children to Have by Rural
and Urban Respondents. (Percent saying "most desirable")

	Rural	Urban
	N=634	N=591
Honesty	42%	34%
Obedience	20%	18%
Good Judgment	12%	16%
Responsibility	8%	6%
Consideration for Others	4%	7%

SOURCE: National Data Program for the Social Sciences, 1975, 1977, and
1978 General Social Survey (University of Chicago, National
Opinion Research Center).

preferences of rural and urban people is a mixed bag. There seems little choice but to agree with the conclusions of Glenn and Hill who, after developing the more precise studies in the literature, caution against the magnification of rural-urban differences but conclude:

> What then is the importance of the rural-urban distinction and of the community size variable to those who would understand and deal with attitudinal and behavioral variation in the U.S.? The answer, clearly, is that the importance is more than negligible and that there is little reason to believe that the importance will soon diminish very much.[27]

Since we are concerned here with rural-urban differences even if they are weakened when other factors (such as income and/or education) are taken into account, the Glenn and Hill study assumes added meaning since it seeks in part to test the independent effect of ruralism. For instance in the NORC data used here, rural respondents displayed lower education levels than did urban respondents (Table 1.1). It seems likely that this difference might explain why rural people are more negative toward social issues such as feminism, sex education, divorce laws, legalization of marijuana, and the pill for teenagers. However, when education is controlled, it turns out that the rural-urban differences persist on most of these issues. In some instances when better-educated urbanites are compared to better-educated ruralites, the attitudinal range between the two groups is actually expanded—as was the case with the attitudes toward the divorce laws in 1978, prayer in the schools and legalization of marijuana in 1975, and abortions for single women in 1977. Yet what is essential to our concerns here is simply that rural and urban people differ on social issues (feminism, abortion, divorce laws, marijuana, etc.), for these issues are the stuff of which politics is made.

Political Views and Behavior

Politics is a specialized component of social life. It involves matters that relate to the allocation of rules backed by some overarching authority that apply to all members of society. When it is decided, for instance, that everyone shall refrain from riding a motorcycle bareheaded, the process whereby this "value" is transferred from an individual or a group concern to a society-wide rule, and also the process whereby it is applied and enforced or not enforced, is politics. Do people who live in the "outback" areas of America differ significantly from those who live in the great population centers on questions of allocating rules that affect all?

Most of the literature on this subject was generated decades ago when there were more ruralites. Generally it was—and still is—believed that rural people are conservative, apathetic, and more easily moved to radicalism. These constructs have not been refined, however, and few descriptive analyses of rural political attitudes and behavior have been forthcoming over the last decade. The task before us is to sketch in the dimensions of political man in the modern rural places. I seek to unearth no strict causal linkage between ruralism and politics — complete with an analysis of antecedent variables. The intent is simply to describe with some precision the markings of rural politics. Once again it seems reasonable to juxtapose these markings with urban ones.

Linkages to the System — Awareness, Concern, Activity

To test the several knots that tie rural people to the political system it is reasonable to speculate that those on the "periphery"[28] of society might participate less in the political process — that living along the dirt roads instead of along the paved ones might breed a lack of concern for and a diminished awareness of activity in the public sector.

Questions put to a sample of rural and urban respondents showed that of those persons living at the extreme rural end of the rural-urban continuum (in outlying areas that are more than fifty miles from the central business area of a central city), 32 percent said they follow what's going on in government and public affairs "only now and then or hardly at all." When the focus was narrowed to a single election (the 1976 presidential election) and the respondents were asked how much interest they had in it, only 34 percent of the ruralites said they were "very interested." Remembering the millions of dollars that were poured into public advertising in the 1976 campaign, these figures appear dismal indeed. Crucial to our understanding of rural politics, however, is the observation that urban people share in the malady. The figures in Table 1.5 exhibit no important differences between the two groups.

Political parties are an important source of political activity in the United States, and areas where they are highly organized and disciplined ought to have higher levels of political participation. One would expect more-advanced participant habits in the urban areas, where parties are more active, than in the countryside, where they often lie dormant. The logistics of contacting voters and other forms of political mobilization are simply more easily handled in city environments. The data show, for instance, that urban citizens are more likely to have been contacted by party workers than are rural citizens. Yet forms of behavior that reflect party activity are not always significantly higher in the city. Equal proportions of both groups indicate that they go to political meetings, rallies, or other such functions, and urban people and rural people share

TABLE 1.5

PUBLIC INTEREST AND CONCERN FOR POLITICS
AMONG RURAL AND URBAN PEOPLE - PRESIDENTIAL ELECTION 1976*

	Rural N=394	Urban N=275
Some people seem to follow what's going on in government and public affairs most of the time whether there's an election going on or not. Others aren't that interested. Would you say you follow what's going on in government and public affairs most of the time, some of the time, only now and then, or hardly at all?		
"Most of the time or some of the time"	68%	72%
"Only now and then or hardly at all"	32%	28%
Some people don't pay much attention to political campaigns. How about you? Would you say that you have been very much interested, somewhat interested, or not much interested in following the political campaigns so far this fall?		
"Very interested"	34%	34%
"Somewhat interested"	41%	41%
"Not much interested"	25%	25%
Generally speaking, would you say that you personally care a good deal which party wins the presidential election this fall or that you don't care very much which party wins?		
"Care a good deal"	56%	57%
"Don't care very much"	44%	43%

*Rural = Respondents living in outlying areas which are more than 50 miles from the central business district of a central city.
Urban = Respondents living in one of the central cities in the twelve largest SMSAs in the United States.
Ns reflect the total sample. Percentages reflect only those responding to the questions. Nonrespondents were very few.

SOURCE: Inter-University Consortium for Political and Social Research, the CPS 1976 American National Election Study (Center for Political Studies, the University of Michigan, Ann Arbor, Michigan).

similar activity levels when it comes to working for a party candidate or giving money to a political party. City respondents may be more apt to wear campaign buttons or put bumper stickers on their cars. But that's about the only difference.

The voting act itself, of course, is the principal measure of political activity in a democracy. Earlier studies of voting in the United States indicated that rural people generally voted less and more inconsistently.[29] However, recent studies, taken in a variety of contexts, show that there are no major differences in participation at the ballot box. Indeed some of the studies show that actually rural people are likely to participate more.[30] When both groups are asked if they vote or not, however, urban residents more often claim they do so, although the evidence is mixed. In 1974 equal percentages of urban and rural respondents said they voted,[31] but in 1976 and 1978 urbanites claimed a voting rate about 10 percentage points higher than rural respondents claimed. Yet a close review of data from various sources (see for example Table 1.6) and a detailed inspection of the literature make it impossible to make a serious claim that participatory rates are significantly higher in the city than in the country.

Political Mind Sets — Trust, Efficacy, Ideology

The scene from the back porch, the town hall, or the snow-filled pasture behind the barn is profoundly set apart from the scene from the rapid-transit railway car or the lobby of a high-rise apartment complex. If environmental situations do relate to attitudes, one's view of the political world ought to vary from the rural to the urban extreme. Three major components of a kaleidoscopic array of political attitudes will be measured here: trust, efficacy, and ideology.

Rural people do not have great trust in the American national government.[32] When asked, "How much of the time do you think you can trust the government in Washington to do what is right?" over two-thirds of them said "only some of the time" (See Table 1.7). Half or nearly half believed that "quite a few" of the people running the government were crooked. This lack of trust may come from an assessment that public officials are incompetent. Large chunks of the two rural samples said that "quite a few of them don't seem to know what they are doing," and over two-thirds of the first sample said they felt that the people in government wasted a lot of money. Table 1.7 shows, however, that urban and rural interviewees feel similarly about the questions of trust, competence, and blame. Esteem for the government may be low, but it is low in both the city and the outback.

Another concept that has received wide attention in the field of

TABLE 1.6

POLITICAL ACTIVITY OF
RURAL AND URBAN PEOPLE 1974, 1976, 1978

	1974		1976		1978	
	Rural	Urban	Rural	Urban	Rural	Urban
	N=345	N=239	N=394	N=275	N=159	N=144
In talking to people about elections, we often find that a lot of people aren't able to vote because they weren't interested or they were sick or they just didn't have time. What about you, did you vote in the elections this fall? (Percent answering "yes")	48%	47%	66%	75%	53%	63%
During the campaign, did you:						
go to any political meetings, rallies, dinners, or things like that? (Percent answering "yes")	5%	5%	5%	2%	8%	7%
do any other work for one of the parties or candidates? (Percent answering "yes")	4%	3%	5%	2%	3%	4%
wear a campaign button or put a campaign sticker on your car? (Percent answering "yes")	4%	9%	6%	5%	8%	10%

		Rural	Urban
		N=394	N=279
Question posed in 1976: In the elections for President since you have been old enough to vote, would you say you have voted in all of them, most of them, some of them, or none of them?	"All or most"	66%	70%
	"Some or none"	34%	30%

SOURCE: Inter-University Consortium for Political and Social Research, the
         CPS American National Election Study, 1974, 1976, and 1978 (Center
         for Political Studies, the University of Michigan, Ann Arbor,
         Michigan).

political behavior is political efficacy, which relates to the individual's
sense of self-worth in the political system. For instance, how did the
respondents react to the statements "People like me don't have any say
about what the government does" and "I don't think public officials care
much what people like me think"? The former statement was associated
with a significant rural-urban dichotomy in the congressional elections of
1974, but that dichotomy melted away in the sample taken during the

TABLE 1.7

OPINIONS OF GOVERNMENT:
TRUST, COMPETENCE, AND BLAME 1976 and 1978

	1976		1978	
	Rural	Urban	Rural	Urban
	N=394	N=275	N=159	N=144
How much of the time do you think you can trust the government in Washington to do what is right--just about always, most of the time, or only some of the time? (Percent answering "only some of the time")	69%	68%	74%	76%
Do you think that quite a few of the people running the government are crooked, not very many are, or do you think hardly any of them are crooked? (Percent answering "quite a few")	54%	43%	46%	46%
Do you feel that almost all the people running the government are smart people or do you think that quite a few of them don't seem to know what they are doing? (Percent answering "don't know what they are doing")	46%	42%	44%	36%
Do you think the people in government waste a lot of money we pay in taxes, waste some of it, or don't waste very much of it? (Percent answering "a lot")	71%	75%	--	--
There has been a good deal of talk these days about Watergate, sex scandals, and corruption in the government in Washington. Do you think these problems are just the result of what individual politicians have done or is it because there's something more seriously wrong with government in general and the way it operates? (Percent answering "in general")	39%	42%	--	--

SOURCE: Inter-University Consortium for Political and Social Research, the CPS American National Election Study, 1976 and 1978 (Center for Political Studies, the University of Michigan, Ann Arbor, Michigan).

1976 presidential election (see Table 1.8). On the latter statement there was perfect rural-urban agreement in 1974, but in 1976 a mild difference materialized. It does appear from the figures that urban respondents are less likely to feel that government is too complicated for them to understand. Yet the gaps between the answers given to questions like these by rural and urban residents are small and inconsistent, so it is impossible to confidently assert that there are rural-urban differences in efficacy.

TABLE 1.8

RURAL–URBAN DIFFERENCES IN POLITICAL EFFICACY

QUESTION: I'd like to read some of the kinds of things people tell
us when we interview them and ask whether you agree or
disagree with them. I'll read them one at a time and
you just tell me whether you agree or disagree.

	Percent Agreeing			
	1974		1976	
	Rural	Urban	Rural	Urban
	N=349	N=239	N=394	N=275
People like me don't have any say about what the government does.	52%	37%	47%	47%
Voting is the only way that people like me have a say about how the government runs things.	66%	59%	55%	65%
Sometimes politics and government seem so complicated that a person like me can't really understand what's going on.	80%	75%	80%	69%
I don't think public officials care much what people like me think.	59%	59%	57%	64%

SOURCE: Inter-University Consortium for Political and Social Research,
the CPS American National Election Study, 1974 and 1976
(Center for Political Studies, the University of Michigan,
Ann Arbor, Michigan).

We know that rural people are more apt to favor the traditional position on many social issues. Moreover, the literature suggests that rural
people are more conservative than are urban people.[33] The usefulness of
the liberal-conservative ideological spectrum as a factor in political
science has often been questioned,[34] but it continues to be used extensively in the popular parlance of politics. The argument is simply that
those who view themselves as "conservative" peer out at the political

world through a different window than those who consider themselves as "liberal."

It is clear that the rural people's perception of their ideological coloring is close to what the scholars predict. The NORC data exhibit a curvilinear pattern, with urban respondents more willing to admit to liberalism than rural respondents are, while equal portions of both groups list themselves as conservative. The CPS data show the predicted pattern at both ends of the spectrum (see Table 1.9). Urban liberals outnumber rural liberals by almost four to one. In 1976 the figures show that the balance between conservatives and liberals in rural and urban places was fairly close. In 1978 there were three times as many rural respondents as urban respondents willing to call themselves conservatives.

Support for the System: Politicians, Groups, Structure

With the coming of the electronic media and the commercialization of politics, images are key political factors. Exposure, visibility, and charisma are the catchwords of a generation that still remembers the Nixon-Kennedy debates of 1960, that watched the "selling of the president" in 1968,[35] and that was on hand as Jimmy Carter's smile outbeamed a bevy of Democratic contenders in 1976. Central to the massification thesis is the premise that a universalized communications grid will level out the regional and spatial lumps in the sauce of American public opinion, yet the support enjoyed by various nationally known political figures is still associated with variations in the rural-urban condition.

The CPS data-collection process employs a useful tool called the "feeling thermometer" that demonstrates that fact. Respondents are asked to rate groups and individuals according to how "warm" their feelings are toward that group or individual; the thermometer scores range from 0 to 100 degrees. The temperatures recorded for important American politicians in the 1974, 1976, and 1978 surveys tell us that significant differences still remain in the rural and urban support levels for U.S. politicians. These differences are reinforced by party and ideology. Rural people tend to rank Republicans higher than Democrats; the reverse is true for urban respondents (see Figure 1.1).

Generally ruralites rank conservatives higher than liberals. In 1978 Ronald Reagan got the highest score recorded for any politician by rural respondents during the three surveys, and in 1974 they rated Gerald Ford far above Nelson Rockefeller. Urban respondents generally score liberal politicians higher than conservative ones, but there are exceptions. In

TABLE 1.9

RURAL-URBAN DIFFERENCES IN PARTY PREFERENCES AND IDEOLOGY

QUESTION: Generally speaking, do you usually think of yourself
           as a Republican, a Democrat, an Independent, or what?

	1974		1976		1978	
	Rural	Urban	Rural	Urban	Rural	Urban
	N=345	N=239	N=394	N=275	N=159	N=144
Republican	22%	7%	25%	15%	26%	13%
Independent	28%	31%	18%	25%	28%	22%
Democrat	35%	46%	44%	53%	38%	53%
Other Responses	14%	16%	13%	7%	8%	13%

QUESTION: We hear a lot these days about liberals and conservatives.
           I'm going to show you a seven-point scale on which the
           political views that people might hold are arranged from
           extremely liberal to extremely conservative. Where would
           you place yourself on this scale, or haven't you thought
           much about this?*

	1976		1978	
	Rural	Urban	Rural	Urban
Liberal	7%	25%	7%	29%
Slightly Liberal	15%	11%	13%	15%
Middle of the Road	35%	35%	29%	37%
Slightly Conservative	22%	15%	20%	10%
Conservative	21%	15%	32%	11%

*Categories "extremely liberal" and "liberal," and "extremely conservative"
and "conservative" were collapsed in order to simplify the table.

SOURCE: Inter-University Consortium for Political and Social Research,
         the CPS American National Election Study, 1974, 1976, and 1978
         (Center for Political Studies, the University of Michigan,
         Ann Arbor, Michigan).

1974 urban people felt warmer toward conservative Ford than liberal
Rockefeller, even though in 1972 Congressman Ford had received a score
of only 6 (out of a possible 100) on the Americans for Democratic Action
congressional rating device, and 68 out of 100 in the ranking developed
by the conservative Americans for Constitutional Action.[36]
    When the same "feeling thermometer" is applied to politically relevant

FIGURE 1.1

RURAL-URBAN DIFFERENCES IN
"FEELING THERMOMETER" SCORES FOR AMERICAN POLITICIANS, 1978*

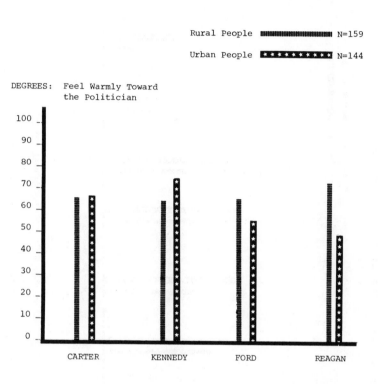

* Scores represent weighted percentages of the respondents falling in each decennial of the scale.

SOURCE: Inter-University Consortium for Political and Social Research,
          the CPS 1978 American National Election Study (Center for Political
          Studies, the University of Michigan, Ann Arbor, Michigan).

groups in society, differences between urbanites and ruralites continue to emerge (see Figure 1.2). Rural people show great warmth toward policemen and the military; their score for blacks is also high. But they are cold in their attitude toward radical students and marijuana users. Urban respondents scored the military and policemen much lower and the radical students and marijuana users much higher than the rural respondents did. Other differences were smaller but still statistically significant. It is important to note that the NORC data showed no difference in the amount of confidence urban and rural people had in the leadership of the military and labor unions. On the other hand, the more

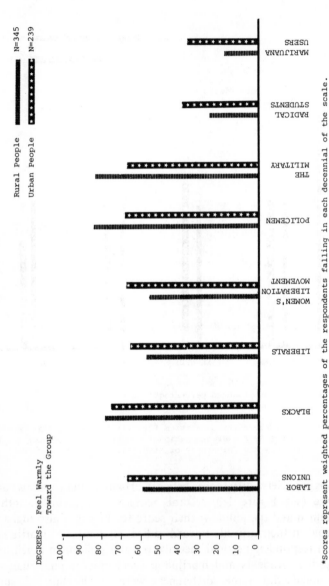

FIGURE 1.2

RURAL–URBAN DIFFERENCES IN "FEELING THERMOMETER"
SCORES FOR VARIOUS POLITICALLY LINKED GROUPS IN AMERICA*

DEGREES: Feel Warmly
Toward the Group

Rural People N=345
Urban People N=239

*Scores represent weighted percentages of the respondents falling in each decennial of the scale.

SOURCE: Inter-University Consortium for Political and Social Research, the CPS 1974 American National Election
Study (Center for Political Studies, the University of Michigan, Ann Arbor, Michigan).

negative reactions of the rural respondents to the women's liberation movement and people who use marijuana were predicted by the data obtained by the NORC questions on social issues. Simply put, the "feeling thermometer" scores for politically relevant groups in American society go a long way in describing the nature of the political value structures of the rural population. The scores also show that rural-urban distinctions can be very important on particular political issues.

A final dimension of support for the system concerns the structure of the government itself. This element may be discussed in two analytically useful ways: support for the levels of government—national, state, and local—and support for the branches of the national government—the presidency, the Congress, and the courts. Rural people can reach their local governments in ways that are impossible in urban places. All of the cities used for our urban sample, for instance, have larger populations than the entire states of Vermont or Wyoming. Citizens of rural America rate their local governments higher than they do their state governments, and they rate the national government last. The seepage of federal power and Potomac politics into the deepest valleys of West Virginia and across the badlands of North Dakota and eastern Montana has not, as the massification hypothesis would suggest, flattened out national opinion on the subject of the federal government's role in political life. In short, rural areas still harbor what has traditionally been called a conservative view of the division of power—governments that are closest to the people are best. The rural people have more faith and confidence in local governments than in state governments, and more in the latter than in the national government. Similarly, ruralites are far more willing to give increased influence and power to state and local governments than to the national government.

Urban people, on the other hand, are not consistent in their views of the division of power. Although they are more likely to say they have faith and confidence in the national government than are the rural people by a two-to-one ratio, the urbanites share the ruralites' disposition to entrust more power and influence to the local and state governments than to the federal. The differences between rural and urban on the parceling out of more influence and power to the various levels of government are not great, although rural people are less willing to give more influence across the board.

The rural-urban differences in attitudes toward the three branches of the federal government are a bit clearer. When the CPS interviewers asked in the 1974 congressional elections survey, Which of the parts of government do you trust to most often do what's right? both rural and urban people said they trusted the Supreme Court the most and the president the least. But the urbanites' support for the Court was significantly higher than that of the ruralites. On an "influence and power" question, the rural-urban variations were more pronounced. Urban respondents again gave the Court their top rating (53 percent said more influence and power should go to the Court), but respondents from rural places ranked the Congress highest (35 percent) and the Court second (29 percent). Despite the leveling forces at work in American society, people in rural areas are still somewhat hostile to the national government as a whole and to the Court in particular.

Political Issues

In drawing a bead on more specific matters—on issues that confront contemporary political decision makers—the answers to questions administered by the NORC surveyors on spending policy are useful. Respondents were shown a list of problems and asked to indicate for each whether they thought the United States was spending too much money on it, too little money, or about the right amount. Space, foreign aid, and welfare stand out as the areas in which rural as well as urban people were likely to indicate that spending was too high (see Table 1.10). The problems that both rural and urban people thought needed the most attention were health and crime.

Overall, two generalities can be made. The first is that ruralites are much more likely to indicate that spending is too high. The second is that the differences between the two population sets have generally increased since 1975. In the 1978 survey blacks, the cities, and welfare all sparked a significantly stronger "too much" response on the part of rural dwellers. In both 1975 and 1977, except for the issues of defense and welfare, spending prioritization was remarkably similar in both rural and urban places.

The matters of civil rights and liberties, however, generate a more consistent pattern. When asked to indicate their preferences along a continuum between protecting the rights of the accused and stopping crime regardless of the rights of the accused, rural-urban distinctions became more clear. The CPS data show that 38 percent of urban respondents and 26 percent of rural respondents indicated preferences in favor of the rights of the accused. A similar gap appeared on the same kind of question for women's rights. When confronted with the polar positions of government should help minority groups and minority groups should help themselves, twice as many urban as rural respondents were in favor of government help for minority groups.

The most poignant illustration of rural-urban differences on political matters concerns the issue of protest action. Rural people are simply less willing to condone modes of interest articulation that do not conform to

TABLE 1.10

SPENDING PRIORITIES OF RURAL AND URBAN PEOPLE
(PERCENT SAYING THE GOVERNMENT SPENDS TOO MUCH)

	1975		1977		1978	
Spending For	Rural	Urban	Rural	Urban	Rural	Urban
	N=317	N=319	N=319	N=261	N=317	N=272
Foreign Aid	75%	75%	72%	67%	69%	68%
Space	67%	66%	59%	56%	52%	55%
Welfare	54%	41%	64%	50%	62%	51%
Blacks	28%	26%	23%	25%	32%	18%
Defense	21%	36%	19%	30%	22%	30%
Cities	16%	10%	23%	18%	26%	12%
Environment	13%	7%	12%	13%	13%	4%
Education	12%	11%	10%	9%	12%	7%
Drug Addiction	9%	11%	9%	13%	10%	9%
Health	6%	5%	8%	6%	7%	6%
Crime	4%	8%	6%	6%	8%	4%

SOURCE: National Data Program for the Social Sciences, 1975, 1977, 1978
General Social Survey (University of Chicago, National Opinion
Research Center).

accepted patterns. Fifty-four percent of the rural people interviewed disapproved of protesting government action by means of meetings and marches, and an equal portion disapproved of protesting by refusing to obey an unjust law. Sixty-six percent disapproved of sit-ins, mass meetings, and demonstrations. Urbanites, on the other hand, were far more willing to accept such activities. These differences stand out as the largest in the array of potential dichotomies that were analyzed.

Summary

Cataloging the political views and behavior of rural dwellers in contrast to those who live in the cities produces a complex picture. Concerning basic linkages to the system, awareness of the public sector, concern for what happens politically, and taking action in the political arena, there do not appear to be major differences based on place of residence. Feelings of trust and political self-worth also exhibit no clear rural-urban breakdown. Very little difference appeared when rural and urban respondents were asked to prioritize government spending.

Nevertheless, rural and urban people do disagree significantly on several matters. They have different ideological views of themselves, and they do not demonstrate a similar warmth for important American political figures. They support the several levels and branches of government with varying degrees of intensity. Finally, on several of the "gut issues" that dominate public concern in America — women's rights, the rights of the accused, minorities, welfare spending, and civil disobedience — rural people still stand to the right of urbanites.

There is little doubt that many of these relationships would wash out under controls. Of course urban people are more positively disposed to Democrats; there are more Democrats in cities. Naturally city dwellers support rights for minorities more than rural residents do; the cities house more minority groups. And so forth. The game plan of this volume is simply to firm up some of the properties of rural political systems in a manner that invites further speculation.

Notes

1. One of the early important articles in this literature is Arthur M. Schlesinger, Sr., "The City in American History," *Mississippi Valley Historical Review* 27 (June 1940), pp. 43–66. J. B. Chitambar describes the antirural-urban bias as follows: "The popular urban expression of rural people is that they are ignorant, slow in thought and action, and very gullible" (J. B. Chitambar, *Introductory Rural Sociology* [New York: Halstead Press, 1973], p. 130).

2. For a series of specific references on this point see the bibliographical essay at the end of the volume.

3. For a series of specific references on this point see the bibliographical essay at the end of the volume.

4. Fern K. Willits, Robert C. Bealer, and Donald M. Crider, "Leveling of Attitudes in Mass Society: Rurality and Traditional Morality in America," *Rural Sociology* 38 (Spring 1973), pp. 36–45. Harold M. Hodges, Jr., disagrees (Harold M. Hodges, Jr., *Conflict and Consensus: An Introduction to Sociology* [New York: Harper and Row, 1971], p. 145).

5. It is important to emphasize that I intend no testing of the model in this book. My concern is simply with describing certain aspects of politics in rural states. I will be involved with the correlational elements of rural-urban differences and political behavior, however. To do more would be greatly pretentious given

the paucity of theorization at hand in the social sciences. By simply establishing the existence or nonexistence of correlations and describing their dimensions in a precise manner, we will be gaining a large measure of ground on the problem.

6. Chitambar, *Introductory Rural Sociology,* p. 130.

7. Louis Wirth, "Urbanism as a Way of Life," *American Journal of Sociology* 44 (July 1938), pp. 1–24. For a development of Wirth's list, see Nels Anderson and K. Ishwaran, *Urban Sociology* (New York: Asia Publishing House, 1965), pp. 6–7. For a critique of Wirth's article, see Harold L. Wilensky and Charles N. Lebeaux, *Industrial Society and Social Welfare* (New York: Free Press, 1965), pp. 121–133.

8. One of the best treatments of the problems involved in the composite approach is Fern K. Willits and Robert C. Bealer, "An Evaluation of a Composite Definition of Rurality," *Rural Sociology* 32 (June 1967), pp. 165–177. Willits and Bealer conclude the following: "Thus despite the popularity, easy verbalization, and apparent sophistication of taking 'rural' to mean a composite or complex of ideas, the empirical utility of such a compound definition appears questionable."

9. The data utilized in this chapter were made available in part by the Inter-University Consortium for Political and Social Research. The data were originally collected at the National Opinion Research Center at the University of Chicago and were distributed by Roper Public Opinion Research Center, Williams College, Williamstown, Massachusetts.

10. The data utilized in this chapter were made available in part by the Inter-University Consortium for Political and Social Research. The data for the CPS American National Election Studies were originally collected by the Center for Political Studies of the Institute for Social Research, the University of Michigan, under a grant from the National Science Foundation. Neither the original collectors of the data nor the consortium bear any responsibility for the analysis or interpretation presented here.

11. For a discussion of problems of definition see Alvin Bertrand, *Rural Sociology : An Analysis of Contemporary Rural Life* (New York: McGraw-Hill Book Company, 1958), pp. 23–24.

12. The NORC data indicate that only about 4 percent of rural (farm and nonfarm) residents are black.

13. T. Lynn Smith and Paul E. Zopf, Jr., *Principles of Inductive Rural Sociology* (Philadelphia: F. A. Davis Company, 1970), p. 351.

14. A. Delbert Samson, *Church Groups in Four Agricultural Settings in Montana,* Bulletin no. 538 (Bozeman: Montana Agricultural Experiment Station, 1958), p. 3.

15. Everett M. Rogers and Rabel J. Burdge, *Social Change in Rural Societies* (New York: Appleton Century Crofts, 1972), pp. 70–71.

16. James D. Tarver, "Gradients of Urban Influence on the Educational, Employment, and Fertility Patterns of Women," *Rural Sociology* 34 (September 1969), pp. 356–367. Rogers and Burdge, *Social Change in Rural Societies,* p. 243. Michael F. Nolan and John F. Galliher, "Rural Sociological Research and Social Policy: Hard Data, Hard Times," *Rural Sociology* 38 (Winter 1973), pp. 491–499. John Stoeckel and J. Allan Beegle, "Urban Dominance and the Rural-Farm

Status Structure," *Rural Sociology* 34 (March 1969), pp. 56–66.

17. Rogers and Burdge, *Social Change in Rural Societies,* p. 377.

18. Charles R. Wright, "The Nature and Functions of Mass Communications," in Jean M. Civikly, ed., *Messages: A Reader in Human Communication* (New York: Random House, 1974), pp. 241–249.

19. Data show that the coming of television to rural America occurred swiftly. In 1950 America's urban families had 160 percent more television sets than did rural nonfarm families and 420 percent more than rural farm families. By 1956 these percentages had decreased to 14 percent and 47 percent, respectively (see Bertrand, *Rural Sociology,* p. 33). In 1968 Irving L. Allen reported that subscription rates to ten selected periodicals were not related to community size (Irving L. Allen, "Community Size, Population Composition and Cultural Activity in Smaller Communities," *Rural Sociology* 33 [September 1968], pp. 328–338).

20. Riesman used the term anomie to refer to that kind of urbanite who "lacks the capacity to conform to the behavioral norms of society" (David Riesman, *The Lonely Crowd* [New Haven: Yale University Press, 1950], p. 278).

21. Harvey Cox, *The Secular City* (New York: Macmillan Company, 1966), pp. 39–40.

22. Lewis Mumford, *The Urban Prospect* (New York: Harcourt, Brace, and World, 1968), pp. 232–233.

23. Johnson and Knop find that optimism for the future is positively associated with urbanism, not ruralism. However, the correlation coefficient was only .15 and was not statistically significant (Ronald L. Johnson and Edward Knop, "Rural-Urban Differentials in Community Satisfaction," *Rural Sociology* 35 [December 1970], p. 547).

24. Robert Lane used a child-rearing item in his four-part AE (authoritarianism-egalitarianism) scale: "What young people need most of all is strict discipline by their parents" (Robert E. Lane, "Political Personality and Electoral Choice," *American Political Science Review* 49 [March 1955], pp. 173–190). In associating conservatism and personality McClosky used items that are clearly definable along an authoritarian-egalitarian continuum (Herbert McClosky, "Conservatism and Personality," *American Political Science Review* 52 [March 1958], pp. 27–45).

25. The patriarchal style of authority in rural families has been noted (Smith and Zopf, *Principles of Inductive Rural Sociology,* p. 295), but also noted is the tendency of women to be socially more active than men in rural communities (Bertrand, *Rural Sociology,* p. 149).

26. David Knoke and Constance Henry, "Political Structure of Rural America," *Annals* 429 (January 1977), pp. 51–62. In Mississippi the reaction to the lumber companies that laid waste to the state's abundant forests helped generate the populist revolt that occurred early in this century (see Albert D. Kirwan, *Revolt of the Rednecks: Mississippi Politics, 1876–1925* [Lexington: University of Kentucky Press, 1951] and John D. Hicks, *The Populist Revolt* [Lincoln: University of Nebraska Press, 1961]).

27. Norval D. Glenn and Lester Hill, Jr., "Rural-Urban Differences in Attitudes and Behavior in the United States," *Annals* 429 (January 1977), pp. 36–50.

28. Lester W. Milbrath, *Political Participation* (Chicago: Rand McNally, 1965).

29. These studies generally established a connection between higher SES levels and participation. Since rural areas tended to be low on the SES measures, ruralism was indirectly associated with lower turnout — Angus Campbell, Gerald Gurin, and Warren Miller, *The Voter Decides* (New York: Row and Peterson, 1954), pp. 70–78; Angus Campbell et al., *The American Voter* (New York: John Wiley and Sons, 1960). The early voting studies are summarized in Bernard Berelson, Paul L. Lazarsfeld, and William N. McPhee, *Voting* (Chicago: University of Chicago Press, 1954), p. 336.

30. In what has become the landmark statement on participation, Verba and Nie show that rural people participate more in politics than one would predict, given their social-economic background. "The small, peripheral community is not the place where participation is most inhibited. Rather, the citizens participate more than their social characteristics would predict" (Sidney Verba and Norman H. Nie, *Participation in America: Political Democracy and Social Equality* [New York: Harper and Row, 1972], p. 236). Other studies at the aggregate level show a negative correlation between participation and urbanism (see Gerald W. Johnson, "Research Note on Political Correlates of Voter Participation: A Deviant Case Analysis," *American Political Science Review* 65 [September 1971], pp. 768–775). For a development of this literature, see Chapter 3.

31. Forty-seven percent of the urban respondents and 48 percent of the rural respondents indicated that they voted in the fall election of 1974. In the NORC data set, a similar question about voting in the 1972 presidential election was asked, and precisely the same percentage (68 percent) of rural and urban people responded that they had voted in the election in which Nixon ran against McGovern (National Data Programs for the Social Sciences, 1975 General Social Survey [University of Chicago, National Opinion Research Center, July 1975]).

32. For an analysis of the role of trust in various parts of the American political system, see Ralph M. Goldman, *Behavioral Perspectives on American Politics* (Homewood, Ill.: Dorsey Press, 1973).

33. Willits, Bealer, and Crider, "Leveling of Attitudes," pp. 36–45; Howard W. Beers, "Rural-Urban Differences: Some Evidence from Public Opinion Polls," *Rural Sociology* 18 (December 1953), pp. 1–11. Beers's article generally contests the rural-urban dichotomy. Conservatism is one area, however, where he finds "strains" of differentiation. Bertrand, *Rural Sociology,* p. 43. Norval D. Glenn and Jon P. Alston, "Rural-Urban Differences in Reported Attitudes and Behavior," *Southwest Social Science Quarterly* 47 (March 1967), pp. 381–400. Glen and Alston focus on farmers as an occupational group. John L. Haer, "Conservatism-Radicalism and the Rural-Urban Continuum," *Rural Sociology* 17 (December 1952), pp. 343–347. Haer's study of residents of the state of Washington is one of the few to question the linkage between size of place and conservatism.

34. Everett Carll Ladd, Jr., "The Changing Face of American Political Ideology," *Massachusetts Review* 8 (Spring 1967), pp. 251–266, and Everett Carll Ladd, Jr., "Hometown, U.S.A.: The Rise of Ideology," *South Atlantic Quarterly* 67 (Winter 1968), pp. 23–39.

35. Joe McGinniss, *The Selling of the President 1968* (New York: Trident Press, 1969).

36. Michael Barone, Grant Ujifusa, and Douglas Matthews, *The Almanac of American Politics* (Boston: Gambit, 1972), p. 481.

2
Rural States in an Urban Nation: Patterns of Politics

Ultimately all political acts are performed by individuals as part of the vastly complex fabric we call human behavior. The proper means of distinguishing these acts from the rest of experience is through an assessment of their collective impact. This is where governments come in. Governments respond to political behavior by producing policy for groups at various geographic levels. We band together to create an SID (special improvement district) to carry off our garbage. We are joined in towns and cities for the purpose of paving our streets or educating our children. We live together in a state that can create, alter, or destroy our local governments, decree educational standards, construct highways, and decide how much money will be set aside for the needy. Beyond this level we hover under a common flag that represents the nation. No matter that many of these government boundaries were conceived irrationally with "happenstance" their only reason for being. They are the units that determine the legal constraints that more and more mold the direction of our lives.

During the period that began with the social revolution of the 1960s, ran through the Vietnam War, and was canopied by Watergate, a structural alteration was at work that affected the balance of influence among these various governments. Almost lost in the chaos of the times, the new structure emerged in the mid-seventies along with the energy crisis. The context of policymaking in America began to refocus on the states—the states as spenders, as conservers, as breeding grounds for bureaucracies, as impediments to and promoters of national policy, as program innovators, and as relatively healthy political systems whose growth had far surpassed Washington's. The states, in short, assumed a new relevance in the federal matrix, and a name was invented, the New Federalism.

In 1972, the State and Local Fiscal Assistance Act was passed, and revenue sharing topped off a new drive to restore power to the states.

Criticism of state governments (always vociferous enough) had reached a crescendo in the early sixties. At that time creditable commentators had felt it safe to assert, for instance, that nearly all the states "have proved beyond a shadow of a doubt that they are basically unfit to govern."[1] But in 1972 a leading political scientist was willing to assert flatly, "If any segment of government promises the resources to meet the most pressing of our social problems, it is the states."[2]

Several elements underscore the growing importance of the states. During this century, the states' share of total expenditures for all governments has increased more than the federal government's. When items such as military spending are removed, the states' cut increases still more.[3] The total number of federal public employees increased by 25 percent between 1902 and 1970; in the states it increased by 60 percent.[4] Grants-in-aid to the states from the federal government have increased dramatically since World War II, marking the decentralization of administrative politics if not the establishment of policy autonomy. State bureaucracies may become the tail that wags the national dog. Moreover, the states have been on a power-snatching binge of their own in recent decades. Local autonomy is eroding as state capitals assume a larger and larger share of the policymaking burden from the towns, cities, and counties.[5] Meanwhile, there is some indication that the people themselves still believe that their state governments are important. Jennings and Zeigler report after a careful study that "it is apparent that the states still loom large in the perspectives of the American public."[6]

To understand better how politics and government work in rural America, states are the most appropriate segment to study. Other units do not suffice. Cities fail by definition; regions have little if any jurisdictional reality; counties lack the legal clout and the cultural coherence to be identified as legitimate polities. But the states have those things and more. They are similar enough and diverse enough to be used as cases for comparative analysis. They share like political structures and are representative democracies. Yet within this uniformity, one finds significant variations. Some states elect their governors for four-year terms, others for two. Some states have small legislative bodies that meet annually, run by lawmakers who are well-paid professional politicians. Others have large legislatures that are run by amateurs and meet biennially, and so forth.

States also have social and economic structures that are uniform enough to help us who study them avoid the charge that we are comparing apples and oranges when we compare, for instance, Vermont and Florida. Yet those structures are different enough to allow us to measure the variations in socioeconomic characteristics and to see if the differences are associated with certain types of public policy. Variation is especially evident in the very subject that most concerns us in this book — ruralism.

Case in point. If one hundred miles is added to the distance between New York and Chicago, the two largest cities in the country, as of 1970, one has defined the distance between one corner of Montana and the other. Scattered over this vast area are only 694,409 people, about the population of the Akron, Ohio, metropolitan area. Montana has fifty-six counties. If all the people of the state were crowded into one of those counties of average size, leaving the rest of the state entirely barren, there would still be nine states in the union more congested than that single Montana county. Put another way, in order to achieve the population density of Montana, the state of California would need a land mass 201 percent larger than the entire United States.

The variation in the land-to-people ratios in the American states is, therefore, demonstrably profound. To develop a catalog of the socio-economic and political differences that accompany this spatial continuum, it is helpful to set a statistical point of differentiation between rural and urban states. How best to do this? First of all, it is not wise to categorize the states by using pure population density as a measure of ruralism. Some states, like Colorado for instance, have low densities despite the fact that most of the people reside in SMSAs (standard metropolitan statistical areas). A better approach is to determine the percentage of a state's population that lives in what is generally accepted to be a city or urban area. Using this approach, Table 2.1 lists which states are called urban and which are called rural. Rural states have more than 56 percent of their population living neither in central cities nor in suburban areas. Urban states have less than 52 percent living outside central cities and suburban areas. Although the demarcation is arbitrary, this particular gap is the widest that appeared in the figures and so seems to be the "natural" location for a statistical break. It is also convenient because, with only three exceptions, it is possible to say that all of the states labeled urban have a majority of their citizens living in the central cities or their suburbs.[7]

Have the rural and urban states retained marked differences in their socioeconomic makeups in an age of demographic dispersion and social massification? A brief catalog of responses to this question, taking into account both the region[8] and the rural-urban dichotomy, reads as follows.

1. Income levels. Both region and ruralism matter. Families in rural, southern states could expect to make about $7,100 a year in 1970. Families in urban, southern states, however, made $1,000 more on the

TABLE 2.1

RURAL STATES AND URBAN STATES - 1970

	RURAL STATES			URBAN STATES	
State	Rank	Percent of Population Outside Central Cities and Suburbs	State	Rank	Percent of Population Outside Central Cities and Suburbs
Alaska	2	100	California	1	8
Vermont	2	100	New York	2	14
Wyoming	2	100	Rhode Island	3	15
North Dakota	4	88	Maryland	4.5	16
South Dakota	5	86	Massachusetts	4.5	16
Idaho	6	84	Connecticut	6.5	18
Mississippi*	7	82	Hawaii	6.5	18
Maine	8	79	Nevada	8	19
Montana	9	75	Illinois	9.5	20
New Hampshire	10	73	Pennsylvania	9.5	20
Arkansas*	11.5	69	Utah	11	22
New Mexico	11.5	69	Michigan	13	23
West Virginia*	13	68	New Jersey	13	23
Iowa	14	65	Ohio	13	23
North Carolina*	15	62	Arizona	15	25
South Carolina*	16	61	Texas*	16	27
Kentucky*	17	60	Colorado	17	28
Kansas	18	58	Delaware	18	29
Nebraska	19	57	Washington	19	34
			Missouri*	20	35
			Florida*	21	36
			Indiana	23	39
			Oregon	23	39
			Virginia*	23	39
			Minnesota	25	43
			Wisconsin	25	43
			Louisiana*	27	46
			Alabama*	28	47
			Oklahoma	29	50
			Georgia*	30.5	51
			Tennessee*	30.5	51

* Southern States. These states were determined by an inspection of Philip W. Roeder's "group assignment probabilities" for his factor analysis of the American states. States which scored .700 or higher on the "Southern" factor were classified as Southern. An exception was Florida, which I included as Southern even though it did not score high enough on the Southern factor. See: Philip W. Roeder, "Classifying the American States: Temporal Stability and Analytic Utility," Western Political Quarterly 29 (December 1976), pp. 563-574.

average. In the nonsouthern region, families in the rural states earned $8,810, and families in the urban states earned $10,362. But it is equally true that families living in rural, nonsouthern states are better off than families living in urban, southern states. Put another way, in 1970 a family moving from an average southern, urban state into a northern, rural state could expect to improve its income by 8 percent.

2. Education Levels. In the South the median number of school years completed by the population over twenty-five was 10.9 in the rural states and 11.2 in the urban states. This is a significant difference. In the non-South, educational levels are not associated at all with rural-urban distinctions between the states; the figure for both is 12.2 years.

3. Occupational Patterns. Both in the South and the non-South, rural states differ from urban states in that, expectedly, the urban states have higher proportions of white-collar workers. But region matters also; and what we find is that both urban and rural southern states have fewer white-collar workers than do the rural states in the non-South. Both rural and urban states have 35 percent of the work force employed as blue-collar workers. However, in the South there is a significantly higher percentage of blue-collar workers in the rural states than in the urban states, 44 percent as opposed to 37 percent. In the North, precisely the opposite is true; urban states have more blue-collar workers than do rural states. The percentage of service workers in the work force shows no relationship to the rural-urban dichotomy in either region or at the national level. Whether South or non-South, urban or rural, all states have close to 13 percent of the work force engaged in service occupations. Finally, the percentage of farmers in the states gives us our first case of a pure rural-urban correlation that is not contaminated by the regional variable. Both nonsouthern and southern rural states have the predicted larger percentages of farmers in the work force.

4. Racial and Ethnic Groups. Region specifies when rural and urban differences predict the percentage of blacks in the population of a state. In the South urban and rural states alike have close to a 20-percent black population. In the non-South, however, the thirteen rural states average only a 1-percent black population, and the twenty-three urban states average 6 percent. Foreign stock in the population is linked to region as well as to ruralism. Urban states have more foreign stock in both regions, although the South itself has very little compared to the non-South.

5. Religious Affiliation. When Elazar's religious affiliation scores[9] are measured against rural-urban and South-non-South classifications for the states, region matters mightily, and ruralism matters not at all. Moralistic and individualistic denominations are heavily clustered in the non-South, and the traditional religions predominate in the southern states. Within the regions, rural-urban distinctions added nothing to our ability to predict where these groupings might be found.

Three summary measures help to wind up this brief discussion of rural-urban differences in the American states. The first is an index of socio-economic-status (SES) diversity developed by John L. Sullivan. Sullivan used five variables similar to the ones discussed above (income, education, occupation, ethnicity, and religion) and added a sixth, kind of housing (home owner or renter), and calibrated the degree to which residents of individual states fall into the wide array of sixteen categories within these variables—in other words, the degree to which individual states have diverse populations. Briefly, states at the lower end of the scale are likely to have citizens who share SES characteristics; and states at the higher end are more likely to have citizens that do not share SES characteristics.[10] The common view of the rural location as a place where social symmetry cancels out the cosmopolitan influences of status and ethnic differences leads to the suspicion that urban states will have a high degree of SES diversity and that rural states will not. In fact, however, the rural southern states of North and South Carolina, Arkansas, and Mississippi lead in SES symmetry, but the rural, nonsouthern states of New Hampshire, Vermont, Montana, and New Mexico are much more diverse than one might expect. In fact, those very rural states have more varied SES mixtures than some states with significantly greater urban populations, such as Ohio, Maryland, Texas, and Utah. Although it is clear that intensely urban states such as New York, California, Massachusetts, and Rhode Island rank highest in SES heterogeneity, it is not possible to conclude that all the very rural states rank lowest. The rural cluster that has a relatively high SES diversity contains nine states that are mainly in two principal regions of the country, northern New England and the great northern plains—Montana, the Dakotas, and Wyoming. It may be significant that the seven most diverse of those nine rural states share a border with a foreign nation. The French-Canadian spillover in Vermont, New Hampshire, and Maine and the Spanish influence in New Mexico add diversity to the ethnic terrain of those states. North Dakota and Montana both have a Scandinavian overlay, and Alaska has a large (16 percent) Indian component.

Nevertheless, the "rural equals nondiversity" pattern is visible if one squints a bit. In the South, rural states average .35 on the index, and urban states score .40. In the North, rural states have an average diversity rating of .44, and the urban states have an average rating of .48. As our analysis develops, this kind of pattern is becoming familiar. Proceeding from rural South to urban South to rural non-South and finally to urban non-South, the quantity of the variable increases. Before we saw this situation to be true in the cases of income, white-collar workers, and foreign stock; now we see it in overall SES diversity. Rural-urban distinctions matter in both regions, but so do the regions themselves.

A second method of establishing summary measures is to create "factor scores," which serve to reduce a series of variables to one umbrella-type statistic. Two factors for measuring SES variations among the American states have been created by Richard Hofferbert. He calls the two factors "industrialization" and "affluence."[11] Think of the industrialization factor as a kind of data basket in which one finds variables associated with economic and occupational activity. The affluence factor includes indicators of wealth and education. Some states have heavier affluence baskets than industrial baskets and vice versa.

It is apparent that there is a relationship between Hofferbert's industrialization factor and ruralism. The average urban state ranks eighteenth on industrialization, and the average rural state ranks thirty-fifth. In the South, the urban connection to industrialization is more tenuous than in the non-South, but there is such a connection in both regions. The exceptions to the pattern are also regional in character. The rural states of Vermont, New Hampshire, and Maine in northern New England are outstanding for their relatively high industrialization rankings, but the urban states of the plains account for massive variations in the direction of a lack of industrialization. It is clear that the great cities of the West are not akin to those of the East. Clear also is the fact that the states ranking lowest on this factor are regionally clustered — the Dakotas, Montana, Idaho, and Wyoming, with New Mexico the exception. Hofferbert's other factor, affluence, shows absolutely no relationship to the rural-urban dichotomy. For this factor regional considerations are totally dominant. All of the least affluent states are in the South; the urban states that rank lowest on the affluence factor are in the East; and the states of the Great Plains and Rocky Mountains (Idaho, Montana, and Wyoming) cluster on the basis of extreme ruralism and on the basis of top rankings on the affluence factor.

A final summary measure has been referred to as a quality-of-life index, which is a factor score that combines a number of measures within such broad categories as individual status and equality, living conditions, agriculture, technology, economic status, education, health and welfare, and government.[12] Legitimate arguments arise concerning the nature of quality of life and the weights assigned to the variables that are said to define it. Nevertheless, the statistic does reflect what is generally viewed to be the "good life" in America — education, money, good health, efficiency in government, egalitarianism, and technological development. The leading state on the quality-of-life index is California with a score of 1.29, and Colorado, Connecticut, Washington, Massachusetts, Montana, Oregon, Rhode Island, Utah, and Wyoming are also high. Ranking lowest are the states of the South — South Carolina scores 0.66; Alabama, 0.69; Kentucky and Mississippi, 0.70; and so forth.

Are there rural-urban differences hidden in this regional split? In the fourteen states of the South, the average quality-of-life score is 0.71 in the six rural states and 0.78 in the eight urban states. In the non-South, the average index in the rural states is 1.05; in the urban states, it is 1.11. Evidently the quality of life does improve as one moves from rural to urban states whether one lives above or below the Mason-Dixon line, although the rate of improvement is a shade higher in the South. Two states of the plains and mountains, Montana and Wyoming, are exceptional rural states. Once again, however, one must recognize that one's quality-of-life environment would generally improve immensely if one moved from an urban state in the South to a rural state in the North.

What we have done is to lay out and analyze the socioeconomic quality of the rural states through a comparison with the urban states, keeping in mind the important role region plays in the dance of statistics. Because the southern, urban states are near the bottom of the urban list and because there is a slight imbalance of rural states in the South anyway, it is easy to mistake what are in reality North-South distinctions in America for rural-urban differences. Given the fact that region does play such a critical role, it is still apparent that rural-urban environments are also important. In five of the nine base variables we tested, there were differences within each region based on a rural-urban classification of the states. The same was true for three of the four summary measures.

But exceptions abound when individual states are considered. Moreover, it is critical to note that in the non-South, where variations among the states along the rural-urban continuum are most profound, socioeconomic variations are no more clearly linked to the rural-urban continuum than in the South. In other words the potential causative energy of the spatial variable, which abounds in the northern and western sets of states, does not explain why the socioeconomic character of those states varies as it does. In a nutshell, although it is possible to identify in the states socioeconomic factors that are associated with the rural condition, the causative linkages between ruralism and socioeconomic environment in the technocratic age remain hidden in a bog of contaminating variables. We note them here and consider them, but not unhappily, the tasks before us lead away from this particular quagmire.

Above all else, the states are political structures. True, they have assumed other social and cultural roles over the years, but their prime reason for being is to establish certain rules and values for the people in them. Given the significant variations in people-to-space ratios of the states and the fact that these variations are tied (however loosely) to socioeconomic structures, it makes sense to argue that the politics of the states will be different as well. Exploration of this argument should cover four areas: political culture and coherence, government structure, political process, and public policy. An extensive treatment of all aspects of these areas would require a full volume, but it is possible here to briefly consider several of the major components.

Political Culture and Coherence

Political culture is to a state what ideology is to an individual. Daniel Elazar, whose work provides the basis for this analysis, defines political culture as "the particular pattern or orientation to political action in which each political system is imbedded."[13] It is a pattern rooted in history, political traditions and myths, and the compounding of policy sets over time. The pattern also reflects more-remote causal forces such as religious affiliation, family structure, physiological and geographical factors, and the character of social interaction. In other words, the term culture describes for political systems "the whole cloth" rather than the individual patches as in a quilt.[14]

Coming up with a conceptual framework that neatly summarizes all qualities and then applying it to the fifty states is a tricky business. Elazar has accomplished it, however, in what is now a well-established cultural map of the American states. He is interested in the systematic answer to three questions: What can we expect the government to do? What kinds of people operate the political system? and How is politics practiced—in a clean or dirty way? If one asks these three questions for each of the fifty states, three patterns of answers (cultures) can be identified: (1) individualistic (I), (2) moralistic (M), and (3) traditional (T). The fourteen states of the South have traditional cultures almost exclusively. The government of these states can be a positive force for good in the community, as long as the goodness is directed toward the proper social cadres. Amateurs are welcome, and the political game is played in a gentlemanly fashion. The idea is to protect the status quo and its traditional moral values. What is important for us to note is that the rural states in the South are not markedly dissimilar to the urban states in this regard, although there are traces of the individualistic culture in the larger cities in the South, and states like Texas and Florida have substantial residues of an I culture.

It is in the nonsouthern states that rural-urban categories are important in locating cultural differences. Seventy-five percent of the nonsouthern, rural states are dominated by what Elazar calls the moralistic culture. These M states have political systems in which the search for the common good is an expected goal. Politics is considered to be a higher good in itself, to be practiced by all with honesty and diligence. Only 35 percent of the urban, nonsouthern states have this type of culture as the foundation of their political activity. The urban states are more likely to have an I or individualistic culture, in which the government is *not* expected to be a positive force that seeks actively to promote the good of society. The government's role is to provide an atmosphere and an environment in which contending private interests can reach compromises on the directions social change should take. Elazar calls this the "marketplace" view. Less than honest practices are accepted as a necessary evil, and only professional politicians are thought to be able to cope with the harsh realities of life in the political marketplace.[15]

It is important to understand that Elazar does not contend that political culture is determined by degrees of ruralism. But the association between the two is unmistakable. Outside the South, this broadest of all political classifications of the states is tied to spatial considerations. States that have a large number of cities are more likely to have the social ecology that leads to the I political culture. And, with exceptions of course, rural states provide the setting for the M culture.

Another question we might ask is, To what extent are the states cohesive political units that promote coherent goals and exhibit unified fronts against threats from other states and/or the national government? Once again Elazar provides the conceptual raw material with which to answer this question as it involves rural-urban differences. In order to develop a measure of "internal unity" he judges to what degree states share common patterns and norms and to what degree these common patterns and norms deviate from those of the nation. As states maximize intrastate sharing and national deviation, the result is a condition called "the civil society." Elazar scores the states from 4 to 11, and the states that have the strongest civil societies receive the lowest scores.[16]

The results show an intensification of the pattern found in the case of political culture. The states with the most developed civil societies are found in the South, and rural-urban differences matter little. In the non-South, however, the rural states are distinctively more cohesive than the urban states are. No rural states are found among the eight states at the bottom of the list in ranks 11, 10, and 9, and only one, Idaho, is found in the eighth rank. The average score for the urban states is 7.87; the average score for the rural states is only 6.62. The very strong civil society scores for the urban, western states of Nevada (4) and Utah (5) influence the latter figure significantly.

Government Structure

There are two more or less established ways of looking at government structure. One is to ascertain the power relationship between levels of government, in this case between the states and their localities. The other is to assess the power relationship between the legislative and the executive branches of the state governments. In other words, where does the power lie in the rural states—in the towns, cities, and counties, or the state capital? And which part of the state government is dominant—the executive branch or the legislative branch? Are the variations in these power relationships based on rural and urban differences?

The best single measure of the state-local balance of power in the states is Stephens's composite centralization index. Using three measures of centralization (financial responsibility, distribution of services, and proportions of total public employment), Stephens is able to score each state on the degree to which the central government controls the localities.[17] There are many individual exceptions, but it is possible to conclude that overall rural states are generally more centralized than urban states; and this finding is true in both the South and the non-South. The strength of the relationship lies in the fact that there are almost no decentralized rural states. In other words the pattern is curvilinear.

It will be recalled that the same phenomenon occurred with levels of state cohesiveness: Although there were several urban states that were very cohesive, there were no rural states that were extremely non-cohesive. In this case there are several urban states that are centralized (for instance, Hawaii and Rhode Island), but only one rural state, Nebraska, is classified by Stephens as decentralized. Stephens's composite centralization index ranges from the least centralized state, New Jersey with a score of 35.0, to the most centralized state, Hawaii with a score of 81.0. Other very centralized states are Alaska (74.9), Vermont (66.7), West Virginia (65.1), and Delaware (61.0). Other extremely decentralized states are New York (36.1), California (39.1), and Ohio (39.9). It seems clear that centralization is also a function of density since the only urban states classified as centralized are territorially very small. Nevertheless, the rural-urban dichotomy as it is defined here is related to the degree to which a state has placed the major burden of decision making on one centralized government. Kansas and Nebraska are the only rural states that have preserved local autonomy on a par with urban states.

In order to gauge the balance of power within state governments, I have used Schlesinger's index of gubernatorial power, which combines elements such as the governor's tenure potential, appointive power, budget control, and veto power,[18] and the ranking of state legislatures by the Citizens Conference on State Legislatures (CCSL), a basic indicator of the distribution of power within state governments. Freedom to establish legislative procedures, relationships with the executive, and capacity to keep track of law once it has left the legislature are some of the elements that go into making up the CCSL ranking.[19] States with the strongest governors are northern, urban states such as New York, Illinois, California, New Jersey, and Michigan. States with weak governors are apt to be southern states; Texas, West Virginia, South

Carolina, and Florida are examples. In both regions the rural states are more likely to have weak governors, although the relationship is more pronounced in the North than in the South.

Legislative power is not so clearly predictable. Although it is true that in each region urban states are more apt to have independent legislatures than are rural states, the relationship is not significant. The southern, urban states of Texas and Missouri rank 45 and 49, respectively, on legislative independence; and Florida, another urban state in the South, ranks 1. In the North, urban Ohio ranks 40, and next door, Illinois, which is only a shade more urban, ranks 2. Montana, Wyoming, and Vermont rank low as can be expected, but Alaska, South Carolina, and Iowa all rank high.

Political Process

There are many ways to look at the political process. Three methods that are especially appropriate are (1) an assessment of which party usually wins elections, (2) an assessment of the size and duration of these victories in each state, i.e., the competitive nature of the party system, and (3) an assessment of the degree to which the citizens of the state participate in the electoral arena. These measures fail, of course, to paint in the subtleties of politics in the rural states, but they are basic, accurate, and comparable, and are surely the way to begin. Moreover, these measures relate to three notions about politics in rural areas that have assumed the posture of stereotypes. One is that rural people participate less in politics than do urban people. Another is that party competition is stronger in urban settings. The final one is that rural states, because of their linkage to agriculture and for other reasons, provide a better footing for Republicans than for Democrats. These propositions are discussed in Chapter 1 as they relate to individuals. What happens in the aggregate?

Austin Ranney's classification of overall party electoral success scores the states on the percentages parties achieve in state gubernatorial races and the percentage of state legislative seats each wins. These scores are combined to form an index of party strength, which ranges from 0.0000 (total Republican domination) to 1.0000 (complete Democratic domination).[20] What we find is that in the South Democrats are still incredibly strong all across the board, despite chinks that have recently appeared in their armor. In the more rural states, southern Democrats score an average of .81, and in the urban states, .83 out of a possible 1.00. In the North, the rural states are well below the urban states (.43 to .53) in Democratic strength.[21]

However, that assessment does not answer the question of whether or not party competition itself is associated with a lack of ruralism. In his analysis, Ranney places considerable weight on the "urban means competition" hypothesis. He says, "The most striking contrast . . . is the fact that the two-party states are substantially more urbanized."[22] When the southern and the nonsouthern states are inspected independently, however, the exceptions to this rule are so flagrant that Ranney's conclusion seems overdone. Mississippi and Texas are close on one-partyism, yet they represent the rural and urban extremes of the South. In the North, Colorado, the Dakotas, and Idaho are equally competitive, but Colorado is vastly more urbanized than the other three. Montana, which is topographically about as far removed from East Coast urbanism as one can get, matches major party ratios with Connecticut and New Jersey; Alaska does the same with California. It takes a careful squint to detect a correlation between ruralism and one-partyism in the North. If one includes the South the relationship fades more deeply still, becoming shadowlike.

Political participation is another variable that is said to be associated with the spatial characteristics of one's living place. Do rural states have the social-political energy to turn out voters at equal rates with urban states? Analysis shows that it is region, not ruralism, that dominates any assessment of voter turnout in the American states. Looking at a measure that combines voting percentages in presidential, congressional, and gubernatorial elections, one notes that the top five participatory states are all in the northern Rocky Mountain and Great Plains regions and the lowest five are all in the South. The Dakotas, Montana, Idaho, and Utah lead, and Georgia, South Carolina, Virginia, Mississippi, and Texas bring up the rear.[23] Although the differences are minor, they do indicate that in either region (the South or the non-South) those states in which the majority of the people live *outside* the central cities and their suburbs have more people going to the polls. Thus in the six rural states of the South the average percentage turnout was 43.8 percent between 1962 and 1972, and in the eight urban states the figure was 40.3 percent. Above the Mason-Dixon line, rural states sent an average of 60.9 percent of their adult populations to the polls, but in the urban states only 58.5 percent voted. Surely these figures establish no case for an increased capacity of rural environments to produce more politically active populations. But the figures do strongly imply that rural areas do not discourage participation, a condition that has been assumed to be true.

Public Policy

So far we have discussed the raw materials of politics in the states (political culture and sense of civic unity), some broad categories of the political process (participation and partisanship), and the relative power status of some of the structures (governorships and legislatures) through which both participation and partisanship find expression. The critical question that remains is, What does all this mean in terms of what the states actually accomplish in the political arena? Can one expect, for instance, that taxes would be more regressive in a rural state? Will less money be spent on education or caring for the poor? Are rural states more or less innovative than urban states in approaching statutory solutions for state problems? In short, have the public agendas of rural states produced policies that set those states apart from the urban states?

A good starting point is financial policy, since nearly every other dimension of state policy is connected with the effort to secure and spend funds. The subject is intriguing. How willing are the people of rural states to tax themselves for public sector activities? How much do the governments of the rural states spend on public services? How deeply are they prepared to go into debt to support public services and activities?

The answer to the question, How much are the citizens of the state willing to tax themselves, tells us much about the political character of the states. It is important to understand that the crucial question is not how much the government takes from its people, but rather how much it takes from what they have. One might be surprised to learn, for instance, that in 1970 Mississippi's combined state and local tax effort was above that of the average American state if Mississippi's very low personal income is taken into account. In that year Mississippi collected in taxes 12.5 percent of the previous year's total personal income. So did Massachusetts. Both states levy the same tax burden on their citizens—Massachusetts in the North, liberal (the only state to support McGovern in 1972), socially heterogeneous, and urban; Mississippi in the South, conservative (the strongest state for Goldwater in 1964), homogeneous, and rural. Vermont had the greatest tax effort in the nation, taking 14.7 percent of the total personal income in state and local tax collections. Alaska had the weakest, collecting only 10 percent. Those two states and Wyoming are the only states with no census-defined "central cities," yet Vermont and Alaska are the farthest apart on their willingness to tax their citizens.[24] What we find when we compare rural and urban states both in and out of the South is a slight negative relationship between tax effort and ruralism, indicating that the people of the rural states are no more tightfisted when it comes to financing their governments than the people of the urban states.

The tax effort of any particular state, of course, does not reflect the amount of funds available for spending since poor states may raise less money with substantial efforts than wealthy states with minimal efforts.

As the decade of the 1970s began, rural states in the South were spending about $20 per person more than the urban states in the South. Outside the South, the rural states were spending about $5 per head more than the urban states.[25] It seems clear that rural states are perfectly willing and able to come up with the money to finance the activities of government, variations in size and wealth notwithstanding.

There remains a final question, How far in debt are the rural states willing to go? Surely it has long been held that this aspect of finance policy reveals hints about the collective political conservatism of government units. Will states with fiscally conservative populations allow the buildup of massive public debts? In 1972 the average American state was in hock for about $788 for every man, woman, and child living in the state. In the South that figure was considerably lower than elsewhere, indicating that those who spend less, owe less. In both regions rural states displayed more fiscal conservatism, although the difference was not substantial in the South. In the North the average urban state's debt was $919 per capita, and in the rural states the figure was $662.[26] What we see, therefore, is that rural states take as much of their citizens' total income in taxes as urban states. They spend as much money per person as the urban states. And they are less likely to wind up in the red.

But where does the money come from? It is possible that rural states are more willing to tax the wealthy than are urban states, and perhaps their ability to keep up with the spending levels of the urban states (on a per capita basis) reflects that fact. On the other hand, many of the poorer states may display prodigious tax efforts because they are willing to soak the have-nots. One way to discover where the money is coming from in the states is to measure the regressivity of the tax structure. Let's nail it down. In 1974 in the state of Oregon, it is possible to estimate that a family earning $50,000 a year paid 10.6 percent of its income in state and local taxes, while a family earning $5,000 a year paid only 6.6 percent of its income in state and local taxes. In neighboring Washington, however, the typical $50,000-a-year family paid only 3.5 percent of its income in such taxes, and the typical $5,000 family paid 10.4 percent. Based on these figures, Oregon has a progressive tax structure, and Washington has a regressive one. The average state taxes its rich and its poor at a ratio similar to Rhode Island's, where wealthy families pay only 8.8 percent of their incomes to state and local governments, and poor families pay 14.3 percent.[27] When it is understood that these figures are based on income only from wages and salaries (discounting the myriad of other income sources enjoyed by the wealthy), the stark regressivity of the tax structure in the average state is magnified.

It may be surprising for some to note that the South is no more regressive than the North in its state and local tax structures and that within the South the more rural states are more progressive than the urban states. The Carolinas have tax systems whereby the poor pay relatively only a bit more than the rich (in South Carolina the $50,000 family pays 8 percent, and the $5,000 family pays about 9 percent), but in more urban Florida and Texas the ratio is heavily biased toward the wealthy (in Florida the $50,000 class pays only 2.6 percent of their incomes in state and local taxes, and the $5,000 class pays 7.5 percent). In the North rural-urban distinctions make almost no difference at all.

Rural states are said to frown on the consumption of alcohol and tobacco and to provide stiffer penalties for violations of laws that involve social mores. It was decided to compare the extent to which rural and urban states make use of taxes on alcohol and tobacco to prop up their tax efforts. About 6.6 percent of the average state's total tax collections consists of money gathered from taxes on alcohol and tobacco.[28] These "sin taxes" account for 7.95 percent of the revenue in the South and 6.05 percent in the North. In neither region are spatial considerations a factor. In the South both sets of states are nearly equal in the employment of "sin taxes," and in the North the urban states lead in their use, but only marginally. If the predisposition against alcohol and tobacco still prevails in the rural states, it does not show up in tax policy.

How to make sense of where the money goes? Across the spectrum of public policies generated by the states and their local governments, no policy sparks controversy like welfare. Government support of the less fortunate in society has been taken as a given in this country almost since its beginning. The question has become one of degree, not principle. But the complexity of modern society has severely tried the capabilities of state and local governments to administer such laws even when matters of degree have been settled. Add the confusion created by fifty different state systems and the growing role of the federal government to this mixture, and it is not difficult to appreciate the turmoil that permeates welfare policy in the American states. Rural states, with their tradition of self-sufficiency and the Protestant work ethic, might well differ on welfare policy from the urban states, in which clustered populations produce highly visible aggregates of potential welfare recipients, who are more easily mobilized politically. In order to properly discover if the rural states do spend less on welfare, it is necessary to take into account the relative wealth of the states and to siphon off federal payments. A useful method is to look at state welfare expenditures per $1,000 of personal income.

In 1972 the average American state government spent approximately

$6.88 on welfare for every $1,000 of income generated in the state. The extremes ranged from a high of $17.43 in Massachusetts to a low of $2.58 in South Carolina. Rural states do seem less inclined to fund welfare programs than are urban states, although in the South the difference is minuscule, and in the North, although it is more substantial, it still falls short of statistical significance. Nonsouthern, rural states support welfare at a rate of $6.62 per $1,000 of personal income, and the urban states budget welfare at $8.35 per $1,000. Within the nonsouthern, rural states there is a clear east-west pattern. The low-density states of northern New England and Alaska spend almost $10 per $1,000 of personal income on welfare, but the rural states of the prairie and plains spend only $5.12 — close to the average in the South. The "urban means high welfare effort" hypothesis is further complicated on the East Coast since states such as New York and New Jersey spend only $7.56 per $1,000, and Massachusetts and Rhode Island average $16.56.

Another way to look at welfare expenditures by the states is to match those expenditures against appropriations for other programs. In this way we are able to ascertain whether or not rural states give the same priority to welfare as urban states do. Robert Albritton's figures provide the foundation for this analysis, and he defines this technique as being indicative of "the relative importance attached to the welfare component of state policy."[29] Using this approach the rural-urban welfare-spending pattern emerges a bit from the shadows cast by the expenditure-per-$1,000 statistic. The nonsouthern, rural states are decidedly less inclined to support welfare programs than are the urban, nonsouthern states. The average rural state in the non-South devotes 15 percent of its state budget to welfare, and the average urban state devotes 21 percent. It is not possible to tie together a neat package of reasons why this difference exists. Many plausible explanations arise, such as the degree to which welfare policy is funded and administered by local governments, the kind of welfare effort expended, the role of the federal government, the kind of budgeting procedures used by the states, and the incremental influence of gross population size.[30] The purpose here is simply to suggest that the rural state governments in the North are not apt to give welfare the same commitment as are the urban state governments.

Figure 2.1 makes that suggestion clear. Ten of the thirteen northern rural states were below the median priority score, and ten were below the median effort score. There were more rural states below par on both priority and effort than there were urban states, even though the urban states in the North outnumber the rural states by almost two to one. Figure 2.1 also indicates that the level of federal help correlates strongly with a state's welfare priority. Rural states tend both to spend less of

FIGURE 2.1

THE RELATIONSHIP BETWEEN WELFARE EFFORT, PRIORITY,
RURAL-URBAN STATUS, AND FEDERAL WELFARE AID IN 36 NONSOUTHERN STATES

State Welfare Expenditures
per $1,000 personal income

Rural States ●
Urban States ○

N = Ranking on Federal
per capita welfare grants

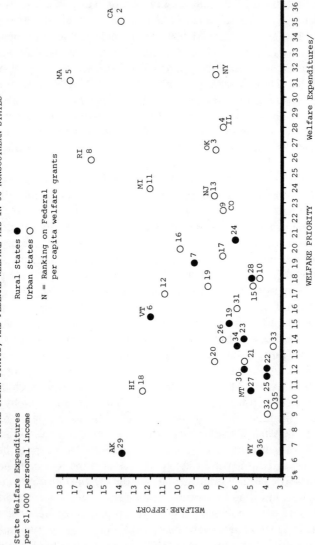

SOURCE: Derived from data found in Robert Albritton, "Welfare Policy," in Herbert Jacob and Kenneth
W. Vines, eds., Politics in the American States, 3d ed. (Boston: Little, Brown and Company, 1976), Table 5 pp. 370-371.

their own money and to receive relatively fewer federal dollars. It may be that a low effort rating signals a lack of hustle in the contest for federal funds, with the result being less money from both sources and an automatic lowering of the welfare priority. Clearly the high priority given welfare in states such as New York, Illinois, Oklahoma, New Jersey, and Colorado results as much from their willingness and ability to tap the national treasury as it does from their own commitment to welfare expenditures. Vermont and Alaska are exceptions to the rural pattern. Their efforts on their own behalf are similar (Alaska extracted $13.78 from every $1,000 of personal income for welfare, and Vermont took $11.75), but Vermont ranks much higher than Alaska in terms of the relative importance of welfare in the total spending picture—coincidentally Vermont ranks much higher as a recipient of federal funds.

The American political ethic on education is sharply different from the political ethic on welfare. Everyone needs an education, it is held, and it is the state's duty to provide it. For the most part, children of the wealthy pay the same price for twelve years of public education as do children of the poor—next to nothing. Indeed, although violations of the principle have abounded historically, universal public education is solidly stitched into the conceptual fabric of the people-ruled polity.

Spending for public elementary and secondary education in the American states is negatively associated with the percentage of the population living outside the central cities and their suburbs.[31] The simple correlation coefficient is −.332. The rural-urban relationship holds up when area is controlled. In the South the average state spent $868 per pupil in average daily attendance (ADA) in 1973-74. The rural states spent $819, and the urban states spent $905. Outside the South the ADA expenditure was substantially more, $1,121, but it was $133 less in the thirteen rural states than in the twenty-three urban states. The relationship between ruralism and spending for education is not overpowering. Yet in the South, six of the seven states spending above the southern median were all classified as urban. In the North only three states above the median were rural—Alaska, Vermont, and Iowa.

When income is controlled, however, the position of the rural states is reversed. Instead of looking at the total spending levels to test educational effort, it is more appropriate to discover, as was done with welfare expenditures, what proportion of a state's income is directed toward public education. To do this the states were arranged according to what percentage of median family income went for ADA expenditure. In New York, for instance, the expenses for public elementary and secondary education based on the average daily attendance figure represented about 17 percent of the state's median family income in 1973-74. This percentage was a high for the states. Vermont, on the other end of the rural-urban continuum, was second highest at 15 percent, and Utah was low at about 8 percent. The average state's percentage was about 11. The data show that the rural states indicate absolutely no tendency to be skimpy when it comes to education if we consider the funds with which they have to work. A footnote to this finding—the kind of fact that is often over-looked by social scientists—is that the urban states outside the South ex-pended no more educational effort than did the rural states in the South.

A final specific policy area, which provides a fresh contrast to those of education and welfare, deals with highways and natural resources. These interests are as rural-directed as welfare is urban-directed. Perhaps the best way to understand the variations in this area as they relate to the spatial characteristics of a state is to employ an umbrella statistic (a factor score), which reduces many different variables to a summary measure. Sharkansky and Hofferbert have produced such a tool, and states that rank high on the factor score also tend to rank high on such variables as rural highway expenditures per rural resident and natural resources expenditures per capita.[32]

It should come as no surprise that a state's ruralism relates strongly to what Sharkansky and Hofferbert call their "highway–natural resources" factor. What may be somewhat unexpected, however, is that this pattern is strictly regional. The average rank for the six rural, southern states is 29.5, and the average rank for the eight more-urban, southern states is 29.9—virtually the same. In the non-South, however, the states diverge sharply on the basis of rural-urban definition. The averge rank for the rural states is 10.3, and for the urban states it is 28.5. The low-density urban states such as Nevada, Utah, Colorado, and Arizona buck the trend and keep the relationship from becoming even stronger. Noteworthy also is the fact that the only states to disrupt the pattern in the opposite direction—that is, they are less interested in natural resources and highways than one would expect given their ruralism—are located in the South. The Carolinas are states of this type. Density is obviously an important component of the rural matrix when it comes to policy on highways and natural resources. The correlation coefficient between density and the rankings, for instance, is .645. So we see states like Nevada, which ranks eighth in the country according to the percentage of its population living in central cities and suburbs, scoring higher on this factor than Vermont, which ties for last-place ranking on urbanism.

Two of the more useful measures of state policy formation developed in the last decade are the Walker innovation score and the Fry and Winters redistribution ratio. Both measures tell us something about policy formation in the broadest sense. The innovation score compares the states on their "tendency to adopt new programs."[33] Which states are

willing to venture into new areas of policy formation and implementation
and which states lag behind, content to use methods that are tried and true?
The Fry and Winters measure arranges the states according to the
"burdens and benefits" of revenues and expenditures.[34] In other words to
whom do the benefits of taxation go and from whom does the money
come to pay for them? In a sense, therefore, this redistribution ratio
combines (at least conceptually) a measure used earlier in this analysis,
regressivity of tax systems, and the class impact of many of the measures
of policy outputs also discussed above.

Walker's innovation score is based on eighty-eight different programs
adopted by the states in all manner of areas, using the list of programs in
the Council of State Governments' *Book of the States*. The score gauges
the relative time it took each state to adopt a program after the first state
had done so. For instance, the first state that adopted no-fault auto in-
surance would receive a score of .000, and the last state to do so would
receive a score of 1.000. States falling between the extremes would
receive a score equal to the percentage of time that had passed since the
first state adopted the program. The scores for all the programs analyzed
are then averaged, and the average figure is subtracted from 1.000. The
results produce a range of scores from .298 for the least innovative state,
Mississippi, to .656 for the most innovative state, New York. Walker
himself poses the central question, "Why should New York, California,
and Michigan adopt innovations more readily than Mississippi, Wyoming, and South Dakota?"[35] Faced with this question and without access to
other data, the pattern seems obvious. Innovative states are urban, nonsouthern states, and noninnovative states are rural, southern states and
rural, low-density western states. Figure 2.2 indicates that the rural-
urban distinction is authentic, especially in the North. Ruralism correlates with innovation at − .59, and that figure holds up under controls
for region. The average innovation score for the twenty-two (Hawaii is
not included) urban, nonsouthern states is .510, and for the rural states it
is .409. In the South the difference is not as great, .403 for the more-
urban states and .379 for the rural states.

Among the very rural, nonsouthern states, it is the northern New
England cluster that is most innovative (more innovative than their
ruralism would predict), and it is the plains and mountain states of the
West that are least innovative. The kind of scatterplot used in Figure 2.2
is valuable in that it graphically points out those states that violate the
pattern. North Dakota's placement in the northern New England group
is just such a case. Why are the two sister states of the prairies and plains,
North and South Dakota, so different from each other in innovation?
The same question can be asked about the northern New England twins
of Vermont and New Hampshire. In the latter case it might well be their

FIGURE 2.2

THE RELATIONSHIP BETWEEN WALKER'S INNOVATION
SCORE AND RURAL POPULATION IN THE AMERICAN STATES

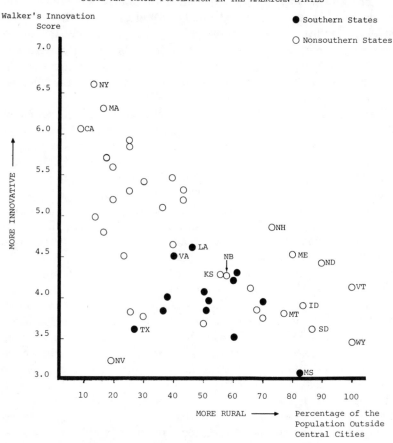

SOURCE: Innovation Scores from Jack L. Walker, "The Diffusion of Innovations Among the American States," Americal Political Science
Review 63 (September 1969), pp. 880-899.

ruralism, since New Hampshire has 27 percent of its population living in
central cities and Vermont has none, but with the Dakotas this explanation is impossible since both are equally rural.[36] Kansas and Nebraska,
on the other hand, tend to demonstrate that adjacent prairie-plains,
rural states with identical ratios of urban-to-rural population will wind
up with nearly identical innovation scores.

Virginia Gray, in an expansion of the Walker study, was able to rank
the states on innovation according to three separate issue areas — education, welfare, and civil rights — as well as according to overall score.

TABLE 2.2

INNOVATION SCORES FOR THE
RURAL STATES AND URBAN STATES CONTROLLING FOR REGION

	SOUTH		NON-SOUTH	
	Rural States	Urban States	Rural States	Urban States
Walker's Score	.379	.403	.409	.510
Gray's Rankings Overall	32.3	33.5	27.2	20.0
Education	25.3	25.3	28.1	22.9
Welfare	32.5	35.1	24.0	18.5
Civil Rights	45.9	46.1	31.3	18.2

SOURCES: Jack L. Walker, "The Diffusion of Innovations Among the American States," American Political Science Review 63 (September 1969), pp. 880-899; Virginia Gray, "Innovation in the States: A Diffusion Study," American Political Science Review 67 (December 1973), pp. 1174-1185. Walker's score ranges from .298 (the least innovative state) to .656 (the most innovative state). Gray's statistics are ranks and range from 1 (the most innovative score) to 48 (the least innovative score).

Gray's summary measure behaves similarly to Walker's composite index. The rural-urban distinction is not important in the South but is important in the non-South since the rural states of the non-South show distinctly less inclination than the urban states of the non-South to adopt new laws first (see Table 2.2). The same is true when education, welfare, and civil rights are isolated into distinct policy sets, although the relationship is not as strong for education and welfare as it is for civil rights. There is simply no other way to say it: Rural states have lagged behind in the adoption of new laws.[37]

Suggested reasons for this lagging behind of course abound. Those people who are imbued with a healthy metro-bias will interpret the findings as proof that rural people are simply inhospitable to change and react in a typically rural and parochial manner to thrusts from the outside that would spell variation from established procedures. Others may argue that rural states simply do not need the kinds of new programs that have defined government activity in this century, which is, therefore, by definition urban activity. But an affirmative interpretation of this latter hypothesis suggests that either (a) rural states have no problems of any sort or (b) they have problems and have innovated programs to solve them but those programs have not been caught by Walker. Other explanations are possible. Perhaps the problems that beset rural states are more likely to be addressed by the federal government. The Department of Agriculture has been active much longer than the Department of Housing and Urban Development, for example. Then, too, there may be a political dimension at work. For instance, if public policy innovation is dependent on certain kinds of relationships between the electorate and the political parties and if these kinds of relationships are found to be lacking in rural states, then it may well be that rural states have not had the mobilization mechanisms necessary for innovation to occur.[38]

The Fry and Winters redistribution index is of special value because it pays attention to a state's policies not only on where funds come from, but also on where the funds are going. In general the index tells us that redistribution is not as solidly connected to rural-urban differences as is innovation. By calculating the ratio of taxes paid to program benefits received, the index is able to show, for instance, that in Kentucky the lower-income classes benefit from the income-outgo process at a rate of 2.43 to 1, but in Michigan the poorer groups benefit at a rate of only 1.92 to 1. In other words the poor in Kentucky get back \$2.43 worth of services for every dollar of taxes paid. In Michigan they get back \$1.92 for every dollar lost because of taxes. Other examples confound expectations. Missouri ranks above California; Mississippi, above New Jersey; Vermont, above Arizona; Alabama, above Pennsylvania; and so forth.

The statistics also reveal that the rural-urban dichotomy is operative only in the North, where rural states do seem to be less inclined to redistribute downward in their societies. The average redistribution ratio in the northern, rural states was only 1.92, while the urban states' ratio was 2.24. None of the nonsouthern, rural states matched the urban mean. In fact the only rural state in the nation that did exhibit a willingness to redistribute at a rate equal to the urban states of the North was Mississippi.

Summary

Socioeconomic differences are still associated with ruralism in the American states with the qualification that the associations are weak and in some cases pretty well camouflaged by other variables. We also have found that the nonsouthern states are no more likely to exhibit rural-urban differences on SES dimensions than are the southern states, despite the fact that the range of the rural-urban statistic is much wider outside the South.

It is also clear that the southern states show little rural-urban variation on political measures. Ruralism matters only in state centralization and overall spending for education. In the nonsouthern states political variables are much more likely to be associated with degrees of ruralism. There are important differences between the rural and urban states on half of the base measures used and minor differences on several others. This situation makes sense because the degree of rural-urban differentiation is clearer outside the South. Therefore, because SES variations are no more rural-linked in the non-South than in the South, perhaps it is the spatial variable (rural-urban) that really matters politically and not the socioeconomic environment. This is a "tiptoe conclusion" at best, however, and is offered only as a cause for worry that the standard SES interpretation of political variation (ruralism is associated with unique SES environments, which in turn cause political outcomes) may be inaccurate. At this point the ice is simply too thin to proceed further. What we can do is concentrate on several individual rural states in different parts of the country with this worry in mind. The remaining chapters of this book undertake just such an exploration.

Notes

1. Christopher Jencks, "Why Bail Out the States?" *New Republic,* December 12, 1964, pp. 8–10.

2. Ira Sharkansky, *The Maligned States: Policy Accomplishments, Problems, and Opportunities* (New York: McGraw-Hill Book Company, 1972), p. 1. The debate over the states is not resolved. See Theodore J. Lowi's categorization of the "systematic" demise of state governments as late as 1969; Theodore J. Lowi, *The End of Liberalism* (New York: W. W. Norton and Company, 1969), pp. 306–307.

3. Herbert Jacob and Kenneth W. Vines, eds., *Politics in the American States,* 3d ed. (Boston: Little, Brown and Company, 1976), pp. 16–17.

4. Thomas R. Dye, *Politics in States and Communities,* 3d ed. (Englewood Cliffs, N.J.: Prentice-Hall, 1977), p. 50.

5. G. Ross Stephens, "State Centralization and the Erosion of Local Autonomy," *Journal of Politics* 36 (February 1974), pp. 44–76.

6. M. Kent Jennings and Harmon Zeigler, "The Salience of American State Politics," *American Political Science Review* 64 (June 1970), p. 535.

7. Several formulas were devised to measure ruralism in the American states, and it was found that all of them correlated at .80 or greater. Therefore, it seemed reasonable to use the most conceptually clear measure and a measure that used basic census definitions.

8. Ira Sharkansky, *The United States: A Study of a Developing Country* (New York: David McKay Company, 1975), p. 61. See also Ira Sharkansky, "Economic

Development, Regionalism, and State Political Systems," *Midwest Journal of Political Science* 12 (February 1968), pp. 41–61; and Ira Sharkansky, *Regionalism in American Politics* (Indianapolis, Ind.: Bobbs-Merrill, 1970).

9. These scores were developed from Elazar's original theoretical formulations in Charles A. Johnson, "Political Culture in American States: Elazar's Formulations Examined," *American Journal of Political Science* 20 (August 1976), pp. 491–509. See also Daniel J. Elazar, *American Federalism: A View from the States* (New York: Thomas Y. Crowell Company, 1966), chap. 4.

10. John L. Sullivan, "Political Correlates of Social, Economic, and Religious Diversity in the American States," *Journal of Politics* 35 (February 1973), pp. 70–84.

11. Richard I. Hofferbert, "Socio-Economic Dimensions of the American States: 1890–1960," *Midwest Journal of Political Science* 12 (August 1968), pp. 401–418.

12. The Quality of Life Index, Midwest Research Institute, Kansas City, Missouri, 1976.

13. Elazar, *American Federalism,* p. 79. See also Ira Sharkansky, "The Utility of Elazar's Political Culture," *Polity* 2 (Fall 1969), pp. 66–83.

14. Everett Carll Ladd, Jr., *Ideology in America* (Ithaca, N.Y.: Cornell University Press, 1969), p. 8. For more on political culture in the states see Samuel C. Patterson, "The Political Cultures of the American States," *Journal of Politics* 30 (February 1968), pp. 187–209.

15. Elazar, *American Federalism*, p. 97.

16. Ibid., chap. 1.

17. Stephens, "State Centralization," p. 74.

18. Joseph A. Schlesinger, "The Politics of the Executive," in Jacob and Vines, *Politics in the American States,* 2d ed. (Boston: Little, Brown and Company, 1971), p. 231.

19. Citizens Conference on State Legislatures, *The Sometime Governments* (New York: Bantam Books, 1971), pp. 44–53.

20. Ranney's device is based on an earlier measure developed by Richard Dawson and James Robinson (see Austin Ranney, "Parties in State Politics," in Jacob and Vines, *Politics in the American States*, 3d ed. pp. 59–61).

21. The simple correlation coefficent between the percentage of a state's population living outside the central cities and Ranney's Democratic strength index is − .12. When the region is controlled, however, it increases to − .39.

22. Ranney, "Parties in State Politics," p. 64.

23. Ibid., p. 51.

24. James A. Maxwell, "The Adequacy of State and Local Tax Effort," *Publius* 1 (Winter 1972), pp. 69–76.

25. Ira Sharkansky, "State Administration in the Political Process," in Jacob and Vines, *Politics in the American States*, 2d ed., p. 254.

26. U.S. Bureau of Census, *Governmental Finances in 1971–72* (Washington, D.C.: U.S. Bureau of the Census, 1973).

27. Stephen E. Lile, "Family Tax Burden Differences Among the States," *State Government* 49 (Winter 1976), pp. 9–17.

28. Murray S. Stedman, Jr., *State and Local Governments* (Cambridge, Mass.: Winthrop Publishers, 1976), pp. 391–392.

29. Robert Albritton, "Welfare Policy," in Jacob and Vines, *Politics in the American States*, 3d ed., p. 369.

30. Ibid., pp. 349–387.

31. ADA expenditures are taken from Frederick M. Wirt, "Education, Politics, and Policies," in Jacob and Vines, *Politics in the American States,* 3d ed., p. 327.

32. Ira Sharkansky and Richard I. Hofferbert, "Dimensions of State Politics, Economics, and Public Policy," *American Political Science Review* 63 (September 1969), pp. 867–879.

33. Jack L. Walker, "The Diffusion of Innovations Among the American States," *American Political Science Review* 63 (September 1969), pp. 880–899.

34. Brian R. Fry and Richard F. Winters, "The Politics of Redistribution," *American Political Science Review* 64 (June 1970), pp. 508–522.

35. Walker, "Diffusion of Innovations," p. 883.

36. Walker argues that some lack of innovation may be explained by poor political communication and refers to Alan Clem's analysis of the isolation of South Dakota's capital, Pierre, as a cause for that state's low ranking on the innovation score. It is clear, however, that North Dakota's more innovative record cannot be explained by the integration of its capital, Bismarck, because it, like Pierre, sits along the Missouri River in almost exactly the same geographical location within the state. Indeed, the isolation of either capital may well unnerve the typical eastern traveler. The isolation hypothesis makes more sense for Vermont and New Hampshire. Although Concord is within the greater Boston orbit and is attached, via Manchester, to intensely urban eastern Massachusetts, the Vermont capital, Montpelier, is a town of fewer than 10,000 inhabitants, is located in the center of the state, and is profoundly detached from the Boston metro-center. Moreover, although southern New Hampshire abuts on urban Massachusetts, southern Vermont borders more-rural western Massachusetts, where the Green Mountains meld into the Berkshires, uninterrupted except for the political border (Walker, "Diffusion of Innovations," p. 898).

37. Virginia Gray, "Innovation in the States: A Diffusion Study," *American Political Science Review* 67 (December 1973), pp. 1174–1185. See also Jack L. Walker's comment on the Gray article, "Comment: Problems in Research on the Diffusion of Policy Innovations," *American Political Science Review* 67 (December 1973), pp. 1186–1191, and Gray's reply to Walker in the same issue of the *American Political Science Review*, pp. 1192–1193.

38. Walker's analysis deals with these and other questions. His data indicate that party competition does not correlate strongly with innovation (Walker, "Diffusion of Innovations" p. 886).

3

Participation in the Rural States

One of the most thoroughly substantiated propositions in all of social science is that persons near the center of society are more likely to participate in politics than people near the periphery.

—Lester W. Milbrath

As we spin toward the twenty-first century, the crisis for participatory democracy becomes more acute. Citizen participation is both the agony and the glory of democratic politics; agony because uninformed publics often upset the policy apple cart, glory because it elevates common people to the stewardship of the society in which they live. Keeping these two elements in balance is critical. Yet in recent times, the country has acted as if the agony is too heavy to bear and the glory has grown tarnished. Americans are becoming disinterested in even deciding who will govern. Everett Carll Ladd, Jr., has been moved to entitle his latest book, *Where Are All the Voters Going?*[1]

The voting act remains the American citizen's fundamental conduit to the political arena. Voting is still the center ring of politics. A careful exploration of voting in rural areas may uncover a key ingredient in the riddle of popular participation in modern society because one immediately runs smack into what has been called "one of the most thoroughly substantiated propositions in all of social science," i.e., rural people participate in politics less because they are on the periphery. If this proposition is true, then perhaps more modernization is called for. On the other hand if the proposition is not true, then perhaps we should seek out contrary elements in order to build a more healthy participatory democracy in the postindustrial age. Perhaps we should replace big with small, complex with simple, mobile with stable, and cosmopolitan with community.

Epigraph: Lester W. Milbrath, *Political Participation* (Chicago: Rand McNally, 1965), p. 230.

The Center-Periphery Model: States and the Nation

Could one imagine better settings in which to test Lester Milbrath's proposition than the three states of Vermont, Montana, and Mississippi? Tiny Vermont is situated above what Arnold Toynbee has called the "optimum" climatic area of the United States. That noted historian claims that the Green Mountain State has contributed little to the lifeblood of the nation, perched as it is so far to the north and so far away from the mainstream of American life. Montana is huge, and it lies out past the great heartland. Cut off by spine-backed Idaho, Montana is isolated from the population clusters of the Pacific, and badlands from Bismarck to Billings guard it on the east. To the south are massive mountain ranges and arid plains, and to the north is Canada. This giant, lonely land is more estranged from the rest of the nation than any other of the forty-seven adjacent states. Mississippi is not set apart by geography. There is a seaport, and there is the Mississippi River, a profound communications network in its own right. Mississippi has been isolated by history (it was one of the states on the wrong side in the Civil War), economic retardation, and racism, which was preserved with gusto far into the twentieth century.

Using the presidential election as a barometer demonstrates that these rural states, far removed from the national "center" of Washington, D.C., do not tend to ignore national politics. The percentage of Vermont's eligible voters casting votes for presidential electors in 1976, for instance, exceeded the percentage in the highly urban, more central states of New York and Pennsylvania. In the West, Montana's voters turned out at a rate of 63.5 percent in 1976, but the most urban of the western states, California, produced only 51.4 percent.[2] Historically these 1976 figures hold up. Vermont continually has matched or exceeded the national election turnout rates of many large, urban, eastern states. Montana's record has likewise been very high when compared with the records of more urban states in the West and profoundly high when matched against nearly every eastern state. Bear in mind, also, that in Vermont's case there is no ingrained two-party system with its mechanisms for mobilization to help bolster participation.

Mississippi, the most rural state in the South, has long shunned the election for president. But is this because Mississippi is on the "periphery" or because there are other social and institutional forces at work? Discrimination against blacks, the election of the governor in the "off" years, no semblance of a two-party system, and the stiffest legal restrictions on voting in the nation cut deeply into the presidential turnout.[3] One study of voting in the election of 1960, for instance, shows that when these kinds of factors are controlled, Mississippi's turnout rate was actually 6 percentage points above the national mean.[4] In 1976, with blacks voting in substantial numbers, Mississippi's turnout was less than 5 percentage points behind the national average. Significant also is the fact that Mississippi's turnout was equal to Florida's, a much more urban and nationally linked southern state that has fewer blacks in the population.

If the outlying states are more likely to ignore national politics, then the turnout at the polls in such states ought to remain fairly stable, more or less untouched by the quadrennial pulse of the national heart. Scanning turnout levels in congressional elections over a thirty-year period indicates that, on the average, turnout increases by 12.9 percentage points in presidential election years. In Vermont the average increase was 15.6 points, Mississippi's jumped by 13.3 percentage points, and Montana's, by 7.5. The lower figure for Montana results from the fact that Montana has high turnout in the off years. Since the governor is elected in presidential years, it is difficult to say whether the increase is the result of national or statewide influence. In Vermont, however, where the governor is elected every two years, it is clear that the increased turnout is because of the national election. The governor's race in Mississippi is also neutralized as a presidential-year magnet since the governor is elected only in the off years. In short it seems apparent that rural, peripheral states respond to the election of the American president in a fashion not at all in keeping with their peripheral status.

The Center-Periphery Model: Outback and the State Capital

What happens within rural states? It could be argued that the capital of Montana, Helena, is more geographically estranged from Montana's outback areas than Helena is from Washington, D.C. Surely the potential for isolation exists. The Great Divide, a ridge of the Rocky Mountains that continually punctures the 10,000-foot level, splits Montana in two. To the west of that range, the water flows to the Pacific via the Columbia River basin. To the east the Missouri ambles northward from the heartland of Montana, through seemingly endless plains, which once were home to the Blackfoot Indians, and then east for distances that would swallow up entire states in other regions of the country.

In the southwestern corner of the state, Beaverhead County is cut off from the rest of Montana by mountain ranges with names that bespeak the western heritage—the Pioneer and Tobacco Root mountains, the Snowcrest, Ruby, and Gravelly ranges, and the Butte Highlands. There is more land mass in this one county than there is in Rhode Island and

Delaware combined. To get to the state capital, the county's 8,187 residents must travel north for a distance nearly equal to that between New York City and Boston, Massachusetts (see Figure 3.1).[5] Beaverhead's turnout for general elections for governor has been one of the poorest in the state, falling below one standard deviation of the mean in most elections. In the northwest, Lincoln County, which touches both Canada and Idaho, is another county with a low participation rate. The same is true for Bighorn County in the southeast and Blaine County on the northern border with Canada.

On the other hand, there are several counties in which location on the geographic periphery is coincidental with very high turnout. With only minor exceptions, these counties are located in the eastern quarter of the state. Although none of the peripheral counties west of the mountains have consistent records of high turnout, counties such as Daniels, Mc-Cone, Prairie, and Fallon in the east often produce a turnout that is above one standard deviation from the mean, even though they are hundreds of miles from Helena. What we have are two very distinctive regions; in the one, being on the geographical periphery is marked by low participation in the state electoral system, in the other, that is not the case.

In order to make sense of the general pattern, turnout figures (percentage of eligible voters voting) were averaged for each of Montana's fifty-six counties for the general and primary elections closest to the decennial years of 1950, 1960, and 1970. These figures were then averaged to create three decennial turnout statistics and correlated with the "as the crow flies" distance from the state capital. Since many other factors may affect a county's political participation, partial correlation coefficients were also produced, which indicate what the effect of distance would be, for instance, if all counties had an equal number of college-educated citizens, equal income levels, equal ratios of party strength, equal numbers of rural residents, and so forth. In none of the three periods of Montana's political history studied was distance from the capital a significant influence on the size of the vote in the general election for governor. When socioeconomic and political variables were controlled,[6] the strongest correlation was .26, the opposite of what was hypothesized (see Table 3.1).

In the two primary elections averaged for the 1970 measurement, however, there is a strong partial correlation coefficient that shows that citizens in the counties of Montana's geographic periphery did tend to vote less. The center-periphery theory may have had some validity in recent years in Montana, when turnout was generally lower and the contest lacked the saliency of the fall elections. Moreover, the drop in the primary turnout, which averages about 25 percentage points, is also

77

Figure 3.1

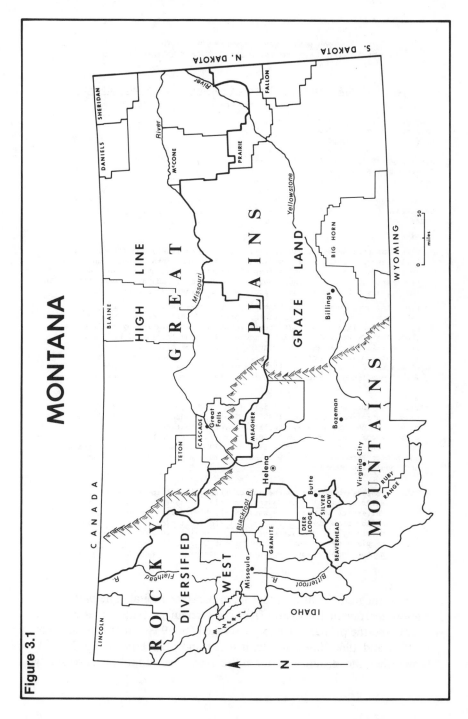

MONTANA

TABLE 3.1

THE RELATIONSHIP BETWEEN TURNOUT IN
GUBERNATORIAL ELECTIONS AND DISTANCE FROM THE STATE CAPITAL

State	Time Periods	General Elections		Primary Elections	
		Simple "r"	Partial "r"	Simple "r"	Partial "r"
Montana*	1950	-.12	-.15	-.16	-.28
Cases=counties	1960	.19	.26	-.03	-.09
N=56	1970	.11	-.18	-.13	-.53
Mississippi**	1950	--	--	-.10	-.11
Cases=counties	1960	--	--	-.05	-.09
N=82	1970	--	--	-.08	-.20
Vermont***	1950	-.02	-.06	-.05	-.08
Cases=towns	1960	-.07	-.11	-.05	-.12
N=246	1970	-.22	-.28	-.22	-.28

* Elections used were: (1948, 1952), (1956, 1960, 1964), and (1968, 1972).
Variables controlled were: median years education, rural population, farmers
in the work force, population over 65, ethnic population, median family income,
Democratic vote for governor, population increase, and party competition. In
the primary a factionalization score was used instead of party competition.

** Elections used were: first Democratic primaries in (1947, 1951), (1959,
1963), and (1967, 1971). Variables controlled were: for the 1950 and 1960
periods--population increase, rural population, population over 65, and a
composite SES variable combining median education levels and median family
income (all for the white population), percentage black population and
factionalism in the primary. In the 1970 period population increase was
eliminated for multicolinearity, and variables measure the entire (not just the
white) population. Farmers in the work force were eliminated in all three
periods for the same reason.

***Elections used were: (1950, 1952), (1960, 1962), and (1970, 1972). Varia-
bles controlled were: for 1970--median years education, population density,
population per dairy herd, population over 65, native Vermonters, median
family income, Democratic vote for governor, party competition, and
population increase; for 1960--same as 1970 minus median years education
and native Vermonters; for 1950--same as 1960 minus median family income
and population over 65.

SOURCES: Montana--compiled by the author from original sources and Ellis
Waldron, An Atlas of Montana Politics Since 1864 (Missoula, Montana:
University of Montana Press, 1958); Mississippi--compiled by the
author from Mississippi Official and Statistical Register (Jackson,
Mississippi: Secretary of State, 1948-1952 to 1972-1976); Vermont--
compiled by the author from Vermont Legislative Directory and State
Manual (Montpelier, Vermont: Secretary of State, 1951 to 1973).

linked to the number of air miles from the state capital. The partial correlation coefficient for drop-off in the turnout percentage between the
general and the primary elections averaged for 1968 and 1972 is .61. For
the 1950 and 1960 time periods, it is .21 and .47, respectively. This indicates that the distance in air miles from the capital is increasingly

enlarging the gap between primary and general election turnouts in Montana.

In Mississippi distances are not as great (it is possible to place three Mississippis in Montana) nor are the impediments to travel nearly so severe. The highest "mountain" is only 800 feet above sea level, and there are no winter snows to clog the highways. Yet with a land mass nearly ten times as large as Connecticut's and a much smaller population base, the problems of distance in Mississippi are not insignificant. Moreover, there are other forces that magnetize the peripheral areas of the state and draw attention away from concerns at Jackson, the capital. The southernmost counties of Hancock, Harrison, and Jackson (not to be confused with the capital city of Jackson in Hinds County) face the sea, and the ports of Biloxi and Gulfport look outward into the haze over the Gulf of Mexico.[7] In the very northwestern corner of the state, the Memphis, Tennessee, metropolitan area has a fix on the concerns of many Mississippians. In the far northeastern corner, the fall line of the Tennessee River slashes at Mississippi. This is a land of sandy red hills covered with oak and pine that tips toward Alabama, lending a mood of isolation to the forests of Tishomingo County.

The four counties within Memphis's orbit — De Soto, Marshall, Tate, and Tunica — are far from the state capital at Jackson (see Figure 3.2). Two of these counties lost population in the 1960-1970 decade. One of them, Tunica, had very low turnouts in the primaries of 1967 and 1971, and the other, Marshall, had relatively high turnouts. The black population in both counties is about equal, and both have lower urban populations than the other two counties in the area. In the two counties in which population increased — De Soto by 50.2 percent and Tate by 2.2 percent — the black and urban populations are about equal. De Soto, which is immediately adjacent to the Memphis SMSA, had very low turnouts, and Tate, buffered by De Soto, was close to the statewide mean.

In other areas on the geographic periphery, the results are somewhat more clear. In the northeastern section, two of the three border counties had turnouts in the 1970 period that were higher than the statewide mean, given the black population.[8] Both counties are essentially rural, and the remaining county is 43 percent urban. In the southwestern portion, the rural counties had above-average turnouts, and the most urban county (Adams, 53 percent urban) had a much lower score. The three counties in the southeast each touch the Gulf of Mexico. The two most urban counties (Harrison and Jackson) had very low turnout scores, and Hancock, with more rural residents, had greater turnouts. This suggests that counties on the periphery will have lower turnouts only if they have

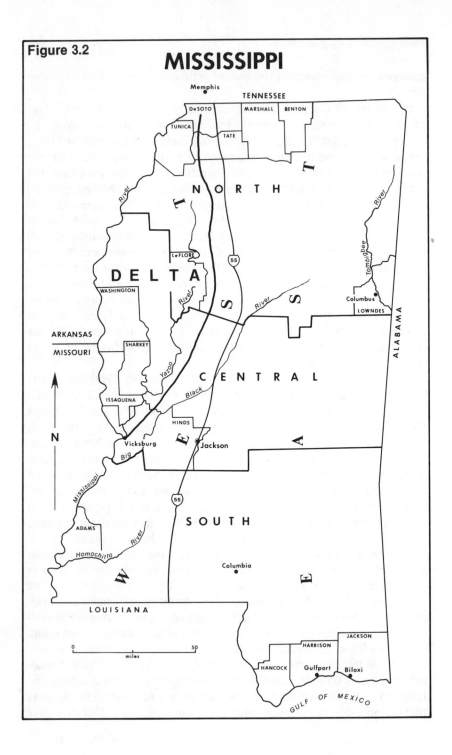

Figure 3.2

MISSISSIPPI

urban populations or are clearly within the influence of a major socioeconomic magnetic force across the state line. Overall, as Table 3.1 makes clear, the actual distance from the state capital in Jackson has little effect on county participation scores.

The capital of Vermont, Montpelier, lies in the center of the state on the Winooski River (see Figure 3.3). Although the total area of the state, 9,267 square miles, is only one-fifth that of Mississippi and although Montana could hold sixteen Vermonts, problems of space are accentuated by a harsh winter climate, very hilly topography, and a scattered population. Although Vermont's mean temperature is higher than that of Montana, the moisture in the winter makes for deep and lasting snowfalls. In a good portion of Montana, the cattle graze on the plains all winter, and fishermen walk the banks of open streams in February. But in Vermont the snows lie deep under cloud-laden skies, the cattle huddle in barnyards, and the streams are icebound. The highways have traditionally followed the contours of the thousands of hills that dominate the landscape like quills on a hedgehog's back. Vermont, like Montana, has a mountain range that cuts the state in two, and east-west travel over the Green Mountains is limited in rural locations. As in Mississippi pockets of the state share socioeconomic linkages with other states. The Northeast Kingdom is set apart from the rest of the state by a range of hills that makes up the western watershed of the Connecticut River, which separates Vermont from New Hampshire.[9] The main north-south highway in this region is on the New Hampshire side (U.S. Route 3). In the very southwestern corner of Vermont, the towns in Bennington County have strong ties with parts of northern Massachusetts and the greater Albany, New York, area. Children in several towns along Vermont's border go to high school in other states on a tuition basis.

Unlike Montana and Mississippi, turnout in Vermont is measured as the percentage of the registered voters who vote, rather than of the eligible voters who vote, since historical data on the population over twenty-one years of age is difficult to obtain for all of Vermont's 246 cities and towns.[10] Benchmark figures were produced for the 1950, 1960, and 1970 periods as they were in the other two states.[11] The distance in air miles to the capital, Montpelier, was then figured for each town and matched against voter participation in both the primary and general elections. The results of this process are given in Table 3.1.

In none of the measurements taken over the three decades do towns on the geographic periphery of Vermont show a strong inclination to participate less in the voting process, whether it be a primary or a general election. However, the correlations in the last period are statistically

82

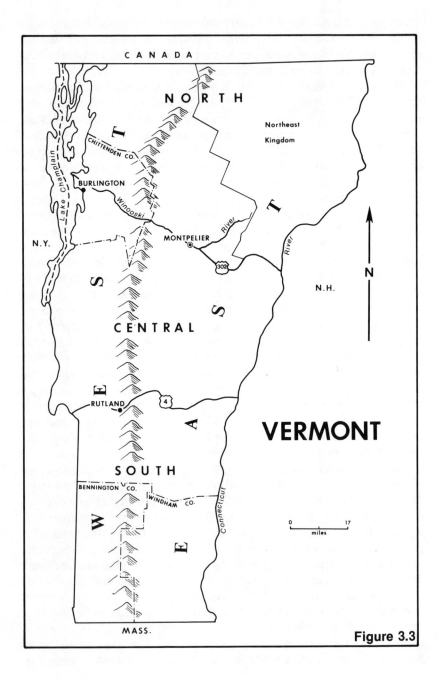

Figure 3.3

significant and vary in the proper direction; that is, as the distance between the town and the capital increases, voting goes down (see Table 3.1).[12] This result confounds some expectations. Surely one might argue that in the early 1950s, when television had yet to penetrate the web of hills and valleys and narrow two-lane highways provided only limited access to Montpelier, the towns on the geographic periphery would be more likely to be on the political periphery than in the post-television, post-interstate-highway decade of the 1970s. The "modernization" of Vermont in the last three decades has not increased the participation of the backbeyond in the culture of the state. If anything, modernization has depressed the participation of the outlying communities.

Vermont's legendary Northeast Kingdom is a good example. This area is made up of forty-seven small towns and one city of under 5,000 population. Most of the towns have fewer than 1,000 residents, and over ten have fewer than 500. It is a land that rolls northward, covered with cedar and fir, marshes, forests, and wildlife. As Vermont has entered the modern era, the Northeast Kingdom has become the "last stand of the Yankees."[13] It is on the periphery both in fact and in spirit.

Yet the Northeast Kingdom towns have historically had slightly higher voter participation scores than have the other towns in the state. In the general elections for governor in the 1950-1952 period, 25 percent of these towns had a turnout that was one standard deviation above the mean, while only 15 percent of the rest of Vermont's towns were in this category. The figures are similar for the primary elections. In the general elections of 1960 and 1962, the Northeast Kingdom had 23 percent of its towns in the high column as against only 12 percent for the rest of the state. In the primaries the figures were 28 percent and 11 percent. The early 1970s found the towns of the Northeast Kingdom more in line with other towns in Vermont. If increased communications and transportation technology have linked this remote area to the rest of Vermont, it has done so coincidentally with a *lowering* of its participation in the electoral politics of the state.

Historically, Vermont's electorate has swelled in the general election, even though the primaries decided the issue in elections of the past. In the 1950-52 period, the general-election turnout was 21 percentage points higher in the average Vermont town. Participation in the primary elections has decreased in the last three decades, and the difference in the turnouts of the two elections has accordingly increased from 21 points in 1950 and 1952 to 36 points in 1960 and 1962 to 39 points in 1970 and 1972. Yet it is not the towns on the geographic periphery that account for the gap in participation between the two elections in Vermont, as was the

case in Montana. When other variables are controlled, only weak and inconclusive correlations appear.

A Note on Method

Throughout the volume "simple" and "partial" correlation coefficients
are used as a shorthand for matching up what goes on in the counties of
Mississippi and Montana and the towns of Vermont. Do not be turned
off by the numbers. They are very useful. A simple correlation coefficient tells us when two phenomena, present in the counties of Montana,
for instance, are related (at least on the face of it). For example, if one
were to measure the amount of rainfall and the height of the hay in July
(the variables) in Montana's fifty-six counties (the cases) and found a
correlation coefficient of .72, one could say that in those counties where
there was more rain there was taller hay. If the coefficient produced was
− .72, one would conclude that the more rain, the shorter the grass (not a
very likely happening). If the coefficient were near zero, one would
assume that there was no relationship between the amount of rain that
fell and the height of the hay in July.

The partial correlation coefficient tests the relationship between two
variables when the other variables are controlled. In other words, might
it not be the case that those counties that had more rain also had more
fertile soil so that it was fertility of the soil and not the amount of rain
that was really associated with the height of the hay? A partial correlation tells us what the relationship between rain and hay would be if every
county in Montana had similar soil types. To be specific, if you controlled for urbanism and education and found a partial correlation coefficient of − .63 between ethnicity and the Republican vote in Montana, it
would mean that if all of Montana's counties had the same percentage of
city dwellers and the same percentage of college graduates, then a higher
percentage of ethnic stock would mean a lower Republican vote.

If you are tempted to shy away from dealing with numbers, think of it
this way. To help you understand, say, the relationship between the
black population of Mississippi and the Goldwater vote of 1964, I could
present two maps of the state, one shading in the counties of Goldwater's
strength and the other shading in the counties where the black population
is high. You could then visually compare the two maps and come to some
conclusion about the association between the two variables. But think of
the imprecision involved! And how does one convey one's findings?
More than that, it would take hundreds of maps to adequately show the
findings of one chapter in this book, and even then the eye could not

critically cover, and therefore the mind could not digest, the infinite complexity of the findings. There is no other way to say it: If we are to be precise and thorough in our analysis of social events, we must use numbers.

Because quantification is such a powerful tool, it is also a very dangerous one. In using correlation coefficients in particular, three dangers are very important to keep in mind. First, the only proper conclusion from tests of this nature is that as one variable changes across a number of counties, another variable changes as well. One is not allowed to claim that there is a causative link between the two. Second, one is not permitted to claim that *individuals* of a certain type in a county account for the fact that, in the aggregate, a county's population acts in a certain way. In other words, if we find that as the percentage of farmers in the work force increases the Republican percentage of the gubernatorial vote increases, the claim cannot be made that farmers are more likely to vote Republican. Of course, the expectation would be that farmers were voting Republican, especially if one is able to control for other potentially important variables by means of a partial coefficient. Third, the correlation coefficients don't account for curvilinear distributions that may be important. Remember the case of the amount of rain and the height of the hay. It is very possible, for instance, that increases in amounts of rain up to a certain point increase the length of the grass but that after that point more water actually stunts growth. When the data for all the counties are compared it may appear in the aggregate that there is no relation between rain and hay because the two tendencies cancel each other out in combination.

Intrastate Regionalism

Regionalism is another explanatory factor that may be used to piece the voter turnout puzzle together. Daniel Elazar has described the phenomenon as geological strata and overlays. Residues of participant cultures are left in particular areas as socioeconomic movements cross and crisscross, advance or recede over the face of the state. We may recall that where M cultures predominate, Elazar predicts greater civic involvement in political life.[14]

Rural states are a promising hunting ground for the connection between region and political culture. The life-styles, economic status, and social behavior of rural people are apt to reflect the land around them. It was the environment that drew them to the land in the first place — the miners to the mountains and now to the plains, the farmers to the river bottoms, and the loggers to the forests. They brought with them particular dispositions toward government. These were remolded by the new topographical conditions, shaped and nurtured by the imperatives of the land and the policies demanded or not demanded of government for the fulfillment of life.

In Vermont the hills have long decreed the nature of human subsistence and, in the process, outlined the character of those who worked and stayed — sending those with differing views outward to the deep sod of the prairies. Most would say that the state's economic conservatism yet gentleness and benevolence for the have-nots in society comes in part from the harsh realities of trying to farm on rocky, mountain pastures and in part from the strength of the sense of community in the small towns, which were themselves created, isolated, and then preserved in the folds of the hills. In Montana the honesty and strength of libertarianism must somehow be fed by the spirit of freedom and self-reliance that is borne on the breezes over bare, rolling, endless plains. That honesty and strength must also be replenished by the spires and solitude of the mountains. There the relationship of man to nature is as everyday as moose grazing in a roadside bog, reports of a grizzly up the river, or a herd of antelope silhouetted on the horizon. In Montana these events are as common as a tollbooth is in New Jersey.

Along the Mississippi River's floodplain, the white men used slaves to grow cotton and to grow rich, while in the hills to the east the "poor whites" scraped a living from the few inches of good soil, northern lumber companies literally ripped away the forests, and the blazing summer sun slowed life to a sleepy crawl. Those people who cleared an opening in the hardwood forests or piney woods for themselves rose to the cry of populism, while those who governed the plantations on the delta protected the existing order. Mississippi's great bifaction of politics (populism versus aristocracy) was from the beginning tied to the saliency of region.

In Montana the most obvious geographic feature is the Great Divide, the range of Rocky Mountains that separates east from west. Nineteen of Montana's counties have a majority of their populations living on the west side of the divide. The other thirty-seven counties are on the east. Those who know the two parts of Montana best describe them as follows. Rocky Mountain Montana

> is a land of high mountains and deep valleys, green forests and sparkling waters, dams and power lines, sawmills, mines, and smelters, irrigated farms and mountain ranches, spectacular scenery and outdoor recreation, heavily populated pockets and virtually uninhabited wild lands.

Great Plains Montana

> is a vast expanse of plateaus and hills, plains and mountain outliners, grass
> lands and park lands, exotic* rivers and flood plain forests, yellow green
> fields and brown fallow strips, vast ranches and narrow, irrigated steeps,
> flower mills and stockyards, oil wells and fuel refineries, coal mines and
> thermal-electric plants . . . it has a cold winter, warm summer, semiarid
> steep climate.[15]

There are other ways of classifying Montana by region. The Montana
Environmental Quality Council has divided the state into seven environmental regions in a refined attempt to distinguish the state's environmentally unique areas. These regions are the Columbia River
Rockies, Broad Valley Rockies, Yellowstone Rockies, the Two Rivers
Region (where the Yellowstone and the Missouri drift toward one
another and almost touch before slipping over the border into North
Dakota), the Big Dry Region, the Sweet Grass Plains (former home of
the Blackfoot Indians), and the Rocky Mountain Foreland.[16] Montana
has other regions that combine aspects of human planning and
geographical imperatives, created to ease the burdens of government activity, which originates at a far-distant capital. There are six conservation
districts and five health-planning districts.[17]

A final regional classification has been established by a keen observer
of the Montanan political system, Ellis Waldron. Waldron employs a
combination of deductive premise and empirical observation and notes
that

> Economic and political life in Montana fortifies the notion that a mountain
> culture encourages localism and diversity among its valley dwellers. It is
> tempting to say that Montana looks outward in three divergent directions,
> rather than inward upon itself as a state. Each of the three largest cities lies
> in a distinct economic and political region, roughly identifiable as one of
> the great river drainages. These cities are service and supply centers and
> they reflect, at least as much as they shape, the particular economic and
> political concerns of their respective regions.[18]

The three regions are (1) the eleven counties west of the Great Divide
that are drained by the Columbia River, with a diversified economy
based on mining, forestry, tourism, manufacturing, and several kinds of
agriculture; (2) the southern counties of Montana (twenty-six of them)

*Used in its geographic sense here to mean arising from humid areas upstream.

that are mountainous in the west where they form the headwaters of the Missouri and the Yellowstone rivers and flat in the east where they compose the Yellowstone watershed (they are rangeland, livestock counties); and (3) the nineteen northern "high line" counties east of the mountains that follow the Missouri eastward to North Dakota (they are dryland, grain-growing, agricultural counties). Each region has its urban influence—Butte and Missoula in the west, Billings in the south, and Great Falls in the north—and each has from 30 percent to 35 percent of the state's population.[19]

In order to make use of these various regional variables to predict levels of turnout, each of Montana's fifty-six counties was classified according to its level of voting for governor and its location in one of the several regions. Tables were then constructed for each of the five regional classifications, and the tables cross-tabulated regions and levels of turnout by county. Fifteen tables were prepared, one for each regional classification for each of the three different time periods we are considering in this analysis. Correlation coefficients were extracted and placed in a summary table (see Table 3.2). As the coefficient increases, it means that we are better able to predict which type of turnout (high, medium, or low) a county has if we know which region it is in. (For purposes of analysis, the smaller Yellowstone Rockies Region was combined with the Broad Valley Rockies Region, which results in six rather than seven environmental regions.)

Table 3.2 indicates that none of the regional breakdowns significantly predicts voter turnout. Although the regions per se are not meaningfully correlated with political participation, the location of the regions in the state are important. If we arrange the regions in terms of their positions on an east-west continuum, we find that counties in the west have a lower turnout than do counties in the east. For example, five percent of the counties in Rocky Mountain Montana had a turnout that was one standard deviation above the mean in the 1970 period. Great Plains Montana had twenty-two percent of its counties in that category. When a "tau" coefficient, which tests for direction and linearity, was applied to the tables for the 1970 east-west division, it was found to be relatively strong, .26, and statistically significant at the .02 level. Thus on closer inspection of the tables that produced the "eta" correlations, it is possible to detect that if the various regions are placed in the table in order of their east-west positions in Montana, the tau coefficient becomes stronger, revealing a statistically significant pattern with the regions of the west displaying lower turnout than those of the east. In classifying eastern Montana as having an M culture, Elazar was on target. People on the sunrise side

TABLE 3.2

THE RELATIONSHIP BETWEEN REGION AND
VOTER TURNOUT IN MONTANA, MISSISSIPPI, AND VERMONT*

		1950		1960		1970	
		Eta	P^{+}	Eta	P	Eta	P
MONTANA (Cases=Counties, N=56)							
Mountains and Plains	(2)**	.04	.26	.22	.09	.27	.14
Environmental Regions	(6)	.32	.30	.34	.54	.33	.21
Conservation Districts	(6)	.25	.44	.42	.07	.29	.38
Health Districts	(5)	.25	.57	.28	.27	.28	.38
Waldron's Divisions	(3)	.17	.48	.13	.15	.23	.34
MISSISSIPPI* (Cases=Counties, N=82)							
East and West	(2)	.22	.01	.18	.03	.18	.18
Delta and Hills	(2)	.10	.05	.14	.09	.17	.30
North to South	(3)	.09	.33	.28	.04	.27	.04
VERMONT (Cases=Towns, N=246)							
Kingdom and Others	(2)	.03	.24	.15	.07	.09	.38
North to South	(3)	.10	.16	.16	.01	.03	.89
Mountain Rule	(2)	.05	.70	.08	.32	.01	.71

† P=probability that the relationship could have occurred by chance.

* For notes on time periods, see Table 3.1.

** (N)=number of divisions in classification.

***Turnout controlled for black population.

SOURCE: Turnout, see Table 3.1; regional classification, see reference in text.

of the divide are more likely to participate in politics.

A final point is worth noting. The east-west division in levels of voter turnout is growing stronger, not weaker. The tau coefficient, which was .26 in 1970, was only .21 in 1960 and .04 in 1950. This fact is important since one would expect that the potential erasure of geographic boundaries by travel and communications technology would blur the impact of such boundaries on social and political life and trumpet a lessening role for physical barriers such as mountain ranges in the political world. But the mountains in Montana mean more now than they did thirty years ago, at least as far as this aspect of political culture is concerned.

There are no regional features in Mississippi that can match for sheer spectacle the sky reachers of the Rockies. But there are features nonetheless, and they are geographically as critical as those of Montana. Montana has its mountains and its plains; Mississippi has its delta and its hills. The Delta region has deep, black soil; the Hills region, thinner, poorer soil. The Delta is perfectly flat; the Hills are rolling or jagged depending on the amount of erosion. The Delta has few trees, only some oak and cypress; the hills are forested with oak, hickory, and pine. The Delta has hard, cool groundwater; the hills have soft water. A solid majority of the people in many Delta counties are black; this is not the case in the Hills. The Delta has been losing population faster than the Hills. Because it is black, the people are generally less educated, generally poorer. In 1970 the median family income of the whites in the Delta averaged over $5,000 above that of the blacks. In the Hills, where the whites are poorer and the blacks are better off, the difference in median family income is cut nearly in half. The differences continue in the realm of politics. The Delta is conservative; the Hills, populist. The Delta voted against prohibition; the Hills, for it.

Depending on one's definition of the Delta region, it can comprise between eleven and twenty-two of Mississippi's eighty-two counties. One writer has commented that it "begins in the lobby of the Peabody Hotel in Memphis and ends on Catfish Row in Vicksburg."[20] Most people agree that it begins at the Tennessee border and continues south to Vicksburg, about two-thirds the way down the state. Just how far east the Delta stretches varies according to whether or not one wishes to include all of the territory west of the Yazoo River. Sticking strictly to a definition based on the soils, I have used the twelve counties included in the Delta region of the land resource map produced by the Agricultural Experiment Station at Mississippi State University.[21]

Two other regional arrangements have been included in the search for an explanation of the ups and downs in voter turnout. One is a more general east-west division marked by the major interstate highway (I-55) that runs from Memphis in the north to the Louisiana border in the south. The second is a three-way north to south arrangement based on Mississippi's major administrative districts for the state Supreme Court and the Highway and Public Service Commission[22] (see Figure 3.2).

Although one must confess to a bit of blind empiricism in establishing the east-west and north-south divisions, the Delta-Hills alignment carries with it a hypothesis concerning turnout. Since the voting-level figures we use here control for the black population, which is very high in the Delta, that region should have a higher turnout than the Hills region because the whites in the Delta are in the higher-income–higher-education brackets. (These variables are discussed in much more detail below.) Moreover, the "planter class" of the Delta is motivated politically by the aspects of Elazar's T culture that prompt involvement, i.e., politics is a good to be practiced by everyone in the governing class.

But the Delta counties actually have a lower turnout than do the other counties in the state. The eta coefficients are very small, however, although in the 1950 period the relationship was significant statistically (see Table 3.2). In that period none of the Delta counties had participation that was one standard deviation above the statewide mean, but eighteen (26 percent) of the Hill counties had turnout in that category. In the 1970 period one of the Delta counties had high participation, but three had slipped from the middle category to the low category (one standard deviation or more below the mean).

The broader east-west division is more important. In 1950, 4 percent of the counties west of what is now I-55 had high turnout, and of the counties in the Hills, 31 percent had high turnout. By moving the line eastward, we have included in the western section fifteen counties of the Loess Bluffs area on the Delta border and portions of the Loess Hills area. All of the counties in the western region share a topographical feature in that they are all a part of the Mississippi River watershed and their land tips west, drained by the Yazoo, Big Black, and Homochitto rivers.

The north to south classifications seem to be becoming more important than the east-west division. The strongest 1970 eta coefficient we find in Table 3.2 is for the north to south relationship. In that period 10 percent of the thirteen northern counties had high turnout, but 40 percent of the thirty southern counties fell in the high turnout group. If we group the northern and middle counties together in order to include all of the Delta counties in the northern section and compare them with the remaining thirty southern counties, we find a 1970 tau coefficient of .26, which is significant at the .01 level. The tau was only .20 in 1960 and .06 in 1950. What we may be seeing regarding voter turnout is a revolving of the regional axis so the line of demarcation lies horizontally east to west across the state, not vertically north to south.

Vermont cannot match either Montana or Mississippi in terms of having distinctive geographic regions. The Great Plains and Rocky Mountains in Montana and the Delta and the Hills in Mississippi mark clearly different environments. If one parachuted blindfolded into any part of Vermont, only the trained eye could locate which part of the state one was in when the blindfold was removed. True, Vermont has its Northeast Kingdom, which tends to fir and cedar rather than to hardwood, and the hills are more gentle in that area than in the rest of the state. But generally speaking, the differences are defined more by man's use of the land than by its natural topography.

Traditionally, the most important regional split in Vermont is defined by the Green Mountains, which cut the state in two along a north-south line. But, unlike Montana, the topography on one side is not markedly dissimilar to that on the other side. The eastern flank of the mountains falls off toward the Connecticut River and New Hampshire, the western flank slopes toward the Champlain Valley and New York State. To be sure, geophysical conditions are not equal on the two sides of the mountains. Corn grows better in the sandy basin of the Connecticut River than it does in the clay of the Lake Champlain basin, for instance. But by and large, the regions are similar.

Nevertheless, the east-west split in Vermont has had a profound impact on the politics of the state, and the linkage between this regional dichotomy and public life is equaled in few other states in the Union.[23] This is because of the nature of the settlement of the two valleys, the Connecticut and the Champlain, and because of the fact that for well over a century the mountains were a formidable impediment to travel and communication between the two. The early settlements in eastern Vermont were well-defined political communities, which were almost direct reproductions of the parent communities in southern New England. These settlers were more conservative than the land-speculating radicals to the west of the mountains who were more adventurers and soldiers of fortune than homesteaders. In the early days of the state, these two regions differed on a host of issues, and their disagreements nearly flared into open warfare on occasion. The towns along the Connecticut River actually seceded from Vermont and, along with equally rebellious towns on the New Hampshire side of the river, created for a time an independent river kingdom.[24] Vermont's political leaders were aware of this regional difference, and they went to great lengths to share important public posts with representatives from both sides of the mountains.

More recently another regional influence, which involves a north to south pattern, has become visible in Vermont. The state's most significant intrastate river, the Winooski, flows east to west across most of the state, cutting a gorge through the mountains, and it provides a natural axis on which to compare north to south. This natural line is continued eastward to New Hampshire by U.S. Route 302, and U.S. Route 4 further south can be used to set apart that region (see Figure 3.3). The towns in the north differ significantly from the towns in the south on variables such as income, education, and influx of newcomers (the north has less of all three), and they have shown an inclination to differ on referenda for amendments to the state constitution. The north has tended to say no; the south, yes.[25]

It was noted earlier that the Northeast Kingdom region had a bit more turnout than the rest of the state in the 1950 and 1960 periods but that by 1970 the differences had leveled out. In order to make more sense of the total picture, a table was constructed for each regional classification for each time period, as was done for Montana and Mississippi. Correlation coefficients and probability figures for the nine tables are recorded in Table 3.2. It is clear that regional divisions in Vermont do not help us understand why some towns have higher voting records than others. The "mountain rule" fails to outline variations in the participant character of the state's political culture. The new north to south regions have shown some potential for use in making predictions of electoral behavior in Vermont, but they are not helpful in distinguishing turnout levels. By 1970 there is simply nothing to be made of the relationship between region and turnout in Vermont. The participant culture of the state seems to be geographically homogeneous.

Political Competition

So far we have looked at the geophysical features of rural states and how those features affect political participation; namely, how far the polling booth is from the center of political activity in the state and the regional context of the places where votes are cast. There is also substantial literature that suggests that competition for office whets the combative appetite of the electorate, stimulating higher turnout.[26] The logic is straightforward. The more divided a town or county is on a slate of candidates, the greater the number of contentious, political, interpersonal contacts. These contacts among neighbors solidify support and identify the opposition. Both factors increase the propensity to vote.

General-election competition in Vermont and Montana was defined as how close the vote for the Democratic candidates was to 50 percent. This device is commonly used to test the competitive tendency of political units. A county in Montana or a town in Vermont that casts 42 percent for the Democratic candidate is deemed identical to a county or town that casts 58 percent for the Democratic candidate. Both of these political units are more competitive than a town that votes 65 percent or

35 percent Democratic. The expectation is that jurisdictions in which the Democrats' share of the vote is close to 50 percent will have the higher turnout. Since there has been no effective competition for the Democrats in Mississippi in the postwar era until very recently, no general-election analysis was made for that state.

For the primary elections, in which there are often more than two candidates, a factionalization score was created for each election, party, and county or town in the three states for each of the elections in each of the time periods. In Montana and Vermont the factionalization scores of the two parties were combined.

In the 1968 gubernatorial primary in Montana, for instance, there were ten candidates in the race—four Republicans and six Democrats. The factionalization score is calculated by summing the squared percent of the total vote received by each candidate within a party and subtracting the total from 1.0.[27] Thus if two candidates are in the primary race and both receive 50 percent of the vote in a particular county, the factionalization score for that party is $1 - [(.50)^2 + (.50)^2]$ or $1 - (.25 + .25)$ or .50. If one candidate gets 100 percent of the vote, the factionalization score is, of course, zero. As more candidates enter the race and/or the candidates divide the vote more evenly, the score increases. Thus a twenty-candidate race in which each receives an equal share of the vote (5 percent) would mean a factionalization score of .95.

Only in Montana and only in the most recent election period considered (1968-1972) did two-party competition in the general election and factionalization in the primary have an effect on turnout. When variables such as education, income, distance from the capital, rural population, and so forth are controlled, factionalization is seen to have some independent effect (the partial correlation coefficient is .33) on the primary election turnout (see Table 3.3). In the general election the partial is .39, which means that in counties in which the two-party vote nears a more even split, the percentage of eligible voters voting in the election increases. Neither relationship is strong, however, and neither occurs in the 1960 or 1950 periods. The primary is more important in Mississippi, but factionalization is not a cause of increased voting. In Vermont neither factionalization nor two-party competition has any effect.

It appears that alternate models must be consulted as we look for an explanation of political participation in the rural states. The signposts left for us by numerous scholars over the last half century do not involve region or competition as much as they do socioeconomic environment. The pathway is not well marked, however, and there is a recent branching that one must be careful not to ignore. I refer to these two "trails," the older route and the new branch, as the standard SES hypothesis and the challenger hypothesis.

TABLE 3.3

COMPETITION AND TURNOUT IN
MONTANA, MISSISSIPPI, AND VERMONT
1950, 1960, 1970 PRIMARY AND GENERAL ELECTIONS FOR
GOVERNOR - SIMPLE AND PARTIAL CORRELATION COEFFICIENTS*

| Time Period | MONTANA | | | | MISSISSIPPI | | | | VERMONT | | | |
| | Primary | | General | | Primary | | General | | Primary | | General | |
	S	P	S	P	S	P	S	P	S	P	S	P
1950	-.17	-.17	.08	.12	.09	.12	--	--	-.15	-.04	-.17	-.03
1960	.14	.19	.10	.06	-.07	.00	--	--	-.19	-.02	-.02	-.01
1970	-.10	.33	.21	.39	.23	.17	--	--	-.07	.01	.04	.03

* Variables controlled: Montana--median years education, rural population, farmers in the work force, population over 65, ethnic population, median family income, population increase, distance from the capital, Democratic party strength. In the 1950 period in Montana, ethnic population was not a control variable. Mississippi in 1950 and 1960--rural population, farmers in the work force, population increase, distance from the capital, population over 65, and a composite SES variable combining median years education and median family income. In 1970--the same except for population increase, which was eliminated because of its rate of multicolinearity. Vermont in 1970--Democratic party strength, population density, population per dairy herd, median years education, population over 65, distance from the capital, median family income, population increase, native Vermonters; 1950--same as 1960 except lacking population over 65 and median family income. Primary competition is measured by the factionalization score. General election competition is measured as the percentage point deviation of the Democratic vote from 50 percent, ignoring the sign.

SOURCE: Same as for Table 3.1.

Standard SES and Challenger Hypotheses

At its widest point, the standard hypothesis involves modernization. The hypothesis began to develop in the 1940s when a series of studies established the core element of the theory—that people in the higher socioeconomic brackets participate more.[28] These findings have been reinforced over time[29] and were still receiving support well into the 1970s.[30] A complementary theme emerged in the late 1950s and early 1960s, and these new studies, generated by students of comparative politics and comparative political development, focused on urbanism as an element of modernization.[31] In a nutshell, the standard view claims that urbanism and higher-status variables (income, education, professional occupations) are invariably intertwined. Although each could have an independent and positive role to play in increasing turnout at the polls, both reinforce the other.

But the 1970s spelled trouble for the standard hypothesis. A growing store of evidence began to suggest that urbanization, socioeconomic development, and increased levels of political involvement are not positively related. In fact, some studies argued that the relationship is actually an inverse one. Research was conducted in many parts of the globe, including the developing countries,[32] and one five-nation study concluded bluntly, "the size of the community in which a citizen lives adds nothing to our understanding of his general level of political participation."[33] In his important analysis of six developing countries Alex Inkeles reported, "our most striking finding is precisely that . . . the larger and more cosmopolitan the city, the less the frequency of active citizenship in the common-man stratum of society."[34]

Scholarship on participation in the United States also began to chip away at the notion that those with more education, higher incomes, and/or living in urban places become more involved in public-sector matters. In American states[35] and cities,[36] structural variables were found to be more important than SES factors. Many other studies have added to the case against the SES[37] hypothesis, and an award-winning volume on participation in America has just about nailed the coffin shut. "The small, peripheral community is not the place where participation is most inhibited. Rather, the citizens participate more than their social characteristics would predict."[38] Thus the challenger hypothesis asserts that small, stable places where citizens have sunk deep roots, joined many local organizations, and developed a "stake" in the community are where political participation will be highest, educational background and cosmopolitanism notwithstanding.

The raw material exists in Montana, Mississippi, and Vermont to put the two conflicting ideas to the test. In all three states there are counties and towns that have gained population sharply over the last twenty years. There are also places where population has decreased substantially. Since population increases threaten the sense of community for those already living in an area and bring in new potential voters who lack a sense of community when they arrive, one would expect (given the Verba and Nie lead) that participation would be lower where population increase is higher. Our task is to place that variable in the context of other SES factors such as income, education, rural population, number of older people in the community (since it has been shown that voting is logistically more difficult for older people and logic tells us that rural residence must maximize this difficulty), farm population (Stickle has shown that farmers vote more, not less),[39] and ethnic population (areas with high ethnic concentrations have been shown to have higher turnout).[40]

In Montana there is an inverse correlation in the fifty-six counties between population increase and turnout, precisely in the manner predicted by the "sense of community" hypothesis. Rural population is negatively associated with population increase and positively associated with turnout. Income, which correlates positively with population increase, is negatively tied to participation, even though the standard hypothesis suggests the opposite. Two questions: Is rural population positively associated with turnout because of its negative association with population increase? and Is income negatively associated because of its statistical link to ruralism?

It is possible to look at counties in Montana with equal percentages of rural people to see if changes in income levels in those counties tell us any more about voting percentages. For instance, if one selects four of Montana's counties (Daniels, Granite, Meagher, and Teton) at random from those counties with no urban population, we find that their average turnout was 78 percent in the general election in the 1970 period. The median family income was $7,295. The four counties with the greatest urban population (Cascade, Missoula, Silverbow, and Yellowstone—all 75-percent urban or more) had an average turnout of 68 percent, 10 percentage points lower despite a median family income of $8,915. Within the rural category, however, we find that the two counties with the lowest median family income ($7,030) had only a 72-percent turnout, and the two with the highest had an 84-percent turnout. The same thing happens in the urban group of counties. The highest turnout is in the wealthiest rural counties; the lowest turnout is in the poorest urban counties. Both variables count.

The partial correlation coefficients in Table 3.4 tell us what the impact of ruralism or income or education would be on voting if every single county in Montana were similar in all other variables. A powerful analytic tool indeed, and the results fall in step with the expectations. When stripped clean of contaminating variables, income shows a mild positive association in 1970 and 1950. The effect of education is strengthened under controls. A strong positive simple correlation between older population and turnout is wiped out; evidently it was the product of a strong association with ruralism. The partials also tell us that the farming population per se has little to do with voting, although a weak, statistically significant association remains in 1970. The relationship of people to space, defined as the percentage of the population living in places of under 2,500 (rural population), also loses some of its influence when it is disassociated from the other variables. Finally, the predictive power of population increase is about halved.

TABLE 3.4

CORRELATIONS BETWEEN VOTER TURNOUT FOR GOVERNOR AND
SES VARIABLES IN MONTANA AND MISSISSIPPI

MONTANA*   TIME PERIODS

Primary Elections	1970		1960		1950	
	S**	P**	S	P	S	P
Education	.24	.26***	.12	.44	.10	.24
Rural Population	.44	.31	.35	.12	.21	.31
Farmers and Ranchers	.56	.33	.51	.21	.18	-.10
Old Population	.53	.12	.31	-.19	.14	.03
Ethnic Population	.31	.33	.34	.50	--	--
Income	-.32	.45	-.18	.07	.17	.30
Population Increase	-.63	-.42	-.54	-.46	-.39	-.53

General Elections

	S	P	S	P	S	P
Education	.24	.39	.04	.43	.12	.49
Rural Population	.48	.34	.46	.24	.36	.41
Farmers and Ranchers	.65	.28	.60	.23	.35	.11
Old Population	.51	-.04	.39	.16	.15	.06
Ethnic Population	.37	.41	.26	.31	--	--
Income	-.32	.37	-.29	.06	.09	.28
Population Increase	-.64	-.34	-.53	-.19	-.45	-.56

MISSISSIPPI (FIRST PRIMARY)****

	S	P	S	P	S	P
Socioeconomic Status	-.49	-.09	-.63	.01	-.53	.05
Rural Population	.72	.59	.78	.53	.69	.39
Population Increase	--	--	-.72	-.31	-.70	-.31
Old Population	.61	.41	.46	.02	.43	.10

*   Also controlled were: distance from the capital and factionalization in
the primary. In the general election, distance from the capital, two-
party competition, and Democratic party strength were controlled.

**   S = Simple Correlation Coefficients; P = Partial Correlation Coefficients

***   Underlined coefficients are significant at the .05 level.

****Variables are for the white population only in the 1950 and 1960 periods.
In all three periods, farmers in the work force were eliminated because of
multicolinearity with rural population. In 1970 population increase was
eliminated because of its multicolinearity with the SES composite variable.
The SES composite combines education and income. Controlled also were distance from the state capital and factionalism.

SOURCE: Same as for Table 3.1.

Under controls the percentage of first- and second-generation ethnics
becomes the strongest independent variable, which supports the findings
of Alford and Lee mentioned earlier. An inspection of individual counties shows this finding to be true. Silverbow County, Montana, where the
city of Butte is perched precariously on the edge of the biggest open-pit
copper mine in the world, has very high turnout, despite the facts that it
is very urban, given Montana standards, and it has lower income levels

than most cities its size in the state. Butte's ethnic component is among the highest in Montana. It has been called the strongest labor city in America, and traditionally it has harbored a political machine akin to those of the cities in the East. Hidden in a deep valley high in the Rocky Mountains in one of the most rural states in the nation, Butte exhibits participatory habits of the large, older, ethnic, machine metropolises.

Over time, in both primary and general elections, the rural variable has lost influence, and some changes have occurred in individual relationships. But generally the findings of 1970 are similar to those of 1950. The traditional hypothesis is supported by moderate to weak associations among education, income, and turnout. The challenger, "loss of boundariedness" school, predicts the positive associations with rural population and the negative correlation with population increase. The combined ability of these five principal variables to explain voter turnout is impressive. The multiple correlation coefficient (R) is .80, explaining 64 percent of the variance in the turnout figures from county to county.[41]

A completely different picture emerges for Mississippi. When three pairs of counties are randomly drawn so that each set has equal percentages of blacks in the counties but varies at the maximum on urbanization, it becomes clear that the percentage of the population classified as rural has a strong and consistent effect on turnout, irrespective of levels of income and education. A brief inspection of Table 3.5 reveals that when highly urban counties are matched against intensely rural counties with equal percentages of blacks, the urban counties are soundly trounced on their turnout percentages, falling an average of 22 percentage points below the rural counties, despite the fact that the urban counties have substantially higher levels of income and education. Turnout levels for sets of counties that don't vary on urbanization but do have different levels of income indicate that sometimes higher income seems to help turnout but at other times it does not. The two Delta counties of Tunica and Issaquena have no urban population, but they differ substantially on the median family income of the whites. In 1970 Issaquena, just north of Vicksburg on the Mississippi, had a median family income among whites of $8,926. Up the river a couple of hundred miles, Tunica's median family income for whites was only $6,670. Issaquena's turnout was 14 percentage points higher than expected, given the number of blacks in the population, and Tunica's was 14 percentage points lower than expected. Sharkey County also had a high income for a totally rural county, $8,346, but fell 11 percentage points behind equally rural Benton County, even though the latter's median family income for whites was only $5,538. On the other end of the urban scale, some counties had a higher turnout coincidental with higher income — Jackson versus Har-

TABLE 3.5

THE RELATIONSHIP BETWEEN VARIOUS SES VARIABLES AND
VOTER TURNOUT IN SELECTED MISSISSIPPI COUNTIES FOR THE 1970 PERIOD**

County Pair	Black Population	Urban Population	Median Years Education	Median Family Income	Predicted* Turnout	Actual Turnout
I George County	12%	0%	10.5	$6,619	71%	75%
Jackson County	16%	71%	12.2	$8,548	70%	45%
II Covington County	33%	0%	10.0	$5,591	64%	75%
Lauderdale County	31%	67%	11.7	$6,621	64%	50%
III Kemper County	56%	0%	8.8	$3,416	56%	66%
LeFlore County	58%	53%	9.6	$5,315	55%	42%

* The turnout expected given the black population and its relationship to turnout in the 1967 and 1971 first Democratic primaries.

** 1967 and 1971 elections combined.

SOURCE: Same as for Table 3.1.

rison and Adams versus LeFlore. In other mostly urban counties, in which income varied substantially, turnout remained stable — Lafayette versus Warren and Washington versus Jackson.

When we submit all the counties and all the relevant variables for each historical time period in Mississippi to a rigorous statistical test akin to what we did for Montana, the profound impact of ruralism on Mississippi's political participation crystallizes (see Table 3.4).

White voters in Mississippi (and they were for the most part the only voters for most of our analysis) display a strong linkage to the "sense of community" hypothesis. Population change affects voting negatively as the model suggests it might. Citizens in counties in which the population is located in small rural communities vote much more than citizens in the larger towns and small cities of the more urban counties. One of the problems in trying to make sense out of politics in Mississippi (and the South generally) has been that scholars have been so concerned (justifiably) with the race variable.[42] Although many scholars have paid lip service to Mississippi's ruralism,[43] the fact is that few have tried to lay aside race and take a hard squint at the political effects of southern ruralism.[44] One who has, V. O. Key, Jr., pointed to the strong relationship between metropolitanism and low voter turnout in the South as early as 1949.[45] Our data confirm Key's findings in Mississippi for the twenty-five-year period following the publication of his *Southern Politics,* and the data suggest one of the purest relationships between rural life and politics found in the post–World War II literature on the topic. In Mississippi the SES hypothesis has been shot full of holes.

The standard model finds smoother terrain in Vermont. Educational levels are the major predictor of higher voting turnout in the general and primary elections for governor. The community boundariedness theory is contradicted by the fact that those towns that have gained the most population over a twenty-year period do not have lower participation, they have higher. The reader will note that these correlations are weaker than those for Mississippi and Montana, yet they still reach levels of statistical significance. This is because the number of "cases" in Vermont is higher. There are 246 cities and towns in Vermont and only 56 counties in Montana and 82 in Mississippi.

Comparisons are hard to make over time in Vermont because the data are more limited. However, it is noteworthy that turnout in the primary election, which was once directed by the same forces that prompted turnout in the general election, is now apt to react to different elements. The figures in Table 3.6 reveal that population density, farming influence, and population increase shared similar coefficients with turnout in the general and primary elections in the 1950 period. This similarity began to

TABLE 3.6

CORRELATIONS BETWEEN VOTER TURNOUT
AND SES VARIABLES IN VERMONT, PRIMARY AND
GENERAL ELECTIONS FOR GOVERNOR 1950, 1960, 1970

TIME PERIODS

Primary Elections	1970		1960		1950	
	S*	P**	S	P	S	P
Population Density	-.15	-.15***	-.53	-.48	-.27	-.22
Per Capita Dairy Herds	-.03	-.04	.09	-.01	.02	.04
Education	.20	.16	--	--	--	--
Old Population	.06	.03	--	--	--	--
Income	.07	.04	-.05	-.05	--	--
Vermont Natives	-.15	-.10	--	--	--	--
Population Increase	.05	-.02	-.28	-.06	-.09	.03

General Elections						
Population Density	.02	-.07	-.19	-.22	-.22	-.28
Per Capita Dairy Herds	.04	.07	-.02	-.02	-.06	-.04
Education	.27	.20	--	--	--	--
Old Population	-.02	.06	--	--	--	--
Income	-.01	-.10	.01	.00	--	--
Vermont Natives	-.09	-.06	--	--	--	--
Population Increase	.23	.17	.01	.09	-.05	-.03

* S = Simple Correlation Coefficients; P = Partial Correlation Coefficients

** Also controlled were the variables: distance from the capital and
factionalization in the primary. In the general election, distance
from the capital, two-party competition and Democratic party strength
were also controlled.

***Underlined coefficients are significant at the .05 level.

SOURCE: Same as for Table 3.1.

shake a bit a decade later. Voter participation was significantly higher in
the low-density towns in both elections but much more so in the primary.
By 1970 density had been wiped out as a factor in the general election but
retained a weak negative association in the primary. Population increase
began to matter also in 1970 in the general election, but it still remained
inconclusive in the primary. The primary seems to be lagging behind the
general election in Vermont in that it retains residues of the density connection and it has not been affected by Vermont's recent population

increases. Vermont's small farming towns are no longer the places of higher participation for which they once were known. Overall, what we have in Vermont is a highly diffused participatory environment with no visible empirical linkages to particular kinds of towns, except for education, which blinks ever so faintly in the statistical sky.

Summary

Rural states like Montana and Vermont are not on the participatory "periphery" in voting for the national leader who sits in faraway Washington. Mississippi has been, but not because it is rural. Within each of these states there is only spotty evidence that distance from the state capital (geographic remoteness) lowers participation. Interestingly, in both Montana and Vermont this evidence has cropped up in the most recent period, meaning that modernization has been accompanied by estrangement of the distant regions within the state. Massification theory predicts precisely the opposite. Also, the expectation that political competition spawns higher turnout held for neither Mississippi nor Vermont, and it held for Montana only in the most recent period.

Finally, the participatory pattern in these rural states completely rejects the urbanization hypothesis. In fact, the data show that it is the rural areas that are the most likely to generate higher participatory habits when other factors are controlled. Moreover, only in Montana are other elements of the SES model (income and education) importantly associated with higher voting levels. In contradiction to the majority of studies that have appeared in the post-World War II period, the evidence shows that small is best for participatory democracy, even when (in terms of SES) small might also be labeled "backward."

Notes

1. Everett Carll Ladd, Jr., *Where Are All the Voters Going?* (New York: W. W. Norton Co., 1978).

2. Richard M. Scammon, ed., *American Votes* (Washington, D.C.: Governmental Affairs Institute, 1948–1978), 1976 volume.

3. Lester Milbrath, "Political Participation in the States," in Herbert Jacob and Kenneth W. Vines, 1st ed. (Boston: Little, Brown and Company, 1965), p. 46. Donald R. Matthews and James W. Prothro, *Negroes and the New Southern Politics* (New York: Harcourt, Brace and World, 1966), pp. 137–138.

4. Jae-On Kim, John R. Petrocik, and Stephen N. Enokson, "Voter Turnout Among the American States: Systemic and Individual Components," *American Political Science Review* 69 (March 1975), pp. 107–123. Bartley and Graham take

special note of Mississippi's participant culture vis-à-vis the rest of the South (See Numan V. Bartley and Hugh D. Graham, *Southern Politics and the Second Reconstruction* [Baltimore, Md.: Johns Hopkins University Press, 1975], p. 17).

5. Robert L. Taylor, Milton J. Edie, and Charles F. Gritzner, *Montana in Maps* (Bozeman: Big Sky Books, Montana State University, 1974).

6. These variables were recorded from census data for 1950, 1960, and 1970. See also Montana, *Montana County Profiles* (Helena, Mont.: State Department of Health and Environmental Sciences, Division of Comprehensive Health Planning, 1973).

7. Sandra H. Brooks, *Handbook of Selected Data for Mississippi* (Jackson: Mississippi Research and Development Center, 1976). See also Irlyn Toner, Loy Moncrief, and Betty Burnett, *Mississippi's Changing Economy* (Jackson: Mississippi Research and Development Center, 1974).

8. The socioeconomic variables used for controls in the partial equations are all supplied by the U.S. Bureau of the Census.

9. Harold A. Meeks, *The Geographic Regions of Vermont:A Study in Maps,* Geographical Publications at Dartmouth, no. 10 (Hanover, N.H.: Dartmouth College, 1975).

10. In 1970 when data were available for both registered voters and eligible voters, the correlation coefficients between the two figures, by town, was .96.

11. Vermont election returns are published in Vermont, *Legislative Directory and State Manual* (Montpelier, Vt.: Secretary of State's Office, 1946–1970).

12. SES data used for controls in the partial equations were found in M. I. Bevins and R. H. Tremblay, *Dairy Farming Trends in Vermont* (Burlington: Vermont Agricultural Experiment Station, 1967); Enoch H. Tompkins, *Income of Families in the Minor Civil Divisions of Vermont, 1959* (Burlington: Vermont Agricultural Experiment Station, 1960); *Vermont Social and Economic Characteristics* (Montpelier, Vt.: State Planning Office, 1971); and relevant census reports.

13. Hal Burton, "Vermont: Last Stand of the Yankees," *Saturday Evening Post* 234 (July 22, 1961), pp. 22–23, 43–45.

14. Daniel J. Elazar, *American Federalism: A View from the States* (New York: Thomas Y. Crowell Company, 1966).

15. Montana, *Montana Environmental Indicators* (Helena, Mont.: Environmental Quality Council, 1975), pp. 26, 27, 67.

16. Ibid., pp. 26–122.

17. *Montana County Profiles,* cover map.

18. Ellis Waldron, "Montana," in Eleanore Bushnell, ed., *Impact of Reapportionment on the Thirteen Western States* (Salt Lake City: University of Utah Press, 1970), p. 175.

19. Ibid., p. 174.

20. James W. Loewen and Charles Sallis, eds., *Mississippi Conflict and Change* (New York: Pantheon Books, 1974), p. 15. See also Edwin Arthur Miles, *Jacksonian Democracy in Mississippi* (Chapel Hill, N.C.: University of North Carolina Press, 1960); James W. Silver, *Mississippi: The Closed Society* (New York: Harcourt, Brace, and World, 1964).

21. Brooks, *Handbook of Selected Data for Mississippi,* p. 56.

22. Ibid., p. 71.

23. Lyman Jay Gould and Samuel B. Hand, "The Geography of Political Recruitment in Vermont: A View from the Mountains," in Reginald L. Cook, ed., *Growth and Development of Government in Vermont,* Vermont Academy of Arts and Sciences, Occasional Paper no. 5 (Waitsfield, Vt., 1970), pp. 19-24.

24. Frank M. Bryan, "The State That Might Have Been," *Vermonter* 4 (December 1966), pp. 9-14.

25. Robert V. Daniels, Robert H. Daniels, and Helen L. Daniels, "The Vermont Constitutional Referendum of 1969: An Analysis," *Vermont History* 38 (Spring 1970), pp. 152-156; Frank M. Bryan, "Reducing the Time Lock in the Vermont Constitution: An Analysis of the 1974 Referendum," *Vermont History* 44 (Winter 1976), pp. 38-47.

26. Lester W. Milbrath, "Political Participation in the States," pp. 25-60. For contrary evidence, see Robert E. Lane, *Political Life* (Glencoe, Ill.: Free Press, 1958), pp. 308-310.

27. Douglas W. Rae, *The Political Consequences of Electoral Laws,* rev. ed. (New Haven: Yale University Press, 1971), pp. 53-58.

28. The early voting studies are summarized in Bernard Berelson, Paul L. Lazarsfeld, and William N. McPhee, *Voting* (Chicago: University of Chicago Press, 1954), p. 336. Other early studies that are representative of those helping to establish the SES linkage are Gordon Connelly and Harry Field, "The Non-Voter—Who He Is, What He Thinks," *Public Opinion Quarterly* 8 (Summer 1944), pp. 175-182; Gerhart H. Saenger, "Social Status and Political Behavior," *American Journal of Sociology* 51 (September 1945), pp. 103-113; Julian L. Woodward and Elmo Roper, "Political Activity of American Citizens," *American Political Science Review* 44 (December 1950) pp. 872-885; John M. Foskett, "Social Structure and Social Participation," *American Sociological Review* 20 (August 1955), pp. 431-438.

29. Some of the early representative studies, listed in chronological order are: Robert E. Agger and Vincent Ostrom, "Political Participation in a Small Community," in Samuel J. Eldersveld and Morris Janovitz, eds., *Political Behavior* (Glencoe, Ill.: Free Press, 1956), pp. 138-148; William A. Glaser, "Intention and Voting Turnout," *American Political Science Review* 52 (December 1958), pp. 1030-1040; Seymour Martin Lipset, *Political Man: The Social Basis of Politics* (Garden City, N.J.: Doubleday, 1960), p. 184; V. O. Key, Jr., *Public Opinion and American Democracy* (New York: Knopf, 1960), p. 330; Alfred de Grazia, *Political Behavior* (New York: Free Press, 1962), p. 169; Edward L. McDill and Jeanne C. Ridley, "Status, Anomie, Political Alienation, and Political Participation," *American Journal of Sociology* 68 (September 1962), pp. 205-213; William Erbe, "Social Involvement and Political Activity: A Replication and Elaboration," *American Sociological Review* 29 (April 1964), pp. 198-215; Phillip Althoff and Samuel C. Patterson, "Political Activism in a Rural County," *Midwest Journal of Political Science* 10 (February 1966), pp. 39-51.

30. William H. Flanigan and Nancy H. Zingale, *Political Behavior of the American Electorate,* 3d ed. (Boston: Allyn and Bacon, 1975), p. 25. See the

bibliographical essay at the end of this volume for other sources.

31. Phillips Cutwright, "National Political Development: Its Measurement and Social Correlates," in Nelson W. Polsby et al., *Politics and Social Life* (Boston: Houghton Mifflin Co., 1963), pp. 569–581; Karl W. Deutsch, "Social Mobilization and Political Development," *American Political Science Review* 55 (September 1961), pp. 493–514; Daniel Lerner, *The Passing of Traditional Society* (Glencoe, Ill.: Free Press, 1958); Lipset, *Political Man*; Samuel P. Huntington, *Political Order in Changing Societies* (New Haven: Yale University Press, 1968).

32. Wayne A. Cornelius, Jr., "Urbanization as an Agent in Latin American Political Instability: The Case of Mexico," *American Political Science Review* 63 (September 1969), pp. 833–857; Elwyn N. Kernstock, "How Migrants Behave Politically: The Puerto Rican in Hartford, 1970," (Ph.D. Thesis, University of Connecticut, 1971); Mark Kesselman, "French Local Politics: A Statistical Examination of Grass Roots Consensus," *American Political Science Review* 60 (December 1966), pp. 963–973; Jun'ichi Kyogoku and Nobutaka Ike, "Rural-Urban Differences in Voting Behavior in Post War Japan," *Economic Development and Cultural Change* 9 (October 1960), pp. 167–186; Bradley M. Richardson, "Urbanization and Political Participation: The Case of Japan," *American Political Science Review* 67 (June 1973), pp. 433–452; Steven W. Sinding, "The Evolution of Chilean Voting Patterns: A Reexamination of Some Old Assumptions," *Journal of Politics* 34 (August 1972), pp. 774–796; Sidney Tarrow, "The Urban-Rural Cleavage in Political Involvement: The Case of France," *American Political Science Review* 65 (June 1971), pp. 341–357; and Jae-On Kim and B. C. Koh, "Electoral Behavior and Social Development in South Korea: An Aggregate Data Analysis of Presidential Elections," *Journal of Politics* 34 (August 1972), pp. 825–859.

33. Norman H. Nie, G. Bingham Powell, Jr., and Kenneth Prewitt, "Social Structure and Political Participation: Developmental Relationships, II," *American Political Science Review* 63 (September 1969), pp. 818–819.

34. Alex Inkeles, "Participant Citizenship in Six Developing Countries," *American Political Science Review* 63 (December 1969), p. 1140. The six countries studied were Argentina, Chile, India, Israel, Nigeria, and East Pakistan.

35. Robert H. Blank, "Socio-Economic Determinism of Voting Turnout: A Challenge," *Journal of Politics* 36 (August 1974), pp. 731–752.

36. Robert P. Alford and Eugene C. Lee, "Voting Turnout in American Cities," *American Political Science Review* 62 (September 1968), pp. 796–813.

37. Warren E. Stickle, "Ruralite and Farmer in Indiana: Independent, Sporadic Voter, Country Bumpkin?" *Agricultural History* 48 (October 1974), pp. 543–570. See the bibliographical essay at the end of the volume for other sources.

38. Sidney Verba and Norman H. Nie, *Participation in America: Political Democracy and Social Equality* (New York: Harper and Row, 1972), p. 236.

39. Stickle, "Ruralite and Farmer."

40. Alford and Lee, "Voting Turnout in American Cities."

41. Gerald Johnson's work on West Virginia was duplicated for Montana on data from the 1930s through 1978. His correlations between a county's mining population and turnout did not appear in Montana (see Gerald W. Johnson,

"Research Note on Political Correlates of Voter Participation: A Deviant Case Analysis," *American Political Science Review* 65 [September 1971], pp. 768–775).

42. See for instance, Lester M. Salamon and Stephen Van Evera, "Fear, Apathy, and Discrimination: A Test of Three Explanations of Political Participation," *American Political Science Review* 67 (December 1973), pp. 1288–1306; and Sam Kernell, "Comment: A Re-evaluation of Black Voting in Mississippi," *American Political Science Review* 67 (December 1973), pp. 1307–1318.

43. Charles W. Fortenberry and F. Glenn Abney, "Mississippi, Unreconstructed and Unredeemed," in William C. Havard, ed., *The Changing Politics of the South* (Baton Rouge: Louisiana State University Press, 1972), p. 472.

44. Those people who have focused on black voting in Mississippi have not agreed about the effects of rural culture on participation. Campbell and Feagin say "as a rule, urban blacks in the South have been politically active longer than rural blacks," and "the greatest progress in black voter registration, and turnout as well, has been made in Southern metropolitan areas" (David Campbell and Joe R. Feagin, "Black Politics in the South: A Descriptive Analysis," *Journal of Politics* 37 [February 1975], pp. 129–162). But in his analysis of black voting in Mississippi, Abney finds a − .30 partial coefficient between urbanism and black turnout. He concludes, "evidently something about the rural environment in the South both before 1965 and since encourages political mobilization" (F. Glenn Abney, "Factors Relating to Negro Voter Turnout in Mississippi," *Journal of Politics* 36 [November 1974], pp. 1057–1063).

45. V. O. Key, Jr., *Southern Politics in State and Nation* (New York: Alfred A. Knopf, 1949), pp. 510–511.

4

Party Competition
in the Rural States

Political parties are, many argue, America's sole contribution to the practice and science of politics; the rest of the American political structures and traditions were copied or salvaged from the European heritage.[1] Yet the contribution is important, for the modern democratic nation-state, as we know it, would be difficult to operate without parties.[2] Political parties recruit candidates and rationalize the competitive thirst for power; they lend coherence and discipline to the rule-making process. They stand by to ferret out and expose the faux pas of those in office (or to trumpet the virtues of the ruling elite), and they provide the voters with cues in the voting booth. Now, in an age when parties are under increasing attack, scholars are actively wondering how the republic would survive without them.

The role of parties in the political process has quite naturally led to their prominence in the literature of political science. It is difficult to find a study of a particular American state or set of states, for instance, in which political parties are not utilized as a major analytical force. Although it seldom leads into rural America, the pathway of scholarship is rich in conceptual lore and empirical findings. Political scientists have dropped on this pathway a central hypothesis—one which bears directly on the rural variable and from which one may strategically develop an approach to a very complex subject.

Party Politics in the
Rural States—The Master Hypothesis

It is generally understood that the linkage between party and society is governed by the competitive balance of the parties in the system. Thus parties that are neck and neck in the race for votes are more likely to keep their act clean, imply choice for the voter and thus inflate political efficacy, and find and reward constituencies among the have-nots. It is also said that rural areas with their homogeneous populations do not have the raw material necessary to support more than one political party. The requisite raw material is socioeconomic diversity, and socioeconomic diversity is an urban phenomenon.

There is a substantial core of literature that explains the magnetism between party competition and urbanism. Thomas Dye has said, "Rural, agricultural states with homogeneous populations do not provide enough social division to support well-organized, disciplined and competitive political parties."[3] The best articulation of the urbanization hypothesis is provided by Heinz Eulau in his early study of urbanism and party competition in Ohio. "It is a most general hypothesis of this study . . . that urban structures are conducive to the existence of competitive party systems and that there is a progressive transition to semi-competitive and non-competitive (one-party) systems as areas are located along an urban-rural ecological continuum."[4]

The urbanism hypothesis is supported by modernization theory when modernism and urbanism are conceptually entwined. Operating at the nation-state level, major scholars in the field of comparative political development hold that modernization produces the social complexity[5] and class differentiation[6] necessary for competitive party systems. For the proposition to be successful, however, two key elements must prevail: SES diversity must in fact produce competitive party systems, and urbanism must be empirically associated with diversity. Until very recently, both propositions have been widely accepted in social science.

In Federalist Paper Number 10, James Madison tied the rise of factions to "unequal distribution of property" or class differentiation.[7] William Chambers accounts for the origins of parties in the United States in terms of SES when he says that the first condition that gives rise to party competition "may be described as the development of socioeconomic structures that involve a substantial variety, differentiation or complexity in society and economy, and consequently a variety of groupings or subgroupings in the population."[8] In his study of politics in the New England states Duane Lockard finds that "The diversity or lack of diversity of economic interests in a state tends to be reflected in the party system and its mode of operation." Lockard sharpens his analysis precisely to the point we are after: "In the first place, of course, it is the diversity in part that creates the atmosphere for two-party competition, and the absence of diversity facilitates one-partyism."[9] An important developmental verification of the SES hypothesis that exposes the urban antecedent is found in the states of the American South, where new

Republican strength was found in the higher SES classes of the cities. Prothro and his colleagues discovered, for instance, that the "Eisencrats" were part of a Republican avant-garde that was both class-based and city-based.[10] Nixon's 1960 vote in the South was located in the metropolitan centers.[11]

The "urban means diversity" leg of the hypothesis is also well established, as is pointed out in Chapter 1. Louis Wirth counts population heterogeneity as one of the basic qualities of urbanism,[12] and Richard Dewey and other sociologists of the metropolis agree.[13] Sullivan's SES diversity index for the American states correlated negatively with ruralism, even though there were some major exceptions to the pattern.

The more this relationship is probed, however, the more it begins to quake and release dissonant soundings. In an important qualification to modernization theory Deane Neubauer finds that above a particular critical level of socioeconomic development, there appears to be no association between political development and socioeconomic progress.[14] Ira Sharkansky shows that within the American states the relationship between economic factors and party competition is seriously weakened when counties are used as cases.[15] Studies that trace the development of the American party system are equally unsteady in pinpointing the roots of partisanship. The decline of the Federalist-Republican dichotomy and the rise of the Democratic-Whig split did not occur, according to Richard McCormick, as a response to shifting characteristics of the SES matrix. Instead, McCormick calls attention to platforms, policies, and candidates.[16] David Cameron believes that the critical factor is mobilization of political "peripherals" against the dominant group (party) at the center. He is direct: "The critical independent variable which gives rise to mobilization efforts involves not the patterns of social cleavage and social change per se but, rather, the context of public policy."[17] Many studies of individual states show competition to be free from SES causation. Rather, the forces of politics — issues and personalities, leadership, and power — give rise to the existence of party competition. In New Hampshire and Texas,[18] Vermont and Ohio,[19] Alaska, Indiana, and North Dakota[20] political scientists have found evidence that is detrimental to the SES diversity hypothesis.

We are left, therefore, in the same intellectual position in which we found ourselves when we investigated the center-periphery hypothesis of political participation in Chapter 3 — besieged by contrary evidence. The problem is best tackled by first taking a close look at Vermont, Montana, and Mississippi to discover if they fit the SES model in the aggregate. Next the curtain will be drawn back on each state to determine if intrastate political units behave in the manner predicted by the SES model.

The SES Diversity Model in the Rural States

Montana, Mississippi, and Vermont exhibit party systems of different colors. Vermont has traditionally been the most Republican of the fifty states and, of those above the Mason-Dixon line, has led in non-competitiveness. Mississippi has been solidly Democratic and one of the three least-competitive states. Montana has always had a two-party system. These three states, which to a large extent hold the rural variable constant, occupy distinct positions on a scale of party competition and thus, at first glance, provide contrary evidence to the hypothesis that competition is urban-dependent. These states also provide an exciting opportunity to view the development of party systems. For Montana has retained its competitive posture over the last half century (1920–1976), but Mississippi has been bound in a one-party mode. Vermont, on the other hand, has in very recent years escaped into the open waters of two-party competition.

Recall from Chapter 2 Ranney's index of party competitiveness for the states. It ranges from 1.00 (no competition, total Democratic control) to .00 (no competition, total Republican control). Perfect party competition is indicated by .50. The figure is derived by averaging for a given time period the average percentage of the vote received by Democratic candidates for governor, the average percentage of the seats occupied by Democrats in both houses of the state's legislature, and the percentage of the terms in which the Democratic party controlled the governorship, the state House, or the state Senate. By subtracting this averaged percentage from .50, it is possible to gauge with considerable precision what the balance between the parties is in any particular state for any given time period. The sign (+ or −) tells which party has the upper hand (see Table 4.1).[21] States with scores of plus or minus .15 or less are said to be two-party states, those in the plus or minus .15 to .35 range are said to be modified one-party states, and those with scores greater than plus or minus .35 are called one-party states.

Over the last half century Montana, Mississippi, and Vermont have displayed three different scenarios. In Montana a steady incease in urbanism coincides with a slight and very unsteady increase in party competition. Mississippi, which has urbanized the most of the three over the last fifty years, has remained buried in one-partyism, although there have been recent gains in competition. The fact that the state has more than tripled its urban population has not been enough to boost it out of

TABLE 4.1

PARTY COMPETITION, URBANISM, AND SES DIVERSITY
IN MONTANA, MISSISSIPPI, AND VERMONT, 1920-1976*

	TIME PERIODS					
	1920-1928	1930-1938	1940-1948	1950-1958	1960-1968	1970-1976
MONTANA						
Competition	+.15	-.09	+.12	+.03	-.02	-.11
Urbanism	31%	34%	38%	43%	50%	53%
SES Diversity	--	--	.46	.48	.54	.51
MISSISSIPPI						
Competition	-.49	-.49	-.49	-.49	-.41	-.40
Urbanism	13%	17%	20%	28%	38%	45%
SES Diversity	--	--	.21	.25	.28	.35
VERMONT						
Competition	+.40	+.32	+.38	+.33	+.17	+.14
Urbanism	31%	33%	34%	36%	39%	32%
SES Diversity	--	--	.41	.43	.50	.46

* Competition is measured by Ranney's technique. See text for explanation. SES diversity is measured by Sullivan's technique. See text for explanation. Urbanism = the percent of the population living in places of over 2,500 population.

SOURCE: SES data compiled by the author from relevant census reports. Political competition data compiled by the author from standard sources, especially the Statistical Abstract of the United States (U.S. Department of Commerce).

the one-party classification. Perhaps the most disquieting case for the urbanization hypothesis, however, is Vermont. There the percentage of the population living in towns of 2,500 or more actually decreased in the 1960-1970 decade and in 1970 was about the same as in 1920. Vermont's transition from a one-party to a two-party state is statistically dramatic, and it is clear that urbanization did not accompany this change. Evidently a state caught tightly in the rural condition can display profound alterations in the competitive balance of its political party system (see Table 4.1).

Sullivan's SES heterogeneity index (see Chapter 2) can be used to plug in the concept of societal diversity.[22] The index ranges from 0 to 1, with a perfect score of 1 meaning that every category of society measured has equally distributed components. For instance, if there are four groups of people grouped according to family income levels, each group would constitute 25 percent of the whole. Sullivan used six categories and sixteen subgroups to design his original index constructed from 1960 data. By reducing Sullivan's categories to four—education, nativeness, income, and occupation—it is possible to stack up the SES heterogeneity of Montana, Vermont, and Mississippi against the dynamics of their party systems from 1940 to 1976.

At first glance, the relationship seems to operate in the predicted direction. In all four time periods, the state with the most SES heterogeneity had the most competitive party system. In Mississippi an increase in heterogeneity occurred at about the same time that competition began to emerge. There are real problems with the data in Mississippi's case, however. Mississippi would be much more heterogenous if blacks were considered an ethnic group, as French Canadians are in Vermont, for instance. Also the fact that blacks have historically inflated the low-education and low-income categories of data—reducing the amount of heterogeneity by creating a massive lower class—but have not been able to vote until recently means that the relationship between party competition and diversity is hopelessly skewed.

In Vermont the largest single gain in heterogeneity occurred at the time of the great breakthrough for the Democrats between 1950 and 1970. Heterogeneity actually decreased in Vermont in the last decade (along with urbanism), however, even though party competition continued to rise. Montana has always been more diverse than Vermont and has had a more competitive party system. In recent years Montana's heterogeneity has decreased along with the competitive balance. The hypothesis, therefore, is punctured by worrisome inconsistencies and weaknesses (see Table 4.1).

Does the partisan nature of the competition in these states fit the generalization that the Democrats do better in urban states and Republicans do better in rural states? Ranney shows, for instance, that modified one-party Democratic states are as urban as the two-party variety. Only the modified one-party Republican states are significantly more rural than are the two-party states.[23] According to this prescription, of course, all three states should be Republican because all three are very rural. But by 1976 Mississippi, Montana, and Vermont were classified, respectively, as one-party Democratic, two-party with a Democratic advantage, and two-party with a Republican advantage. Thus two of these three rural states show a stronger link to the

Democratic party than to the Republican party. It is clear that Mississippi's Democratic nature can be explained by region. As a state of the Deep South, the political imperatives of the Civil War are still operative. The strength of the Democrats in Montana and Vermont cannot be so easily explained away. Montana is a strong Democratic state in which three-quarters of the people live outside the central cities and suburbs. Vermont, which is more rural, is now a two-party state.

Table 4.1 displays statistics that allow us to visualize the character of the partisan division in these states over time. The shiver of competitiveness that has swept across Mississippi in the last quarter century was generated by the Republican candidates for president (Goldwater and Nixon carried Mississippi) or other statewide Republican candidates that managed to win respectable percentages of the two-party vote—one even winning in 1978. The Republican party in this period did not make inroads into legislative territory; its strength has been a surface blaze, a top fire, which nowhere has penetrated to the floor of the Democratic forest.

On the face of it, it is not possible to argue that the Democrats in Vermont have risen to a position of electoral respectability on the shoulders of an urban renaissance with its presumed concomitant increase in socioeconomic heterogeneity. The Vermont of two-party competition is not much more urban than the Vermont of one-party Republican domination. Although there is still slightly more heterogeneity of social groups in the competitive period, that factor has actually declined substantially since 1960. On the other hand, the decade that saw the greatest increase in party competition, the 1960s, followed the decade of the greatest SES diversity upsurge.

The success of the Democrats in Montana—except for an impressive surge during the era of the New Deal, a surge Vermont experienced in a milder form—has been due to a slow erosion of Republican power. Over the years the parties occupying the high ground in Montana have switched. Yet the system is still competitive. The Democrats have seen their dominance of the early 1970s threatened by a Republican resurgence later in the decade. In Vermont a strongly entrenched Republican party was dislodged in only two short decades. The GOP has regrouped and still holds a slight advantage, although the political landscape is now dotted with Democratic forces. But in Montana blazing battles on all fronts (state legislative, gubernatorial, congressional, and presidential) have always been common. Slowly the Democrats began to win more of these skirmishes than they lost. This process of glacial realignment was accompanied by a steady increase in urbanism and, until the 1960s, increases in SES heterogeneity.

Roughly sketching these three political party systems preludes an analysis guided by three themes. In Mississippi the task is to portray the changing of a sleeping system at first dawn. In historical perspective, competition is still only a faint glow in the East. Has it been ignited in the cities? Among the wealthy? In the counties where blacks are beginning to vote? Vermont is a state still gasping for breath after the upheavals of the 1950s and 1960s. Its political fabric, which was so securely stitched in one pattern, has been radically altered to another. The chore here is to retroactively plot that breakthrough. Montana represents still a third circumstance. There the assignment is to monitor robust parties in a competitive context; to watch the political coloration of this giant rural state mold and alter like a Rocky Mountain sunset. Infancy, adolescence, and maturity—these are the stages of partisan development in Mississippi, Vermont, and Montana as the last fifth of the twentieth century begins.

Mississippi—Competition at First Dawn

The first glint of a Republican dawn fell over the green-brown land of Mississippi in the autumn of 1952.[24] In that year Eisenhower's share of the two-party vote in the average county was 37 percent. In 1944 the Republicans had mustered only 6 percent and Dewey had managed a mere 2 percent in 1948. 1952 marked a profound breakthrough. Never again would the partisan balance in presidential politics be so lopsided. Eisenhower's poorest county in 1952 chipped in with 15 percent, and his strongest county, Lowndes, gave him 62 percent of the vote.

Significantly, Lowndes County on the state's eastern border violated a sharp regional pattern in Eisenhower's strength, which was anchored in the western counties. Thirty-one percent of the fifty-five eastern counties recorded an Eisenhower vote that was at least one standard deviation below the mean, but only 7 percent of the twenty-seven western counties fell in that category. Overall, the relationship produced a correlation coefficient (gamma) of .67. Scholars who have begun the task of charting the rise of Republicanism in the South point to the "black belts" as a seedbed or source of emerging GOP power in the presidential election of 1952.[25] Whether the term is measured by the color of the soil or by the color of the population, western Mississippi contains the state's black belt. Viewed from afar, at least, the pattern in Mississippi clicks with expectations.

Yet Lowndes County pierces the generalization cleanly. Why? First of all, Lowndes County is severed by the Tombigbee River, which has created its own black belt. Lowndes County borders Alabama, and the major economic conduits eastward to Tuscaloosa and Birmingham are found there. It is the home of Mississippi University for Women, it is influenced by Mississippi State University in an adjacent county, and it is the location of a U.S. Air Force base. The county seat, Columbus, is the largest city in the northwestern region.

Along with these characteristics (and perhaps because of them), Lowndes County exhibits all the factors that define the second great historical seedbed of early presidential Republicanism in the South—populations that are relatively high on the socioeconomic status ladder. Lowndes County was one of only two counties in the northern Alabama border region to grow in population between 1950 and 1960. Family income increased faster than in most counties in the region, and by 1969 Lowndes County had the highest median family income of any county on the Alabama border except for the Gulf Coast county of Jackson. In 1950 the median years of education for whites in Lowndes County was one standard deviation above the statewide mean. Forty-three percent of employed whites were white-collar workers while the statewide figure was 30 percent. Finally Lowndes County is the most urban county in the northeastern quadrant of Mississippi.

Although much of the vote for Eisenhower may have been influenced directly by institutions in the area, the existence of a black belt along with a growing, high SES, urban population validates in capsule form what the leading scholars on emergent Republicanism in the South have had to say—that early in the game white southerners in heavily black counties were most apt to shift to the GOP and, beyond that, urbanism, complete with its SES trappings, has been the chief carrier of political change into the Deep South. These authors contend that the rural areas in the South have stood guard over the one-party system.[26] The literature on Mississippi, although limited, is in step with the southernwide hypothesis.[27]

Yet because of methodological differences, variations in scope (both in terms of time and place), and a lack of research that takes apart the variables in a consistent manner over time, a clear picture of the political breakthrough in this state, the most rural of the southern states, is yet to be had. Indeed, Louis M. Seagull, who has written the most thorough election-based study of southern Republicanism, claims that Mississippi's Republican presidential voting results reveal "a unique pattern among the states of the South."[28]

Presidential Republicanism

Note that Mississippi differs from the other southern states on several of the ingredients in the mixture that is said to have predicted the early Republican vote. First, it had less black voting during the period than any other southern state. In fact, outside of Hinds County, the black vote approached zero. We may be certain that in Mississippi the black-belt votes for Eisenhower were white votes only.[29] Second, Mississippi had the weakest Republican party in the South prior to 1952. The party lacked what Oliver Garceau calls the "traditional bedrock of Southern Republicanism," the highland or hill Republicans typical of the Ozarks and the Appalachians.[30] Nor was migration from the North a factor, as it was in Florida, for instance. Third, Mississippi occupies the rural anchorage of the rural-urban continuum in the South. If ruralism affects the mixture that causes breakthrough in the South, Mississippi offers the best chance to find out how.

In the attempt to secure a firm grip on the interplay of forces that have so dramatically reshaped the competitive balance in Mississippi, several questions rise immediately to face us. Just how intense was the rural resistance to Eisenhower and was it pure or a function of other factors that typify rural counties? Has the strength of the urban-rural split been maintained over time? Have the forces at work on the presidential level trickled down to races for statewide office?

By matching socioeconomic data in Mississippi's eighty-two counties with the Republican vote for president, it is possible to be fairly precise about the extent to which selecting the Republican option in the polling booth was an upper SES, urban phenomenon. Education and income levels, percentages of rural and rural farm population, age, population increase, and the percentage of white-collar workers employed were all measured for the white population. The percentage of the black population was also used. We do find that Eisenhower's totals were higher in counties with more urban population and fewer farmers, in which the population increase was greater, and in which there were more white-collar workers, higher incomes, and higher education levels for whites (see Table 4.2).

The problem, of course, is that these variables are highly correlated themselves. Is it ruralism or low socioeconomic status that accounts for the low Republican vote in the rural counties that have lower SES levels? To answer this question, partial correlation coefficients were figured for a selected group of variables. Those items not included were cast off because they were too highly intercorrelated ($r = \pm .80$) with other more conceptually important variables. Thus in a choice among white-collar workers or the rural percentage or the rural farm percentage, the rural percentage variable was retained.[31] Education and income were combined to form a single composite variable and when 1970 data were used, it was necessary to discard population increase.

TABLE 4.2

CORRELATES OF THE REPUBLICAN PRESIDENTIAL VOTE IN MISSISSIPPI

Cases = Counties N = 82

Variables*	Eisenhower 1952**		Eisenhower 1956		Nixon 1960		Goldwater 1964		Nixon 1968		Nixon 1972		Ford 1976	
	S	P	S	P	S	P	S	P	S	P	S	P	S	P
Percent Black Population	.42	.57	.43	.36	.05	.18	.40	.27	-.17	-.22	-.88	-.74	-.29	.27
Percent Rural Population***	-.55	-.23	-.40	-.07	-.63	-.38	.30	.30	-.74	-.63	-.04	.10	-.42	.05
Percent Over 65 Years Old	-.20	-.13	.33	-.22	-.46	-.18	.21	.00	-.47	-.24	.01	.07	-.26	.24
SES (A Composite Measure of Education and Income)	.53	.29	.58	.26	.55	.01	.02	.32	.49	-.19	.54	.03	.61	.51
Population Increase (20 Years)	.44	.02	.37	-.03	.57	.12	-.29	-.21	.42	--	.34	--	.39	--
Percent White-Collar Workers in Work Force	.77	--	.69	--	.61	--	-.02	--	.71	--	.00	--	.48	--
Percent Rural Farm Population	-.70	--	-.61	--	-.57	--	.12	--	-.38	--	-.19	--	-.46	--
Median Education Level Attained	.36	--	.56	--	.38	--	.24	--	.44	--	.52	--	.68	--
Median Family Income	.51	--	.51	--	.55	--	-.11	--	.49	--	.51	--	.53	--

* Prior to 1968 these variables (except for percent blacks) measure data for the white population only.

** S = simple correlation coefficients, P = partials, (--) = variable was excluded from the partial equations due to multicolinearity. Coefficients significant at the .01 level are underlined.

***Percent of the population living in places of 2,500 or less.

SOURCE: SES data compiled by the author from: U.S. Census Reports, 1930-1970. Electoral data compiled by the author from: Mississippi Official and Statistical Register (Jackson, Mississippi: Secretary of State, 1947-1979).

The partials show that the relationship between ruralism and emergent presidential Republicanism is not a strong one. In 1952 it moves in the proper direction, but it is not strong enough to be statistically significant, and in 1956 it disappears almost completely. Does this tendency suggest that the title of Donald Strong's pioneering work *Urban Republicanism in the South* is misplaced? Probably not. Strong's analysis is based on large cities in the South generally (New Orleans, Jacksonville, Mobile, Charleston, Dallas, Birmingham), and as has been noted, Mississippi lacks large cities.

However, as Strong himself perceptively shows for the case of Jackson, Mississippi's largest city, it was the SES levels in Jackson that were responsible for the Eisenhower vote (not including the "black-and-tan Republicans") and not its "cityness." Jackson's citywide vote (37 percent) precisely matched the statewide county average.[32] It is not possible to argue, therefore, that the rural condition as such is responsible for blocking the inroads of early Republicanism in Mississippi. Nor were SES levels a major factor statewide; under controls the SES statistic loses much of its punch. The most important variable, by far, was the black population. The more nonvoting blacks there were surrounding the white voting public in a county, the more that county's totals were likely to favor Eisenhower — SES levels, rural population, population increase, and the age of the electorate notwithstanding (see Table 4.2).

Throughout the South support for Eisenhower shifted between 1952 and 1956.[33] The nature of that shift as it was defined for 1956 and as it was extended to predict the future involves an increasingly solidified urban factor (or, more precisely, the SES factor) and an increasingly unreliable black-belt factor. Strong writes off the black belt after 1952,[34] and Seagull claims that not only will the white-collar variable (or urban variable since he uses these terms interchangeably) intensify its capacity to predict Republican strength, it will form the basis for a durable realignment in the South much akin to the post–New Deal alignment in the North.[35]

How do these dual predictions stack up for the Mississippi example? Better than could be expected given the explosive nature of racial politics during the period. Who, for instance, could have predicted that a Republican candidate for president would carry Mississippi by a four-to-one ratio in 1964?[36] Thus, the roadway of statistical trends is bumpy indeed, and given the nature of aggregate analysis, it may never be honed smooth. Yet the black-belt vote did decrease steadily. In 1964 the partial correlation between the black belt and Goldwater's percentages was only .27. After Goldwater, blacks began to vote, and in 1968 the partial between the black population and the Republican vote is negatively associated for the first time.

The Civil Rights Act came home to roost with a vengeance in 1972. The black population in the counties correlated at $-.74$ with the Republican vote, with SES, rural population, and age held constant. Numbers favored the whites, and the blacks were soundly defeated. (Nixon's vote in the average county was 77 percent). Remarkably, given the current wisdom, the black belt shifted back in the direction of the Republicans in 1976. Here the problems inherent in any aggregate analysis are critical. Did the blacks in the black belt support Ford equally with the whites there? Or was it a combination of solid white voting (the old white reaction in the black belt) and a low turnout of blacks?[37] Survey research indicates that the blacks voted for Carter, but whatever the reason, on this dimension the counties in Mississippi behaved in the same manner as in 1964, producing in both years a weak but positive partial correlation coefficient between the percentage of a county's black population and the Republican vote for president.

Much in the manner Seagull predicts, an upper SES class core may be developing from which Republicans may consistently launch forays onto Democratic turf. But there is a twist; it does not rely on an urban environment. The 1964 Goldwater vote raised havoc with the electoral map in Mississippi. In some respects it leveled class status differences and produced a vote that varied little from group to group.[38] What seems to have been most important is that the partial correlation coefficients for both SES and ruralism are positive and significant. The Goldwater campaign legitimized Republicanism for rural Mississippi. This finding is supported by other work that deals with Goldwater's appeal to rural southerners.[39] Still, when push came to shove, as it did in the 1968 election in which Wallace stripped off the racist vote, the rural population was the only variable that was important. The strong negative correlation between the Nixon vote and rural population, however, is the product of a powerful rural populist vote for Wallace and says little about the Democratic-Republican balance. In fact the impact of Wallace and the statistical problems of counting the electorate as the total voting-age population of a county, when in fact blacks were just gearing up to vote, make any attempt to interpret the 1968 election extremely hazardous. The operative point seems to be that Ford's vote in 1976 generated a strong (.51) partial coefficient with SES (the composite of income and education) and the rural variable, which correlated at $-.42$ before controls were introduced, is washed out when there are controls. Among counties with similar charcteristics Republicanism has been spatially dispersed. The Strong-Seagull hypothesis turns out to be accurate, given this qualification. It is especially apparent when the 1952 and 1976 partial coefficients are compared for three of the component variables in Table 4.2.

	Partial Correlation Coefficients	
	1952	1976
Percent Black Population	.57	.27
SES (Income and Education)	.29	.51
Percent Rural Population	− .23	.05

As Seagull predicted, the black-belt and SES variables have swapped intensities almost perfectly. As Strong predicted, the black-belt influence has weakened substantially. What was not predicted is that the rural variable has disappeared.

Gubernatorial Republicanism

It is well known that presidential politics often deviate remarkably from local politics; that party strength in the election of the U.S. president may not reflect party strength at the grass roots. In Mississippi, the Republican vote for governor has lagged well behind the Republican vote for president. Although Eisenhower picked up over 30 percent of the Mississippi vote in 1952 and 1956 (and Nixon over 20 percent in 1960), the Republicans failed to even run a candidate in the general elections for governor. When a serious Republican challenge was raised in 1963, however, it was very successful. Rubel L. Phillips, the first Republican in memory to brave the electoral waters in the governor's race with an intent to win, earned over one-third (35 percent) of the vote in the average county. This was a remarkable showing. Phillips ran again in 1967 but did not do as well, picking up 26 percent in the average county. No Republican ran for governor in 1971, but Gil Carmichael tried for the U.S. Senate the next fall and won 38 percent of the vote, and Thad Cochran surprised the nation when he slipped away with the 4th Congressional seat in the same election. It is worth noting that Cochran did so on the strength of his strong showing in the state's most urban area, Hinds County. In 1975 Carmichael gave the Democrats a real scare by winning 47 percent of the popular vote (40 percent in the average county) in his try for the governorship. Because the gubernatorial election is held in odd-numbered off years (1959, 1963, 1967, etc.), it is more or less uncontaminated by national influences and allows us to peek briefly at the nature of the linkage between environmental context and new

TABLE 4.3

CORRELATES OF THE REPUBLICAN GUBERNATORIAL VOTE IN MISSISSIPPI

Cases = Counties   N = 82

Variables*	Phillips 1963		Phillips 1967		Carmichael 1975	
	S	P	S	P	S	P
Percent Black Population	-.04	-.14	.37**	.36	-.14	.21
Percent Rural Population	-.56	-.06	-.53	-.27	-.73	-.33
Percent Over 65 Years Old	-.40	-.34	-.35	.03	-.48	.03
SES (A Composite Measure of Education and Income)	.17	.16	.16	.36	.36	.36
Percent for the Loser in the Second Democratic Primary	.78	.75	.58	.34	.41	.15
Percent White-Collar Workers in Work Force	.44	--	.48	--	.75	--
Percent Rural Farm Population	-.39	--	-.28	--	-.59	--
Median Education Level Attained	.22	--	.09	--	.66	--
Median Family Income	.36	--	.15	--	.56	--
Population Increase (20 Years)	.54	--	.16	--	.46	--

* For an evaluation of the measures used to construct these variables, see Table 4.2.

**S = simple correlation coefficients, P = partials. Coefficients which are significant at the .01 level are underlined.

SOURCE: SES data compiled by the author from: U.S. Census Reports, 1930-1970. Electoral data compiled by the author from: Mississippi Official and Statistical Register (Jackson, Mississippi: Secretary of State, 1963-1979).

Republicanism on the intrastate level.

Simple correlation coefficients (Table 4.3) for the governor's vote are similar to those for the presidential vote, although in 1963 and 1967 they are generally weaker. In 1975, however, the coefficients are consistently strong and conceptually interlocked. The white-collar, education, income, and population-increase variables are all powerfully associated with the Republican vote, and farm workers and rural population are negatively associated. From the appearance of things, the SES syndrome is clearly at work in Mississippi's Republican voting, although the combined SES variable is not as strong as might be expected.

There is another variable operating in the governor's races, however, that makes for lumps in the pudding. This is the tendency for disgruntled Democrats whose candidate lost the primary to use the Republican ballot as a protest vehicle.[40] For instance, in 1963 when J. P. Coleman lost the second Democratic primary contest to Paul Johnson, receiving 42 percent of the vote in the average county, those counties that supported Coleman were the very counties in which the Republican vote against Johnson in the general election was the strongest ($r = .78$). Coleman's vote in the Democratic primary explained, in fact, 62 percent of the variance in Phillips's vote in the general election. When other variables are controlled, the protest-vote element remains an overwhelming source of explanatory power, and the other variables are eliminated.

Although this kind of protest vote is still highly visible on the surface for 1967, ($r = .58$), it is reduced significantly when controls are applied, so the partial for 1967 is only .34. Other factors are at work in 1967 as well. Both black population and rural population are working on the Republican vote—the former, positively, and the latter, negatively. By 1975 the protest vote had disappeared. The Republican vote for governor (Gil Carmichael's totals) was not importantly linked to the vote for the loser in the second Democratic primary, William Winter. Other variables were much more relevant; namely, socioeconomic status and ruralism. What began as a protest vote had evolved by 1975 into a familiar Republican statistical landscape. There is similarity in the Carmichael vote of 1975 and the Ford vote of 1976. Black population is mildly associated with the votes of both candidates. SES is the dominant variable, although it is considerably weaker at the gubernatorial level. The principal difference in the two votes is that rural dwellers seem to have remained negatively disposed toward the Republicans when voting for governor.

One way to judge the properties of the presidential and gubernatorial votes is to match the sources of their gains over time. The gain in the Republican vote for president is correlated strongly with both ruralism (the partial correlation is .40) and SES (the partial correlation is .47). The Republican presidential vote has strengthened the weak linkage it had to SES in 1952 by making gains in precisely those areas where (other things being equal) SES is higher. The result, it will be remembered, is that the 1976 partial coefficient between SES and Ford is .51, whereas in 1952 it was only .29 between SES and Eisenhower. At the same time,

Republicans had extended their influence into the outback from a base in the urban areas, so that a 1952 partial of − .23 between ruralism and Eisenhower became a 1976 partial of .05. Thus the strong rural gain canceled out the old urban linkage.

The dawn of political competition in Mississippi came first in the presidential election and some ten years later penetrated the election for governor. It began originally in the black belt, and it carried the seeds of a socioeconomic imperative, which seemed to include ruralism. As time passed, these seeds grew, but the negative association with ruralism became unstuck, and (despite some alterations in the 1960s) by 1975 presidential Republicanism was no longer independently associated with the rural-urban dichotomy. In fact the rise of Republicanism at the presidential level in Mississippi may be in part defined as a ruralization process rather than as an urbanization process.[41] To the extent that urban areas have higher SES status variables, urbanism will seem to be important. But when placed under controls, we find that the urban influence has no independent impact on the Republican vote. Gone, too, is the black-belt association, which served as an early incubator for the Republican party. Gubernatorial Republicanism likewise needed an incubation period to legitimize its existence. In this case it was the Democratic protest vote, but it, too, like the black-belt vote, was shed like a cracked eggshell as time passed. Now the development of the Republican gubernatorial vote lags behind that of the presidential vote only in that its SES connection is weaker, and it has not yet proved mature enough to jettison its urban linkage and become, like presidential Republicanism, spatially diffused. The prediction is that as the competition expands to cover other elections for state offices, the urban-rural factor will disappear for those as well, like meadow dew under a morning sun.

Vermont — Competition in Adolescence

Far to the north of Mississippi in a land of hills bristling granite, a land huddling against the cold between New York and New Hampshire and profoundly estranged from the warm flatness of the deep-soiled delta and gentle piney woods, politics was on the move, too. The pivotal year for Vermont, like Mississippi, was 1952. Both states were in the process of casting off the political habits of a century, habits cast by precisely the same mold — the Civil War. The air above these rural kingdoms was uncluttered by the sound pollution of the Industrial Revolution, and if one listened carefully, one could still heart the echoes of cannons over Charleston Harbor and the death cries on Cemetery Ridge.

Although Vermont and Mississippi picked the same year to break free from the past, similarities begin to blur quickly otherwise. Vermonters stepped to the tune of a Republican drummer, not a Democratic one. The Democrats in Vermont had always had a base to work from, unlike the Republicans in Mississippi, and prior to their first major successes, Democrats ran for statewide office, earning anywhere from 10 percent to 30 percent of the vote. They also occupied from 5 percent to 15 percent of the seats in the Vermont legislature. Finally, with the possible exception of the Johnson landslide, there was no vanguard vote to run interference for the Democrats in Vermont as "presidential Republicanism" did for the GOP in Mississippi.

The Democratic Breakthrough—An Overview

The major breakthrough for the Democratic party in Vermont occurred in 1952. There had been an earlier Democratic "wave" that had crested in the mid-thirties and had receded between 1936 and 1950. It swelled to even new heights in the 1950s, never to slip backward or to "trough" again. James L. Sundquist, in an artful and thorough analysis of party realignment in the North, refers to these phenomena as "aftershocks of the New Deal earthquake."[42]

Following 1952 a period of realignment took place, and as V. O. Key, Jr., explains, the new pattern developed "inexorably and almost imperceptibly, election after election."[43] In 1962 Philip Hoff reaped the fruits of this process when he was elected Vermont's first Democratic governor in a century. Working on the off-year surge in the Democratic percentage of the votes for governor, the Democrats made a slow climb up the electoral ladder. Hoff must be credited for bringing the Democrats credibility outside the northwestern part of the state. No other Democratic candidate before or since has increased the Democratic vote outside the northwestern section as much as Hoff did.

The gain that created the original New Deal wave in Vermont was unrelated to the pre–New Deal base. In other words those towns that gained the most in Democratic percentage of the vote between the elections of 1928-1930 (averaged) and 1934-1936 (averaged) were not necessarily the towns that already possessed a Democratic base in 1928-1930. Thus the concept of a "wave" flowing evenly over the political terrain seems to be valid.

The towns that were gainers in 1934-1936 tended to be losers in the next decade. Interestingly, the 1952 breakthrough, in which the average Vermont town increased its Democratic vote by 15 percentage points, was similar to the New Deal increase in that it was not associated with the earlier base (1948-1950). The breakthrough wave was not associated with the New Deal wave either. Those towns that gained the most between 1928–1930 and 1934–1936 were not the towns that gained the most between 1948–1950 and 1952–1954. It does not appear that this was a reawakening of a New Deal imperative grown dormant during World War II — an "aftershock" of the New Deal as Sundquist suggests. There were two independent waves, each geographically distributed in a random fashion from each other on a map on which the settings of the votes (the towns) had not shifted socioeconomic characteristics in any profound sense (see Figure 4.1).

After the 1952 breakthrough, the Democratic base continued to grow. Moreover, a "ceiling effect" took place as Democratic gains became negatively associated both with previous gains and with previous bases. The correlations between gains and bases for each set of elections (1952-1954, 1960-1962, and 1974-1976) change direction from +.50 to +.11 to −.28 while the coefficients between each of these gains and the previous period's base increase from .03 to −.35 to −.82 (see Figure 4.1). In the elections of 1974 and 1976, for instance, those towns that gained the most for the Democrats showed a mild tendency to have been Republican towns in the elections held twelve years earlier.

The Correlates of Breakthrough

The growing influence of the Democrats in Vermont could have taken several routes. Which trail to follow? Two principal responses guide such a speculation. One is that a new class division appeared to feed Democratic growth. Either people moved into Vermont creating a new social class, or the state underwent such profound change internally that a different type of class was created. Another is that the Democrats somehow convinced voters that were originally Republicans to vote Democratic, even though the voters' place in life had not changed. Beginning with the New Deal, the task is to nail down the character of the Democratic base over time and to assess the nature of the gain from that base.

But first it should be recognized that the original New Deal wave was not a sour-grapes reaction akin to the one uncovered in Mississippi in 1963. It was not a thrust generated by the losers of a majority party primary. There were struggles within Vermont's GOP (more on that later), but the most vociferous of these in the New Deal period, the Smith-Wills contest in 1934, is not associated with either the Democratic vote for governor in 1934 ($r = -.04$) or the gain in the Democratic vote ($r = -.01$).

Second, it does not appear that Franklin Delano Roosevelt's candidacy drew out Democrats or legitimized the Democratic party for hesitant

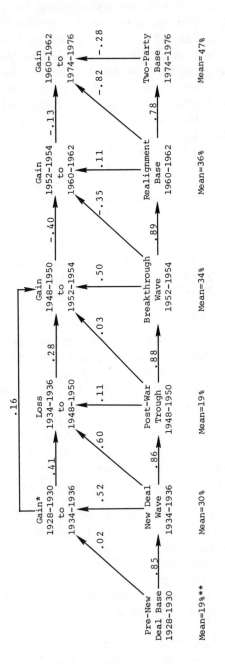

FIGURE 4.1

THE RELATIONSHIP AMONG DEMOCRATIC VOTES IN VARIOUS ELECTIONS
FOR GOVERNOR IN VERMONT BY TOWN, N = 239, SIMPLE CORRELATION COEFFICIENTS

* Gains are measured as percentage point gains.

**The means are the average town vote. Since the Democratic vote is negatively related to town size, the statewide percentage for the Democrats is higher than the average town vote.

SOURCE: Election results were compiled by the author from: Vermont Legislative Directory and State Manual (Montpelier, Vermont: Secretary of State, 1927-1976-77).

Republicans looking for alternatives during the Depression. The Democratic candidates for governor in 1934 did nearly as well as Roosevelt in 1936 and the Democrats' candidate for U.S. senator in 1934 received 49 percent of the vote, 7 percentage points higher than Roosevelt's 1932 score.[44] Meanwhile in the contest for Vermont's solitary congressional seat, Democrats received over 40 percent of the vote in both 1934 and 1936. New Deal increases were a ticketwide phenomenon in Vermont.

Third, although the Democratic bases of both 1928–1930 and 1934–1936 were significantly associated with higher turnout, the increase in the Democratic vote between those periods is not. The electorate in Vermont was clearly larger in the mid-1930s — by 15 percentage points (59 percent to 74 percent) of the registered voters voting. But those towns where turnout increased the most between 1928-1930 and 1934-1936 are not more likely to have higher Democratic totals when other variables are held constant (partial r = .08) — see Table 4.4. One must, of course, be wary of "ecological inferences" that are made with aggregate data. It is perfectly possible, for instance, that the great majority of those voting in 1934-1936 but not in 1928-1930 were Democrats emerging from cover and that when this occurred in a particular town the gains were offset by traditional Democratic voters switching to the Republican side and thus, when the votes were counted, camouflaging the relationship between the new voters and the Democratic party. My hunch is, however, that this scenario is by far the more unlikely circumstance. The stronger argument is that the ratio of new Democratic to new Republican voters did not lean significantly in favor of the Democrats.

That leaves socioeconomic analysis. Much of the literature outlined at the beginning of this chapter directed us to look for Democrats in the urban places and Republicans in the rural places. It also suggests that increases in the competitive balance depend on injections of urbanism and different SES groupings. But will this be true in such an incredibly rural state as Vermont, where in the 1930s the largest town had fewer than 30,000 inhabitants and the average town of the 246 had fewer than 1,500?

Indeed, the correlations in Table 4.4 show that Democratic percentages of the two-party vote in Vermont, both prior to and during the New Deal years, were higher in the larger towns, where more people were on relief and where the population was increasing. When other factors are controlled in both time periods, however, town size loses its influence. Towns with more farms and farmers were more likely to stick with the GOP, whether they were big towns or small towns, growing or declining. The Democrats did better in towns in which larger ratios of the popula-

TABLE 4.4

CORRELATES OF THE NEW DEAL WAVE IN VERMONT
1928-1930 to 1934-1936 GUBERNATORIAL ELECTIONS

Cases = Towns and Cities N = 246

Variables	Pre-New Deal Base 1928-1930		New Deal Wave 1934-1936		Gain Between Base and Wave	
	s	p	s	p	s	p*
Increase in Voter Turnout 1928-1930 to 1934-1936	--	--	.05	-.09	.13	.08
Voter Turnout 1928-1930 (1934-1936)**	.22***	.26	.21	.25	.05	.04
Percent of the Population on Relief, 1935	.40	.18	.45	.21	.21	.13
Town Population 1925 (1935)	.37	.09	.42	.10	.11	.05
Percent Farming Population (1935)	-.45	-.23	-.51	-.26	-.25	-.12
Population Increase 1920-1930	.23	.06	.32	.15	.23	.15
Per Capita Delinquent Taxes 1932-1933 (1934-1935)	-.12	.00	-.07	.04	-.07	.00

* Controlling for all the variables in the table plus the Democratic base 1928-1930.

** Dates in parentheses indicate data were changed for correlations with the 1934-1936 base and the 1928-1930 to 1934-1936 gain.

***Coefficients significant at the .01 level are underlined.

SOURCE: Selected electoral data were compiled by the author from: The Vermont Legislative Directory and State Manual (Montpelier, Vermont: Secretary of State, 1927-1937). Other data were obtained from the tapes of the Vermont Elections Project, ed. Garrison Nelson (Burlington, Vermont: Government Research Center, 1926-1930). SES data: U.S. Department of Commerce, U.S. Census of Agriculture (Washington, D.C., 1935) and Census of Population, 1921-1940; Vermont State Planning Board, A First Stage in State Planning for Vermont (Montpelier, Vt., 1937); Vermont Development Commission, Financial Statistics of State, County, and Local Government 1932-36 (Montpelier, Vt., 1938).

tion were on relief. It seems that the size-of-place variable is important primarily because it houses other more active variables.

It may raise eyebrows to note, however, that it is impossible to locate Democratic gains in any particular segment of Vermont's rural society. They came not from the big towns or the little towns, the towns with more farmers or fewer farmers, the rich or poor towns. The gains came from everywhere. It was, as Sundquist predicted it might be, a true wave, an across-the-board 11-percent increase in the Democratic vote. It is hard to argue that Vermonters who changed parties between 1928-1930 and 1934-1936 saw the Democratic party as a savior from the Depression. Towns with higher proportions of the population hurting economically were more likely to vote Democratic, independent of other factors. But this tendency was not strong enough to propel those towns into the category of towns that changed the most in favor of the Democrats. Again we do not know, nor will we ever know, whether or not those people who were on relief were *already* voting Democratic in the 1920s and, therefore, could not swell the percentage of new Democratic voters.

The electorate's behavior in the Green Mountain State proved to be "deviating" rather than "realigning." No sooner had the Democrats gained respectability than they melted back into the shadows. The decrease in the Democratic vote in the post–New Deal "trough" averaged 11 percentage points, the same percentage gained in the New Deal wave. Like the gain that produced the wave, the loss that produced the trough was uncorrelated with SES factors as far as can be known. By and large the Democrats seem to have come and gone in the 1930s without leaving a ripple on the socioeconomic surface of Vermont's rural society.

Between the 1948-1950 and 1952-1954 bases, the Democrats in Vermont made their first lasting breakthrough. It was the largest, most uniform, and most durable in the state's history. They increased their vote by 14 percentage points in the average town and continued to hold that plateau in subsequent elections. This jump, like the earlier New Deal vote, came in the form of a wave. It is critical to understand, given high expectations for a linkage to SES variables, that the breakthrough was not linked to social and economic conditions in Vermont. Causation can never be nailed down with aggregate data. But the figures in Table 4.5 strongly suggest that the phenomenon was politically inspired; that a political upheaval is possible in the most rural of environments without the aid of concomitant socioeconomic alterations in the population.

On the other hand, there are indicators that political causation was at work in the chemistry of breakthrough. Historians of the period point out that for the first time in memory a Democratic candidate for governor, Robert Larrow, campaigned long and hard for the post. A serious

TABLE 4.5

CORRELATES OF THE DEMOCRATIC VOTE
IN VERMONT'S BREAKTHROUGH ERA 1948-1954

Cases = Towns and Cities   N = 246

Variables	Democratic Loss 1934-36 to 1948-50		Democratic Pre-Breakthrough Base 1948-1950		Democratic Breakthrough Base 1952-1954		Democratic Breakthrough Gain 1948-50 to 1952-54	
	S	P*	S	P	S	P	S	P**
Town Population 1950	.28***	.05	.32	.30	.38	.30	.21	.11
Per Capita Dairy Herds 1953	-.11	.02	-.13	.13	-.16	.13	-.09	.03
Voter Turnout 1948-50 (1952-54)	-.12	-.21	.27	.21	.30	.29	.10	.10
Population Increase 1930-1950	.10	-.02	.08	.06	.19	.13	.27	.16
Dairy Herd Stability 1935 to 1953	.04	-.06	.17	.15	.16	.19	.02	.02
Decrease in Voter Turnout 1934-36 to 1948-50	.14	-.01	-.05	.16	--	--	--	--
Increase in Voter Turnout 1948-50 to 1952-54	--	--	--	--	.10	-.02	.31	.25
Vail's Percentage, 1952 (The Republican Primary Loser)	--	--	--	--	.18	.19	.37	.34

* Controlling for all the variables in the table, plus the Democratic base of 1934-1936.

** Controlling for all the variables in the table, plus the Democratic base of 1948-1950.

***Coefficients significant at the .01 level are underlined.

SOURCE: Electoral data were compiled by the author from: The Vermont Legislative Directory and State Manual (Montpelier, Vermont: Secretary of State, 1935-1955). SES data: U.S. Department of Commerce, Census of Population, 1930-1950, and Census of Agriculture, 1935, 1945, 1955.

Democratic candidate for governor who made noises like a winner was as strange in Vermont as a balmy January, and Larrow's candidacy must have had an impact on the breakthrough, although there is no way to package it statistically.

Whether it was caused by Larrow, the Eisenhower candidacy, or the rift in the Republican party (see below), turnout jumped dramatically from 1948-1950 to 1950-1952, and for the first (and last) time the correlation coefficient between the gain in turnout and the gain in the Democratic vote is relatively strong (partial r = .25). The new post–World War II electorate in Vermont, unlike the new New Deal electorate, was Democratic in character.

Important, too, was a bitter struggle within the Republican party. In 1948 Lee Emerson of Vermont's Northeast Kingdom challenged the popular and progressive Ernest Gibson and lost in a close race. By 1950 Gibson had resigned to take a judgeship, and this time Emerson won the primary and the governorship. In 1952 Henry Vail challenged Emerson, and a deep ideological split, reinforced by regional hostility, developed. (Vail, like Gibson, was from the southern part, and Emerson was the first governor since the institution of the primary to represent the northern half of the state.) Emerson entered the general election of 1952 with the smallest plurality in the Republican primary in history, 41 percent. Correlating the Vail vote in the 1952 primary with the Democratic vote in the general election and holding other variables constant produces a partial correlation coefficient of .34, stronger than any other partial coefficient produced by SES variables at any time during the half century between 1926 and 1976. Shades of Mississippi.

The interplay between increased voting, the Republican intraparty shootout, and the Larrow campaign and the effect of those factors on the Democratic breakthrough may never be known. But it is clear that those dynamics overshadowed the social and economic forces. The drama of politics that propelled the Democratic party into the position of legitimate contender forevermore in Vermont was played out on a socioeconomic stage that had changed very little with the passage of time. What socioeconomic markings there were on the face of Vermont and what alterations occurred in those markings simply do not match up with the breakthrough vote.

The next point of measurement is a decade later at the beginning of the Hoff administration. Hoff was to Vermont what Muskie was to Maine, the symbol of an emergent Democratic party. His election, however, was not astounding. It was clearly predictable given the slow but continual growth of the party, especially in off-year elections. But the Democratic election results for 1960 and 1962 (Hoff's victory year) are important because they represent a convenient benchmark between the original breakthrough (1952-1954) and the coming of the competitive period.

Three points concerning those results should be made. First, the towns that gained the most between 1952-1954 and 1960-1962 were negatively associated with the towns that made up the 1952-1954 base and the towns that scored the highest 1948-1950 to 1952-1954 gains. This, plus the fact that the towns making the greatest gains between 1952-1954 and 1960-1962 were not associated with the 1960-1962 base, demonstrates the ceiling phenomenon and the resultant shotgun pattern of the Democratic gains during the period of realignment. Second, the 1960-1962 results reinforce the non-SES character of the Democratic party's climb to maturity. The 1960-1962 base Democratic vote is once again loosely stitched to town size (partial $r = .30$), but that is about all. Finally, Hoff's main electoral contribution was the activation of many potential Democratic votes in Vermont's Northeast Kingdom and other outlying regions of the state, especially in the south. In what was a mild déjà vu of the early 1950s, a Republican personality from the romanticized Northeast Kingdom (Arthur Simpson) defected (after a primary loss in 1960) to Hoff and, Pied Piper–like, took many votes along with him. His home county in the Northeast Kingdom, Caledonia, led the state in Hoff gains. On a smaller scale, Simpson in the north was to Hoff what Vail in the south had been to Larrow a decade earlier. Whereas Vail's effect was a critical element in the chemistry of the breakthrough, Simpson was more a catalyst in the continuing postbreakthrough reaction. The key point is that the chemistry itself was uncontaminated by social and economic factors.

Precisely a decade later in 1972, the Democrats once more accepted the gift of a bloc of votes from disgruntled Republicans. Liberal James Jeffords fought it out with the more conservative Luther Hackett in the Republican gubernatorial primary. Jeffords lost. In the general election the correlation between his vote and the vote for Thomas Salmon, the second Democrat to be elected governor in Vermont since the Civil War, was .39 with nine other variables held constant. This coefficient held up when region was controlled. At the beginning of every decade since World War II, on the nose, the Republicans have become engaged in primary battles that steered voters into the Democratic camp. In this occurrence, Vermont and Mississippi are similar. They differ in that in Mississippi the Democrats seemed to have learned their lesson early and the "disgruntled vote" soon weakened. In Vermont it did not.

The Democrats' rise to power continued after 1972. Losses in statewide elections are now evidence of a malfunction in electoral strategy more than symptoms of basic inadequacies in the electorate. As the decade of the 1970s ended, the Republicans had no more advantage in any single election than the dealer at a blackjack table.

The base Democratic vote looks similar to those of the past in terms of its association with SES variables. Town size is strongest (partial r = .27) followed by per capita dairy herds and Vermont natives at −.16 and +.16, respectively (see Table 4.6). Those are the only correlations that are statistically significant, and all are very weak—none explain even 10 percent of the variance in the Democratic vote. Correlations for the gain in Democratic votes between 1960-1962 and 1974-1976 are more important for they show for the first time that the Democrats snatched more additional votes from Republican than from Democratic towns. In their final vault into electoral parity, the Democrats began to raid the small towns in a consistent fashion (partial r with town size is −.22). They also gained fewer votes in towns with increasing populations and Vermont natives and more votes where dairy farming showed more stability. The SES variable, which is a composite of income and education statistics, proved meaningless. In short, the Democrats gained the most in the smaller, stable farming communities. The Democratic base, which was established by a wavelike increase in 1952 and grew in a hit-or-miss fashion in all manner of Vermont towns and "cities" during the 1950s and early 1960s, was topped off with a rural component during the 1960s and early 1970s.

Although it is useful to point out that the Democratic base in Vermont shows inklings of similarity to the Democratic bases in the more urban states—negative associations with dairying (−.16) and higher SES (−.13) and a positive association with town size (.27)—the point of this analysis is that (1) those associations are minuscule, (2) they have not grown coincidentally with increases in the size of the Democratic base, (3) the increases that have gone to make up the base are not linked to socioeconomic factors as far as these data show, and (4) the only variables measurably associated with the gain (other than political factors) came at the last stage of the breakthrough and came from distinctly nonurban sectors of Vermont's society. Vermont became competitive not because Vermont became more urban, not because the Democrats absorbed the influx of outsiders that flooded Vermont from the 1960s onward, and not because the hill farm died away. Vermont became more Democratic because Vermont's Democrats were able to expand their influence *within* the rural environment, using politicians' tools. If they had waited for Vermont to urbanize or for a core of socially similar types to arrive, it appears they would still be holed up in some of the larger towns, content to snap up patronage bones tossed down from Washington. Vermont owes its competitive electoral system to Democrats who changed

TABLE 4.6

CORRELATES OF THE
DEMOCRATIC VOTE IN VERMONT 1974-1976

Cases = Towns and Cities   N = 246

	Democratic Base 1974-1976		Democratic Gain 1962-1976	
Variables	Simple r	Partial r	Simple r	Partial r
Town Population	.25*	.27	-.32	-.22
Voter Turnout	-.23	-.07	.22	.11
Per Capita Dairy Herds	.07	-.16	-.14	.06
Population Increase 1950-1970	.02	.08	-.06	-.15
Dairy Herd Stability	-.04	.00	.14	.19
Decrease in Voter Turnout	.19	.09	-.21	-.13
Vermont Natives	.21	.16	-.20	-.20
Socioeconomic Status**	-.12	-.13	-.02	-.04
Percent of the Population over 65 years old	-.07	.01	.04	-.04

* Coefficients significant at the .01 level are underlined.

**Socioeconomic status is a composite of education and income variables.

SOURCE: Election data compiled by the author from: The Vermont Legislative Directory and State Manual (Montpelier, Vermont: Secretary of State, 1961-1977). M. I. Bevins and R. H. Tremblay, Dairy Farming Trends in Vermont (Burlington: Vermont Agricultural Experiment Station, 1967). State of Vermont Planning Office, Vermont: Social and Economic Characteristics (Montpelier, Vermont, 1971). Enoch H. Tompkins, Income of Families in the Minor Civil Divisions of Vermont, 1959 (Burlington: Vermont Agricultural Experiment Station, 1960). Relevant SES data compiled by author from U.S. Census publications, 1960-1970.

history, not to the inexorable working out of some mystic socioeconomic imperative.

Montana: Mature Partisanship in a Rural Setting

Montana started late; it became a territory only in 1864, the year before the Civil War ended, and it did not become a state until 1889, exactly one century after the ratification of the U.S. Constitution and only thirteen years after Custer fell in the grasses of the Little Bighorn. Far into the twentieth century, the political systems of Mississippi and Vermont pulsed to energies emitted by America's "big boom" in politics, the Civil War. But it is a long way from Appomattox to Virginia City, the largest "city" (actually a sprawling mining camp) in Montana at the time of Lee's meeting with Grant. And it was not until 1877 that the "Red Napoleon," Chief Joseph of the Nez Percé, surrendered in the Bear Paw Mountains, marking the end of the Indian wars with his incandescent words, "From where the sun now stands, I will fight no more forever."[45] Separated by time and space, one might expect that Montana would have escaped the fallout of the Civil War; that its party system would have derived from beginnings as fresh and different as the immense topography of that most northern and most spectacular of the states in the plains-mountain region.

Not so. The Civil War and early politics in Montana were securely yoked together. Historians Malone and Roeder claim that "To a surprising extent . . . here, on the most remote frontier, the fierce political feuds of the Civil War echoed resoundingly."[46] Remember, it is *Virginia* City that still exists as a tiny tourist town in southwestern Montana. Or consider the fact that one of the most important early mining districts was named Confederate Gulch. The last words of tough Boone Helm, a second before a Montana vigilante noose broke his neck were, "Every man for his principles—hurrah for Jeff Davis! Let her rip!"[47] Jeff Davis Gulch and the town of Dixie add name flavor to the existence of strong Southern sentiment in early Montana. The barren plains west of Bismarck, North Dakota, and the war cries of the Sioux kept direct immigration into Montana from the northern half of the eastern United States at a minimum. When reports of gold began to drift out of Montana, they came from the western part, in or within sight of the Rockies, and they drew adventurers and fortune seekers from the border, southern, and other mining states *up* from the south and the Oregon Trail rather than across from the east.

In Mississippi and Vermont the Civil War set the dimensions of one-partyism in a rural environment. In Montana, where ruralism is different in character but equally dominant, the war fashioned the dimensions of a two-party system. That system was greatly similar to the national system after the New Deal (a Democratic party dependent on a nervous coalition between a southern tradition and an urban ethnic component versus a more-or-less rural, agrarian, and business-based Republican party). Montana was like a vast wilderness laboratory into which the forces that were to control American politics in the mid-twentieth century spilled after 1864, unencumbered and free to evolve and mature quickly. Montana's particular brand of ruralism, frontier ethic, and economic development left profound marks, but the outlines of the basic pattern remained clear for decades. It should be noted, too, that between 1900 and 1960 Montana did not miss voting for a presidential winner.[48]

Montana's political beginnings set the tone for contemporary analysis. Elements such as populism, progressivism, corruption, and wildly colorful intraparty warring between economic interests (for instance, the warring among the "copper kings") constantly weave in and out, appear and reappear to confuse and even startle the observer, like the northern lights over a cold, Great Plains nighttime. The essential elements, however, are never far off the horizon. They are (1) an intense interparty competition defined by (2) an SES base and (3) geographical location. The very first election held in Montana Territory (1864) resulted in a perfect split in the Territorial Assembly. The Democrats won the Council but only by one seat. The Republicans controlled the House, also by only one seat. Thus Montana was born competitive. When statehood was achieved in 1889, a Democrat won the governorship with 51 percent of the vote. A Republican won the only congressional seat with 52 percent of the vote. Almost unbelievably the state Senate was exactly cut in two, eight against eight, and so was the House, in which twenty-five Democrats were matched by twenty-five Republicans.

Competition was delicately balanced on a fulcrum of socioeconomic status and geographical location. One circumstance that sounds very familiar even today, in many parts of America, is that Montana's first territorial representative to Congress, a Democrat, won 59 percent of the vote by carrying only two counties. The Democrats were building strength in the more populous mining areas of the Rocky Mountain region where ethnics abounded. This strength was reinforced by a strong tradition of Catholicism, which had been built up by half a century of missionary work among the Indians in western Montana.

The Republicans came as the railroads pushed westward into eastern Montana from the northern states. Thus geography accented political configurations. The Democrats controlled the west and the mountains, and the Republicans held the east, especially the "high line"—a vast stretch of plains country, generally north of the Missouri, that reaches from the Rockies to the North Dakota border. The Republicans were also strong in the area adjacent to North Dakota south toward gaunt, lean Powder River country and Wyoming. In fact no county in Montana that begins east of the Rockies and touches either Canada and/or North Dakota voted Democratic in any of the twenty statewide electoral contests held from 1889 to 1910. What was true of the high line was true of the rest of eastern Montana to a lesser extent. Montana's geography defined the character of politics in that state and is responsible for the genesis of an oddity in American state politics—the coexistence of intense ruralism and intense party competition.

The New Deal

The Great Depression, like the Civil War, allows social scientists to take a shot at one of their most basic hypotheses, that societal catastrophes cause political change. In Vermont, however, the impact of the Depression on the two-party balance is difficult to establish. The thirties came and went with only a bubble appearing in the lava of Republican control that lay over the state. In Mississippi the Depression butted up against a condition of endemic poverty and an ironclad Democratic party. It did not even twinge Mississippi's one-party system, and it caused only a ripple in the bifactional struggle within the Democratic party there.

The Depression began early in Montana. A substantial shift in political alignment had already taken place by 1928, and it accompanied the minidepressions caused by droughts and economic disasters that occurred when the plains were plowed up in good times (wet) and blew away in bad times (dry). Between 1900 and 1928, the high line, which was particularly susceptible to these kinds of cycles because it supported farming rather than cattle agriculture, switched from being an area with a solid Republican base to an area in which Democrats did as well as Republicans and often better. Realignment had been forewarned by the Populists (1896), and the Progressives became the vanguard of it in 1912 and 1916.[49] In 1912 Taft carried only one of the high line counties, Teddy Roosevelt got three, and Wilson, two. In 1916 Wilson carried them all. In the gubernatorial race in 1912, Republicans split the high line with the Progressives. In 1916 the Republicans lost seven of the nine high line counties to the Democrats.

During the Depression the Democratic gubernatorial percentage actually went down. Roosevelt won impressively in 1932, but no more so than Wilson had in 1916. On the other hand, Montana's eastern congressional district had never gone Democratic before but did so in 1932, and it remained Democratic until 1946. Previously the Republicans had scored well in contests for state legislative seats, but in the elections of 1934, 1936, and 1938 the Democrats carried both houses. They would not do so again until 1956. The Democrats' grip on the high line held fast after the Depression, but elsewhere Democratic gains began to erode.

Importantly, Democrats in Montana, unlike those in Vermont, emerged from the period with a new territorial stronghold. In every gubernatorial election except two from 1932 through 1976, the Democrats carried the high line. Eighteen statewide senatorial and presidential elections were held from 1948 through 1976, and the Democrats did not lose the high line once. In Vermont the Depression left no new geographic encampment of Democrats. The high line, remember, is intensely rural and agricultural, and Montana shows that ruralism and bedrock Democratic strength are compatible even outside the South.

The shift of many agricultural counties to the Democrats between 1890 and 1940 confused the early alignment. Neither the Democratic New Deal base (the gubernatorial elections of 1932 and 1936 averaged) nor the Roosevelt percentages (1932 and 1936 averaged) hooked up with the expected SES indicators. Population increase during the decade was significantly associated with the Democratic gubernatorial base but not with the Roosevelt vote. Roosevelt's percentage was weakly tied (not statistically significant) to ethnicity. Neither vote was associated with urbanism, mining population, or education. Only the New Deal gain (Roosevelt's percentage-point increase over the gubernatorial score for the period) was ethnic-urban based (see Table 4.7). With only minor exceptions, high Democratic percentages during this period are no more likely to be found in more-urban than in more-rural counties, counties in which the population is better educated or where education levels are lower, mining or nonmining counties.

Regional Variations in Montana's Two-Party Vote

An inspection of regional political enclaves in Montana is vital since it allows us to determine if the statewide competition level hides one-party environments. This has been a traditional characteristic of the American system, with many states like Vermont and Mississippi locked into a one-party category while the nation as a whole exhibits, on the face of it, a stiffly competitive arrangement. Second, Montana presents a golden opportunity to determine if environmental characteristics invite certain kinds of settlement patterns, which in turn promote social and economic activities that then could (hypothetically) be translated into partisanship.

Finally, the massification hypothesis suggests that as time passes, communications facilities grow, modernization takes place, and regional political enclaves will break up. We can look to see if counties hidden in the deepest mountain valleys or lost below the horizon on isolated prairies have been able to escape the leveling processes of communications technology and population dynamics.

By using the percentage of the two-party vote cast for Democratic candidates for governor, president, and senator within various regions in Montana as an indicator of partisanship and matching it with the

TABLE 4.7

THE RELATIONSHIP BETWEEN DEMOCRATIC VOTES
AND SELECTED SES VARIABLES IN MONTANA IN THE
NEW DEAL: SIMPLE AND PARTIAL CORRELATION COEFFICIENTS

Cases = Counties N = 56

Variables	Average Democratic Vote for Governor 1932-1936		Average Vote for Roosevelt 1932-1936		New Deal Vote*	
	S	P	S	P	S	P
Median School Years Completed	-.06	-.11	.01	-.05	.07	.06
Percent Ethnic Population	.02	-.07	.26**	.20	.27	.30
Percent Urban Population	-.11	-.11	.11	.11	.23	.24
Percent Employed in Mining	-.11	-.06	.11	.09	.23	.16
Population Increase 1930-1940	.28	.30	.17	.11	-.08	-.19

* The percentage point difference between the gubernatorial vote and Roosevelt's vote.

**Coefficients significant at the .05 level are underlined.

SOURCE: SES data compiled by the author from: U.S. Census Reports, 1920-1940. Election data found in: Ellis Waldron, An Atlas of Montana Politics Since . . . 1864 (Missoula, Montana: Montana State University Press, 1958).

Democratic percentage outside each region, it is possible to judge if regions are the anchor points for party voting, what kinds of elections cause regional distinctions, and the extent to which regional distinctions are changing.

The 1976 governor's race, for instance (see Table 4.8), produced a probability coefficient of .251 when the high line is compared with the rest of Montana. What this figure means is that the gap between the Democratic percentage in the high line counties and the Democratic percentage in the rest of the state was so small that it would occur in any random selection of counties 25 out of 100 times. Also in 1976, however, the gap between that region and the rest of the state in the race for president was wide enough so that it could have occurred by chance only 3 times in 100 random selections of counties.

Overall regional differences were statistically significant in only 27 of the 104 election-by-region analyses conducted. Moreover, 16 of the 27 "successes" involved the high line counties. In fact, sixteen of twenty-six

142

TABLE 4.8

THE SIGNIFICANCE OF REGIONAL DIFFERENCES
IN THE DEMOCRATIC VOTE IN MONTANA 1944-1976*

Cases = Counties   N = 56

Regional Dichotomies

Democratic Candidates	Year	I Rocky Mountain MT vs Great Plains MT	II East & North Central MT vs West & South Central MT**	III Eastern MT vs Central & Western MT***	IV High Line vs the Rest of MT****
GOVERNORS' RACES					
Bonner	1948	.025	.096	.001	.363
Bonner	1952	.914	.261	.950	.042
Olsen	1956	.104	.992	.514	.458
Cannon	1960	.690	.979	.691	.021
Renne	1964	.091	.291	.138	.191
Anderson	1968	.751	.181	.592	.009
Judge	1972	.008	.001	.001	.067
Judge	1976	.983	.316	.253	.251
PRESIDENTIAL RACES					
Truman	1948	.089	.014	.844	.000
Stevenson	1952	.515	.858	.240	.017
Stevenson	1956	.020	.003	.090	.001
Kennedy	1960	.740	.790	.370	.005
Johnson	1964	.340	.550	.110	.057
Humphrey	1968	.200	.410	.170	.036
McGovern	1972	.130	.450	.280	.232
Carter	1976	.882	.780	.760	.033
SENATORIAL RACES					
Murry	1948	.200	.023	.896	.001
Mansfield	1952	.037	.506	.030	.105
Murry	1954	.935	.224	.988	.007
Mansfield	1958	.090	.431	.510	.030
Metcalf	1960	.340	.450	.800	.006
Mansfield	1964	.790	.800	.740	.036
Metcalf	1966	.640	.680	.490	.021
Mansfield	1970	.400	.150	.470	.029
Metcalf	1972	.999	.490	.820	.034
Melcher	1976	.163	.887	.203	.399

*   Data are probability coefficients based on the "Student's T" distribution.

** Combines the Two Rivers, Big Dry, and Sweetgrass Plains regions and the Rocky Mountain and Rocky Mountain Foreland regions.

*** Compares District three (the Eastern District) of Montana's Health Planning Districts with the rest of Montana.

****I have used a strict geographic definition of the high line, which includes only twelve counties, all north of the Missouri and east of the mountains.

SOURCE: Election data, 1948-1956, Ellis Waldron, An Atlas of Montana Politics Since ... 1864 (Missoula: Montana State University Press, 1958). Selected 1960-1976 elections compiled by the author. Other selected election data were made available by the Inter-University Consortium for Political Research, Ann Arbor, Michigan.

of the elections for governor, senator, and president caused the high line region to vary significantly from the rest of Montana in favor of the Democrats. Regions other than the high line affect the party balance in Montana very little.

Two other important observations are evident in the data. First, there is the question of which office is associated with the greatest regional difference. In three of the four regional dichotomies used, the gaps between the two regions grow more significant the further removed the office is from the state. Evidently, the closer the election is to home, the more apt it is to break down regional differences in the partisan division of the vote.

Second, it is possible to discover if important regional differences in Montana have existed in the past but have weakened over time, producing the weak coefficients for the entire post–World War II period. When the probability coefficients for the twenty-six elections are regressed against time, very weak negative correlations are produced, and there is some decline in the significance of the high line dichotomy in presidential and senatorial elections ($r = -.49$ in both cases). But the presidential voting in 1972 (when Nixon swept Montana and leveled out the vote) and the 1976 vote for Melcher account for a great deal of this.

Another regional classification with multiple components is Waldron's tripartite arrangement. Waldron views Montana much like a pie cut in three wedges with the sections roughly set apart by the watersheds of the state's three great river systems.[50] The summary statistics for twenty-six tables (one for each senatorial, presidential, and gubernatorial election from 1948 to 1957) cross-tabulate a county's Democratic vote as high, medium, or low. (High equals three-quarters of one standard deviation or more above the mean; low equals three-quarters of one standard deviation or more below the mean; medium equals all other counties.) With this three-way regional breakdown, it can be demonstrated that Waldron's geographic schema is a better predictor of the two-party vote than any of the other regional classifications, a fact that testifies to the salience of judgments made on the basis of a general and long-standing competence in the field of local political culture. Waldron has grafted this kind of talent onto geographic and economic considerations and significantly swelled our capacity to tie region to political behavior.

Waldron also contends that the Democrats should do most poorly in the Yellowstone watershed, better in the Columbia watershed, and best along and especially above the Missouri River. Table 4.9 contains tau b correlation coefficients for the same set of data when the regions are arranged from weakest Democratic (according to the Waldron hypothesis) to strongest Democratic. Tau b will register a strong score only when

TABLE 4.9

TAU B CORRELATION COEFFICIENTS:
WALDRON'S TRIPARTITE CLASSIFICATION
BY DEMOCRATIC PARTY STRENGTH IN MONTANA
1948-1976

Cases = Counties   N = 56

| YEARS | ELECTIONS | | |
	Gubernatorial	Senatorial	Presidential
1948	.41	.69	.52
1952	.53	.42	.47
1954	--	.47	--
1956	.39	--	.46
1958	--	.43	--
1960	.43	.48	.58
1964	.45	.41	.44
1966	--	.46	--
1968	.37	--	.46
1970	--	.36	--
1972	.04	.37	.35
1976	.33	.16	.38

SOURCE: Election data, 1948-1956, Ellis Waldron, An Atlas of
Montana Politics Since ... 1864 (Missoula: Montana
State University Press, 1958). Selected 1960-1976
elections compiled by the author. Other selected
election data were made available by the Inter-University Consortium for Political Research, Ann Arbor,
Michigan.

counties with Democratic percentages at or below one standard deviation of the mean tend to fall in the first region (the Yellowstone watershed) and when counties with Democratic percentages at or above one standard deviation of the mean fall in the third region (the Missouri watershed). These coefficients confirm that Waldron was right in his analysis. They also show that the pattern has been breaking up in recent years.

Illustrative of that breakup is the high line region's inability to withstand the pressure of a "friends and neighbors" impulse in favor of the Republicans. There is a neat comparative match available in the 1960 and 1972 gubernatorial elections. In both years the Republicans nominated a candidate from the high line region. In both years, also, the Republican candidate received a strong friends-and-neighbors vote in the primary. A strong local vote in the general election should slash deeply into the Waldron hypothesis in both instances, since these Republicans lived in high line counties. In 1960, however, the high line didn't budge. The Republican candidate, Donald Nutter, who won the election, received only average support in his home county, and none of the three adjacent counties voted strongly (percentage at or above one standard deviation from the statewide county mean) for him either. This fact is more remarkable when it is known that Nutter's Democratic opponent, Paul Cannon, was from Silver Bow County across the continental divide, as far away from Nutter's home county as Boston is from Richmond. Most of Nutter's own neighbors chose a Democrat from another world—a warmer, wetter, mountainous, timbered land where the water flows toward the Pacific. In 1972, however, when Republican Ed Smith ran from the high line region, his home county and the two adjacent counties all fell in the strong Republican category. A "home-town" candidate was, for the first time, able to crack Democratic control in the high line counties.

The Modern Period—Party and Society, SES Linkages

If Democratic strength is not natural to the rural condition, why are the Democrats so successful in Montana? The answer may lie in the fact that the state is not without urban places. It has two cities that are relatively large, Billings and Great Falls with 1970 populations of about 60,000 each, and several smaller cities such as Butte, Helena, and Missoula, which are nearly as large, for instance, as Vermont's largest city. Yet we know that Democrats in Montana are not urban-bound because the high line area has been a consistent source of Democratic votes and most of the high line is anything but urban.

In order to be more certain about the arrangement between societal factors and the two-party vote, seven variables were created for the coun-

TABLE 4.10

SES CORRELATES OF THE DEMOCRATIC VOTE FOR GOVERNOR
IN MONTANA 1948-1976 SIMPLE AND PARTIAL* CORRELATION COEFFICIENTS

Cases = Counties N = 56

Variables	1948 S	1948 P	1952 S	1952 P	1956 S	1956 P	1960 S	1960 P	1964 S	1964 P	1968 S	1968 P	1972 S	1972 P	1976 S	1976 P
Percent Urban Population	.24	-.21	.21	.11	.17	.01	.15	-.09	.37**	.02	.09	-.27	.47	.04	.41	.05
Median School Years Completed	.18	-.05	-.05	-.20	-.18	-.17	-.14	-.05	.02	-.05	-.27	-.19	.03	-.13	-.16	.23
Median Family Income	.35	.34	.43	.46	.10	-.05	.11	-.03	.32	-.09	.23	.33	.27	-.06	.38	.14
Percent Agricultural Occupations in the Work Force	-.39	.18	-.25	-.08	-.26	-.32	-.29	-.33	-.51	-.40	-.18	-.31	-.61	-.13	-.48	-.28
Percent Ethnic Population	.25	.18	.25	.17	.38	.32	.29	.34	.24	.29	.24	.34	-.25	-.02	.03	.08
Percent over 65 Years Old	.15	.24	-.18	-.18	-.09	-.20	.15	-.28	-.26	-.22	-.15	-.34	-.23	-.10	-.22	.04
Population Increase (20 Years)	.19	.18	.05	-.00	.08	-.13	.10	-.17	.36	-.04	.02	-.34	.41	-.10	.34	-.02

* Whenever there was a significant cross-over vote between the primary and the general election (closest loser's counties voting more for the opposition party), this too was controlled.

**Coefficients significant at the .01 level are underlined.

SOURCE: Election data, 1948-1956, Ellis Waldron, An Atlas of Montana Politics Since ...1864 (Missoula: Montana State University Press, 1958). Selected 1960-1976 elections compiled by the author. Other selected elections were made available by the Inter-University Consortium for Political Research, Ann Arbor, Michigan. SES data compiled by author from U.S. Census publications, 1930-1970.

ties over three decades for correlational purposes. The expectation is that urbanism and ethnic population should correlate positively with the Democratic vote and the SES variables of income, education, and agricultural occupations in the work force should correlate negatively. How old the population is and population increase are used to set apart counties on the decline from growing counties.

Democratic votes, indeed, are more likely to be found in counties that have more urban dwellers and fewer farmers (see Table 4.10). Yet during the first half of the post–World War II period the association between urbanism and the Democratic vote was very weak and on the decline. The variable for agricultural population behaved more as it should, but the partials were significant only in the middle years — 1956, 1960, and 1964. More importantly, the partial coefficients in the modern period show that although the Democratic vote comes from the urban places, it is not a function of urbanism itself, for when the other variables are controlled, the simple coefficients are wiped out. Nor are agricultural counties as importantly linked to the vote when controls are applied. In 1972 an r of − .61 becomes a partial of − .13. In 1976 an r of − .48 becomes a partial of − .28.

The ethnicity measure shows weak positive associations with the Democratic vote throughout the period. Only in 1956 and 1960 are they statistically significant, however, and in the last two elections they disappear completely when other variables are considered. Early in the period, 1948 and 1952, Democrats did unexpectedly well in the wealthier counties, but this tendency has not proved to be a significant pattern. It appeared again in 1968, but in the last two elections, 1972 and 1976, it is gone again. The other "achieved" variable, education level, shows no inclination to predict with any degree of authority the success or nonsuccess of Democratic candidates, although the coefficients are negative, as is expected. Except for 1968 the two variables used to measure population dynamics (population over sixty-five and population increase) are likewise unimportant.

There are fifty-six counties in Montana that vary widely on the kinds of socioeconomic variables contained in Table 4.10. But the lesson the table gives is that the partisan division of the vote in those counties is generally not associated with the socioeconomic environment. The competitive balance is relatively free-floating in Montana, and its linkages with society are unstable and unpredictable. What we have is a rural society that began competitive and remains competitive to this day. Yet it also remains impossible, using traditional models, to adequately explain why Democrats are stronger in some counties and weaker in others.

In Vermont and Mississippi, it is difficult to statistically separate competition from the minority-party vote. In Montana, however, competitiveness as such (measured as the absolute percentage-point deviation from perfect competition—a 50-50 split in the two-party vote) is not strongly related to either party's strength. It is possible, therefore, to determine if it is a function of societal structure. The Democratic percentage of the vote was subtracted from .5 for each county for each gubernatorial election in Montana between 1948 and 1972, and the sign ignored. To help avoid irregularities caused by individual elections, these figures were averaged for elections clustered at the decennials 1950, 1960, and 1970. Simple and partial correlation coefficients were then figured for the relationships between these county competitiveness statistics and various SES indicators.

For the 1950 and 1960 periods, the partial coefficients show absolutely no linkage to socioeconomic factors. Urbanism and competitiveness are simply unrelated. In the 1970 period, one glimpse of the society-politics connection is possible; a simple correlation of .34 between ethnic population and competitiveness is strengthened under controls to .45. But the coefficient between competition and urbanism is − .24, indicating a weak tendency for the counties that house the large centers like Billings, Great Falls, Butte, Missoula, and Helena to be *less* competitive. Pound another nail in the "urbanism equals competition" coffin.

The concept of SES diversity is an important component of the competitiveness model. An SES variable was devised from the equation used for the American states in Chapter 2, and Montana's counties were the unit of analysis. The items included were occupation, education, age, and ethnicity. The potential range of the diversity scale is from 0 to 1. Unfortunately, as in the cases of both Mississippi and Vermont, there is much too little variation in the scale so that its use allows only the most speculative conclusions to be drawn. Given this important caveat, SES diversity was a relatively important predictor of the Democratic vote in both the 1960 and the 1970 periods. The partials, controlling for urbanism, were − .33 and − .48, respectively. Notice, however, that they correlated in a direction opposite to that predicted. Democrats do better in Montana in the more homogeneous districts, and Republicans, in the heterogeneous. SES diversity, it turns out, is higher in rural than in urban counties in Montana. In neither set of elections did competitiveness itself show a link with diversity large enough to be statistically significant. In Montana, the urban diversity competition syndrome confounds expectations because the relationship of the two independent variables, diversity and urbanism, are confounded.

One factor that muddies the water in Montana is the crossover vote from primaries to general elections. This crossover has occurred in

Mississippi, especially in 1963 and 1967, and had important consequences in Vermont in 1952 and 1972. In Montana this phenomenon is more developed, and in many cases a county's general-election total is more predictable from knowledge of how well the primary runners-up did than from any or all of a wide variety of social and economic clues.

Primaries can have a dual effect on the Democratic general-election vote. Supporters of the loser in a Democratic primary may vote for the Republican candidate in the general election or vice versa. In over half the elections held for governor between 1950 and 1976, there was a crossover vote that had an important effect on the election. In 1952 those counties that supported the runner-up in the Democratic primary the most were also the counties that showed the strongest vote for the Republican candidate for governor ($r = .42$). This coefficient remained strong when controls were applied ($r = .46$). At the same time, the correlation between the primary vote for the Republican runner-up and the Democratic vote in the general election was .38 under similar controls. In 1964 there was a very strong connection (partial $r = -.65$) between the percentage earned by Mike Kuchera, the loser in the Democratic primary, and that earned by Roland Renne, the Democrat who lost the general election to Tim Babcock. In 1972 Frank Dunkle ran a close second to Ed Smith in the Republican primary for governor. When the general election totals were counted, Dunkle's percentage correlated at .81 with that of Thomas Judge, the eventual Democratic winner. The partial was .66.

Because we are using aggregate data, the flow of causation in these analyses is impossible to pick up, and conclusions based on a strict interpretation of "crossover" would be inconclusive. Nevertheless, the figures do indicate that there is a great deal of overlap between the two sets of elections and that this overlap is not linked to socioeconomic environments. All of this places in further jeopardy any hope one might have to satisfactorily firm up a society-politics connection in the rural empire they call Montana.

Summary

On balance it seems impossible to lay out a firm statement about the central concern of this chapter—the linkage of rural social systems to partisanship. Although it is true that one can locate party division in different social strata and that urbanism plays a role as well, these ties are very weak in most cases and flutter about the statistical landscape like August butterflies over rowen. More importantly, the dynamics of breakthrough are at best very uneasily associated with increasing urbanization and/or SES change. Mississippi's struggle to cast off the one-party yoke has been somewhat hitched to urbanization and more strongly marked by socioeconomic considerations. But Mississippi has a long way to go, and already the urban connection is fading. In Vermont, moreover, where a more complete breakthrough has run its course, it is impossible to conclude that a necessary antecedent was urbanization or changes in the SES composition of the population. In high, wide Montana, party competition floats freely over socioeconomic variables and recently may have cast off its principal regional pattern—Democratic strength in the high line region.

In all three states there are strong indications that political overlays are the critical factor. Mississippi's incubator for Republican gubernatorial votes prior to 1970 was the losers' percentage in the second Democratic primary. In Vermont there were strong associations between second-place finishers in the Republican primary and Democratic electoral successes. Montana has shown powerful and persistent crossover voting from primary to general elections. All of these tendencies seem to indicate that political systems, even of the most rural variety, need not wait on urbanization or the influx of differing socioeconomic groups. Profound alterations in politics can take place without them. One thing is for sure: Mississippi, which "urbanized" the most between 1920 and 1970, changed the least, and Vermont, which urbanized the least, changed the most. Montana, meanwhile, shows that a northern rural area can house the Democratic party and that a tightly competitive political environment can thrive under rural skies.

Notes

1. Everett Carll Ladd, Jr., *American Political Parties* (New York: W. W. Norton, 1970), pp. 15–16.

2. Jeane Kirkpatrick, "Dismantling the Parties: Reflections of Policy in the Process of Party Decomposition," (Paper presented at the Annual Meeting of the American Political Science Association, New York, September 1978).

3. Thomas R. Dye, *Politics in States and Communities,* 3d ed. (Englewood Cliffs, N.J.: Prentice-Hall, 1977), p. 98.

4. Heinz Eulau, "The Ecological Basis of Party Systems: The Case of Ohio," *Midwest Journal of Political Science* 1 (August 1957), p. 126. See also Malcolm E. Jewell, *Legislative Representation in the Contemporary South* (Durham, N.C.: Duke University Press, 1967), p. 21.

5. Phillips Cutwright, "National Political Development: Its Measurement and Social Correlates," in Nelson W. Polsby et al., *Politics and Social Life* (Boston: Houghton Mifflin Co., 1963), pp. 569–581; Karl W. Deutsch, "Social Mobiliza-

tion and Political Development," *American Political Science Review* 55 (September 1961), pp. 493–514; Daniel Lerner, *The Passing of Traditional Society* (Glencoe, Ill.: Free Press, 1958); Seymour Martin Lipset, *Political Man: The Social Basis of Politics* (Garden City, N.Y.: Doubleday, 1960). For more recent refinements of this literature, see Lee Sigeleman, *Modernization and the Political System: A Critique and Preliminary Empirical Analysis* (Beverly Hills, Calif.: Sage Publications, 1971).

6. David Butler and Donald Stokes, *Political Change in Britain* (New York: St.Martin's Press, 1969), especially chaps. 5 and 6; Heinz Eulau, "Perceptions of Class and Party in Voting Behavior: 1952," *American Political Science Review* 49 (June 1955), pp. 364–384. Charles E. Merriam and Harold F. Gosnell, *The American Party System*, rev. ed. (New York: MacMillan Company, 1929), p. 3.

7. Edward Mead Earle, ed., *The Federalist Papers* (New York: Modern Library, 1941), p. 55.

8. William Nisbet Chambers, "Party Development and the American Mainstream," in William Nisbet Chambers and Walter Dean Burnham, *The American Party Systems* 2d ed. (New York: Oxford University Press, 1967), pp. 8–9.

9. Duane Lockard, *New England State Politics* (Princeton: Princeton University Press, 1959), p. 337. See also V. O. Key, Jr., *American State Politics: An Introduction* (New York: Alfred A. Knopf, 1956).

10. James W. Prothro, Ernest Q. Campbell, and Charles Grigg, "Two-Party Voting in the South: Class vs. Party Identification," *American Political Science Review* 52 (March 1958), pp. 131–139.

11. Bernard Cosman, "Presidential Republicanism in the South, 1960," *Journal of Politics* 24 (May 1962), pp. 303–322. See also Anthony M. Orum and Edward W. McCranie, "Class, Tradition, and Partisan Alignments in a Southern Urban Electorate," *Journal of Politics* 32 (February 1970), pp. 156–176.

12. Lewis Wirth, "Urbanism as a Way of Life," *American Journal of Sociology* 44 (July 1938), pp. 1–24.

13. Richard Dewey, "The Rural-Urban Continuum: Real but Relatively Unimportant," *American Journal of Sociology* 66 (July 1960), pp. 60–66.

14. Deane E. Neubauer, "Some Conditions of Democracy," *American Political Science Review* 61 (December 1967), pp. 1003–1009.

15. Ira Sharkansky, "Economic Development, Representative Mechanisms, Administrative Professionalism, and Public Policies: A Comparative Analysis of Within-State Distributions of Economic and Political Traits," *Journal of Politics* 33 (February 1971), pp. 112–132.

16. Richard McCormick, "Political Development and the Second Party System," in Chambers and Burnham, *American Party Systems,* p. 97.

17. David R. Cameron, "Toward a Theory of Political Mobilization," *Journal of Politics* 36 (February 1974), p. 169. See also Ladd, *American Political Parties.*

18. Robert Dishman and Robert P. Ford, "New Hampshire: Republican Schisms, Democratic Gains," in George Goodwin, Jr., and Victoria Schuck, eds., *Party Politics in the New England States* (Durham, N.H.: New England Center for Continuing Education, 1968), p. 62; John R. Todd and Kay Dickenson Ellis,

"Analyzing Factional Patterns in State Politics: Texas, 1944–1972," *Social Science Quarterly* 55 (December 1974), pp. 719.

19. Frank M. Bryan, "Ecological Causation and Partisan Breakthrough: Vermont—A Case Study" (Paper presented at the Annual Meeting of the Northeastern Political Science Association, Rutgers University, New Brunswick, N.J., November 1975); Thomas A. Flinn, "Continuity and Change in Ohio Politics," *Journal of Politics* 24 (August 1962), pp. 521–544.

20. Herman E. Slotnick, "Alaska: Empire to the North," in Frank H. Jonas, ed., *Politics in the American West* (Salt Lake City: University of Utah Press, 1969); V. O. Key, Jr., and Frank Munger, "Social Determinism and Electoral Division: The Case of Indiana," in Eugene Burdick and Arthur J. Brodbeck, eds., *American Voting Behavior* (Glencoe, Ill.: Free Press, 1959), pp. 281–299; Ross Talbot, "North Dakota—A Two-Party State?" *North Dakota Quarterly* 25 (Fall 1957), pp. 93–104.

21. Austin Ranney, "Parties in State Politics," in Herbert Jacob and Kenneth W. Vines, eds., *Politics in the American States,* 3d ed. (Boston: Little, Brown and Company, 1976), pp. 60–61.

22. John L. Sullivan, "Political Correlates of Social, Economic, and Religious Diversity in the American States," *Journal of Politics* 35 (February 1973), pp. 70–84.

23. Ranney, "Parties in State Politics," pp. 61–100.

24. As late as 1975 Monroe Billington still argued that "one-party politics is not about to die" (Monroe Lee Billington, *The Political South in the 20th Century* [New York: Charles Scribner and Sons, 1975], p. 179).

25. William J. Keefe, "Southern Politics Revisited," *Public Opinion Quarterly* 20 (Summer 1956), pp. 405–412; Louis M. Seagull, *Southern Republicanism* (New York: John Wiley and Sons, 1975), p. 24; Donald S. Strong, *The 1952 Presidential Election in the South* (University, Ala.: Bureau of Public Administration, 1955); Donald S. Strong, *Urban Republicanism in the South* (University, Ala.: Bureau of Public Administration, 1960), especially chap. 3, "Black-Belters Into Republicans?" pp. 30–35.

26. Both Seagull and Strong accept the urbanism hypothesis completely (see Seagull, *Southern Republicanism,* pp. 1–19, and Strong, *Urban Republicanism in the South*). Seagull, however, makes the point that in some respects Mississippi strays from the general southern model.

27. F. Glenn Abney, "Partisan Realignment in a One-Party System: The Case of Mississippi," *Journal of Politics* 31 (November 1969), pp. 1102–1106; Charles W. Fortenberry and F. Glenn Abney, "Mississippi, Unreconstructed and Unredeemed," in William C. Havard, ed., *The Changing Politics of the South* (Baton Rouge: Louisiana State University Press, 1972), pp. 472–524. Donald S. Strong, "Durable Republicanism in the South," in Allan P. Sindler, ed., *Change in the Contemporary South* (Durham, N.C.: Duke University Press, 1963), p. 194.

28. Seagull, *Southern Republicanism,* p. 43.

29. Ibid., p. 24; Strong, "Durable Republicanism in the South," p. 33.

30. Frank Munger, ed., *American State Politics: Readings for Comparative Analysis* (New York: Thomas Y. Crowell Company, 1966), p. 21.

31. I do not agree with Seagull that white-collar workers may be used as a surrogate for urbanism. Nor do all rural areas have high percentages of farmers in the work force (see Seagull, *Southern Republicanism,* pp. 12, 25).

32. Strong, *Urban Republicanism in the South,* pp. 17–20.

33. Munger, *American State Politics,* p. 20.

34. Strong, *Urban Republicanism in the South,* pp. 30–35.

35. Seagull, *Southern Republicanism,* pp. 1–19.

36. Strong himself, in a better position to make predictions than anyone else in those days, says that the Republican Party will have to tone down its racial appeal and "of course, no Republican nominee can be expected to . . . receive quite the same degree of support [as] Eisenhower" (Strong, *Urban Republicanism in the South,* p. 57).

37. There is evidence for both possibilities. Bruce Campbell shows that black voting in the South dropped twice as fast as white voting between 1972 and 1976 (Bruce A. Campbell, *The American Electorate* [New York: Holt, Rinehart and Winston, 1979], p. 26). Thus blacks may have supported Carter heavily, but a disproportionately heavy white vote in the black counties swung the correlation coefficients toward Ford. On the other hand, Gerald Pomper in his early analysis of the 1976 election holds that "It is unlikely that Carter would have carried any region, even the South, without black support." Nationwide, claims Pomper, blacks gave 90 percent of their vote to Carter (Gerald M. Pomper, *The Election of 1976: Reports and Interpretations* [New York: David McKay, 1977], pp. 60–61, 139).

38. Bernard Cosman, *Five States for Goldwater* (University: University of Alabama Press, 1966), p. 86.

39. Munger, *American State Politics,* p. 24; Cosman, *Five States for Goldwater,* p. 59. See especially the survey data in Everett Carll Ladd, Jr., and Charles D. Hadley, *Transformation of the American Party System* (New York: W. W. Norton, 1973), pp. 164–165.

40. Jack Bass and Walter De Vries, "Mississippi: Out of the Past," in Bass and De Vries, *The Transformation of Southern Politics* (New York: Basic Books, 1976), pp. 186–218. Fortenberry and Abney, "Mississippi, Unreconstructed and Unredeemed," p. 497.

41. Thus in Mississippi, the data seem to suggest a different interpretation from the claim that the "metropolitan Republicanism that appeared so decisively in 1952 has proved to be solid and reliable" (James L. Sundquist, *Dynamics of the Party System* [Washington, D.C.: Brookings Institution, 1973], p. 259). That claim is true when one looks at the raw source of Republican strength. But urbanism as an independent correlate of Republican voting has been on the demise. Only if one means SES, when one says urban, may one call the metro-base of Mississippi presidential Republicanism "solid and reliable." See also Donald S. Strong, "Further Reflections on Southern Politics," *Journal of Politics* 33 (May 1971), pp. 239–256. Strong's factor analysis for Mississippi shows the Nixon vote

in 1968 to be negatively associated with a factor Strong calls "rural poverty." I accept his corollary that Nixon "was listed as having done well among high-status, urban people" (p. 198).

42. Sundquist, *Dynamics of the Party System,* pp. 218–244.

43. V. O. Key, Jr., "Secular Realignment and the Party System," *Journal of Politics* 21 (May 1959), pp. 198–199.

44. See George T. Mazuzan, "Vermont's Traditional Republicanism vs. the New Deal: Warren Austin and the Election of 1934," *Vermont History* 39 (Spring 1971), pp. 128–141.

45. Dee Brown, *Bury My Heart at Wounded Knee* (New York: Holt, Rinehart and Winston, 1970), p. 329.

46. Michael P. Malone and Richard B. Roeder, *Montana: A History of Two Centuries* (Seattle: University of Washington Press, 1976), p. 63.

47. Ibid. For further documentation on the Confederate influence in Montana, see Clark C. Spence, *Territorial Politics and Government in Montana, 1864–89* (Urbana: University of Illinois Press, 1975), pp. 20–25.

48. Ellis Waldron, *An Atlas of Montana Politics Since 1864* (Missoula: University of Montana Press, 1958), p. 3.

49. See K. Ross Toole's two chapters on the progressive movement in Montana in K. Ross Toole, *Twentieth Century Montana: A State of Extremes* (Norman: University of Oklahoma Press, 1972), pp. 233–271. Michael Malone points out that Montana was the only state to lose population during the 1920s (see Michael P. Malone, "The Montana New Dealers," in John Braemon, Robert H. Bremner, and David Brody, eds., *The New Deal* [Columbus: Ohio State University Press, 1975], pp. 240–268).

50. Ellis Waldron, "Montana," in Eleanore Bushnell, ed., *Impact of Reapportionment on the Thirteen Western States* (Salt Lake City: University of Utah Press, 1970), p. 175.

5
The Primary Systems

Within democratic systems, conflict is good, probably essential. Even better is organized conflict. Conflict that is stable over time, packaged, and labeled gives the citizen direction, information, and purpose. Many people contend that it is on the battle for votes waged by political parties of near-equal strength that the poor must hang their hopes. Sometimes, however, single-party systems established in a profound societal blast such as the Civil War dominate the landscape far past the point where the state, through socioeconomic development, has accumulated the raw material (social heterogeneity) for multiorganizational conflict.

This is where primaries come in. If competition within a totally dominant party has been capped and removed from popular control, the direct primary removes the lid and allows the people to use their votes as chips and play the game of politics to their own advantage. Until very recently in two of the three states we are studying, Mississippi and Vermont, the primary was the arena in which the struggle for power was played out. This is the reason why I have left the primaries until last in the discussion of elections in this volume. They may have come first in time, but in two of the states studied they were the determining elections.

As societies grow more complex, they begin to generate competing clusters of interests. These clusters may find expression in the rise of a second party, or a bifactional situation may develop within the majority party. If a multifactional situation exists within the majority party as a new second party begins to grow, the many power centers within the majority party may jell into two factions, one seeking to lead in the struggle against the new contender and another composed of opposition groups. These are complex generalizations, and they have never been satisfactorily arranged in a deductive pattern that could be called a theory. Nevertheless, a lot of good thinking has gone into the genesis and refinement of these models, with the result that we have at hand some very useful grab hooks for analysis. The question is central: To what degree has organized conflict in rural societies been camouflaged by the general election? We need to look at this problem in three different settings: (1) where one party has been totally dominant, Mississippi; (2) where one party has dominated an ever-present but never-successful minority party, Vermont; and (3) where two parties have been well matched, Montana.

Mississippi — A Legacy of Chaos

Mississippi is one of the most multifactional of America's one-party states. Conflict exists all right, but party label will not identify it. Intraparty warring from the slash pines of the coast to the hickory forests of the north and from the delta to the Tombigbee River has been chaotic. The factions will not sit still long enough to be properly labeled. Watching them is like watching fireflies flash and drift in the humid air above a deep-grassed June pasture at twilight. What should cause great excitement, however, is the fact that we have in Mississippi a perfect opportunity to make a judgment on the hypothesis that the dual forces of modernization and a growing opposition party (forces that are themselves, of course, theoretically tied) will alter the nature of the factional struggle within the Democratic party. For Mississippi is modernizing, and the Republican party is poised to do extreme damage to the Democratic party, as the election of Thad Cochran to the Senate in 1978 so clearly documents. Yet despite the fact that the GOP hangs on the horizon like a growing storm, factionalism in the Democratic primary has decreased not at all since the end of World War II.[1]

Society and Conflict in the Mississippi Primary

Mississippi holds two primaries, a contest in early August to narrow the field for a second runoff primary near the end of the month between the top two vote-getters in the first primary. Primary number one has traditionally been analogous to the only primary in a two-party state, and primary number two plays the role of the final election since its winner used to be guaranteed victory in the general election to follow. Although interparty competition for major state offices has been nonexistent until very recently, competition in the primaries has been fierce. By any criterion the primary elections are usually very close. Logic says that rural, agricultural counties will be more noncompetitive and urban counties will house the hottest competitive environments.

To test these notions it would be helpful to be able to use Sullivan's SES heterogeneity measure. When applied to Mississippi counties, however, it lacks range and variation. Nevertheless, since SES factors such as income and education seldom pass the 50-percent level, it can be said with some validity, for instance, that those counties in Mississippi that have more college graduates are by definition more heterogeneous. To measure factionalism, Douglas Rae's index of factionalization is applied to each of Mississippi's eighty-two counties for the first primaries from 1951 through 1975. The index accounts for both the number of candidates and the evenness of their percentages of the total vote.[2] To measure party competition in the runoff primary, where there are always two candidates, the technique of using one winner's absolute percentage-point deviation from 50 percent has been used (see Chapter 3).

The first primary in Mississippi has averaged a field of six candidates since 1947. A quick search through the list of nine social and economic indicators over the eight primaries held in Mississippi between 1947 and 1975 turns up very few clues as to the kinds of environments that produce factionalism in wide-open political contests. The composite SES variable that was created to register the combined values of income and education levels is completely unrelated to factionalism. In 1947 the simple correlation between SES and factionalism was .09; in 1975 it was .06 (see Table 5.1). One might expect that counties with small populations would not be able to mobilize the kind of support for individual candidates needed to match the statewide totals. In 1947 and 1951, for instance, before television helped universalize campaigns, it would seem that localized appeals combined with relative isolation would increase the likelihood of one-candidate counties. This possibility, coupled with the potential of the larger urban counties to draw candidates and therefore increase factionalization, should have created a negative relationship between ruralism and factionalism. But that is not the case. Only the primary election of 1971 reveals any coherent pattern at all, a negative relationship between white-collar workers and factionalism and positive relationships between factionalism and rural counties and counties with older populations. The message that Table 5.1 leaves, however, is that there is no way to predict factionalism from the socioeconomic character of a county. This conclusion is upheld when controls are applied (see Table 5.2).

Competition in the second primary, however, is more urban-related. The simple correlation coefficients show that in three of the last four second primaries there was a statistically significant negative relationship between a county's population living outside places of 2,500 people or more and competition between the two candidates. This result meets the expectations of the SES model. The percentage of white-collar workers in the work force is reinforcing since it correlates strongly with competition in two of the last four elections. Under controls for SES, black population, age, and population increase, the rural linkage holds up. It

TABLE 5.1

THE RELATIONSHIP BETWEEN SES VARIABLES AND FACTUALIZATION AND COMPETITION
IN THE FIRST AND SECOND MISSISSIPPI GUBERNATORIAL PRIMARY ELECTIONS 1947-1975*
(SIMPLE CORRELATION COEFFICIENTS)

Cases = Counties   N = 82

Variables	1947** 1st	1951 1st	1951 2nd	1955 1st	1955 2nd	1959 1st	1959 2nd	1963 1st	1963 2nd	1967 1st	1967 2nd	1971 1st	1971 2nd	1975 1st	1975 2nd
Percent Black Population	-.64***	.17	-.17	.10	-.15	-.04	-.09	.09	.06	-.20	.24	-.19	.09	.04	.28
Percent White-Collar Workers in Work Force	-.34	.21	-.28	.08	-.25	.02	.22	.17	.32	.01	.24	-.38	.13	.02	.44
Median Education Level Attained	.06	.09	-.18	.17	-.17	.04	.05	.14	.17	.16	-.08	.00	.11	.11	.07
Median Family Income	.08	.08	-.09	.17	.18	.01	.05	.16	.13	.17	-.01	-.04	.08	.02	.07
Percent Rural Population	.08	-.16	.14	-.08	.16	.01	-.23	-.15	-.42	-.15	-.33	.28	-.12	.05	-.46
Percent Rural Farm Population	.08	-.21	.17	-.12	.13	.00	-.14	-.08	-.13	-.10	.04	.14	-.12	.02	-.11
Percent Over 65 Years Old	.15	-.04	.06	-.02	-.15	.09	.01	-.10	-.11	-.01	-.26	.33	-.27	-.01	.36
Population Increase (20 Years)	-.14	.14	-.07	.08	-.06	-.04	.12	.14	.25	.11	.09	-.15	.15	-.02	.17
SES (A Composite of Education and Income)	.09	.09	-.14	.20	-.08	.03	.08	.18	.18	.17	-.03	-.03	.10	.06	.07

* Factionalism = Rae's index. Competition = 1.00 minus the statewide winner's deviation from 50 percent.

** In 1947 no second primary was held for governor.

***Coefficients significant at the .01 level are underlined. Before 1967 variables measure white population only.

SOURCE: Data for the socioeconomic variables were compiled by the author from U.S. Census Reports, 1930-1970. Data for selected elections were provided by the Inter-University Consortium for Political and Social Research (Center for Political Studies, the University of Michigan, Ann Arbor, Michigan). Other data for selected elections were compiled by the author from Mississippi Official and Statistical Register (Jackson, Mississippi: Secretary of State, 1947-1979).

TABLE 5.2

THE RELATIONSHIP BETWEEN SES VARIABLES AND FACTUALIZATION AND COMPETITION
IN THE FIRST AND SECOND MISSISSIPPI GUBERNATORIAL PRIMARY ELECTIONS 1947-1975*
(PARTIAL CORRELATION COEFFICIENTS)

Cases = Counties N = 82

Variables	1947** 1st	1951 1st	1951 2nd	1955 1st	1955 2nd	1959 1st	1959 2nd	1963 1st	1963 2nd	1967 1st	1967 2nd	1971 1st	1971 2nd	1975 1st	1975 2nd
Percent Black Population	-.71***	.09	-.22	.14	-.04	-.08	.06	.10	.27	-.12	-.01	.00	.11	.21	.13
SES (A Composite of Education and Income)	.25	.01	-.09	.22	.34	.09	-.17	.02	-.32	-.01	-.26	.19	.05	.23	-.17
Percent Rural Population	.13	-.07	.08	.10	.28	.02	-.28	-.05	-.44	-.12	-.38	.25	.04	.18	-.43
Percent Over 65 Years Old	.16	-.05	.11	-.05	-.29	.08	.13	-.02	.09	.07	-.24	.30	-.19	.10	-.25
Population Increase (20 Years)	-.15	-.02	.10	-.02	-.18	-.04	.11	.03	.20	--	--	--	--	--	--

* Factionalism = Rae's index. Competition = 1.00 minus the statewide winner's deviation from 50 percent.

** In 1947 no second primary was held for governor.

***Coefficients significant at the .01 level are underlined. Before 1967 variables measure white
   population only.

SOURCE: Same as for Table 5.1.

seems clear that in recent years in the second Mississippi primary, competition for the governorship has been more intense in the urban counties.

Friends-and-Neighbors Politics in Mississippi

One of the monkey wrenches tossed into the workings of these correlative equations is friends-and-neighbors politics, the tendency in rural societies for people to vote for candidates they know — candidates who live nearby. Implicit in the friends-and-neighbors theory is the concept of ruralism. Communication flows, it is held, are more limited in rural areas, and politics in general is more personalized. Rural people distrust strangers and may vote for someone they know over another candidate who might hold views that are closer to their own. Friends-and-neighbors politics is most often found in rural states with multifactional systems in which strong factional and/or party pressures are absent.

Raymond Tatalovich's rigorous analysis of friends-and-neighbors voting in Mississippi for the period we are concerned with (1943–1973) shows that in three-fifths of the elections for senator, governor, and lieutenant governor, candidates' percentages in the eighty-two counties correlated negatively with distance from the candidate's home county.[3] The first primary, when more candidates were in the field, exhibited the highest incidence of friends-and-neighbors politics. In the period between 1943 and 1958, 65 percent of all elections studied had friends-and-neighbors influences at work. Between 1959 and 1973, 54 percent fell in the friends-and-neighbors category. Tatalovich calls this a "sharp" decline and attributes it to improved socioeconomic status, the development of two-party competition, and the rise of blacks as a force in the electorate. Nevertheless, half the primary elections in Mississippi still have a significant friends-and-neighbors ingredient in the behavioral mixture, a factor that serves to disrupt attempts to uncover electoral foundations in the social structure of the state.

Delta and the Hills

If in the absence of two-party competition, rural areas are to benefit from the existence of conduits between polity and policy, then enduring and visible factional alignments must exist. Where these have been found there is usually a geographic base of support. Mississippi has such a regional dichotomy, which in the past has caused political activity to vary. Most observers agree, however, that the dual mind-sets and life-style differences in the Delta and the Hills have never supported factional structures that survived over time to provide an approximation of a party system. In the post–World War II period, the Delta-Hills pattern has weakened still further. In 1951 a liquor amendment to the Mississippi Constitution caused a significant Delta-Hills split in a statewide referendum, which explained 25 percent of the variance in the vote. In a 1960 right-to-work referendum, a similar result occurred. In the average Delta county, the vote was 91 percent affirmative; in the Hills, it was 71 percent affirmative. A series of voter qualification referenda in the 1960s, however, emphasize the demise of the Delta-Hills distinction as an important predictor of the vote. Referenda to extend the length of legislative sessions (1968) and to give the franchise to eighteen-year olds (1972) produced percentage splits of 53 to 51 and 81 to 80 between the Delta and the Hills.

One way to assess the political homogeneity of the Delta and therefore its potential as a cornerstone for a factional alignment is to determine whether or not the counties of the Delta are more likely to agree on candidates. If the twelve counties of the Delta have evolved political cultures to match the symmetry of the environment, then the people of those counties ought to have less factionalism in the first primary and less competition in the second. Only in the first primary of 1971, however, were the Delta counties significantly less factionalized than the state's remaining seventy counties, and even then the eta-squared coefficient was only .17. The second primary fits the hypothesis no better. In the elections for governor of 1951 through 1975, there was an important Delta-Hills difference in competition only once, and that was in 1975 when the voters of the Delta counties were *less* in agreement on their choice of gubernatorial candidates than other counties around the state.

There does seem to be some tendency for the Delta region to stand out from the rest of the state on its actual choice of candidates. In the last four second primaries the Delta cast significantly fewer votes for the winners than did the rest of the state. In 1971, for instance, the Delta voted 57 percent for the eventual loser, Charles L. Sullivan. It may be that the black vote, which began to count in 1967 and which is disproportionately strong in the Delta, is behind the new (and still weak) tendency for Delta counties to end up on the losing side of runoff primary votes. With that exception, however, it is clear that the traditional differences between planters and red-necks have been lost amid the dynamics of Mississippi's political atmosphere. Data readings from the Delta do not register indications that the raw material exists there to support a factional base.

Can a Bifactional Pattern
Be Empirically Derived in Mississippi?

Even though the Delta-Hills factional base seems to be sterile, the possibility remains open that bifactionalism exists in other forms in

Mississippi. Remember, we are interested in testing the proposition that the second primary approximates the conditions of a general election. In a general election in a two-party state, discovering the existence of factions is simple since the parties are the factions. But in a nonpartisan election such as Mississippi's second primary, we are forced either to deduce the hypothetical existence of factions and then check to see if they exist (we did this above in the Delta-Hills case) or to make an empirical (inductive) search of the data to see if factional patterns exist to which we may then attach labels. In short if the second primary in Mississippi approximates a two-party situation, then the two candidates in the race should represent visible, enduring dimensions in the vote. Put another way, the county votes for a candidate of one faction should be positively related to the votes over time of other candidates representing that faction. For instance, we find in Montana that the correlation coefficients between candidates representing the Democratic "faction" are consistently strong over time.

If something close to this pattern occurs in Mississippi, then we should be able to plot out similar interrelationships and label the candidates who share the relationships as components of a faction. But in Mississippi enduring relationships over time between winners and losers in the second primary are somewhat hard to find. One candidate's percentage of the two-candidate vote seldom explains more than 20 percent of the variance in another candidate's vote in another election. Although Cliff Finch's votes (1975) were more likely than not to come from the same counties as John Bell Williams's (1967), the relationship between the two is not great (r = .45).

A more precise exercise is to factor analyze the data with the election totals for the contestants in each second primary defined as independent variables. Factor analysis will tell if there is one underlying "dimension" or factor that explains a significant portion of the variance in all the elections. Again, Montana provides a good comparison. Factor analysis there shows that there is but one common dimension underlying the seven elections for governor between 1952 and 1976. That factor explains 70 percent of the variance in the data. Since Republican candidates are negatively associated with that dimension or "factor," Democrats are positively associated, and both kinds of relationships are very strong, we may conclude that parties are absolutely critical in understanding the dimensions of Montana elections.

If the second primary in Mississippi approximates the two-party condition that exists in Montana, a common unifying factor should appear in the data for Mississippi as well, a factor with which one of the candidates is positively associated in most elections and the other candidate is negatively associated. Such a factor does not appear, however. Instead of one factor that explains 70 percent of the variance as was the case in Montana, three factors appear in Mississippi that explain 63 percent, 21 percent, and 15 percent of the variance. (The original matrix was rotated to a final solution using the varimax technique.) The dominant factor loads high (is strongly associated with) the three most recent (1967, 1971, 1975) second-primary winners in Mississippi and the loser of the 1951 primary. The second factor is most strongly associated with the winners of the 1959 and 1963 primaries, with positive loadings of .68 and .78. The third factor is positively associated with the 1951 and 1955 guber- natorial winners, Hugh White and James P. Coleman. What is obvious is that the common dimensions are winning and losing and these change in sequential fashion over time. There are "winner coalitions" in Mississippi that appear regularly and disappear just as regularly.

It may be, however, that the last set of winners, Williams, William L. Waller, and Finch, represent more than a passing wave on the political sea that has traditionally been so factionalized it appears smooth. What the factor analysis tells us is that those three individuals have won sup- port from generally the same areas of Mississippi, that in the electorate they share a somewhat similar base. That base is mildly associated with the base of the winners in 1959 and 1963, not at all associated with the winner of the 1955 primary, and negatively associated with the 1951 win- ner. One must remember when reviewing these data that the factoring routine does not consider winner or loser status or the time the elections were held. That the technique has uncovered a dimension on which the three most recent winners score high (representing twelve years of ruler- ship in Mississippi) is important. Although for now the Mississippi sec- ond primary has not been typified by a bifactionalism that meets the dual criteria of visibility and endurance, it may be that this sequence of win- ners represents a bifactional arrangement in embryo.

The Second Primary—Correlates of Winners' Support

Beginning in 1959 every winner of the second Democratic primary in Mississippi has received more than average support from the rural coun- ties in Mississippi. Partial correlation coefficients are consistently strong and significant at the .01 level. As an example, when Cliff Finch won the second primary in 1975 with 57.7 percent of the statewide vote, he lost the county with the state's largest city, Jackson. The SES composite variable is also associated with the winner's vote and is significant at the .01 level in three of the last five elections (see Table 5.3). The consistent support for Mississippi's governors from the rural areas since 1959 tempts one to relabel the common factor found in the county returns for

TABLE 5.3

THE RELATIONSHIP BETWEEN THE WINNER'S PERCENTAGE OF THE
SECOND PRIMARY VOTE IN MISSISSIPPI AND SELECTED SOCIOECONOMIC VARIABLES 1951-1975

Cases = Counties   N = 82

YEAR AND WINNER

VARIABLES	1951 White		1955 Coleman		1959 Barnett		1963 Johnson		1967 Williams		1971 Waller		1975 Finch	
	S	P	S	P	S	P	S	P	S	P	S	P	S	P
Percent Black Population	.57*	.64	.38	.34	.12	-.03	-.09	-.35	-.47	-.17	-.44	.03	-.29	-.17
Percent Rural Population	-.21	-.06	.07	-.13	.46	.35	.41	.49	.33	.42	.11	.31	.50	.44
SES (A Composite of Education and Income)	.24	.28	-.16	-.10	-.28	.16	-.11	.43	.15	.29	.29	.45	-.10	.13
Percent Over 65 Years Old	-.04	-.19	.30	-.15	.24	-.02	.11	-.08	.27	.30	.29	.51	.34	.19
Population Increase (20 Years)	.10	-.18	-.25	-.12	-.38	-.16	-.24	-.25	-.02	--	.04	--	-.16	--
Percent White-Collar Workers in Work Force	.51	--	.09	--	-.33	--	-.31	--	-.25	--	-.15	--	-.49	--
Median Education Level Attained	.37	--	.14	--	-.09	--	-.13	--	.23	--	.32	--	-.09	--
Median Family Income	.12	--	-.28	--	-.32	--	-.08	--	.09	--	.24	--	-.09	--

* S = Simple correlation coefficients; P = Partials; (--) = variables were omitted from partial equations due to multicolinearity. Coefficients significant at the .01 level are underlined. Prior to 1967 variables measure white population only.

SOURCE: Same as for Table 5.1.

the second primary as the "rural-based winners" factor. Beginning with 1959 the tendency for governors to get relatively more votes from counties with larger percentages of their populations living outside places of 2,500 or more is a reversal of the condition in the early 1950s.

Others who have swiped at the cobwebs covering these relationships argue that the candidacies of White (winner, 1951), Johnson (loser, 1955), and Barnett (winner, 1959) demonstrate a probusiness and industrialization movement in Mississippi's electorate. Barksdale claims that Coleman's 1955 victory was due to a perception that he was a better manager and more qualified to bring industrialization to Mississippi.[4] Bass and De Vries point to the business-directed accomplishments of Ross Barnett (1960–1964) and Paul Johnson, Jr. (1964–1968).[5]

In their chapter on Mississippi in Havard's important *Changing Politics of the South,* Fortenberry and Abney argue that one's stance on business-labor issues may have been more important than the racial question in the mid-1950s.[6] This could have happened because both candidates tried to "out-racist" the other, thus neutralizing the effect of that issue. In 1955 Paul Johnson, Jr., who was to win in 1963, tried to pin a prolabor tag on Coleman and failed. According to Fortenberry and Abney, that attempt, coupled with White's strong economic development campaign in 1951, erased "any doubt that the political scene was changing." There was a decline in neopopulism as a result of industrialization, urbanization, and racial politics. Created was a "new division" in the state in the 1950s; it was "consolidated" in the elections of 1959 and 1963 but appeared again in 1967, an election that was different in tone but the same in "cleavage."[7]

Although Fortenberry and Abney are correct in their assessment that patterns were changing, there is no way of knowing from their work what direction those movements were taking in Mississippi. Their notation that voting "patterns" correlated more significantly in 1959 with the level of urbanization than in previous elections is incomplete. The "patterns" should have been identified in terms of the vote for a particular candidate, and the correlation with level of urbanization should have been defined as positive or negative. For it was the loser's vote that was strongly associated with urbanism, and it was the rural counties that cut down populism and fed the business-oriented rulership. If, as Fortenberry and Abney claim, voting in the second primary between 1950 and 1967 demonstrates a decline in neopopulism and the rise of a dominant cadre of industrial elites, then politically it was a rural industrialism not an urban one.

Bothersome to the "business cadre buries populists" hypothesis is that many view the winning candidates Waller (1971) and Finch (1975) as populists, not capitalists, at least at the electoral stage. Yet we know that they too had rural-based support like Barnett, Williams, and Johnson. Bass and De Vries portray the William Waller-Charles L. Sullivan campaign as "Waller running against the establishment, the 'Capital Street Gang.'" Waller, they claim, had "genuine populist instincts." Cliff Finch ran a clear workingman's campaign, a populist "lunch pail" effort.[8] Even John Bell Williams (1967), whom Fortenberry and Abney claim represented a continuation of the new industrialism breakthrough, won an election that represented "redneck know-nothings vs. enlightened progress" (according to one state newspaper editor), in which Williams was associated with the red-neck know-nothings.[9]

Another way to shed light on the nature of bifactionalism in Mississippi with specific reference to the Fortenberry and Abney hypothesis is to look at referenda voting for amendments to Mississippi's constitution. Three of these votes are particularly relevant — for the prohibition amendment of 1951, the right-to-work amendment of 1960, and the annual-sessions-of-the-legislature amendment of 1968. The first we might call a morality issue and expect the "business-industry" vote to be yes and the populist vote to be no. The second gives a clear labor versus business reading, and the third is a "good government" amendment, on which the business-industry vote should be yes, and the populist vote, no. On the morality vote, White's county percentages (1951) are consistent with the model. The correlation between the White vote and the vote for liberalizing restrictions on the sale of alcohol was .39 (see Table 5.4). The Coleman vote, however, showed no tendency in either direction. After that every winner's vote in the Mississippi second primary for governor has been (in the populist tradition) stronger in the antiliquor counties. The right-to-work amendment received stronger support in the White, Coleman, and Barnett counties, but in later elections the winners' counties fell on the prolabor side of the issue.

The good-government vote shows a significant break in the relationship taking place in 1959 with the election of Ross Barnett. Since that time, none of the governors of Mississippi has done well in "good government" counties; they all have done better, on the other hand, in those counties that voted more negatively on holding annual sessions of the legislature. Fortenberry and Abney may be correct in their assessment that a populist versus "business-industrial-managerial-progressivism" split exists in Mississippi. But to include Ross Barnett, Paul Johnson, Jr., and John Bell Williams in the business cadre as an extension of a movement that began with White and Coleman is questionable. The more correct judgment seems to be that Barnett and Johnson were pivots between the strong business-managerial governors,

TABLE 5.4

THE RELATIONSHIP BETWEEN
THE WINNER'S VOTE IN THE SECOND MISSISSIPPI
PRIMARY AND THREE SELECTED REFERENDA ISSUES

Cases = Counties N = 82

WINNERS		REFERENDA ISSUES		
		Liquor	Right-to-Work	Legislative Sessions
White	1951	.39*	.30	-.11
Coleman	1955	-.03	.39	.19
Barnett	1959	-.29	.21	-.51
Johnson	1963	-.41	-.17	-.23
Williams	1967	-.46	-.37	-.28
Waller	1971	-.56	-.33	-.25
Finch	1975	-.49	-.18	-.22

*Pearson product moment coefficients.

SOURCE: Same as for Table 5.1.

White and Coleman, and the rural populists, Williams, Waller, and Finch.

In short, if the White, Coleman, Barnett, and Johnson governorships represent the flowering of a new politics in Mississippi — a conservative, antipopulist capitalism — it seems to have been a morning-glory movement that was ended rather quickly by a rural-based populism. How long the Finch brand of populism will last is best left to the judgment of those who, like we have been, are blessed with the opportunity for hindsight. Agreeing to cast predictions about the second primary in Mississippi is like agreeing to sail the Bermuda Triangle; erratic currents and sudden electoral storms can swallow one up. Such a judgment, of course, is itself the only safe description of the second primary today.

Vermont: Where a One-Party Primary System Has Disappeared

Vermont triggers a conceptual leap forward in the developmental sequence. There the Republican primary, like the Democratic primary in Mississippi, has traditionally been the election that counted. But, unlike Mississippi, the minority party was an established force, and although it could not win statewide elections, from time to time it had to be reckoned with. Vermont is a rural state in which the minority has moved well past the competitive threshold, but the greater portion of the story of politics in America's most rural northern state has still been staged in the Republican primary. If we are to understand rural politics, we must understand that process.

Society and Conflict in the Vermont Primary

The principal enterprise of our discussion of parties and elections in rural states is to discover if ruralism is an inhospitable environment for political conflict. We know from Chapter 4 that it is difficult to trace the competitiveness of the two-party vote in the general election to particular kinds of societal environments. The logical explanation for this difficulty is that it is the primary that houses the critical society-conflict linkage. Since conflict itself has been transferred from the general election to the primary, perhaps the empirical linkage of conflict to social structure had been shipped along with it. The hypothesis is straightforward: Small, rural, agricultural towns with populations that are stable or declining will be less factionalized than larger towns with more-diversified economic structures and growing populations.

As a first step, town population, population increase, people per farm, the increase in people per farm, and the Democratic percentage of the two-party vote were plugged into simple and partial correlation equations for primaries from the pre–New Deal period (1926–1930) through the breakthrough period (1948–1952). A total of eleven primaries in which the median index of factionalization was .498 were analyzed. In the 1926 and 1928 primaries the only variable that was important was the Democratic-strength variable, which correlated at .17 (p = .004) with factionalism in the Republican party in 1928 when other variables were controlled. It may be that some crossover existed, whereby Republicans supporting a candidate who lost in the primary voted for the Democratic candidate in the general election. Or it may be that the Democrats entered the Republican primary, although Vermont's form of "open primary" discourages this. The most profound dynamic in rural Vermont in the first half of the twentieth century was the disappearance of the hill farm. Yet areas suffering from this condition did not respond politically within the Republican primary by registering a more factionalized response to candidates.

The New Deal primaries (1932–1936) were absolutely void of any empirical ties between kinds of towns and factional response. The strongest partial correlation coefficient in the entire array of twenty associations (five variables times four elections) was .13 between Democratic strength and factionalism in 1932. The Republican primary vote seemed to float above social structure. For instance, when Vermont's most significant politician of this century, George Aiken, ran for governor in a four-person primary in 1936, factionalization was the highest it had ever been, .659. Yet the association between that intraparty dynamic and SES variables was nonexistent. The partials for town size, farming, herd stability, and population increase were .08, −.09, −.04, and .05, respectively. Barren ground, indeed.

In the years preceding the Democratic breakthrough of 1952, some structure appeared in the findings. But it is spotty and may be explained in some instances by varieties in each election. In the 1944 contest, for instance, there was a positive .25 correlation between dairy-herd stability and factionalism. However, in that two-candidate race, the loser lost by a substantial margin. This means that factionalism was also a measure of the loser's percentage. The loser, Arthur Simpson, was a farmer from the Northeast Kingdom, where the loss of dairy herds had not been as great as in other parts of the state. In 1952 there was a relatively strong partial coefficient for population increase and factionalism, .26, $p = .001$. This relation is more like it since it fits the theory very well—people moving in may create the basis for a new factional alignment.

In the modern period we are left once again with a virtual wasteland of factional society linkages, even though a more complete set of independent variables allows a precise testing of the hypothesis. The Republican primary was no longer the final election during this period, but the change did not alter the fact that factionalism seemed to be unaffected by the environmental context of the vote. The only variable that correlated with factionalism was Vermont natives, the percentage of a town's population born within the state. There again, however, what is probably being measured is candidate strength rather than factionalism per se. In the two elections in which the Vermont-natives variable was most important (1968 and 1970), the same candidate was the winner both times, Deane Davis. Since his opponents rarely received more than 50 percent of the vote, higher percentages for them caused a higher factionalism score.

One of the ways we can verify the paucity of factional ties to society is to look at the correlation matrix for factionalism among elections. Seldom does factionalism in one election predict factionalism in another. Since we know that society does not change that quickly, one would hypothesize that if certain societal contexts promote factionalism, there would be strong correlations between elections across time. If factionalism is high in Sharon and Newbury in 1970, for instance, because of the kind of towns they are, then it should be high in those towns in 1972, 1974, and so forth. The correlations show that factionalism bounced here and there across the geographic face of Vermont in a completely unpredictable manner.

The Nature of Factionalism Prior to Breakthrough

A rural society like Vermont's, generally lacking in socioeconomic diversity, carved into tiny bits and pieces by the granite hills, and hosting a tiny and scattered population, ought to have had trouble maintaining durable factions within the majority party, especially if the minority party were strong enough to siphon off a goodly amount of socioeconomic diversity. Prior to the Democratic breakthrough of 1952 (1926–1952), there were fourteen Republican primary elections. The median factionalization score was only .493. There were two elections in which there was only one candidate, and in the other twelve elections the top two candidates earned over 90 percent of the vote nine times and 100 percent of the vote eight times. Compare this situation to Mississippi's multifactional system, in which the average number of candidates in the first primary was 5.5, the median factionalization score was .734, and the top two candidates never got over 90 percent of the vote.

If not multifactional, what? Vermont appears to be bifactional. If we choose to call a bifactional election one in which there are only two candidates running and the winner receives less than 70 percent of the vote, or one in which there are more than two candidates but the top two get at least 90 percent of the vote with the runner-up getting at least 30 percent, then a majority of the elections (eight of fourteen) were bifactional from 1920 to 1952. Yet this record does not match the record of the southern states, where bifactionalism is known to be dominant. Malcolm Jewell has shown, for instance, that in Kentucky's bifactional system the top two candidates almost always receive well over 90 percent of the vote and elections are never left uncontested.[10] Vermont cannot match this record. Every ten years or so during the prebreakthrough era, the Republicans in Vermont got caught up in a three-way contest in which the split was always very nearly 43 percent–33 percent–24 percent, something close to multifactionalism. This has never occurred in Kentucky.

Vermont is caught in the middle with a party that has flirted with multifactionalism, exhibited a tendency toward bifactionalism, but engaged in unifactionalism also. Theory tells us this may be an appropriate finding. The Democrats were strong enough to stimulate the maintenance of a Republican apparatus. That apparatus (the "establishment") kicked off its own reaction within the GOP (the natural tendency for large organizations to stir up their own opposition), but since Vermont lacked the socioeconomic raw material to institutionalize that opposition, it danced across the electoral history of the state sporadically, at times disappearing altogether.

But an opposition faction could appear inconsistently and still maintain the qualities of a faction if it was tied to a certain sector of society and therefore identifiable geographically, if the votes its candidates received were intercorrelated, and if it exhibited longevity. Therefore, the next step is to determine, as we did for Mississippi, if there were *sets* of candidates in Vermont. For instance, was there a winning set and a losing set, two sets that rotated victories regularly, one dominant set and another set that challenged from time to time—if so, did the challenger set win or lose—or were there no sets at all, simply winners and losers?

In Mississippi the search for a factional pattern was guided by the notion that there was (1951–1975) a populist-business split in the second primary. In Vermont, too, there is a guide to factionalism in the early period (1920–1952). The theory is that the Republican party was composed of two "wings," a conservative, probusiness, "Proctor" wing dominated by forces sympathetic to the Proctor Marble Company and a progressive wing, typified by opposition to the Proctor machine and led by such important governors as George Aiken (1936–1940) and Ernest Gibson (1946–1949). Aiken was cast as the rural agricultural opposition to the business-oriented "machine" candidates controlled by the Proctors.[11]

But this bifactional pattern eludes the grasp of the most sensitive statistical techniques. In the period beginning in 1934 and ending only fourteen years later in 1948, candidates intimately involved in this hypothesized arrangement ran in six of the eight contested Republican primaries for governor. But correlation coefficients among the town-by-town election returns for all the candidates throughout the period exhibit no factional arrangement at all. Candidates associated with the two wings of the party do not appear to be keyed to the same electorates. For instance, in 1944 Mortimer Proctor, president of Proctor Marble Company, won the primary. Just two years later, as an incumbent, he lost in the primary to progressive Ernest Gibson, the leader of the opposition faction. But the Proctor vote of 1944 correlated at only − .09 with the Gibson vote of 1946. This figure also means, of course, that the two Proctor electorates of 1944 and 1946 correlated at only .09. The only important indicator in the direction of the bifactional hypothesis is the negative (− .44) correlation between the Proctor towns of 1946 and the Gibson towns of 1948. But this is hardly surprising since Gibson had denied Proctor what was normally taken for granted — a second term.

When the primary returns for Vermont's 246 cities and towns for all candidates in all primaries are passed over the heat of a data-reductive factor analysis, no bifactional pattern appears in the parchment. What would be expected, given the Proctor versus Gibson-Aiken model, is a single factor on which the candidates of one faction load positively and the candidates of the other faction load negatively. Yet, when the correlation matrix is rotated to a terminal solution, three factors are found explaining 51 percent, 31 percent, and 18 percent of the total variance in the data, indicating that several crosscurrents were at work in the Vermont Republican primaries rather than a single one. Moreover, the dominant factor cannot be labeled a Proctor versus Gibson-Aiken factor, for neither the Proctor 1944 vote nor the Benjamin Williams (vice-president of Proctor Marble Company) 1934 vote loads on this factor at all, the Aiken 1936 vote loads positively, and the Gibson votes of 1946 and 1948 load negatively.

A final check on the existence of bifactionalism in Vermont can be made by uncovering the ties each of the candidates had to the socioeconomic conditions in the Vermont towns. Clearly if the Proctor candidates generated support from a particular kind of town and the Gibson-Aiken candidates from another, then the bifactional model would be more credible. But the data continue to paint a picture of completely unstructured politics. Whether the candidate was Gibson or Aiken or Williams or Proctor, there is no way of predicting the direction of a town's vote by knowing whether or not it is a big town or little town, a farming town or nonfarming town, or a growing or declining town. An array of partial correlation coefficients turns up no important linkages between seven Republican primary winners and socioeconomic indicators for Vermont towns in eleven primary elections between 1926 and 1952. Nor is it possible to identify, as we did for Mississippi, a cadre of winners in the primary. Not even once between 1920 and 1952, a period in which thirteen primaries for governor were held, was there a significant positive correlation between the votes of one winner of a Republican primary and the votes of that candidate's immediate successor. There was nothing, in other words, approaching the Johnson-Williams-Waller-Finch matrix in Mississippi.

Yet we know there was order in the Vermont primary system. Two almost uncanny patterns indicate this. One was the apprenticeship system, and the other was the "mountain rule." Republican governors in Vermont followed a clear route through a hierarchy of offices before they ran for governor, usually beginning in the state House of Representatives. Speakership of the House, a seat in the Senate, and the lieutenant governorship usually followed.

The second pattern was geographical. Vermonters had, since the formation of the state as the independent Republic of Vermont in the nineteenth century, been aware of the cultural dichotomy caused by and marked by the Green Mountains, which bisect the state north to south. Accordingly, Vermonters doled out political offices by the "mountain rule," which was a "wait your turn" principle whereby Republicans were nominated and then elected first from one side of the state and then from the other. So hard and fast was this rule that it was never broken in the first thirty-four years of this century, despite the fact that there were twenty-two opportunities to do so. Even after the institution of the direct primary, when the decision was handed over to the electorate, the mountain rule held. Two decades and nine primaries passed before the electorate snapped the pattern. In 1944 a westerner, Mortimer Proctor, did not wait his turn. He challenged W. Arthur Simpson, the eastern candidate, and defeated him. The eastern part of the state got its revenge in 1946 when Proctor lost his bid for a second term to the Connecticut Valley progressive, Ernest Gibson. After this event the mountain rule was maintained fitfully until the Democrats plowed it under for good in 1962, ending one of the most intriguing patterns of geographic politics in American political history.

What Vermont had was neither a wide-open, "every man for himself" multifactionalism nor a bifactional arrangement. It had a benevolent unifactionalism, whereby a cadre of office holders, under traditional constraints such as the apprenticeship system and the mountain rule operated to minimize conflict. There were two prevalent attitudes within the Republican elite—a more or less progressive populism and a more or less conservative elitism. But they were in no way society-based, electorally linked, or visibly enduring to the electorate. In the context of history those attitudes rarely caused serious conflict. Except for the mountain rule and the apprenticeship system, there was little order in Republican primary politics in Vermont—no pattern the voters could count on, no continuing apparatus one could turn to. It was distinctly not the kind of arrangement that many people contend is necessary for the betterment of the underprivileged.

The Vermont Primary in the
Context of the Republican Slide

The hinge between the old and the new in Vermont Republican primary politics is the three candidacies of a Northeast Kingdom resident, Lee Emerson, in 1948, 1950, and 1952. Northerners in the Republican primary were not popular, and Emerson lived in the shadow of Canada. His candidacies did three things. They helped latch the casket of the mountain rule, since governors preceding and following Emerson were both from the eastern part of the state. They broke up any possibility that the Gibson-Proctor feud would get out of hand. Since Emerson's principal political contests were to be with southerners, the struggle in the party shifted from an east-west battle in the south to a north-south battle in the east. Proctor in the southwest warmed the bench. Finally, Emerson's candidacies set the stage for the first major Republican defection to the Democratic party in the southern counties (see Chapter 4).

Prior to 1952 the Republicans seemed to go about their business quite nonchalantly vis-à-vis the Democrats, and Vermont affords an excellent opportunity to trace the breakthrough process through the next logical step. What happens to majority-party factionalism after minority breakthrough? Does a bifactional system develop? Or does the party coalesce into unifactionalism?

Immediately after the Democratic breakthrough — with the disruptive Emerson primaries and the Gibson-Proctor confrontation well within memory, the mountain rule and the apprenticeship system gone, and the Democrats at the gates — the Republican primary entered a decade of disorientation. The party switched violently between the extremes of factionalism. After this period, however, there seems to have been, at least for a brief time, the development of some order. Simple correlation coefficients between the winners of the Republican primary in the quarter century following 1952 exhibit a phenomenon that never occurred in the quarter century preceding the breakthrough (1920–1952). Three different candidates in succession were positively tied together by simple correlation coefficients (see Figure 5.1). Although the associations between successive candidates are weak, they are the closest thing to evidence of a factional arrangement in the Republican primary electorate that has ever appeared in Vermont.

Factoring the data for the period produces a major factor that explains 60 percent of the variance. Expectedly, the major factor loads high on the votes for Richard Snelling, Deane Davis, and Luther Hackett. Given a ten-year lag after the original breakthrough, but during the term of Vermont's first Democratic governor in a century (1963–1967), some structure began to appear in the Republican primary. Two of the members of the Snelling-Davis-Hackett group are responsible for the only significant candidate-society connection in the postbreakthrough period. Despite the fact that we have a broader array of SES indicators to use for the modern period, there is a remarkable lack of ties between candidates' votes and the social and economic ecology of the communities from which the votes come.

Partial correlation coefficients between an array of SES variables and seven winners of the Republican primary in eight elections indicate that

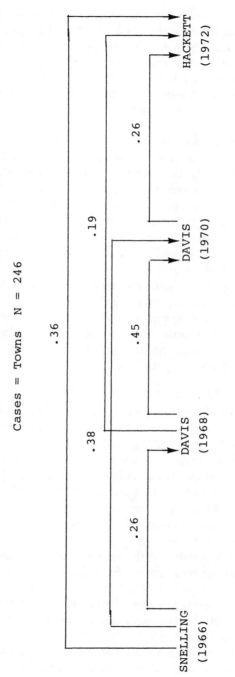

FIGURE 5.1

LINKAGES AMONG WINNERS OF THE
REPUBLICAN PRIMARY IN VERMONT, 1966-1972

Cases = Towns   N = 246

linkage occurs with only one variable in the Snelling election of 1966 and the two Davis elections of 1968 and 1970. Town size, the educational and income levels of a town's citizens (the SES composite variable), the age of the population, the number of family farms, and whether or not the town was growing made no difference in the Republican primary vote. When all these variables are held constant, however, it is found that towns with more native Vermonters were likely to vote for Snelling and Davis.

The appearance of this cadre of Republicans as a unifying force in the electorate was a fleeting thing indeed. Four years after the Hackett primary of 1972, Snelling ran for governor again, and surprisingly his totals of 1976 showed no association with his totals of 1966 nor with the totals of Davis or Hackett. The electoral map had shifted again. In short, there seems to have been in the last half of the 1960s and early 1970s a conservative-moderate wing of the Republican party and a more liberal wing. These two wings had an unsteady regional flavor that helped produce a statistical association. The candidates opposing and losing to members of the winning cadre were all associated more or less with the liberal wing. But the point seems to be that this loosely knit ideological dichotomy, although very real within the party hierarchy itself and dominating the parlor talk of politics, lacked (except for a brief period) a visible and enduring base in the state's communities and it does not meet the criteria of bifactionalism.

The End of Friends-and-Neighbors Politics

The great disruptive force on the electoral map of rural politics has always been friends-and-neighbors voting. In Vermont this phenomenon has caused substantial mischief for those people who seek uniformity and patterns. The tendency for the electorate to support friends and neighbors irrespective of socioeconomic and political considerations has been the only pattern one could count on since the mountain rule and the apprenticeship system have fallen. Now for the most part, the state has shucked friends-and-neighbors politics, and the electorate has been cast free.

A hawk's-eye view of the decline in friends-and-neighbors politics can be had by exploring the notion of a difference between factionalism for the state as a whole and factionalism within each individual town. For instance, in 1950 factionalism based on the candidates' statewide percentages was .643, but the factionalism score for each town averaged .531. If there is no relationship between town size and a particular candidate's vote—that is, if town size is not associated with factionalism—the average town factionalism will always be lower than the statewide score to the extent that individual candidates do better in particular towns. Even though, for instance, the minority candidate loses the statewide election 70 percent to 30 percent (a factionalization score of .42), he might carry his home county towns, thus increasing factionalism there, and do more poorly in distant towns, thus decreasing factionalism in a great many more towns and pulling the average town factionalism down.

Between 1926 and 1976 in the twenty contested Republican primaries, statewide factionalism averaged .075 points above the average town score of .447. But the major differences in these scores occurred in the past. The correlation between the passage of time and the difference between the two scores is $-.52$ (p = .01). In the first four Republican primary elections in Vermont, the difference between state and local factionalism averaged .150. In the last four Republican primary elections, it averaged .025. Localism in the Vermont Republican primary is becoming extinct. Also the Democrats have shown no tendency to engage in friends-and-neighbors politics in their primary since 1970.

Montana: Dual Primaries in a Rural State

Montana represents a third conceptual environment—a rural state in which two primaries have flourished for decades. The circle is thereby closed: Mississippi, a single primary system; Vermont, a transitional primary system; and Montana, a dual primary system. Montana is a double enigma. Not only does this spatially massive state with its tiny population muster up enough political diversity to support a rough-and-tumble two-party system, it also has shown a capability to maintain a high degree of competitiveness in both primaries. Where, one might ask, does it get this kind of political moxie?

Factionalism—An Overview

Montana's Democratic primary is so highly factionalized that it looks similar to the first primary in Mississippi. The key difference between Mississippi and Montana is that Montana's primary usually has two candidates that stand out and capture a significant percentage of the vote. The percentage for the top two candidates in Montana seldom dips below 70 percent and in Mississippi it seldom rises above 70 percent. The Democrats in Montana lean toward bifactionalism in the primary but are kept from that posture by a plethora of minor candidates. The Republican party is much less factionalized. Since 1940 the combined scores of the top two Republican candidates fell below 90 percent only once, and they have fallen below 70 percent only twice since 1920 (see Table 5.5). The Republican primary in Montana is very close on these

TABLE 5.5

FACTIONALISM IN THE MONTANA PRIMARY 1920-1976

YEAR	PARTY							
	Democratic				Republican			
	No. of Candidates	Winning Percentage	Top Two Percents	Factionalism Index	No. of Candidates	Winning Percentage	Top Two Percents	Factionalism Index
1920	3	61%	92%	.520	6	35%	65%	.680
1924	5	35%	59%	.761	2	56%	100%	.500
1928	2	51%	100%	.500	4	46%	70%	.688
1932	4	46%	67%	.686	2	69%	100%	.420
1936	5	38%	72%	.698	2	72%	100%	.400
1940	3	38%	75%	.660	6	33%	62%	.759
1944	3	47%	77%	.640	2	88%	100%	.200
1948	5	37%	67%	.715	3	72%	92%	.430
1952	1	100%	100%	0	2	72%	100%	.400
1956	4	45%	87%	.520	1	100%	100%	0
1960	6	35%	67%	.708	2	50%	100%	.500
1964	2	56%	100%	.500	1	100%	100%	0
1968	6	38%	73%	.708	4	55%	95%	.500
1972	5	60%	90%	.545	4	41%	79%	.656
1976	1	100%	100%	0	2	57%	100%	.491
Median	4	46%	77%	.640	2	57%	100%	.500

SOURCE: Ellis Waldron, *An Atlas of Montana Politics Since ... 1864* (Missoula: Montana State University Press, 1958). Selected 1960-1976 elections were compiled by the author. Other related election data were made available by the Inter-University Consortium for Political Research, Ann Arbor, Michigan.

dimensions to its counterpart in Vermont.

Factionalism in both parties is declining. Since 1948 each primary has gone uncontested twice, something that never happened in either primary before World War II. The correlation coefficient between the passage of time and factionalism in the Democratic primary is −.37. For the Republican primary it is −.28. Over time there seems to be no relationship between factionalism in one primary and factionalism in the other. The correlation coefficient between factionalism in the two parties, using the fifteen primaries held since 1920 as cases, is .06.

When an incumbent is running, factionalism is lower in the incumbent's party, especially since World War II. In both Democratic primaries held after 1950 in which there was a Democratic incumbent on the ticket he was unopposed. Prior to that time, incumbent Democrats faced stiff primary opposition each time they ran for reelection. When no incumbent was running in the Democratic primary prior to 1950, the factionalism score was .607. After 1950 it was .596. The same pattern holds true for the Republicans. Since 1950 they have had incumbents running in three primaries, and in two of the three instances the incumbent ran unopposed. Primary politics seems to be mellowing in Montana, partly as a result of the modern tendency not to oppose an incumbent within one's own party.

It is clear that factionalism in one party may benefit the other party in the general election. It was noted in Chapter 4, for instance, that on several occasions county percentages for the runner-up in one primary correlated strongly with the county percentages of the opposition party's candidate in the general election. Over the past half century the correlation between the Democratic vote for governor and factionalism within the Democratic primary is −.22. The more the factionalism, the lower the vote in the general election. The correlation between the Democratic general-election vote and factionalism within the Republican party was .20. The higher the Republican factionalism, the higher the Democratic vote in the general election.

What is needed is a score for either party that combines the factionalism indexes for both parties. Thus the optimum situation for the Democrats existed in 1976 when the Republican factionalism score was .491 and theirs was 0. The most potentially damaging situation for the Democrats took place in 1956 when their own factionalism was .520 and the Republicans' was 0. By subtracting the Democrats' index of factionalism from 1.0 and adding the Republicans', an index was created that ranges from 0 (where the Democrats are totally factionalized and the Republicans have only one candidate in the primary) to 2.00 (where the Republicans are totally factionalized and the Democrats have no factionalism). This index correlated at .30 with the Democratic percentage in the general elections. This figure indicates that there is a mild tendency in Montana for factionalism in the primary to disrupt a party's chances in the general election.

SES Linkages to Factionalism in Montana

The opportunity to hunt down the social and economic basis for primary-election factionalism in a two-party rural state is excellent in Montana. The counties exhibit widely diverse social ecologies. There is a flourishing two-party system in a rural setting, and the parties display different kinds of factionalism. By calculating a factionalization score for each of Montana's fifty-six counties for each contested primary in the quarter century following 1950, it is possible to determine what kinds of environments housed factionalism.

Since 1950 each party has had five contested primaries for governor. The two counties with the highest factionalization scores for the Democratic primary are Cascade and Yellowstone. Cascade County has Great Falls and Yellowstone has Billings, Montana's largest cities. Both counties have educational levels that are above the state's average and median family incomes that are about $1,000 higher than the norm.

The two counties with the lowest Democratic-primary factionalism are Deer Lodge in the Broad Valley Rockies of southwestern Montana and Sheridan in extreme northeastern Montana. Deer Lodge has a large ethnic population, and the percentage of the work force employed in manufacturing is the highest in the state. Mining is also very important. Population decreased by 5 percent between 1960 and 1970, and most of the population (63 percent) lives in urban places. There is almost no farming. It is, in a nutshell, a Rocky Mountain approximation of a traditional, urban, blue-collar county in the East. Over 600 miles and the Continental Divide separate Deer Lodge County from Sheridan County. Environmentally, the two counties are profoundly dissimilar. Nowhere in Sheridan County are people grouped in a place of even 2,500 population, and the total population is only 6,500 scattered over an area of the Great Plains above the Missouri River about the size of Delaware. It is rough, plateau country bordering both Canada and North Dakota. Thirty-four percent of the population lives on farms while the statewide county average is 24 percent. What Sheridan County has that Deer Lodge County also has is a large ethnic population. In fact at 34 percent it is substantially greater than Deer Lodge's and one of the largest in the state.

The pattern seems obvious, and it fits the expectations of the SES model: It takes the urban populations of Cascade and Yellowstone counties to support high levels of factionalism. Deer Lodge County is a Democratic stronghold, and the organization there produces both overwhelming Democratic majorities (Deer Lodge has been the most Democratic county in Montana in the post–World War II period) and a consensus at primary time; thus the county's ranking at the bottom of the factionalism list. Sheridan County, with its tiny, highly ethnic, rural population and homogeneous economic base, doesn't have the diversity to produce factionalism.

Yet when expanded to include all of Montana's counties, the SES model begins to fade badly. Although the percentage of a county's population classified as urban in 1970 is still associated with factionalism, the coefficient is weak, .29. Simple and partial correlation coefficients (see Table 5.6) indicate that factionalism in the Democratic primaries throughout the period studied is not firmly attached to the socioeconomic ecologies of the counties. When the data are broken down into individual elections, only one Democratic primary, the primary of 1972, reveals an association between factionalism and society. A matrix of correlation coefficients verifies this lack of association by showing that factionalism in a county in one election tells us little about its degree of factionalism in the previous election or the next election to come.

The two counties with the highest factionalism in the Republican primaries in 1952–1976 are Lincoln and Prairie. They are horizons apart, both in terms of their geography and in terms of their socioeconomic and physiological environments. Prairie County is the far eastern Great Plains section of Montana, dusty and hot in summer, frigid and windswept in winter. Lincoln County is perched in the very northwestern tip of the state bordering Canada and Idaho in the Columbia Rockies. It is warmer in winter and cooler in summer than Prairie County, and it is a land of great Pacific mountains, forests, and grazing land. Lincoln County has one of the fastest-growing populations in the state and the second-highest median family income. Its population is less ethnic, less urbanized, and much younger than that of the average county.

Four hundred miles to the east of Lincoln County as the eagle flies, Prairie County has 1,752 residents and 1,727 square miles of territory. They are as factionalized as the 18,000 people of Lincoln County, and Prairie County's median family income is well below the state average. Prairie County's education levels are subpar, and there are substantially more ethnics and farmers there than in Lincoln County.

The counties with the lowest Republican factionalism, Sheridan and Daniels, are twins. We already know Sheridan. Daniels is next door. They are similar on nearly every socioeconomic indicator, differing only on median family income (by about $1,000). Although Prairie and Lin-

TABLE 5.6

SOCIOECONOMIC CORRELATES OF FACTIONALISM IN MONTANA

DEMOCRATIC PRIMARIES	1956		1960		1964		1968		1972		1956-1972*	
	S	P	S	P	S	P	S	P	S	P	S	P
% Urban Population	-.18**	-.13	.02	.05	.09	.28	.08	.25	.34	.03	.23	.29
% Farmers in Work Force	.22	.30	.00	.03	.08	.06	.16	.29	-.58	-.42	-.16	.09
Median Education Level	.08	-.07	.15	.13	.07	.06	.05	.09	-.02	-.01	.10	.06
Median Family Income	.11	.26	-.07	.00	.00	.13	-.04	-.25	.24	-.14	.00	-.30
Population Increase	.04	.16	-.04	.15	-.19	-.30	-.04	.10	.53	-.03	.20	.11
% Over 65 Years Old	-.18	.00	.35	.40	.09	-.02	-.19	-.19	-.46	-.22	-.21	-.09
% Ethnic Population	-.12	-.02	-.07	-.22	.00	-.11	.14	.26	-.46	-.31	-.27	-.15

REPUBLICAN PRIMARIES	1952		1960		1968		1972		1976		1952-1976*	
	S	P	S	P	S	P	S	P	S	P	S	P
% Urban Population	-.09	.10	.03	-.07	-.06	.22	.18	.20	-.14	-.17	.07	-.15
% Farmers in Work Force	.08	-.20	-.10	-.07	.15	.27	-.24	.09	.18	.16	-.12	.06
Median Education Level	-.30	-.20	.21	.14	.20	.09	-.06	-.06	-.07	-.06	.06	-.11
Median Family Income	-.26	-.18	.09	-.02	-.18	-.25	.00	-.12	.17	.17	.02	-.06
Population Increase	-.35	-.33	.13	.07	.00	-.21	.20	.01	.09	.06	.22	.14
% Over 65 Years Old	.22	.10	-.01	.09	.08	.19	.07	.22	-.24	-.14	-.07	.30
% Ethnic Population	.10	-.20	-.24	-.22	-.24	-.24	-.44	-.48	-.11	.04	-.48	-.49

* The factionalism score averaged for the five primaries.
**Coefficients significant at the .01 level are underlined. S = simple correlation coefficients. P = partials.

SOURCE: Election data, same as for Table 5.5. SES data taken from U.S. Census Reports, 1950-1970.

coln counties belie the theory (similar socioeconomic surroundings should generate similar political outcomes), Sheridan and Daniels support it.

By considering all counties in the analysis and subjecting each socioeconomic variable to controls for every other variable, one discovers that there is a strong relationship between ethnicity and a lack of Republican factionalism for the 1952 to 1976 period. The election of 1972 seems to explain a considerable amount of this relationship (see Table 5.6), although weak negative coefficients are found between ethnicity and factionalism throughout the period. This relationship was also apparent in the Democratic primary, although to a lesser degree. Evidently high rates of ethnicity in the counties serve to focus candidate selection and discourage factionalism. Otherwise, it is impossible to discover any socioeconomic-based predictors of factionalism in the data.

Seeking Out the Nature of Factionalism in Montana

In the Democratic primaries in Montana the top two candidates usually earn close to three-quarters of the vote, smoke signals of bifactionalism. But the correlation coefficients among the electorates of all candidates in all contested primaries between 1950 and 1976 tend to support the multifactional model. Returns for Arnold Olsen, Paul Cannon, and Roland Renne in 1956, 1960, and 1964 are positively associated but weak. The largest is between Cannon and Renne ($r = .40$). Each of those candidates won his primary contest. The Forrest Anderson and Thomas Judge electorates of 1968 and 1972, however, are disassociated with each other and with the three previous winners. More importantly, none of the losers in 1968 or 1972 was strongly associated with the votes for any of the earlier three, indicating that the 1968 and 1972 elections did not simply represent the switching of winners in a continuing bifactional arrangement. Factoring these election totals for major candidates produces, expectedly, one dominant factor and a subsidiary one, with Olsen, Cannon, and Renne loading positively on the strongest factor. This cluster is much like the Snelling-Davis-Hackett grouping in Vermont, a weak, impermanent island in a sea filled with unpredictable currents. Neither cluster has the strength or longevity of the winner's cluster in the second Mississippi primary.

For the most part, candidates in the Montana Democratic primaries do not solicit votes on the basis of electorates that can be identified by their socioeconomic trappings. The candidacy of Paul Cannon in 1960 is important because Cannon was strongly associated with the Farmers Union vote in Montana. His county percentages in the highly factionalized primary of 1960 are strongly associated with population decline and the number of older people in the population. His percentages are weakly

184

TABLE 5.7

SOCIOECONOMIC CORRELATES OF THE WINNER'S VOTE IN CONTESTED
DEMOCRATIC AND REPUBLICAN PRIMARIES IN MONTANA, 1952-1976, PARTIAL CORRELATION COEFFICIENTS

	DEMOCRATS					REPUBLICANS				
	Olsen 1956	Cannon 1960	Renne 1964	Anderson 1968	Judge 1972	Aronson 1952	Nutter 1960	Babcock 1968	Smith 1972	Woodahl 1976
Percent Urban Population	-.06	-.20	-.15	.02	.10	-.02	.09	-.26	-.16	.04
Percent Farmers in the Work Force	-.10	.17	-.09	-.10	-.38*	.24	-.25	-.22	.24	-.25
Median Education Level	.08	-.17	.12	.13	-.06	.22	-.18	-.18	-.06	-.11
Median Family Income	-.02	.04	-.10	-.17	.01	.11	-.06	.35	-.03	-.17
Population Increase (20 Years)	-.03	-.43	.17	-.10	.01	.31	-.12	-.29	.02	.01
Percent Over 65 Years Old	-.03	.41	-.13	-.12	.20	-.08	-.18	-.21	-.07	.17
Percent Ethnic Population	.26	.04	.23	-.01	.26	.19	.18	.20	.29	.05

*Coefficients significant at the .01 level are underlined.

SOURCE: Same as for Table 5.6.

associated with urbanism (negatively) and farmers in the work force (positively). What we have with Cannon is the hub of the rural, agrarian Democratic cluster that included Olsen before him and Renne who followed. Political historian of Montana, Richard Roeder, claims that those three winners of Democratic primaries (all of whom lost the general election) represent the swan song of Farmers Union power in Montana and that the two most recent Democratic gubernatorial primary winners, Forrest Anderson and Thomas Judge (both of whom won the general election) represent a newer, "old style," more-urban Democratic influence in the party.[12] Catholic Thomas Judge's strong negative correlation with farmers in the work force in 1972 and weak but positive association (.26) with ethnicity supports this view (see Table 5.7).

The Republican primary in Montana has a much simpler structure. Even though there are fewer candidates to disrupt the percentages, the associations among winners of the Republican primary are weaker than those of the Democratic primary. The last four winners of the Republican primary, however, do share positive correlations among their electorates. Reducing the data produces a single factor on which these four load positively and Hugo Aronson (the 1952 winner) loads negatively. Since the electorates of Donald Nutter (1960) and Ed Smith (1972) contribute the most to this factor, it may be properly labeled "the Republican conservative center."

This extremely weak "coalition" of Republican winners is in no way fastened to any identifiable component of society. Typical of the general pattern is the fact that Nutter's partial correlation coefficient with farmers in the work force is $-.25$, and Smith's is $+.24$. Simply stated, although the statewide pattern indicates a potential for bifactionalism (usually two candidates taking all or almost all of the votes), what the Montana Republican primary has really been all about in the last few years is the candidacy of a conservative who wins. Those candidates share no common SES-based electorate.

Friends-and-Neighbors Politics in the Montana Primary

If friends-and-neighbors politics is the politics of space and isolation, of protected enclaves of those who know the candidate close up, then Montana would seem to be a likely setting for such politics. Distances in Mississippi and Vermont pale before the immensity of the land under "the big sky." Communication networks in the first two states must appear close-knit to those who live where blizzards can white out the sun in May or September. On the face of it, it would seem inconceivable that a candidate from the Pacific mountains of western Montana, where the people think "Seattle," would receive the strongest support on the flat plains of the eastern part of the state, where people think "Minneapolis."

Knowing more about friends-and-neighbors politics in Montana helps to unlock some important secrets about politics there. It will tell us if the party system has been able to universalize politics. It will tell us if the passage of time and increased communication facilities have helped break down pockets of localism. It will tell us, indeed, if such pockets ever did exist, under what conditions, and in which party. All of these things provide clues as to the nature of the impact of modernization on the political system of massive rural polities. We noted above, for instance, that the two Republicans with the closest (r = .42) primary electoral ties were Nutter (1960) and Smith (1972). Friends-and-neighbors analysis shows us, however, that those men were neighbors in the extreme northeastern corner of the state. We know that the two Democrats with the strongest correlation coefficients were Renne and Cannon, but geographic analysis shows us that they had home counties that are relatively close, Gallatin and Silver Bow. Although those two counties do not border one another, they share two adjacent counties. Perhaps these associations between candidates represent, not evidence of a weak coalitional structure within the parties, but simply coincidental home turfs where regional loyalties brought the voters together.

Using simple mapping techniques to check out the voting returns for the thirty-seven candidates that have participated in the Republican and Democratic primaries in the quarter century between 1952 and 1976 turns up a mixed bag of results. For instance, the 1972 Republican primary appears to have been heavily influenced by friends-and-neighbors voting. Each of the three major candidates received a significantly larger proportion of the votes in their home counties and counties adjacent to their home counties. In that same year the Democratic primary winner, Tom Judge, found his strongest counties scattered far and wide over the entire state. In only one case (Dick Dzivi) did the runner-up have his strongest counties adjacent to his home county.

To bring more precision to bear on the problem, each candidate's home-county and adjacent-county percentages were averaged and matched against their average percentage in all other counties. Eta-squared coefficients were calculated to measure the strength of the differences between the two sets of counties. Probability coefficients were also produced to test the significance of the gaps. Whenever two or more candidates in the same primary shared home counties, those counties were eliminated from the calculations. Forty-two percent of the Republican candidates in the 1952–1972 period received significantly more votes in their home and adjacent counties. Exactly half of the Democratic candidates produced home county–distant county gaps that were statistically significant at the .01 level.

Importantly, there has been no tendency in either primary for friends-and-neighbors voting to diminish over time as the modernization theory would suggest. In general we can say that friends-and-neighbors voting has taken place in Montana about one-half of the time, that this level has remained constant since 1952, and that the Democrats have had a bit more friends-and-neighbors voting than the Republicans have had. The parties differ on one important dimension, however. The correlation coefficient between the share of the vote a Democratic candidate received in the primary and the friends-and-neighbors score is strongly negative, $-.52$, but the Republican's is positive, .38. What this means is that major candidates in the Republican party rely more heavily on local voting than do leading candidates in the Democratic primary. The stronger friends-and-neighbors tendency in the Democratic primary results from the fact that the minor candidates are locally based and the major candidates are not. Winners and runners-up in the Democratic primary are more likely to be statewide candidates rather than candidates whose major appeal comes from their home counties and other surrounding counties.

This finding suggests an answer to the question posed earlier: Was the linkage between candidates in what was called the conservative center (Nutter and Smith) the result of the geographic proximity of their home counties? Was the same true for what was called the Farmers Union coalition of Cannon and Renne in the Democratic primary? The findings of the friends-and-neighbors analysis indicate that the Republican connection was regionally based since both Nutter and Smith received strong regional support. But precisely the opposite was true for Cannon and Renne. They lived in the same region of Montana, the Broad Valley Rockies, but the correlation between their votes happened because they both received strong support from the same far-distant counties. In fact the candidacies of Renne and Cannon actually produced a negative friends-and-neighbors relationship—they received proportionally fewer votes in home-territory counties.

Summary

On its face party politics in many rural systems has been placid. In states like Mississippi and Vermont, however, powerful currents have existed below the surface. These currents are best identified and monitored by soundings from the primaries, in which conflict is apt to rush and swirl within the majority party while the minority party eddies quietly on the outskirts. In Montana, of course, white water abounds at both levels. The task of associating degrees of conflict in the primary with socioeconomic variables and/or urbanism turned up positive results in the second Democratic primary in Mississippi and the Republican primary in Montana. In the first primary in Mississippi, Vermont's Republican primary, and Montana's Democratic primary, however, it was impossible to snap this catch between society and politics.

One reason may be the traditional hold friends-and-neighbors politics has had on all three rural states. In Vermont that phenomenon, which served to mightily confuse the alleged bifactional pattern, has all but disappeared. In Mississippi it has declined but still exists, and in Montana, perhaps because of the magnified importance of space and distance, it has remained fairly steady over the last three decades.

Attempts to type the nature of factionalism in Vermont and Mississippi and then to gauge its reaction to a strengthening minority party reveal that Mississippi's chaotic multifactionalism has not diminished with the rise of the Republicans and that Vermont's peculiar unifactionalism has remained essentially unchanged in the face of the Democratic challenge — although a wisp of empirical evidence of order emerged in the 1960s in both states. In Montana, factionalism has declined somewhat in recent years in both primaries, and there is evidence that it hurts a party's chances in the general election. Patterns in Montana's primaries have been limited to a weak Farmers Union coalition in the Democratic party and to what I have called a Republican conservative center. In general it seems that the interface between society and politics and the existence of patterns of political behavior at the macro level in modern rural systems are probably less evident than ever before. With some exceptions, modernization seems to have cast rural politics afloat from its docking to friends-and-neighbors voting with no clear anchorage to SES landfalls in sight.

Notes

1. A similar conclusion was reached in Florida; see Margaret Thompson Echols and Austin Ranney, "The Impact of Interparty Competition Reconsidered: The Case of Florida," *Journal of Politics* 38 (February 1976), pp. 142–152. This study has been expanded to include all the states of the South with similar results. See Bradley C. Canon, "Factionalism in the South: A Test of Theory and a Revisitation of V. O. Key," *American Journal of Political Science* 22 (November 1978), pp. 833–848.

2. Douglas W. Rae, *The Political Consequences of Electoral Laws,* rev. ed. (New Haven: Yale University Press, 1971).

3. Raymond Tatalovich, "Friends and Neighbors Voting: Mississippi, 1943–1973," *Journal of Politics* 37 (August 1975), pp. 807–814.

4. E. C. Barksdale, "The Power Structure and Southern Gubernatorial Conservatism," in Harold M. Hollingsworth, ed., *Essays on Recent Southern Politics* (Austin: University of Texas Press, 1970), p. 38.

5. Jack Bass and Walter De Vries, *The Transformation of Southern Politics* (New York: Basic Books, 1976), pp. 196–202.

6. Charles W. Fortenberry and F. Glenn Abney, "Mississippi, Unreconstructed and Unredeemed," in William C. Havard, ed., *The Changing Politics of the South* (Baton Rouge: Louisiana State University Press, 1972), p. 506.

7. Ibid., pp. 506–514.

8. Bass and De Vries, *Transformation of Southern Politics,* pp. 211–214.

9. Barksdale, "The Power Structure," p. 40.

10. Malcolm E. Jewell, *Legislative Representation in the Contemporary South* (Durham, N.C.: Duke University Press, 1967), pp. 56–76.

11. See Duane Lockard, *New England State Politics* (Princeton: Princeton University Press, 1959), pp. 8–45, and Melvin S. Wax, "Vermont's New Dealing Yankee," *Nation* 168 (June 1949), pp. 659–660.

12. Richard Roeder, telephone interview, July 17, 1978.

6
The Legislature: People Who Serve

Conceptual Windows for a Rural Landscape

No one long involved in the business of making sense of mankind's behavior in the aggregate has failed to lament the absence of laboratories for the social sciences. If only we could gauge and adjust the inputs, filter the controls, condition the environment, and precisely measure the outcomes. Without such power, we are cast into the roll of ghost-rider cowboys seeking out those rare and relatively stable pools of clear water, windows through which we can see the processes we long to understand. Caked with uncertainty, we are condemned to chase a devil's herd of events across an empirical sky that never stands completely still.

There are but a limited number of conceptual water holes, and one finds political scientists huddled around them like thirsty hands under an August sun. One of the clearest of these water holes is the legislature. Although legislatures seem to be having less and less to do with the rule-making process as the courts and bureaucracies grow more important, it is in the statutes and their formation that the best record of what society *intends* to have done or not done is found. It is in the process of forming those statutes that the most open and informative public debate concerning that agenda is to be had.

Most importantly, legislatures are where the catch between society and policy is snapped. It is a principal arena of conversion into which interests are funneled on one end and out of which policy emerges on the other. It is true that legislatures have even subdelegated some of their linkage function to bureaucracies, demanding in law that agencies assess public input before acting. Nevertheless, when the people ask what happened and why, their eyes still turn to the legislatures. It remains appropriate that they do. In short, legislatures are like giant magnets drawing to them the phenomena that make up the science of politics.

Mississippi, Vermont, and Montana, like many rural states, have large legislative bodies despite their skimpy populations. This fact makes for much smaller population-to-representative ratios. In Mississippi, there is one senator for approximately every 42,000 citizens of the state. In Vermont and Montana the ratio is 1 to 15,000 and 1 to 14,000, respectively. The national median is 1 to 69,000. In Vermont the House has been recently reduced from 246 members to 150, but there still remains a tiny constituency for each member, approximately 3,000 people. In Montana the ratio is 1 to 7,000, and it is 1 to 18,000 in Mississippi. The national median is 18,000 people per member of the lower legislative chamber.[1]

In most other respects, however, these bodies are structurally indistinguishable from other American state legislatures. Montana is one of only a few states to stick with biennial sessions, Mississippi's legislature has twice as many standing committees as the average legislature, and in Vermont, where there are five representatives for every senator, the two houses rank third in the nation on being numerically out of balance. But these represent exceptions that relate more to regional variations than to any rural bonding. In the South, for instance, many state legislatures are loaded with committees. Small senates and large houses are a phenomenon that exists particularly in New England. New Hampshire, with 400 representatives in the House and only 24 in the Senate, has the most unbalanced legislature in the nation; Massachusetts' is next with a 240/40 split.

The legislatures of these three rural states may also be judged in terms of power. Wayne Francis has developed an index he calls "legislative centralization," which is based on questions asked of legislators in the fifty states. He wants to know where the most important decisions are made—in the governor's office, in the party caucus, in regular committee hearings, or "on the floor." To the extent that legislators indicate that decisions are made on the floor or in regular committees, the legislature itself is ranked as being decentralized. But low rankings on the index may also be interpreted as an indication of perceived power; that is, where decisions are made. On Francis's index, Montana ranked thirty-first, Mississippi, thirty-seventh, and Vermont, forty-fourth, which means that members of those bodies viewed the legislature more as a center of decision-making power than did members of legislatures from other states.[2] On Schlesinger's index of gubernatorial power, Vermont and Mississippi are shown to have weak governers while Montana's governor is stronger than that of the average state. The index ranges from 7 to 20. Montana scores 16, Vermont 13, and Mississippi only 10. Evidently the perception of Montana legislators that the legislature is not so much the center of power as in the other two states was on target, since the governor is quite strong in that state.[3]

The best way to compare the legislatures of Mississippi, Vermont, and Montana is to use a technique specifically designed for the task by the

Citizens Conference on State Legislatures. The CCSL ranking measures each state legislature on five dimensions: (1) functional capacity, (2) accountability, (3) potential to be informed, (4) independence, and (5) representativeness. The legislatures of our model rural states rate very poorly on the CCSL device. Mississippi ranks forty-second, Montana ranks forty-first, and Vermont ranks only thirty-seventh among the fifty states. Mississippi ranks above the mean (twentieth) on only one dimension, independence, which reflects its freedom from the control of the governor. Montana ranks low on representativeness (forty-ninth) and independence (forty-sixth) and is above the mean on none of the five criteria. Vermont is more "functional" and "accountable" than the average state but not very independent (forty-second rank) or representative (forty-seventh rank).[4] There is great danger, both real and semantic, in making too much of these rankings. Why, for instance, does Mississippi rank far above Vermont and Montana on representativeness when there are almost no women, blacks, or Republicans in the Mississippi legislature? Or, can Mississippi's legislature be so much less accountable than Vermont's when roll calls in Mississippi are mandatory on the final passage of all bills and in Vermont they are not? Nevertheless, the scores do represent the single best rational attempt to rate the legislatures we have, and they do reflect the views of people deeply concerned with the legislative process in the American states.

The Reapportionment Bubble

There has occurred in recent history in nearly all state legislatures a structural change so profound in its implications for theories of governance that no treatment of legislative systems can ignore it. The very foundation of the state legislatures was changed by the U.S. Supreme Court in 1962. The states were forced to radically alter their representative base to meet the "one man–one vote" criterion laid down in *Baker v. Carr* (1962) and levied on both houses of the legislatures in *Reynolds v. Sims* (1964).[5] Think of the ramifications of this move for social and, in particular, political science. In the broadest sense, one might ask, What if we engineered the most radical change in a core political institution that that institution has ever undergone and did it swiftly, not through process of pluralistic give-and-take but by a court order? What if we shook up the structure of state political systems as they had never been shaken up before? What if we pulled off the greatest coup for raw egalitarianism in the history of American political institutions? What if we chopped and cut, twisted and reformed, squeezed and expanded the representative base of the state legislatures and nothing happened at all?

In a narrower sense, but of critical importance to the concern of this book, the "reapportionment revolution"[6] puts to the test the most important assumption concerning rural political behavior to appear in this century, that rural legislators were a prime causal factor in the demise of the American urban place. The story is familiar. As the people moved from the rural areas to the cities, the state legislatures failed to reapportion their seats accordingly. That failure resulted in vast discrepancies from the normal one man, one vote in many states. It also meant that the urban places were greatly underrepresented in state governments and the rural areas were substantially overrepresented. The verdict was clear. Rural areas retard the development of social services in the cities because they control the state legislatures. Give urban districts equal representation, and their fair weight in numbers will mean new and progressive urban policies. It seemed logical. How could the cities hope to solve their problems when they were beset at every turn by hostile state legislatures controlled by farmers? Rid the state capitals of their rural majorities, and their replacements from the cities would begin to deal effectively with urban problems. The propostion that malaportionment has hurt the cities and reapportionment would help them was widely accepted.

Jack Kennedy in 1959 said it well in a speech before the American Municipal Congress in Denver: "our state legislatures, still rural-dominated in most states, will neither expand municipal taxing power nor distribute to our cities and suburbs a fair share of the tax dollars collected within their boundaries."[7] Interest groups,[8] urban politicians,[9] established journals of opinion,[10] political scientists,[11] and others joined in overwhelming agreement: Things would be a lot better for the cities when state capitals no longer housed artificial majorities of backwoods lawmakers.[12]

Lost in the shuffle of the reapportionment revolution during the 1950s were several studies that would have caused some nervousness within urban circles had they been noticed. The studies generally indicated that rural lawmakers did not fit the expected behavior pattern.[13] Even as the Court acted (*Baker* v. *Carr,* 1962), items began to appear that seemed to hedge the bet that had been on the table for so long. Noel Perrin,[14] Robert S. Friedman,[15] Daniel P. Moynihan,[16] and Duane Lockard[17] all contributed to a rethinking of the problem. From this point on, the reapportionment thesis carried a burr under its saddle.

In the decade following *Reynolds* v. *Sims* (1964), a new sequence of studies appeared that retested the reapportionment thesis in the major journals of political science. By measuring overall legislative performance in terms of policy outputs in the malapportioned states against policy outputs in the fairly apportioned states, the studies were able to determine if urban-oriented legislation was as likely to be forthcoming from the former as from the latter. The verdict was generally that it was.[18] The article by David Brady and Douglas Edmunds entitled "One Man, One Vote — So What?" echoes the underlying theme of the new research.[19]

By 1970 the reapportionment bubble had truly burst. The bursting was noisy simply because the bubble itself had been huffed and puffed into gigantic proportions. Understand, the fact that the bubble has burst does not mean that the "skeptics"[20] have made a solid case that reapportionment will have no impact. But the point is they never intended to. What they have done is to demonstrate that the charge against rural America — and it was precisely that — was for the most part a bum rap. In short, rural America had been convicted without a trial and with only the skimpiest circumstantial evidence. New findings, which grow more reliable as time passes, are a mixed bag,[21] but they establish beyond much doubt that Ward Elliott is on target.

> The available evidence seems more than sufficient to put the reapportionists' expectations of a great revitalization of state and local government into a more realistic perspective, which should rank reapportionment as a trivial political influence compared to such forces as parties, personalities, interest groups and the perversities of popular fashion.[22]

Keeping an eye on the effect of reapportionment in Mississippi, Vermont, and Montana is made potentially more profitable by three factors. First, a considerable amount of time has passed since *Reynolds* v. *Sims,* and our data base includes several legislative sessions held after reapportionment in each state. Second, scholars have established a hypothesis that is particularly relevant to rural states. That is, in rural, homogeneous states in which agricultural elements have had consistent influence and in which urban places never had even a potential for majority status, the effect of reapportionment will be minimal. Third, rural states have been largely ignored by scholars seeking to apply more-rigorous and precise quantitative techniques to the question of reapportionment. In the pages that follow, the reapportionment thesis will be treated as an exercise to accompany exploration of the very basic question, What kinds of people do ruralities choose to govern them? In Chapter 7 the thesis will be kept aboard as aspects of legislative behavior are considered.

The Policymakers — Mississippi

Half of Mississippi's population is female, 37 percent is black, and probably at least 20 percent is Republican. Yet in the 1975 elections not a single woman, not a single black, and only 2 Republicans were elected to the 52-member Senate. In the House, where 122 individuals are elected every four years, 2 women, 4 blacks, and 3 Republicans were elected in 1975. Although a woman (Evelyn Gandy) has been elected lieutenant governor, and a Republican from Mississippi (Thad Cochran) sits in the U.S. Senate, other indications of the opening of recruitment channels for state legislative personnel in Mississippi are not evident.

Overview of Legislative Types

In the legislature that met between 1976 and 1980, about 17 percent of the members were over fifty-five years old and about 26 percent were under thirty-five. A huge majority in both houses (about nine out of ten) had been born in Mississippi. Lawyers were heavily represented; over one of every three legislators serving in 1979 were attorneys. Farmers and holders of professional occupations other than the law had about 18 percent of the membership, businessmen had 13 percent, and all other occupations had 13 percent. Baptists were by far the strongest religious group, having half again as many members as the next closest denomination, the Methodists. Only 6 percent were Catholics; 13 percent were Presbyterians. Mississippi, like other states, has a high rate of turnover. Thirty-eight percent of the legislators who came to Jackson after the 1975 elections were new to their respective chambers.

On several dimensions the two houses appeared to be very similar. Religious denominations seemed to match up fairly well. Both bodies had less than 8 percent Catholics and both ranked Baptists first, Methodists second, and Presbyterians third. The Senate had less diversity of religious background than did the House. Eighty percent of all senators were either Methodists or Baptists, but only 68 percent of the lawmakers in the House were. Both houses were nearly equal on percentages of those who were over fifty-five years old, lawyers, and professionals. On the other hand, the House had a much larger percentage under the age of thirty-five than did the Senate, fewer businessmen, and more farmers. The House also had more nonnatives[23] (see Table 6.1).

Overall, the legislature was considerably younger than the adult (over twenty-five) population in Mississippi. Thirty-five percent of those over twenty-five years old in Mississippi are also over fifty-five years old, but only 17 percent of the legislature was over fifty-five. Mississippi legislators are more likely to have been born in Mississippi than is the average citizen of the state, especially in the Senate. In 1970 about four-fifths of all Mississippians had been born in Mississippi, and 96 percent of state Senate members were native sons. Lawyers were enormously overrepresented. Lawyers made up about one-half of 1 percent of the

TABLE 6.1

CHARACTERISTICS OF MISSISSIPPI LEGISLATORS
1948-1979 (PERCENT OF TOTAL MEMBERSHIP BY HOUSE)

CHARACTERISTIC	1947*		1951		1955		1959		1963		1967		1971		1975	
	H	S	H	S	H	S	H	S	H	S	H	S	H	S	H	S
Age																
Under 35	30	18	30	27	30	16	35	27	25	27	21	18	31	20	33	12
Over 55	27	39	27	33	27	24	22	22	25	23	24	14	18	18	17	19
Born in Mississippi	91	87	91	88	83	84	83	86	88	90	87	84	93	88	87	96
Occupation																
Farmer	35	38	32	28	43	24	37	21	32	27	26	18	16	24	20	14
Businessman	10	13	13	13	13	22	12	21	19	11	20	14	20	14	8	24
Lawyer	20	30	31	43	28	33	23	42	27	42	30	57	32	41	37	41
Professional	12	15	12	8	9	16	8	6	11	8	7	4	15	6	19	18
Other	23	4	13	9	7	4	19	10	11	12	17	6	17	16	16	4
Religion																
Catholic	2	9	4	4	4	2	3	4	4	0	6	2	9	2	7	4
Methodist	32	30	34	29	35	38	27	39	36	26	33	33	26	37	27	34
Baptist	49	44	44	33	44	38	48	37	43	54	40	43	46	43	41	46
Presbyterian	7	18	11	19	10	13	10	2	9	4	9	8	9	12	15	10
Other	5	10	8	14	6	10	11	17	8	16	12	14	9	6	11	6
Freshmen (No prior experience)	56	57	56	67	55	67	65	67	42	40	41	47	34	49	42	29
House N	141		140		140		140		122		122		122		122	
Senate N	49		49		49		49		52		52		52		52	

YEAR ELECTED

*H = House; S = Senate

SOURCE: Compiled by author from biographical sketches found in Mississippi Official and Statistical Register (Jackson, Mississippi: Secretary of State, 1947-1978).

work force in 1974, but they occupied 38 percent of the chairs at the capital in Jackson. There was also an imbalance in favor of farmers and professionals.[24]

The percentage of Catholics in the Mississippi legislature was close to the percentage of Mississippi's 1,132,375 reported church members who are Catholics.[25] Baptists make up 61 percent of church membership in Mississippi but only about 43 percent of the state legislature. Methodists were overrepresented, but it was the Presbyterians who exceeded their "quota" the most. They claim well under 3 percent of total church membership in Mississippi, yet they had 13 percent of the church membership in the 1976-1980 legislature.

Mississippi is in line with the truism that state legislators generally reflect the population on birthright characteristics and differ on a number of acquired characteristics.[26] Thus we find that Mississippi's legislature exhibits a closer image of Mississippi society on religious background than it does on occupation categories. Findings from other states, although sometimes dated, tend to indicate that the occupations of Mississippi's legislators are similar to their counterparts elsewhere. In Georgia legislative religious categories are nearly identical to those in Mississippi, and the percentages of lawyers, farmers, and professionals in both state legislatures do not differ greatly either. Mississippi legislators are younger and there are fewer freshmen in the Mississippi Senate; otherwise, the two state legislatures are very close.[27]

However, another southern state, Arkansas, is substantially different from Mississippi. For the period 1957-1965, there were over twice as many farmers in the Mississippi legislature and only a third as many businessmen as there were in the Arkansas legislature. The percentages of lawyers were close. Mississippi is closer to Georgia than to Arkansas on this dimension, however, even though Georgia is more urbanized than is Arkansas.[28] Across the river in Louisiana, legislators are substantially older than in Mississippi. The large Catholic population in Louisiana is reflected in its legislature; in 1964-1968 about 45 percent of both houses were Catholic, as compared to only 5 percent in Mississippi. What a difference a river makes.

Mississippi's legislature had more farmers and fewer businessmen and lawyers than Kentucky's,[29] more professionals and fewer farmers than Kansas's,[30] more lawyers and fewer farmers than South Dakota's,[31] and equal percentages of lawyers, fewer professionals, and more farmers than Ohio's.[32]

District-Lawmaker Linkages

Clearly, if populations in the districts vary, then kinds of legislators should vary by district type also. Two kinds of district dissimilarities are of special concern, regional and rural-urban.[33] Mississippi's clearest regional enclave is the Delta. Delta legislators differ from legislators from the Hills region in both houses of the legislature in that they are more likely to be middle-aged, born in Mississippi, and Methodist. In the Senate, Delta members are more likely to be lawyers. In the House they tend more to be farmers or businessmen (see Table 6.2).

Urban legislators are said to be younger, more mobile, and more professional than are rural legislators. This statement seems to be true in Mississippi, especially in the Senate. In 1975 senators representing urban districts were more likely to be under thirty-five and less likely to be over fifty-five. All the senators born outside of Mississippi and all the Catholics in the Senate came from urban districts. Seventy-four percent of the urban senators were either lawyers or professionals, and only 46 percent of the rural legislators were in those categories. For the most part, these occupational differences were the same in the House. The figures in Table 6.2 seem to indicate that rural-urban differences based on district type will predict differences in the types of legislators elected.

Legislative Types over Time

The problem with this kind of analysis is that it is limited to a single session of the legislature and may be governed by circumstances surrounding one particular election or apportionment pattern. Mississippi has undergone substantial developmental changes since World War II.[34] Can the membership of the state legislature be fastened to them? To make sense of the wider picture, 1,279 additional biographical sketches were coded and analyzed for all Mississippi representatives and senators serving from 1947 to 1971 (these figures are included in Table 6.1).

Over the last quarter century, the percentage of legislators under thirty-five years of age in Mississippi has varied considerably, especially in the Senate, but in the 1976-1980 session it was essentially unchanged from what it had been in the 1948-1952 session. But in both houses, the percentage of members over fifty-five has gone steadily down. Occupational groups have also changed dramatically in Mississippi in the last thirty years. In 1947 one-third of all successful House candidates were farmers, and farmers led lawyers in the Senate by 8 percentage points. This was to be the last time farmers outnumbered lawyers in the Mississippi Senate, however, and the 1963 election was the last time farmers would win more seats in the House than lawyers did. The impact of these changes is made clear in Figure 6.1. The increase in the percentage of legislators with professional occupations in both houses adds to the growing professionalism of the legislature. This development seems

TABLE 6.2

CONSTITUENCY TYPES AND
CHARACTERISTICS OF MISSISSIPPI LEGISLATORS 1975-1979*

CHARACTERISTICS	SENATE N=52				HOUSE N=122			
	Legislators From:				Legislators From:			
	Rural Districts N=29	Urban Districts** N=23	Delta Districts N=13	Hills Districts N=39	Rural Districts N=74	Urban Districts N=48	Delta Districts N=31	Hills Districts N=91
Age								
Under 35 years old	3%	22%	0	15%	39%	24%	13%	39%
Over 55 years old	26%	9%	8%	23%	17%	16%	7%	20%
Native Mississippians	100%	91%	100%	95%	86%	88%	93%	85%
Religion								
Catholics	0	9%	0	5%	0	17%	3%	8%
Methodists	36%	32%	45%	31%	31%	24%	34%	26%
Baptists	46%	45%	36%	49%	37%	47%	34%	46%
Presbyterians	7%	14%	9%	10%	17%	14%	14%	16%
Occupation								
Farmers	21%	4%	15%	13%	26%	10%	29%	17%
Businessmen	26%	17%	8%	29%	8%	8%	13%	7%
Lawyers	32%	52%	62%	34%	34%	42%	35%	38%
Professionals	14%	22%	15%	18%	14%	27%	6%	23%
Freshmen	28%	30%	23%	31%	49%	31%	29%	46%

* Percentages do not total 100 because "other" categories were omitted to save space.

**Urban districts are those districts in which 50 percent or more of the population lives in places of over 2,500 population. Rural districts are all others.

SOURCE: Same as for Table 6.1.

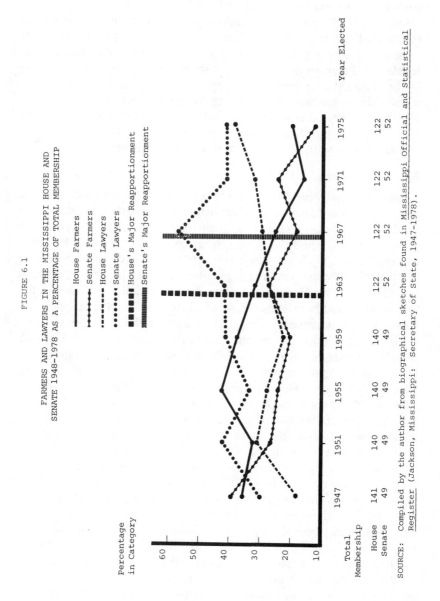

FIGURE 6.1

FARMERS AND LAWYERS IN THE MISSISSIPPI HOUSE AND
SENATE 1948-1978 AS A PERCENTAGE OF TOTAL MEMBERSHIP

House Farmers
Senate Farmers
House Lawyers
Senate Lawyers
House's Major Reapportionment
Senate's Major Reapportionment

Percentage
in Category

60
50
40
30
20
10

1947   1951   1955   1959   1963   1967   1971   1975   Year Elected

Total
Membership

	1947	1951	1955	1959	1963	1967	1971	1975
House	141	140	140	140	122	122	122	122
Senate	49	49	49	49	52	52	52	52

SOURCE: Compiled by the author from biographical sketches found in Mississippi Official and Statistical
Register (Jackson, Mississippi: Secretary of State, 1947-1978).

to move in tandem with Mississippi's urge to promote economic and technological development and with the reemergence of the prewar BAWI (balance agriculture with industry) movement.

On the two "birthright" variables, place of birth and religion, the legislature looks much like it did right after World War II. It still makes sense to be a homegrown Mississippian if one intends to run for the legislature. There are more Baptists in the Senate now and fewer Baptists in the House, but overall, the changes are small, and no trend is apparent. Mississippi has been fashioning younger legislatures in recent years, and one is more and more likely to find lawyers and professionals serving for longer periods of time. But they are basically the same kinds of people — native Mississippians with similar religious backgrounds.

Reapportionment

Reapportioning the Mississippi legislature on a one-man–one-vote basis has been a slow, tooth-pulling affair. As in many other states, the legislature was based on the "federal analogy" — the House was geared to population ratios, and the Senate, to geographic boundaries. By 1960, however, even the House was badly apportioned because of neglect in redrawing district lines to match population shifts. In 1962 Mississippi reapportioned the House to redress these imbalances[35] and left the Senate with land-based representation. Prior to the 1962 reapportionment, districts representing only 29 percent of the state's population elected a majority of the membership in the House; after 1962 it took districts representing 41 percent of the population to elect a majority. In the Senate the figure changed from 35 percent to 37 percent.[36] The 1962 plan was wiped out by the language of *Reynolds* v. *Sims,* and in 1967 a court-ordered plan brought both houses close to equity in terms of population-lawmaker ratios.[37] Subsequently, a series of redistributing plans have come and gone as the system is fine tuned to deal with the problem of race. The largest single gain for the cities in Mississippi came in 1963 in the House and four years later in the Senate.[38]

Probably the most universal effect of reapportionment on American state legislatures concerns the turnover of legislative personnel. Such different kinds of states as Georgia, New York, and Wyoming indicate that reapportionment brought a group of new, inexperienced lawmakers to those state legislatures.[39] In California the "most dramatic effect of reapportionment" was "a record turnover of legislators."[40] Other states such as New Mexico and Nevada have shown a decrease in legislative experience in at least one branch.[41] Thus reapportionment interrupted a general trend downward in the number of freshmen in state legislative assemblies across the United States.[42]

But in Mississippi the percentage of legislators with no prior experience dropped sharply during the reapportionment era. In the House the percentage of freshman legislators remained remarkably constant between 1947 and 1955. In 1959, under the same apportionment system, it rose sharply. Then it plunged drastically in 1963 after the initial reapportionment plan was installed. The percentage of freshmen in the Senate took the same dive in the same year, despite the fact that the reapportionment plan actually *decreased* the power of the large districts in the Senate. The 1967 court-ordered apportionment vastly increased large district representation in the Senate, but there was only a mild flutter upward in the percentage of freshmen. In the House, where the large districts gained still more power, the percentage didn't budge much at all. By cutting out the two sessions of the legislature elected during the reapportionment era and comparing the 1956–1962 sessions with the 1972–1979 sessions, there can be no doubt that the Mississippi legislature has become much less amateurish. The actual connection to reapportionment, however, is much less obvious.

Nor did Mississippi experience an influx of younger legislators as was the case in other states.[43] Although in Georgia the percentage of legislators under thirty-five increased in the House from 13 percent immediately prior to reapportionment to 20 percent immediately after, and the Senate increased its younger category of lawmakers too (from 9 percent to 15 percent),[44] in Mississippi the percentages fell, from 35 percent to 25 percent in the House and from 27 to 18 percent in the Senate.

The evidence of the impact of reapportionment on the occupational backgrounds of legislators is varied. In Wyoming the number of businessmen increased, and the number of farmers decreased.[45] The chances of farmers and ranchers being elected were also hurt in Idaho,[46] but in Washington reapportionment had little impact on the occupations of the legislators.[47] Thomas Dye found that reapportionment did not alter "the predominance of business and professional men in the Georgia legislature," but it did have a "noticeable effect" on the percentage of farmers.[48]

The number of farmers in the Mississippi House began to slide after 1955 and has continued steadily downward without registering even a twinge in response to the several reapportionments that have occurred. Reapportionment may have reversed a negative trend in the number of lawyers in the House, but in 1971, after two reapportionments, the percentage of lawyers in the House was almost the same as it had been two decades earlier in 1951 (see Table 6.1 and Figure 6.1). The percentage of farmers in the Senate was also declining steadily prior to reapportionment, and projections from the trend do not indicate that reapportionment accelerated the process. It does appear that the proportion of lawyers in the Senate did react sharply to reapportionment as it increased from 42 percent to 57 percent between 1963 and 1967. But in 1971 it fell back to the pre-reapportionment level and has remained there. The percentage of professionals increased sharply in the House in 1971, one full session after the most significant reapportionment for that body had taken place in 1963. Exactly the same thing happened later in the Senate. The number of businessmen increased in the House with reapportionment in 1963, but the major increase in the proportion of businessmen in the Senate came almost a decade before reapportionment.

Finally, Dye has found that in Georgia reapportionment made a difference by increasing the number of non-Protestants in the legislature.[49] In Mississippi there seem to be slightly more Catholics in the House since reapportionment, but in the Senate no important change has taken place in that category for thirty years. In short, although changes in the kinds of legislators have occurred coincidentally with the reapportionment era, it is next to impossible to associate them with reapportionment itself.

The Policymakers — Vermont

Vermont's lower chamber is set at 150 members for a 1970 population of under one-half million. Prior to reapportionment, the legislator-citizen ratio in the House was under 1,500 to 1, and the average district had a population of fewer than 800. Each town was a district; each district got one vote in the assembly. Many representatives came from towns with only a couple of dozen families. The smallest district had a population of 38; the largest, about 38,000. The Senate's thirty members have always been elected from the state's fourteen counties on a population basis. Since each county is entitled to at least one senator and since there are fourteen counties and only thirty Senate seats to distribute, the one-man–one-vote principle has often been violated. Both houses elect all their members every two years.

Overview of Legislative Types

In the most recent period (1973–1978), 50 percent or more of the membership of both houses of the legislature was over fifty-five years old. There were very few young legislators in either chamber. In the Senate only one member of the three-session sequence was under thirty-five when elected (see Table 6.3). About 60 percent of both houses were born in Vermont. In terms of their occupations, senators and representatives were not markedly different, although senators were more likely to be businessmen, lawyers, and professionals. In general the House dif-

TABLE 6.3

CHARACTERISTICS OF VERMONT LEGISLATORS,
HOUSE AND SENATE, 1973-1978 (IN PERCENTS)*

CHARACTERISTICS	HOUSE N=450	SENATE N=90
Party		
Democrats	42	31
Republicans	51	69
Independents**	6	0
Age		
Under 35 years old	17	1
Over 55 years old	52	57
Native Vermonters	60	59
Occupation		
Farmers	9	12
Businessmen (including real estate)	23	29
Lawyers	5	12
Housewives, Blue-Collar Workers, and Students	14	6
Professionals	10	17
Retired	25	19
Others	13	6
College Graduates	39	67
Religion		
Catholics	34	40
Jews	2	0
Methodists	10	6
Congregationalists	13	20
Other Protestants	32	19
NA	9	10
Women	14	7
Freshmen	32	21

* Percentages represent averages for the three sessions.
  Legislators were counted each time they served.

**Often classified as Democrat-Republicans or Independent-
Democrats, etc.

SOURCE: Data compiled by the author from The Vermont
Legislative Directory and State Manual
(Montpelier, Vermont: 1973-1977).

fers from the Senate in that it has a less-homogeneous occupation base with a larger percentage of members being in "lower status" occupations. Catholics were the largest religious group in both houses; Congregationalists were second, and Methodists, third. There were relatively more women in the House (14 percent) than in the Senate, and on the average, more newcomers.

The major differences between the legislatures of Mississippi and Vermont are that the Mississippi legislature is very much younger and has a much smaller variety of legislator types. The former is probably true, at least in part, because of the large number of lawyers in the Mississippi legislature. It has been demonstrated that lawyers enter state legislatures at a very early age, for reasons of professional visibility.[50] The diversity of Vermont's legislators is evidenced by the fact that the three largest occupational groups in the House and Senate compose only about half the membership. In Mississippi, the top three occupational groups make up about three-quarters of the membership. Moreover, in Vermont there are two parties, two sexes, and a host of nonnatives to lump the mixture. The only characteristic in the Mississippi data that suggests more variety in the legislative elite is the higher rate of turnover. Even that factor is muted, however, by the fact that Mississippi's lawmakers are elected once every four years and Vermont's are elected every other year.

Perhaps the most important distinguishing characteristic of the Vermont legislature is the tiny number of lawyers elected. Only about 5 percent of the members are attorneys. In Mississippi well over one-third of the legislators are lawyers. There are other rural northern states, such as South Dakota[51] and Wyoming,[52] in which lawyer legislators are hard to find. Vermont also has fewer lawyers than such a diverse group of states as Wisconsin, Indiana, and Kansas.[53]

The percentage of women legislators in Vermont is high compared to the average American state but more or less in line with the state's ruralism and its New England regional location.[54] There is evidence however that Vermont's legislators are considerably older than are legislators of other rural states. Although educational levels in the Vermont Senate are close to those of the average state, in the House they are considerably lower. Only about 40 percent of the representatives in the 1973–1977 sessions had college degrees. This may be caused in part by the fact that Vermont has so few lawyers in the legislature.

Vermont legislators are considerably older than the population at large. Thirty-three percent of all Vermonters twenty-one years old or older are over fifty-five, but 52 percent of the House and 57 percent of the Senate are over fifty-five. Farmers and lawyers are overrepresented in the legislature but not by as much as in Mississippi. The percentage of professionals in the House just about matches the percentage statewide (11 percent) but exceeds the 11-percent quota in the Senate by 6 percentage points. Catholics are overrepresented in the Senate by 7 percentage points but fall close to their mark (33 percent statewide) in the House. Congregationalists (the United Church of Christ) exceeded societal ratios in both houses. Less than 7 percent of the Vermonters are estimated to adhere to the Congregationalist denomination, but 13 percent of Vermont's state representatives and 20 percent of the senators list themselves as Congregationalists. College graduates are overrepresented in both houses, and women are underrepresented. Those representations fit expectations generated by the situation in other states. What defies expectations is that Vermonters elect more nonnatives than is warranted on the basis of their ratio in the population.

Party and Size of Place

Three major variations exist between members of the two parties in the Vermont legislature. Democratic legislators are clearly based in the larger towns and cities; twice as many Democrats as Republicans represent districts in which a majority of the population lives in places of 10,000 or more (see Table 6.4). Second, 65 percent of the Democrats serving in the Vermont legislature between 1973 and 1978 were Catholics; only 13 percent of the Republicans were. Finally, although 61 percent of the Republicans were over fifty-five years old, only 43 percent of the Democrats were. There are other differences of lesser magnitude. Democrats were more likely to be women and nonnatives and less likely to be farmers, or to have attended college (see Table 6.4). These findings are in tune with the traditional view of the two-party split in America: Democrats are more likely to be urban, Catholic, and younger; represent minorities (in this case, women); and have less education and less-prestigious occupations. In the 1977 session of the legislature, for instance, two-thirds of the housewives, students, and blue-collar workers in the Vermont House of Representatives were Democrats.

The task of discovering whether or not legislators' backgrounds are tied to rural-urban differences in Vermont is complicated by the strong Democrat-urban correlation. The question is not only, Are there rural-urban differences? but also Do they hold up when party is controlled? From Table 6.4 we find that legislators from the larger communities are more likely to be nonnatives, women, and Catholic and less likely, of course, to be farmers. There is some very slight tendency for the percentage of legislators with no college education to increase as the districts get more rural. When controls are applied, the rural-urban effect on the election of Catholic legislators survives. Seventy-three percent of all urban

TABLE 6.4

BIOGRAPHICAL CHARACTERISTICS OF VERMONT LEGISLATORS
HOUSE OF REPRESENTATIVES (1973-1978),* BY POLITICAL PARTY AND DISTRICT TYPE

Characteristics	Party**		District Type***		
	Dem. N=191	Rep. N=231	Urban N=155	Large Town N=148	Rural N=147
From Urban Districts	50%	23%	--	--	--
Native Vermonters	55%	62%	50%	63%	65%
Freshmen	34%	31%	30%	34%	32%
Over 55 Years Old	43%	61%	52%	57%	47%
Women	18%	11%	19%	12%	10%
Catholics	65%	13%	52%	30%	20%
Farmers	6%	13%	3%	6%	19%
No College Education	45%	39%	39%	41%	43%

*   Legislators were counted each time they served. Thus the total cases =
    450 (150 members x 3 sessions).

** Independents and members listing themselves as belonging to both parties
    were not considered.

***Urban = majority of the population of the district lives in towns or cities
        of over 10,000 population.
    Large Town = majority of the population of the district lives in towns or
            cities of from 2,500 to 10,000 population.
    Rural = majority of the population of the district lives in towns of less
            than 2,500 population.

SOURCE: Same as for Table 6.3.

Democrats are Catholics. Similarly, there are relatively more Catholics
within the urban Republican group than in the rural Republican group.
What the urban variable does is reinforce a strong Catholic-Democrat
linkage in Vermont. On the other hand, the tendency for Democrats to
be nonnatives is a function of the fact that they are more likely to be urban, and urban representatives are more likely to be nonnatives irrespective of party. Republicans from urban areas are nearly as likely to be
originally from out of state as are urban Democrats.

Rural districts elect fewer female representatives. This is not because
there are more Republicans from rural districts and Republican
legislators are less likely to be women; the fact is that there are no party-

related sex differences outside the urban places. But in the urban places, party seems to matter since 28 percent of the urban Democrats are women and only 9 percent of the urban Republicans are women. Finally, the Republican relationship to the election of farmers is a real one, but it is severely weakened outside rural areas where Democrats are as likely to elect farmers as are Republicans, although neither party elects many from the larger communities.

Changes over Time

Vermont legislators have changed substantially. In the 1947–1949 sessions, 77 percent of the House members and 70 percent of the senators were born in the state; thirty years later in the 1973–1978 sessions about 60 percent had been born in Vermont (see Table 6.5). Farmers have decreased from 43 percent to 9 percent in the House and from 28 percent to 12 percent in the Senate. College graduates are up from 23 percent and 48 percent to 39 percent and 67 percent. Catholics now compose 34 percent of the House membership and 40 percent of the Senate; three decades ago they composed 12 percent and 10 percent, respectively. The percentage of freshmen has fallen in both chambers during the period studied. The number of Democrats, of course, has increased dramatically; that of lawyers has not. Surprisingly, women held almost exactly the same percentage of seats in the 1973–1978 period as they did in the 1947–1949 period. Age levels were about the same as well.

Reapportionment came in 1965, dropping like a cyclone on the House but leaving the Senate relatively untouched. In the lower chamber 96 seats were scratched as the membership was reduced from 246 to 150. The percentage of seats held by Vermont's five largest towns and cities (with 23 percent of the population) increased from 2 percent to about 22 percent. The Northeast Kingdom, etched by village and wilderness, had controlled 21 percent of the seats with only 13 percent of the population; its percentage of seats fell to 13. Although reapportionment came like an August thunderclap, the Democrats came like a New England springtime — very slowly. Is it possible to discern to which call, reapportionment or party change, the Vermont House responded?

There are two items that were probably unaffected by either party or reapportionment. The percentage of lawyers has remained constant over time and didn't flinch at either reapportionment or Democratic increases. The percentage of college graduates has changed substantially, but did so prior to the coming of the Democrats or reapportionment. A third category, the percentage of freshmen, is logically tied to the increases in the number of Democrats, who by definition were newcomers for the most part. It is also linked to reapportionment by evidence from other

TABLE 6.5

CHARACTERISTICS OF VERMONT
LEGISLATORS, HOUSE AND SENATE, 1947-1978*

CHARACTERISTICS	YEAR ELECTED											
	1946-1948		1950-1954		1956-1958		1960-1964		1966-1970		1972-1976	
	H**	S	H	S	H	S	H	S	H	S	H	S
Over 60 years old	41	35	47	50	51	45	58	49	49	50	37	47
Native Vermonters	77	70	72	68	72	75	75	59	65	63	60	59
Occupation												
Farmers	43	28	40	34	35	20	29	13	15	18	9	12
Lawyers	4	7	5	10	6	17	4	14	6	8	5	12
College Graduates	23	48	38	48	38	68	38	76	41	66	39	67
Religion												
Catholics	12	10	8	18	16	33	20	29	31	38	34	40
Congregationalists	27	45	26	40	25	39	24	33	22	27	13	20
Women	12	7	17	7	19	10	19	10	12	9	14	7
Freshmen	54	37	48	38	43	48	33	36	25	19	32	21
Democrats	13	14	9	12	16	23	22	32	33	26	42	31
House N	492		738		492		738		450		450	
Senate N		60		90		60		90		90		90

* Percentage of total membership in each two-year session averaged for each period.

**H = House   S = Senate

SOURCE: Same as for Table 6.3.

states that experienced an influx of freshmen after reapportionment. Yet percentages of freshmen were decreasing steadily prior to 1965, and that curve slipped through the restructuring process unscathed. And if the party variable was at work, why is it that the percentage of freshmen decreased as Democrats increased until the 1973–1978 period?

There are also several categories on which it is fair to speculate that reapportionment had a direct impact. The percentage of legislators over sixty years old had steadily increased between 1947 and 1965. After reapportionment, that trend was sharply reversed. The percentage of native-born Vermonters also took a dive after reapportionment. In both cases, the downward curve has continued. The ratio of women to men, which fell sharply after reapportionment, reversed that slide in the 1973–1978 years. Perhaps in that case reapportionment was the villain and the rescuer was the Democratic party.

Reapportionment seems to have affected three other factors in a catalytic manner by increasing the speed of a reaction already under way. Between 1947 and 1965, for instance, fewer and fewer farmers were being elected to Vermont's 246-member legislature, probably a result of the disappearance of family farms. Reapportionment, however, accelerated the process. Percentages of Democrats and Catholics were also on the rise well before reapportionment, moving upward in perfect tandem between 1951 and 1965. But reapportionment gave them an additional boost. Catholics benefited from reapportionment because the Democrats did, and they benefited to about the same degree. Indeed, Figure 6.2 demonstrates a classic case of a minority group's use of a political party as a conduit to political influence. The growing gap between the Catholic percentage and the Democratic percentage, especially evident in the 1973–1978 period, marks both the peak of the Catholic ratio — that is, the legislative ratio began to equal the societal ratio — and the growing maturity of the Democratic party. Democratic gains in legislative seats in the recent decade, like their gains in statewide election returns, are beginning to come from outside their areas of core strength.

Prior to 1965 the Senate reflected the one-man–one-vote principle much better than the House did. The Senate serves, therefore, as a kind of control. If the same kind of changes occurred to the same degree in the Senate as in the House, that fact will dampen any inclination to credit changes in the House solely to reapportionment.

Overall the Senate did change about as much as the House. Moreover, in eight of the nine categories of biographical data, the two bodies changed in the same direction. The critical difference between the House and the Senate is that the major alterations in the Senate took place before reapportionment. In six of the eight categories that shifted substan-

212

FIGURE 6.2

PERCENTAGES OF DEMOCRATS, CATHOLICS,
AND FARMERS IN THE VERMONT LEGISLATURE 1947-1977

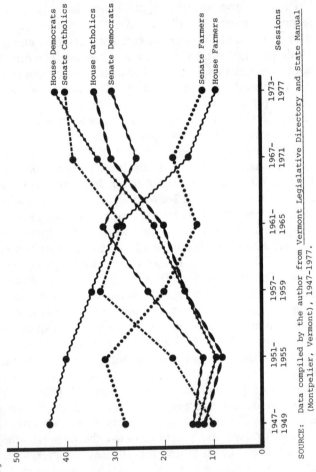

SOURCE: Data compiled by the author from Vermont Legislative Directory and State Manual
(Montpelier, Vermont), 1947-1977.

tially in the House, the greatest percentage-point fluctuations came immediately after reapportionment. In the Senate only seven categories changed substantially between 1947 and 1978, and in six of them the change happened prior to reapportionment in the mid-1950s and early 1960s. The impact of reapportionment itself was negligible, and the small changes that did take place were not expected; farmers, native-born Vermonters, and Republicans gained a few seats.

Since the Democratic increases came in the Senate precisely at the same time that personnel types changed, one must conclude that it was the party in both houses that was the crucial ingredient. In other words, changes in the Senate occurred in the presence of party gains and in the absence of reapportionment, which reinforces the conclusion that reapportionment accelerated processes already under way in Vermont. The Senate responded to the changing nature of Vermont society a decade prior to the House, where the response was muffled by malapportionment. When that obstacle was removed in the mid-1960s, the chemistry bubbled more furiously. The key to understanding the reapportionment revolution in Vermont, however, is the fact that the bubbling had been going on before reapportionment and it has continued afterward. The chemical causing this reaction must be party, not the removal of rural legislators from Montpelier.

The Policymakers – Montana

With its 100 representatives and 50 Senators, the Montana legislature looks much more like Mississippi's than Vermont's. Since 1974 legislators have been elected from single-member districts. Lower-house occupants serve two-year terms, and members of the upper body serve staggered four-year terms; one-half of the Senate faces election every two years. Montana, like Vermont and Mississippi, struggled through the reapportionment revolution in the 1960s. The House was geared to population ratios from the beginning, but each of the fifty-six counties had at least one representative. This arrangement, plus the failure to reapportion on a decennial basis, meant that by 1960 the House was badly malapportioned. The Senate, with its "one county–one vote" system was of course profoundly and intentionally skewed.

Like so many things political in Montana, the legislature is set apart from other legislatures in America by the perversity of space. Senator Carroll Graham, elected to the Montana legislature in 1960 and still serving in 1979, is a rancher and a Democrat. He lives in Lodge Grass on the Little Bighorn River in Bighorn County. He represents 13,740 people. His constituents are scattered over more than 10,000 square miles of territory, an area larger than nine of the American states and bigger than Massachusetts and Rhode Island combined. At last count, 2,733 of the people of his district lived in Hardin, the largest city. When he is in Helena representing them, some of Graham's constituents are over 320 miles away as the eagle flies and much further by road. Directly to the north, a colleague represents a district of 16,435 square miles with a population density of .8 per square mile. His district is bigger than the three southern New England states of Massachusetts, Connecticut, and Rhode Island combined, plus Delaware: this is the price one pays for one man, one vote. It is not unimportant to remember that under the fragile sod of these two huge state senatorial districts there are massive deposits of subbituminous and lignite coal.

Overview of Legislative Types

The kinds of people Montanans choose to occupy the House and Senate chambers are quite similar on a number of items. Percentages of native-born legislators and college attenders are very close as are the percentages of businessmen, lawyers, and professionals. The party balance in the Senate was closer for the period 1975–1979 than it was for the House, and there were more women and freshmen in the House than in the Senate. The greatest difference between the two were in the age and occupation categories. There were more young (under thirty-five) and fewer old (over fifty-five) representatives than senators. Farmers and ranchers were more heavily represented in the Senate than in the House, and the House had a larger proportion of occupations that did not fit the major categories (see Table 6.6).

Similarities exist between the legislators of Montana and Mississippi, and of Montana and Vermont. Percentages of freshmen and professionals in Montana and Mississippi match fairly well, and Montana's legislators are almost identical to Vermont's with respect to place of birth and percentages of women legislators. Montana, like Vermont, has a scarcity of lawyers in the legislature. Montanan lawmakers are substantially older than Mississippi's on the whole and considerably younger than Vermont's. The other dimension on which Montana stands apart from the other two states is the extent to which the agricultural component of the economy has held on to legislative seats. In Vermont less than 10 percent of the total seats are held by farmers; in Mississippi the figure was about 18 percent for the 1975–1979 sessions. For the same period in Montana, however, 32 percent of the membership of the House and Senate claim they are farmers or ranchers or some combination of both. The percentage of farmers and ranchers in another western state legislature, Colorado, is less than half that of Montana's.[55] Neighboring

TABLE 6.6

BIOGRAPHICAL CHARACTERISTICS OF MONTANA
STATE LEGISLATORS 1975-1979 BY POLITICAL PARTY*

CHARACTERISTICS	SENATE			HOUSE		
	Dem.	Rep.	Total	Dem.	Rep.	Total
	N=79	N=71	N=150	N=179	N=121	N=300
From Urban Districts	52%	31%	42%	51%	32%	43%
Region						
High Line (Crop land)	24%	39%	31%	28%	39%	32%
Grazeland	33%	41%	37%	33%	38%	35%
West	43%	20%	32%	39%	23%	33%
Native Montanans	63%	52%	58%	61%	56%	59%
Freshmen	39%	28%	34%	41%	39%	40%
Over 55 Years Old	40%	44%	42%	28%	44%	34%
Women	8%	1%	5%	14%	8%	12%
Occupation						
Farmers and Ranchers**	36%	45%	40%	17%	45%	29%
Businessmen (including real estate)	12%	30%	21%	17%	21%	18%
Lawyers	12%	7%	10%	8%	2%	5%
Professionals	21%	13%	17%	26%	11%	20%
Others	18%	6%	12%	32%	21%	27%
No College Education	22%	19%	21%	26%	19%	23%

* Legislators were counted each time they served. Thus for the House,
  total cases = 300 (100 members x 3 sessions). For the Senate,
  total cases = 150 (50 members x 3 sessions).

**Also includes a small number of farm or ranch plus a small business.

SOURCE: Data compiled by the author from Lawmakers of Montana (Anaconda,
         Montana: Office of Governmental Affairs, The Anaconda Company,
         1975-1979).

Idaho, on the other hand, has almost exactly the same ratio of famers and ranchers to total membership in its lower legislative body as is found in Montana's.[56]

In 1970 32 percent of the population over twenty-five in Montana was less than thirty-five years old, but only 19 percent of the House and 13 percent of the Senate were in that cohort. In both houses, but especially in the Senate, the percentage of the membership over fifty-five years old exceeded the percentage of those over twenty-five who were also over fifty-five in the population. The percentage of farmers and ranchers in the legislature was far above the percentage in the state. Lawyers were vastly overrepresented. Educational levels were also much higher in the legislature than in the adult population. Native-born legislators, over-represented in Mississippi and underrepresented in Vermont, were right on the nose in Montana. The 1970 census shows that 59 percent of Montana's citizens were born there, and in the legislature 59 percent of the House seats and 58 percent of the Senate seats were occupied by native-born Montanans in the 1975–1979 period.

Party, Size of Place, and Region

In Montana the Democratic party is boisterous, mature, and successful, and in Vermont it is tentative, young, and victories still taste fresh. Yet the differences in legislative types based on party affiliation are remarkably similar between the two states. Like Vermont, Montanan Democrats in the House of Representatives are significantly younger than are the Republicans. As in Vermont, the Democrats are more likely to be women and less likely to be farmers. The Democrats in both states tend to represent the populous districts in the legislature, and a greater percentage have professional occupations even though they are less likely to have attended college. The only difference is that in Montana there is a weak tendency for more Democratic legislators to have been born in Montana, but in Vermont the reverse is true.

There also seems to be a tie between region and party. Thirty-nine percent of the House Democrats in Montana represented districts in the west in 1975–1979, but only 23 percent of the Republicans did so. Only 28 percent of the House Democrats came from their old fortress, the high line region, but House Republicans counted 39 percent of their members from that area. Relationships between party and legislator type are remarkably similar in both houses of the Montana legislature.

The tie between party and legislator in Montana is complicated, as it was in Vermont, by the size-of-place variable. Rural legislators in 1975–1979 were found to be twice as likely as urban legislators to be over fifty-five years old, half as likely to be women, and three times as likely to not have attended college (see Table 6.7). The percentage of urban legislators who had professional occupations was triple that of rural legislators. Farmers were almost exclusively rural, and lawyers, urban. There was a slight tendency for more urban legislators than rural legislators to be nonnatives, and a still slighter tendency for urban lawmakers to be businessmen. Seventy percent of the urban legislators and only 48 percent of the rural legislators were Democrats.

Since there is an urban-Democrat linkage and since both urban and

TABLE 6.7

BIOGRAPHICAL CHARACTERISTICS OF MONTANA STATE LEGISLATORS
HOUSE OF REPRESENTATIVES (1975-1979) BY DISTRICT TYPE AND REGION

CHARACTERISTICS	DISTRICT TYPE*		REGION		
	Urban	Rural	High Line	Grazeland	West
Democrats	70%	48%	51%	55%	71%
From Urban Districts	--	--	36%	48%	46%
Region					
High Line	27%	36%	--	--	--
Grazeland	38%	32%	--	--	--.
West	35%	31%	--	--	--
Native Montanans	55%	62%	68%	45%	65%
Freshmen	47%	35%	41%	35%	44%
Over 55 Years Old	21%	45%	37%	36%	31%
Women	16%	8%	10%	15%	9%
Occupation					
Farmers and Ranchers	4%	47%	46%	27%	13%
Businessmen	21%	16%	21%	20%	8%
Lawyers	9%	2%	1%	7%	14%
Professionals	35%	9%	10%	23%	26%
Others	30%	25%	22%	22%	39%
No College Education	9%	34%	27%	19%	24%

*Urban = a majority of the district's population living in a city of 20,000
     population or more.

Rural = all other districts.

SOURCE: Same as for Table 6.6.

Democratic legislators as groups are more likely to be young, women,
and professionals, it is necessary to untangle those associations. In four
of the five cases in which there is multicolinearity among party, district
type, and dependent variables such as age, education, etc., the party
association is very weak or nonexistent among rural legislators. For instance, it is clear that the Democratic legislators are younger than the
Republican legislators in either context, urban or rural. But because a
larger percentage of Democrats than Republicans are urban-based, the
differences between the parties are magnified. In fact a smaller proportion of urban Republicans are over fifty-five (32 percent) than are rural
Democrats (40 percent). Among rural legislators the tendency for the
Democrats to count themselves as being in professional occupations

and the Republicans not to is practically wiped out. Forty-two percent of all urban legislators who are also Democrats are professionals, but only 19 percent of urban Republicans are. Once again it is instructive to point out that urban Republicans are more likely to be professionals than are rural Democrats. Democrats are no more likely to be women than are Republicans if both are from rural districts. Almost one out of every five urban Democrats, however, is a woman, as compared to about one out of ten for the Republicans.

A variant of this tendency for parties to distinguish legislators within the urban context is evident in the place-of-birth category. In rural areas there is very little difference between the parties on place of birth, but among urban legislators, the Republicans are much more likely to be nonnatives than are the Democrats. Another case demonstrates the party differences that exist exclusively within the rural delegation. Urban representatives have more formal education, irrespective of party. The reason the Republican legislators seem to be somewhat better educated overall is that the rural members of the party serving in the House of Representatives in Helena are better educated than their Democratic counterparts are. District type again specifies under what conditions the party variable is important, but in the case of education it is the rural districts that house the party differences.

Finally there is the question of farmers and ranchers. Is it the case that Democratic legislators are less likely to be in those agricultural occupations because they are more likely to come from urban districts where farmer or rancher representatives are scarce? Are the Democrats from rural areas as likely to be farmers or ranchers as are the Republicans from rural areas? The data show that about one-third of the rural Democrats and about two-thirds of the rural Republicans are farmers or ranchers. Although it is true that if all Democrats and all Republicans were rural, the gap between the proportions of farmers in the two parties would be relatively smaller, it is also true that the Republicans from rural areas are much more likely to be farmers than are the Democrats. Party makes an important difference.

If regions spawn political cultures that in turn produce political behavior and events, then one might expect that we would find, as we did to some extent for Mississippi, that legislators can be identified by the regions from which they come. In Montana high line legislators are more likely to be farmers or ranchers and less likely to be professionals or lawyers. Graze-land legislators tend to have more formal education and to have been born outside the state. The western delegation is heavily Democratic (71 percent) and has most of the lawyers. In general, as Waldron would predict, the western group displays a more diversified occupational background. Breaking down dependent variables by region, party, and district type to determine if the variations are solid or melt away under controls is hazardous, since the "Ns" in particular cells of any given table become very small. A thumbnail look at the two most prominent relationships, the tendency of the high line region to send farmers and the tendency of the graze-land region to send nonnatives, indicates that both relationships hold up fairly well under controls. Graze-land representatives, for instance, are more likely to be nonnatives, irrespective of party or district type. The high line region is more heavily rural than are the other regions; we also know that overall, farmers and ranchers tend to be Republicans. Although the size-of-place indicator holds under controls for region as one might guess, the party variable does not. The high line region sends farmers and ranchers to the statehouse, party label notwithstanding.

Changes over Time

Making a judgment about the effect of radical structural changes such as reapportionment on the kinds of people serving in rural legislative systems is made difficult in Montana by a lack of biographical data for legislators elected before 1971. Sex and occupation are the only categories of personal information that can be traced over time. Both of those are important dimensions, however, and will allow at least a peek at the impact of the reapportionment revolution. In 1960 voters representing approximately 37 percent of the population could elect a majority in the House of Representatives, and voters representing only 16 percent of the population could elect a majority in the Senate.[57] After reapportionment this situation improved to 47 percent in the Senate and 48 percent in the House.[58] Thus any tremors caused by redistricting should register most strongly in the Senate.

It is a surprise, given the billing reapportionment received, how completely unaffected the partisan balance in the Senate was when the one-man–one-vote principle was implemented. The percentage of Democrats slipped from 57 percent in 1965 to 55 percent in 1967 (see Figure 6.3). The only possible argument that could be made for the reapportionment thesis is that a steeper downward slide by the Democrats was somewhat arrested. But even that limited effect is clouded by the fact that the "downward trend" was in reality a drop from an all-time Democratic peak in 1959 and 1961. Any assessment of the effect of reapportionment on partisanship in the House is complicated by the eruption in the number of Democratic seats that occurred in the 1964 election.[59] Percentages fell for the Democrats following reapportionment in 1967, but only to levels clearly in line with projections made on the basis of the sessions

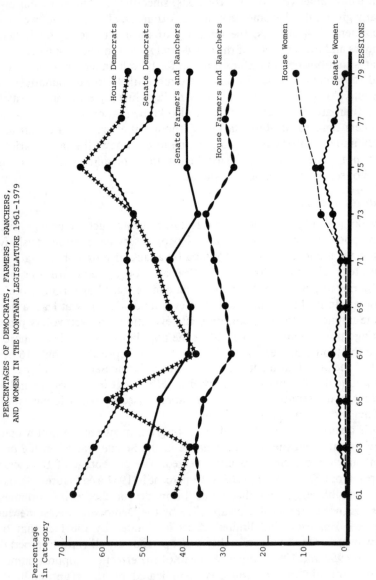

FIGURE 6.3

PERCENTAGES OF DEMOCRATS, FARMERS, RANCHERS, AND WOMEN IN THE MONTANA LEGISLATURE 1961-1979

SOURCE: Data compiled by the author from *Lawmakers of Montana* (Anaconda, Montana: Office of Governmental Affairs, Anaconda Company, 1975-1979).

of 1961 and 1963. Figure 6.3 demonstrates with profound emphasis the independence of political events from structural arrangements.[60]

The percentage of farmers and ranchers sank in both the House and the Senate after reapportionment. This result was unexpected for the Senate underwent a much greater reduction in rural representation; it behaved much like Vermont's House in that reapportionment seems to have accelerated a trend already in progress. Since 1967 the percentage of farmers and ranchers has remained fairly steady in both houses. Finally, the percentage of women in the legislature did not change as a result of the reapportionment process.

In 1972 the voters of Montana approved a new state constitution that brought many reforms to the legislature, including open committee hearings, annual sessions (since repealed), and single-member districts. The constitutional convention that spawned the changes was a critical event in the history of the state. The noted historian of Montana, K. Ross Toole, claims that "the first session of the new legislature, 1973, bore about as much resemblance to previous sessions as Congress bears to the Politburo."[61] Most people view the constitutional convention as both the symbol of a new progressivism in Montana and the seedbed for a highly eclectic reform movement that swept over the face of the state in the first half of the 1970s like a chinook.[62] One full session (1973-1974) of the "new" legislature (the first and only session to meet annually) met prior to the formation of single-member districts. It is, therefore, possible to measure both the effect of the statewide mood on the types of people elected to the legislature in 1973 and the effect of structure plus mood in 1975 when single-member districts were introduced.[63]

The 1972 legislative elections caused little change in the partisan-balance trend. The increase in the number of Democrats in the House in 1969 and 1971 continued, and ratios of Republicans to Democrats in the Senate barely flickered. The number of farmers and ranchers in the Senate fell to pre-1971 levels, but given past patterns, it would be hard to attribute anything new to that occurrence. In the House a slow rise in the percentage of legislators with agricultural occupations remained steady. The number of women in the House, however, leaped to an all-time high in 1973. It seems clear that in that case the "mood" effect was operating, and there seem to be direct linkages between feminine involvement in politics in Montana and the constitutional convention.

In the Senate the coming of single-member districts correlated with an upward Democratic blip on the screen, which faded immediately. In the House the Democratic climb was accelerated in the 1974 elections to produce a Democratic majority of 67 percent, a high that had not been equaled since the election of 1936. In two subsequent elections (1976 and

1978), that percentage dipped to a more natural level. The impact of single-member districts on the elections of farmers and ranchers was negligible in the Senate but more important in the House. In fact the percentage of farmers and ranchers in the House, which by 1973 had climbed steadily from its postreapportionment low of 29 percent in 1967 back up to its pre-reapportionment level of 36 percent in 1965, fell sharply and precisely in 1975 back to its postreapportionment low of 1967. Single-member districts may have opened wider the doors of the Senate to women, but after 1975 the doors swung shut again. In the House changes in the sex balance favoring women continued throughout the 1970s, single-member districts notwithstanding. Distilled, the massive structural changes laid on the political system of this giant rural state seem to steam off in the analysis of legislative types. With the limited data we have (occupation, sex, and party), the only truly new phenomenon is the arrival of significant numbers of women in the House of Representatives. They were carried not by reapportionment nor on the shoulders of single-member districting; the winds of political change whispered the times were right.

Summary

Biographical profiles of the membership of legislatures in the rural states reveal much about the tone of rural politics. The profiles also speak to the imprint that partisan, rural-urban, and regional variables may leave on rural political systems. Finally, the profiles document the effect of one massive structural change, reapportionment. In Mississippi we find a younger legislature filled with professional types (mostly from the urban places) and lawyers. Both regional and spatial influences were at work in the selection process. The Mississippi legislature has changed substantially over time on achieved characteristics of its members, but it has remained essentially the same on birthright characteristics.

In Vermont the legislators are much older, much more likely to have been born out of state, and much less likely to be lawyers. There the party variable is important in the recruitment process, and the spatial variable operates as a qualifier and specifier of that basic relationship. Montana's legislators are younger than Vermont's, older than Mississippi's. The party variable is most important within the urban delegation and weakens among the legislators from rural areas. In all three states the number of legislators with agricultural occupations has dropped steadily throughout the post–World War II period. But in Montana those legislators remain relatively strong, holding about twice as large a percentage of seats as in either Mississippi or Vermont.

The importance of reapportionment has been, at best, very spotty indeed. In Mississippi it is impossible to link changes in legislative personnel to reapportionment as such. In Vermont partisan breakthrough was critical, and reapportionment played an essentially catalytic role. In Montana the reapportionment revolution in no measurable way interrupted the forces that have shaped the nature of that state's legislative cadre over the past thirty years. In a nutshell, when one charts the various categories of biographical data for these three states over time and then steps back to locate reapportionment visually, it is impossible to do so. When changes are found that coincide with reapportionment, other variables usually prove more meaningful. On the dimension of legislative personnel at least, reapportionment seems to have been, as Elliott says, a "trivial political influence."[64]

Notes

1. Council of State Governments, *The Book of the States* (Lexington, Ky.: Council of State Governments, 1978), pp. 13–14.
2. Wayne L. Francis, *Legislative Issues in the 50 States* (Chicago: Rand McNally, 1967), pp. 74–75.
3. Joseph A. Schlesinger, "The Politics of the Executive," in Herbert Jacob and Kenneth W. Vines, eds., *Politics in the American States,* 2d ed. (Boston: Little, Brown and Company, 1971), pp. 210–237.
4. Citizens Conference on State Legislatures, *Report on an Evaluation of the 50 State Legislatures* (Kansas City, Mo., 1971).
5. Baker v. Carr, 369, U.S. 186 (1962); Reynolds v. Sims, 377, U.S. 533 (1964).
6. Gordon E. Baker, *The Reapportionment Revolution* (New York: Random House, 1965).
7. Quoted in Daniel R. Grant and H. C. Nixon, *State and Local Government,* 2d ed. (Boston: Allyn and Bacon, 1968), pp. 285.
8. Gordon E. Baker, *Rural vs. Urban Political Power* (Garden City, N.Y.: Doubleday, 1955), p. 27; *Newsweek* 59 (April 9, 1962), pp. 29–30.
9. Baker, *Rural vs. Urban Political Power,* p. 281; Howard D. Hamilton, ed., *Reapportioning Legislatures* (Columbus, Ohio: Charles E. Merrill Books, 1966), p. 142.
10. Helen Hill Miller, "The City Vote and the Rural Monopoly," *Atlantic Monthly* 210 (October 1962), pp. 61–65. See the bibliographical essay at the end of this volume for additional sources.
11. Baker, *Rural vs. Urban Political Power*; Malcolm E. Jewell, *The Politics of Reapportionment* (New York: Atherton Press, 1962); William J. Keefe and Morris S. Ogul, *The American Legislative Process,* 2d ed. (Englewood Cliffs, N.J.: Prentice Hall, 1968), p. 95; Byron H. Marlow, "What Do Political Scientists Say?" in Hamilton, *Reapportioning Legislatures,* p. 39.

12. William C. Havard and Loren P. Beth, *The Politics of Misrepresentation: Rural-Urban Conflict in the Florida Legislature* (Baton Rouge: Louisiana State University Press, 1962).

13. John B. McConaughy, "Certain Personality Factors of State Legislators in South Carolina," *American Political Science Review* 44 (June 1950), pp. 897–902; Murray C. Havens, *City vs. Farm* (Tuscaloosa: University of Alabama Press, 1957); David R. Derge, "Metropolitan and Outstate Alignments in Illinois and Missouri Legislative Delegations," *American Political Science Review* 52 (December 1958), pp. 1051–1065; Robert J. Pitchell, "Reapportionment as a Control of Voting in California," *Western Political Quarterly* 14 (March 1961), pp. 214–235.

14. Noel Perrin, "In Defense of Country Votes," *Yale Review* 52 (Autumn 1962), pp. 16–24.

15. Robert S. Friedman, "The Reapportionment Myth," *National Civic Review* 49 (April 1960), pp. 184–188.

16. Daniel P. Moynihan, "The Question of the States," *Commonweal* 77 (October 12, 1962), pp. 65–68.

17. Duane Lockard, *The Politics of State and Local Government* (New York: Macmillan Company, 1963), p. 319. See also "No Miraculous Cure," *National Civic Review* 54 (October 1965), p. 464, and Alfred de Grazia, "Righting the Wrongs of Representation," *State Government* 38 (Spring 1965), pp. 113–117.

18. Thomas R. Dye, "Malapportionment and Public Policy in the States," *Journal of Politics* 27 (August 1965), pp. 586–601. See the bibliographical essay at the end of this volume for further sources.

19. David Brady and Douglas Edmonds, "One Man, One Vote–So What?" *Trans-Action* 4 (March 1967), pp. 41–46.

20. The labels "skeptics" and "reformers" are borrowed from William E. Bicker's excellent article "The Effects of Malapportionment in the States—A Mistrial," in Nelson W. Polsby, ed., *Reapportionment in the 1970's* (Berkeley: University of California Press, 1971), pp. 151–201.

21. For an excellent example of this "mixed bag," see Brett W. Hawkins, ed., *Reapportionment in Georgia* (Athens, Ga.: Institute of Government, University of Georgia, 1970). See also Eleanore Bushnell, ed., *Impact of Reapportionment on the Thirteen Western States* (Salt Lake City: University of Utah Press, 1970).

22. Ward Y. Elliott, *The Rise of Guardian Democracy* (Cambridge, Mass.: Harvard University Press, 1974), p. 223.

23. Biographical data for Mississippi legislators for occupation, religion, age, and sex are aggregated for the 1944–1968 period in Charles W. Fortenberry and Edward H. Hobbs, "The Mississippi Legislature," in Alex B. Lacy, Jr., ed., *Power in American State Legislatures* (New Orleans: Tulane University, 1967), pp. 81–119.

24. Farm workers are not included in the figures for the labor force, since only farm managers or owners are found in the legislature.

25. Figures for religious groups were compiled from *Churches and Church Membership in the U.S.* (Washington, D.C.: Glenmary Research Center, 1974).

26. Thomas R. Dye, *Politics in States and Communities,* 2d ed. (Englewood

Cliffs, N.J.: Prentice-Hall, 1973), p. 122.

27. Thomas R. Dye, "The Impact of Reapportionment on the Characteristics of Georgia Legislators," in Hawkins, *Reapportionment in Georgia*, pp. 43–60.

28. Donald T. Wells, "The Arkansas Legislature," in Lacy, *Power in American State Legislatures*, pp. 1–41.

29. Malcolm E. Jewell and Everett W. Cunningham, *Kentucky Politics* (Lexington: University of Kentucky Press, 1968), pp. 217–220.

30. Marvin Harder and Carolyn Rampey, *The Kansas Legislature* (Lawrence: University Press of Kansas, 1972), p. 12.

31. George M. Platt, "South Dakota's 1965 Legislative Session," *Public Affairs* (May 15, 1965), found in Charles R. Adrian, *State and Local Governments*, 4th ed. (New York: McGraw Hill Book Company, 1976), p. 335.

32. Thomas A. Flinn, "The Ohio General Assembly: A Developmental Analysis," in James A. Robinson, ed., *State Legislative Innovation* (New York: Praeger Publishers, 1973), pp. 226–278.

33. Leonard I. Ruchelman, "Lawyers in the New York State Legislature: The Urban Factor," *Midwest Journal of Political Science* 10 (November 1966), p. 486–497.

34. John R. Skates, Jr., "World War II as a Watershed in Mississippi History," *Journal of Mississippi History* 37 (May 1975), p. 135. See also the section on Mississippi in Ira Sharkansky, *The United States: A Study of a Developing Country* (New York: David McKay Company, 1975), pp. 63–65.

35. Fortner v. Barnett, no. 59, 905 (Ch. Ct., 1st Jud. Dist., Hinds Co., Mississippi, 1962); cited in Robert B. McKay, *Reapportionment* (New York: Simon and Schuster, 1965), p. 356.

36. *Compendium on Legislative Apportionment* (New York: National Municipal League, 1962).

37. Connors v. Johnson, 256 F. Supp. 962 (S. D. Mississippi, 1966); cited in Robert G. Dixon, Jr., *Democratic Representation* (New York: Oxford University Press, 1968), p. 610.

38. For a good summary of this process see John Quincy Adams, "The Mississippi Legislature," in David M. Landry and Joseph B. Parker, eds., *Mississippi Government and Politics in Transition* (Dubuque, Iowa: Kendall/Hunt Publishing Company, 1976), pp. 57–88. An excellent early treatment of reapportionment in Mississippi is Edward H. Hobbs, *Legislative Apportionment in Mississippi* (University, Miss.: Bureau of Public Administration, University of Mississippi, 1956).

39. Dye, "Impact of Reapportionment on the Characteristics of Georgia Legislators," pp. 43–60; Richard Lehne, *Reapportionment of the New York Legislature: Impact and Issues* (New York: National Municipal League, 1972); John B. Richard, "Wyoming," in Bushnell, *Impact of Reapportionment*, pp. 307–327.

40. John F. Gallagher and Louis F. Weschler, "California," in Bushnell, *Impact of Reapportionment*, p. 87.

41. Richard H. Folmar, "Legislature '67 — A New Mexico Profile," in Susanne A. Stoiber, ed., *Legislative Politics in the Rocky Mountain West* (Boulder, Colo.:

Bureau of Government Research, University of Colorado, 1967), pp. 51–62; Eleanore Bushnell, "Nevada," in Bushnell, *Impact of Reapportionment,* pp. 105–206. See also Allan Dines, "A Reapportioned State," *National Civic Review* 55 (February 1966).

42. David Ray, "Membership Stability in Three State Legislatures: 1893–1969," *American Political Science Review* 68 (March 1974), pp. 106–112. See also Jack E. Holmes, *Politics in New Mexico* (Albuquerque: University of New Mexico Press, 1967), p. 232, and Alan Rosenthal, "Turnover in State Legislatures," *American Journal of Political Science* 18 (August 1974), pp. 609–616.

43. Samuel C. Patterson, "American State Legislatures and Public Policy," in Jacob and Vines, *Politics in the American States,* 3d ed. (Boston: Little, Brown and Company, 1976), p. 155. Bruce B. Mason and Leonard E. Goodall, "Arizona," in Bushnell, *Impact of Reapportionment,* p. 66. In Washington State James J. Best found reapportionment made little difference on the age of legislators (James J. Best, "The Impact of Reapportionment on the Washington House of Representatives," in Robinson, *State Legislative Innovation,* pp. 136–182).

44. Dye, "Impact of Reapportionment on the Characteristics of Georgia Legislators," p. 44.

45. Richard, "Wyoming," p. 325.

46. Bernard C. Borning, "Idaho," in Bushnell, *Impact of Reapportionment,* p. 159.

47. Best, "Impact of Reapportionment," p. 151.

48. Dye, "Impact of Reapportionment on the Characteristics of Georgia Legislators," p. 46. In New Mexico farmers were hurt by reapportionment but still remained a force in the 1970s (see Paul L. Hain, "The Legislature," in F. Chris Garcia and Paul L. Hain, eds., *New Mexico Government* [Albuquerque: University of New Mexico Press, 1976], pp. 27–53).

49. Dye, "Impact of Reapportionment on the Characteristics of Georgia Legislators," p. 51.

50. Heinz Eulau and John D. Sprague, *Lawyers in Politics: A Study in Professional Convergence* (Indianapolis, Ind.: Bobbs-Merrill Co., 1968).

51. Adrian, *State and Local Governments,* p. 335.

52. Ralph M. Wade, "The Wyoming Legislature," in: Stoiber, *Legislative Politics,* pp. 112–113.

53. Malcolm E. Jewell and Samuel C. Patterson, *The Legislative Process in the United States* (New York: Random House, 1966), p. 109; Kenneth Janda, Henry Teune, Melvin Kohn, and Wayne Frances, *Legislative Politics in Indiana* (Bloomington, Ind.: Bureau of Government Research, Indiana University, 1961); Marvin A. Harder and Raymond G. Davis, *The Legislature as an Organization* (Lawrence: Regents Press of Kansas, 1979).

54. Dye, *Politics in States and Communities,* 3d ed. (Englewood Cliffs, N.J.: Prentice-Hall, 1977), p. 120.

55. Victor S. Hjelm and Joseph P. Pisciotte, "Profiles and Careers of Col-

orado State Legislators," *Western Political Quarterly* 21 (December 1968), pp. 698–722.

56. Borning, "Idaho," pp. 157–164.

57. Ellis Waldron, "How the Montana Legislative Assembly Became Malapportioned," *Montana Business Quarterly* (Winter 1965). Waldron has contributed a series of excellent sources on reapportionment in Montana, including Ellis Waldron, "Montana's 1966 Legislative Apportionment Amendment," *Montana Business Quarterly* (Spring 1966); Ellis Waldron, "100 Years of Reapportionment in Montana," *Montana Law Review* (Fall 1966); Ellis Waldron, *The Montana Legislative Assembly* (Missoula, Mont.: The Montana-Idaho Assembly on State Legislatures in American Politics, 1966).

58. For figures for all the states, see the table in Jacob and Vines, *Politics in the American States,* 2d ed., p. 170.

59. The 1964 election had massive negative effects for Republicans in individual legislative chambers in other states also (Samuel C. Patterson, Ronald D. Hedlund, and G. Robert Boynton, *Representatives and Represented* [New York: John Wiley and Sons, 1975], p. 24).

60. In a careful analysis of partisan changes in the House, Waldron concludes, "it appears that the Republican gain of 26 seats in the House was the product of factors other than reapportionment" (Ellis Waldron, "Reapportionment and Political Partisanship in the 1966 Montana Legislative Elections," *Montana Business Quarterly* [Fall 1966], pp. 13–27).

61. K. Ross Toole, *The Rape of the Great Plains* (Boston: Little, Brown and Company, 1976), p. 217.

62. For analyses of the amendment process, see Robert E. Eagle, "Public Opinion and the 1972 Constitutional Convention" (Paper delivered at the Annual Meeting of the Rocky Mountain Social Science Association, El Paso, Texas, April 25–27, 1974); Elizabeth Eastman, "The 1971–1972 Montana Constitutional Convention," *Montana Public Affairs* (January 1972); Leo Graybill, Jr., "The New Montana Constitution," *State Government* 46 (Spring 1973), pp. 89–94; Ellis Waldron, "Montana's 1972 Constitutional Election" *Montana Public Affairs* (June 1972).

63. In a study of the 1975 session, Jerry Calvert was less than enthusiastic about the impact of reform on the issue of accountability (see Jerry W. Calvert, "The Linkage Between Legislative Choices and Constituent Preferences: Does Reform Make a Difference?" (Paper delivered at the 1976 Annual Meeting of the Western Political Science Association, Sheraton Palace Hotel, San Francisco, California, April 1–3, 1976).

64. Elliott, *Rise of Guardian Democracy,* p. 223.

7
The Legislature:
Voting Behavior and Public Policy

Legislatures are where the demands and supports generated by society are finally hammered into formal public policy. The hammering itself is of primary concern in this chapter. Is it done in unison by identifiable groups such as political parties? Do those groups shift according to the kinds of policy constructed? If so, is it possible to identify a rural-urban factor involved in the shifting? Questions such as these are best answered through roll call analysis. The roll call vote is "when push comes to shove" in the policymaking process. It is pretty much agreed that roll call votes are the best yardstick we have. They are available over time and allow for a meaningful time-series analysis. They are the only precise comparative indicator at hand since cross-state attitudinal studies are expensive and scarce. Their validity as data points is high because they do not rely on verbal reports or interpretations of actions.[1]

Published studies of roll call voting in individual state legislatures are not plentiful, and although exceptions can be found, the field generally suffers from an urban bias in the kinds of states studied, limited data bases both in terms of which house is analyzed and in terms of the number of sessions used, and the employment of differing methodologies and quantitative techniques. These problems add up to trouble for comparative analysis. I seek to overcome them by (1) analyzing both houses of the legislatures, (2) treating a series of legislative sessions over time, and (3) using similar techniques of analysis for each state. To do this 8,059 roll calls were recorded representing forty-four years of legislative activity in three states. The individual yes, no, absent, or abstain responses of legislators, representing a total of 9,321 years of service and over 700,000 separate decisions, were coded by party, region, and district type (urban or rural).

Voting Behavior in State Legislatures

From a wide variety of research on the U.S. Congress and legislatures

in the American states, it has been concluded that the best single predictor of roll call voting responses is the political party.[2] Party voting
behavior is critical because it is a key element in the "competition equals
policies for the have-nots" hypothesis that has been a dominant
epistemological force in the study of state politics for three decades.[3]
Such studies usually rely on the assumption that competitive party
systems outside the legislature equal competitive party systems inside the
legislature.[4] This is a dangerous assumption, however, since there is little
chance that the logic of the essential hypothesis can hold unless party
cohesion is expressed in the arenas in which policies that will help the
poor are created.[5]

How cohesive are the political parties? In Kansas John Grumm found
partisanship overshadowed other considerations such as rural-urban
conflict.[6] Bruce Robeck reported that the party label was strong enough
in California to survive tests of regional diversity and rural-urban differences in district makeup.[7] In other urban states such as Connecticut,
Massachusetts, and Ohio partisanship has been demonstrated to be the
most important predictor of legislators' voting behavior.[8] In some states
party cohesion is qualified by institutional factors such as the house in
which the voting takes place[9] or the coming of a partisan-minded governor.[10] Yet even in a nonpartisan setting such as the Nebraska unicam-
eral legislature, party has been called "the most important reference
group."[11]

There are many states, however, that have little or no partisan voting
in their legislatures. In the southwestern states, studies show that party
conflict is either limited (New Mexico) or nonexistent (Arizona).[12] In the
central part of the nation, Emil Lee Bernick found party conflict in
Oklahoma to be limited to a tiny percentage of the roll calls and concluded that the data "support the general hypothesis that parties are
unimportant voting references across the entire universe of roll calls."[13]
The same kind of conclusion has been reached for Missouri.[14]
Elsewhere, the political parties seem to be involved in little more than a
cold war in the halls of the state legislatures. In South Dakota, Utah, and
Washington, studies have shown that party packs little punch when the
voting takes place.[15]

It has been observed that the more-urban states have greater party
cohesion and interparty conflict in the legislature.[16] The rural-urban
dichotomy is also an identifier of bloc voting, often competing with
party as the principal agent of roll call behavior. In a study of California,
New Jersey, Ohio, and Tennessee, rural-urban differences received the
highest overall rating when members were asked to identify the most important conflict in their legislatures.[17] It is more difficult to nail down explicit cases in which rural-urban conflict manifests itself, however.

Thomas Page found it existed in Kansas as a function of tax legislation.[18] Perhaps the clearest example of a visible rural-urban split in a state legislative system is the Florida Senate prior to reapportionment, but even there region played an important role.[19]

Those people who see the massification process as a leveler of rural-urban differences in society argue that a reduction in legislative conflict results from such leveling.[20] Some claim that the spatial characteristics of the districts will be especially relevant only in the vacuum created when party is not a factor.[21] Murray Havens found, however, that even in the absence of two-party competition in Alabama rural-urban distinctions rarely appear.[22] Most scholarship indicates that when rural-urban warfare erupts it does so on specific kinds of issues only. Patterson found rural-urban differences on public-morals questions in Oklahoma in the late 1950s, and Kirkpatrick found those differences cropping up again on specific issues (such as local-government affairs and taxation) a decade later in the same state.[23] In an extensive review of roll call voting in Alabama, Tennessee, and Iowa, Glen T. Broach shows that party is the critical factor, except in Alabama, and that rural-urban dimensions in the roll call structure of those states were decidedly issue-specific. "Even in one-party Alabama" when rural-urban conflict was great, "it occurred over a rather restrictive range of stereotyped issues."[24] The issues mentioned most in the literature as triggers for rural-urban conflict are associated with questions of public morality.[25]

Yet, although party seems to be more important, constituency differences generally and rural-urban differences specifically do affect the character of partisan groups within state legislatures.[26] Frank Sorauf contends that "perhaps the key to the entire riddle of legislative party cohesion is the type of constituencies the parties represent."[27] Lack of party unity in legislative systems has been attributed to the fact that social and economic characteristics in the districts tend to divide party organizations. Thomas R. Dye states the hypothesis as follows.

> The evidence seems to indicate that party influence is only effective where the parties represent separate and distinct socio-economic conditions. Where the constituencies of a state are divided along socio-economic lines and where party divisions coincide with these constituency divisions, only then will party program and discipline be effective in shaping policy in legislative chambers.[28]

For instance, in Massachusetts Edgar Litt ascribes party cohesion to "the likelihood that a lower-level, Irish-Catholic and Boston corps of legislators will unite in opposition to an upper-level, Yankee-Protestant, and outstate Republican group."[29]

Rural and urban population distributions diluted party cohesion in Michigan, where Becker and his associates have reported that when Democrats are elected from districts atypical of the party's districts in terms of urbanism, they seem to deviate from the party's position.[30] John Fenton says that Michigan's urban Republicans had more difficulty toeing the party line than did the rural Republicans.[31] A similar situation has appeared in Ohio and Washington.[32] M. Margaret Conway has contributed the important finding that of four constituency variables in Indiana (manufacturing, urbanism, owner-occupied residences, and population increase), urbanism was far more able than the others to explain variations of voting behavior within both parties.[33] In Kansas Harder and Rampey have demonstrated that the metro-rural split is basic to the existence of two Republican party blocs instead of one.[34] A variant is reported for Minnesota where the conservative coalition is weakened by rural-urban tensions.[35]

The state legislatures of Mississippi, Vermont, and Montana lend unique opportunities to explore these questions in rural settings. Montana's legislature is as traditionally competitive in its two-party balance as that of any urban state, and in Vermont a new Democratic cadre has materialized from the fog of an unstructured, one-party system. The absence of party differentiation in Mississippi denies a most basic guideline for analysis and entices the exploratory urge.

Mississippi: Seeking Out Patterns in Chaos

Thousands of roll call votes were held in the Mississippi legislature between 1964 and 1977, and hundreds of thousands of responses to those roll calls were recorded in the Senate and House journals. How to make sense of them? To get started, it seemed reasonable to require that a minority of at least 25 (20 percent) of the 122 House members vote against the majority and that 10 (20 percent) of the 52 senators be on the losing side for any given roll call for a vote to be chosen for analysis. This requirement left 2,809 "competitive" votes to be analyzed, 918 for the Senate and 1,891 for the House.

There has been an apparent decrease in the number of competitive roll calls recorded per yearly session. In actuality the legislature had no more competitive votes in the 1960s than in the 1970s; they simply held the same number in less time in the earlier period when the legislature met only once every two years. Only in the 1976 and 1977 Senate sessions can we see a clear drop in the number of competitive roll calls. The Senate has traditionally recorded fewer competitive roll calls than has the House although variations in the number of competitive votes in each chamber seem to be somewhat synchronized over time. Finally, within the list of generally competitive roll calls there seems to be a substantial amount of intense conflict in both chambers. In the House the outcome of about one-third of the 1,891 competitive roll calls would have been different if ten members had switched sides. With so many roll calls being decided by a handful of votes, the Mississippi legislature does not want for drama. The problem is making sense of the groups that define the script.

Legislative Voting: Delta and the Hills

The Delta is Mississippi's most noticeable geographic region. Historically, unique social and economic patterns rose to complement a topographical distinctiveness that is etched in flatness and undulates west toward the river in rhythm to the heat waves of a mid-morning July. Fashioned too was a politics different in tone and substance from the rest of the state. It is possible that the Delta might fade away as a predictor of election tallies but reappear as a cohesive force in the policymaking process when the legislature meets. The effect of the Delta region in the rural politics of Mississippi should emerge when its elected representatives vote on issues of public policy.

A series of questions comes immediately to mind. To what extent do representatives from the Delta vote cohesively on competitive roll calls? To what extent do Hills representatives vote in unison? On what percentage of the competitive roll calls do the two groups oppose one another and how intense is the struggle when they do? How successful is the Delta when its legislators vote cohesively? Has the Delta been able to win when it confronts the Hills representatives head on? What kinds of issues are associated with the Delta-Hills conflict in Mississippi? Overlaid on these questions are two additional chores. We must pay attention to variations in the answers over time and judge the impact reapportionment has had.

The Rice index of cohesion was applied to each group of legislators for each of the 2,809 competitive roll calls taken between 1964 and 1977. The Rice index is calculated by subtracting the percentage of a group voting in that group's minority from the percentage voting in the majority. If 30 percent of the Delta legislators in the House voted yea and 70 percent voted nay, the Rice index would register 40. Thus the measure's range is from 0 (50 percent–50 percent) to 100 (100 percent–0 percent). The average Rice index for Mississippi Delta-based legislators for the average session between 1964 and 1977 was 39 in the Senate (approximately a 70-percent–30-percent split) and 35 in the House (approximately a 68-percent–32-percent split). Although these figures are generally lower than the cohesion reached by political parties in many state legislatures, it is higher than party cohesion in some. The Hills legislators were much

The Legislature: Voting Behavior and Public Policy

less cohesive in both houses. The percentage of the time that a majority of the Delta legislators voted on the opposite side of an issue from the Hills legislators averaged 27 percent in the Senate and 35 percent in the House (see Table 7.1). These figures are not out of line with percentages of party opposition roll calls based on the same criterion in both houses of the U.S. Congress and some state legislative bodies.

TABLE 7.1

MEASURES OF DELTA AND HILLS VOTING IN THE
MISSISSIPPI LEGISLATURE ON COMPETITIVE* ROLL CALLS: 1964-1977

								Measures of Cohesion and Conflict**		Delta Victories***			
Years	N****		Delta Cohesion (average)		Hills Cohesion (average)		Index of Likeness (average)		Majorities in Opposition (percentages)		Type I		Type II	
	S	H	S	H	S	H	S	H	S	H	S	H	S	H
1964	150	222	41	34	28	22	79	82	37	39	43	33	77	74
1966	160	235	43	36	22	20	78	81	41	41	46	36	76	74
1968	126	184	39	35	25	23	83	81	24	41	30	41	81	76
1970	87	151	43	34	23	23	79	83	36	36	39	42	76	79
1971	60	115	51	37	28	22	81	82	23	34	29	46	83	82
1972	71	186	34	31	26	22	82	85	27	38	47	35	83	75
1973	52	132	36	32	27	21	90	85	31	34	14	36	75	78
1974	89	224	33	32	26	22	85	85	19	32	34	32	83	79
1975	70	144	39	30	24	23	86	84	17	42	40	28	91	70
1976	40	162	32	37	29	25	85	86	25	24	11	36	77	85
1977	32	131	41	45	27	30	85	83	19	27	50	36	90	82
Mean	85	172	39	35	26	23	83	83	27	35	35	36	81	78

 * Competitive roll calls are all roll calls taken when at least 20 percent of the membership voted in the minority.

** Cohesion measured by the Rice Index of Cohesion.
Likeness measured by the Rice Index of Group Likeness.
Majorities in Opposition = the percentage of roll calls on which a majority of Delta legislators was opposed by a majority of Hills legislators.

*** Type I = the percentage of times the Delta delegation voted on the winning side on all competitive roll calls when majorities of both groups were in opposition.

Type II = the percentage of times the Delta delegation was on the winning side on all competitive roll calls.

**** N = number of competitive roll calls recorded. S = Senate H = House

SOURCE: Roll calls were compiled by the author from Mississippi House and Senate Journals, 1964-1977.

The Delta legislators found themselves on the winning side of competitive votes (those roll calls on which at least 20 percent of a chamber's membership voted against the prevailing view) a great deal of the time. In the House they were successful on 78 percent of the votes, and in the Senate they were successful on 81 percent. Since the Delta delegation never measured more than 30 percent of the membership of either house, their record of voting with the majority is important. What is more impressive is the fact that even though they could at best control only three out of ten votes, they lost but one roll call of the 2,809 when 80 percent of them balloted similarly. When the index of group likeness was low, of course, they could not hope to win. (The Rice index of group likeness equals the percentage voting affirmative in one group minus the percentage voting affirmative in the other subtracted from 100. Thus with both groups voting 60 percent yes, the difference between the two is 0 and 100 minus 0 is 100 or perfect likeness.) In fact on votes where majorities of both groups were in opposition, the Delta representatives' cohesion was strong enough to win only 36 percent of the time. What we have is a legislative ball game in which the dominant theme concerning the Delta-Hills competition is a more cohesive Delta group usually voting as the winner on most legislation. When the Hills legislators draw a line in the sand, however, they create the conditions for an intense Delta-Hills conflict and can count on winning.

The principal dynamics involved in these data over time read as follows. Since 1962 the cohesion of the Hills legislators has increased moderately but unevenly in both houses, and the percentage of Delta victories when majorities of both groups were in opposition has predictably decreased. Yet, because the dominant association is a sharp decrease in the number of roll calls on which the Delta opposed the Hills, the overall position of the Delta has improved. The percentage of all competitive roll calls on which a majority of Delta representatives voted with a majority of the legislature averaged 74.0 percent in the 1964 and 1966 sessions and 83.5 percent in the 1976 and 1977 sessions. For senators the percentage was 76.5 for 1964 and 1966 and 85.5 for 1976 and 1977. In short, competition between the Delta and the Hills falls off sharply between 1964 and 1977, and that fact has ensured an even more advantageous position for the Delta overall, although when the Hills legislators do vote together against the Delta, they do so with more cohesion. What was a fairly visible source of legislative conflict in the mid-1960s is fading away.

The coming of reapportionment seems to have had little direct impact on that trend. The Delta was able to protect its numbers through the several reapportionments in both houses, and newly reapportioned sessions did not display marked differences in the Delta-Hills conflict. Yet it is difficult to dismiss entirely the notion that the reapportionment process has had an effect, for the Delta-Hills conflict in the legislature has been weaker since reapportionment.

Questions involving the production, sale, and use of alcohol have traditionally been used to separate Hills politics from Delta politics. V.O. Key, Jr., specified a statewide vote on prohibition to outline the Delta-Hills division in 1934, and he comments, "The preachers of the Hills fight demon rum and their followers vote for prohibition, while the sinful Delta votes for liquor."[36] Historically, taxes and government expenditures have also been sources of Delta-Hills division. Key's analysis has held up two decades beyond his own research. In the 1964 session of the Senate, for instance, over two-thirds of the votes that caused intense Delta-Hills competition were on matters involving liquor or taxes. Of the 2,809 votes analyzed, the one associated with the greatest Delta-Hills conflict occurred in the Senate in 1966. One hundred percent of the Delta delegation voted together against 67 percent of the Hills delegation on an amendment to a local-option bill to submit the question to a statewide referendum. As conflict between the two regions diminished in the Senate, so too did any tendency for one issue to dominate. Many times in more recent years conflict results only on bills that have a regionally specific thrust, affecting, for instance, a highway or public institution located within the Delta.

The same patterns can be seen in the House. In 1964, for instance, the Delta representatives voted 29 to 2 against reconsidering the passage of a bill to allow judges to sell contraband liquor outside the state; Hills representatives voted 51 to 32 for reconsideration. An example of a vote based more or less on a geographic rather than on an ideological imperative was the 1966 vote whereby the Delta voted 6 to 21 against an amendment to an appropriations bill that would have increased funding for East Mississippi State Hospital; the Hills representatives voted 57 to 15 for the amendment. That vote caused the lowest index of group likeness score for the session, 43.

Although liquor and tax questions were the most obvious sources of the Delta-Hills conflict in the 1960s, many other issues were associated with instances of Delta members voting against Hills members. Questions on social welfare matters were important in 1968 and 1970, and Delta-Hills battles over control of the fire ant occur consistently in both houses. The vote causing the greatest Delta-Hills division in the House over the fourteen-year period was in 1964 and dealt with the geographic distribution of the membership of the state executive committee of the Democratic party—the index of group likeness was only 38. But the general pattern has been that of a Delta-Hills division based to a great extent on "wet-dry" and tax questions, and that pattern has been diminishing over time. In the mid-1960s smoke from Delta-Hills skirmishes could still be seen rising over well-worn legislative battlegrounds. A decade later, except for a random wisp here and there, the skies were clear.

Legislative Voting, Urban Versus Rural

Mississippi ought to be a prime hunting ground for rural-urban legislative conflict. With no party whips to tug at the members' coat sleeves, with the chief regional division of the state as a reinforcing factor (since the Delta is predominantly rural), and with a long tradition of rural populism set against attempts to industrialize (as, for instance, BAWI represents), the terrain looks inviting indeed.

In order to provide a clear distinction between urban and rural members in the House of Representatives, those legislators from districts having between 30 percent and 60 percent of the population living in places of 2,500 or more were eliminated from the analysis. This created a circumstance whereby the most rurally based group of the legislators could be compared to the most urban group. In the Senate a strict dichotomy was employed. Those from districts where over 50 percent of the population lives in places of more than 2,500 were called urban, and the remainder were called rural.

The average index of cohesion for Mississippi's urban delegation for the 1964–1977 period was 39 in the Senate and 36 in the House, remarkably similar to the figures for the Delta. This means that on the average, two-thirds of the urban delegation voted similarly when a roll call was recorded. Rural cohesion was considerably lower, 28 in both chambers. There was somewhat more conflict between urban and rural legislators than there was between Hills and Delta legislators. Majorities of both groups opposed one another on 34 percent of the competitive roll calls in the Senate and on 43 percent of the competitive roll calls in the House. The index of group likeness averaged 80 in the Senate and 77 in the House (see Table 7.2). When the criteria for classifying roll calls as rural-urban conflict votes are stiffened to include only those votes in which two-thirds of one group opposed two-thirds of the other, about 11 percent of the generally competitive votes in the Senate and 9 percent of those in the House measured up.

We have seen that studies of other states show that when urban delegations vote cohesively, they usually wind up on the winning side of the vote. This situation has also been the case in Mississippi. When the members from cities like Jackson, Biloxi, Meridian, and Gulfport and the other urban places around the state voted with an index of cohesion

TABLE 7.2

MEASURES OF RURAL AND URBAN VOTING IN THE
MISSISSIPPI LEGISLATURE ON COMPETITIVE ROLL CALLS: 1964-1977*

			Measures of Cohesion and Conflict							Urban Victories			
			Urban** Cohesion (average)		Rural Cohesion (average)		Index of Likeness (average)		Majorities in Opposition (percentages)		Type I		Type II	
Years	N													
	S	H	S	H	S	H	S	H	S	H	S	H	S	H
1964	150	227	42	34	26	28	80	78	33	44	26	61	76	74
1966	160	235	44	33	21	27	79	79	32	44	24	43	71	75
1968	126	184	37	33	28	31	82	79	27	49	29	37	71	68
1970	87	151	37	36	24	33	81	72	38	51	50	32	79	60
1971	60	115	45	32	32	25	80	82	28	32	13	46	75	71
1972	71	186	31	37	29	24	84	76	30	35	20	52	70	85
1973	52	132	38	31	28	28	81	78	44	45	57	54	78	76
1974	89	224	38	42	24	26	82	70	29	58	50	65	83	83
1975	70	144	34	36	29	33	84	74	23	53	24	42	71	81
1976	40	162	40	40	32	26	75	81	40	32	31	50	72	86
1977	32	131	44	44	35	32	74	78	50	35	38	61	69	87
Mean	85	172	39	36	28	28	80	77	34	43	33	49	74	77

* For a definition of terms, see Table 7.1.

** Urban = Senate - legislators from districts where more than half the population
   lives in places of 2,500 or more; rural = all other legislators. House -
   legislators from districts in which 60 percent or more of the population lives
   in places of 2,500 or more. Rural = (1968-1977) - legislators from districts in
   which 30 percent or less of the legislators lives in places of 2,500 or more;
   (1964-1966) - legislators from districts where none of the population lives in
   places of 2,500 or more.

SOURCE: Roll calls were compiled by the author from: **Mississippi House and
         Senate Journals**, 1964-1977.

of 60 or higher, they won 91 percent of the time, and when their index of
cohesion was at least 80 (90 percent agreement), their yearly ratio of wins
to losses was 94 to 6. Even though a distinct numerical minority, they
averaged a victory rate of 75 percent for each of the eleven sessions in the
entire set of 2,809 competitive roll calls analyzed. In those situations in
which the two groups opposed each other, each with indexes of cohesion
of at least 30 (meaning the rural legislators were voting together too), urban success was much more limited. Under those conditions on a yearly

average they prevailed only 49 percent of the time in the House and 33 percent of the time in the Senate. With group cohesion held constant, the rural members could never lose because of their greater numbers. The urban legislators are successful because they are, on the average, more cohesive as a group than are the rural legislators.

The urban delegation has improved its winning percentage appreciably in Mississippi's House of Representatives in the 1964–1977 period. In the 1964 and 1966 sessions they were on the winning side of 74.5 percent of the 462 competitive roll calls recorded. In the 1976–1977 sessions the urban delegation voted with the winning side 86.5 percent of the time. Pearson's "r" between years and their winning percentage is .63, not because urban members strengthened their relative numerical position to any great extent but rather because their cohesion increased while that of the rural members did not ("r" between years and urban cohesion is .65 and between years and rural cohesion is .09). Competition between the two groups, measured as the percentage of the time a majority of the urban representatives faced off against a majority of the rural representatives, seemed to rise and fall in two large swells, cresting in 1970 and 1974 and falling in 1971 and 1976.

In Mississippi's Senate, reapportionment has increased the number of urban-based legislators substantially. Prior to reapportionment (1964 and 1966) the urban delegation was successful on about one-quarter of the roll calls recorded when urban majorities faced rural majorities. The urban success increased dramatically after reapportionment to 29 percent in 1968 and 50 percent in 1970 but crashed even more dramatically in 1971 to 13 percent. The same urban delegation that voted on the prevailing side only 20 percent of the time in 1972 found itself in the winning position 57 percent of the time in 1973 and half the time in 1974. In 1975 their wins tumbled sharply again, making a limited recovery in 1976 and 1977. Thus there is some slight improvement ($r = .27$) in the urban delegations' chances of victory when they are confronted by a more or less cohesive rural bloc. Their average success in 1964–1966 was 25 percent; it was 34 percent in 1976–1977.

Overall, however, a rise in the rural legislators' cohesion ($r = .63$ between years and rural cohesion) matched by a slight decrease in urban cohesion ($r = -.20$) has meant that urban legislators are no more likely to vote with the majority on all competitive roll calls in 1977 than they were in 1964. Moreover, urban representatives voted with the winning side when they voted together at high levels of cohesion prior to reapportionment and they have made no improvement in that area since. In fact in 1964 an urban delegation of eleven in the fifty-six-member Senate voted with the winners 95 percent of the time. In 1977 an urban delegation of twenty-three in an equal-sized chamber with equal cohesion was victorious 90 percent of the time. The lesson to be learned seems to be that the reapportionment of the Mississippi Senate, with its concomitant swelling of the urban cadre, tripped a cohesive cord within the shrunken rural delegation, which reacted to subdue urban successes. The caveat is that urban legislators have been a bit more successful after reapportionment on winning head-to-head confrontations.

Although the Delta-Hills conflict was clearly on the wane in both houses between 1964 and 1977, the picture regarding rural-urban voting is more cloudy. In the House of Representatives the MIO (majorities in opposition) statistic is down ever so slightly, but the index of likeness has fallen a bit too. The only sharp evidence that the rural-urban conflict is diminishing is the fact that in the last legislature studied, which was elected in 1975 and for which data are available for 1976 and 1977, only thirteen roll calls were held in which intense rural-urban division was recorded (two-thirds of one group opposed two-thirds of the other). The Senate showed a healthy rural-urban conflict in 1976 and 1977, however. In fact, there were as many highly divisive roll calls taken in 1977, eight, as there had been in 1964. Relatively there were more since there has been such a large drop in generally competitive roll calls in recent years. The MIO score for the Senate has increased slowly, and the group likeness index has decreased. Simply stated, there is no way to conclude from these figures that the rural-urban conflict has ended in the Mississippi legislature.

In Mississippi, as in other states, the rural-urban conflict has taken place on "morality" issues more than on any other single kind of issue. A bill to allow playing golf and tennis on Sunday passed 29 to 22 in the Senate in 1973; the urban delegation voted for it 15 to 3, and the rural senators opposed it 14 to 19. Divorce, the death penalty, regulation of marijuana, and of course, alcohol are other subjects that have caused rural-urban divisions in the legislature. In 1964 an amendment to a bill specifying that "persons who shall become parents of an illegitimate child shall be guilty of a felony" caused two-thirds of the rural members of the House to line up against two-thirds of the urban members.

A classic example of rural-urban voting on liquor questions with heavy moral overtones occurred in 1966 when H.B. 112, which would "permit counties to vote themselves out from under" the prohibition law, was amended by a vote of 65 to 45 as follows: "provided that no permit shall be issued to any person, persons, or firm or firms to manufacture, sell or store for sale any intoxicating liquor as specified in this Act within eight hundred (800) feet of any church, school, kindergarten or funeral home."[37] Rural members of the House voted 8 to 23 against reconsidering the vote on that amendment, and the urban representatives were in favor 21 to 5. The vote produced an index of group likeness (IGL) of 45. The motion to reconsider passed, and an amendment to the amendment cutting the distance from churches, schools, kindergartens, or funeral homes from 800 to 400 feet was quickly offered and passed 82 to 53. On that roll call the urban group voted 25 to 4 in favor, and the rural group voted 6 to 26 against (the IGL was 33).

Other types of legislation that have been associated with the rural-urban conflict center on issues that are more interest-specific. For instance, the organization, funding, and power of the Mississippi Milk Commission have caused continual rural-urban voting in the Mississippi legislature. Issues involving the highway system, taxes (especially on land and property), and real estate have often been linked to rural-urban voting divisions. In 1966 a vote on daylight savings time caused the greatest rural-urban battle of the session as the IGL dropped from an average of 79 for the year to 24 for that vote. Reapportionment has also been responsible for raising rural-urban conflict to a white heat. The lowest IGL recorded in the fourteen-year period studied was 11, and it occurred in 1968 on the floor of the House on a vote that dealt with a proposed reapportionment plan. Representatives from the most-urban districts voted 25 to 1, and representatives from the most-rural districts voted 3 to 37. Funding for education, especially when it involves colleges and universities in particular areas of the state, and some aspects of local-government power and control are also important stimulators of rural-urban conflict. Otherwise, one must look for direct urban-benefit issues, which are rare, to find rural-urban divisions. As an example, in 1977 the House of Representatives divided sharply on rural-urban lines twice on a bill (H.B. 89) that would have placed a 3-percent tax on admission receipts at the sports arenas in Jackson and Biloxi, Mississippi's two largest cities.

It is difficult to nail down any clear trends in the evolution of rural-urban voting defined in terms of issue areas, although two tentative patterns may be set forth. First, it seems that issues of private morality are cropping up less as sources of rural-urban conflict. In 1977 a bill allowing the sale of alcohol on election days in resort areas sparked a rural-urban division in the Senate (along with a proposal for a 3-percent tax on liquor sold by the Alcoholic Beverage Commission), and in the House there was a rural-urban split in 1975 on a liquor question. Nevertheless, the incidence and intensity of these kinds of divisions is weakening. Second, there appears to be a narrowing of the range of issues associated with rural-urban conflict toward a category that might be labeled "good government." It seems that more rural-urban splits are appearing on issues of governance and fewer on substantive policy, with taxes and education being the principal exceptions.

Vermont: The Coming and Going of Democratic Cohesion

The central question Vermont poses for students of politics in rural areas is, Will the development of interparty competition at large spawn a competitive framework within the legislature? We also need to know if and how that potential cause-and-effect sequence is marked by rural-urban divisions and reapportionment. To get at these matters 2,081 roll calls were recorded for the twenty seatings of the legislature in the twenty-four-year period from 1955 through 1978. Only those roll call votes on which 20 percent of the membership voted on the losing side were selected for use in the analysis.

In the House during the decade prior to 1957, an average of only nineteen competitive votes were taken during each biennial session; the Senate recorded more than fifty on the average. Since 1967, when the first regular session of the legislature was held after reapportionment, the House has averaged fifty-one competitive roll calls, and the Senate, fifty-four. The percentage of the roll calls (20 percent in opposition to the prevailing view) that displayed more intense conflict (at least a 40-percent–60-percent split) has increased slightly in the later period, too, indicating that the quantity and the quality of the conflict have risen together. In comparison to Mississippi, however, Vermont displays substantially less conflict.

Legislative Voting: Democrats and Republicans

Between the time the Democrats gained statewide political respectability in the early 1950s and the time they first elected a speaker of the House of Representatives in the mid-1970s, their Rice index of cohesion in the House ranged from a low of 24 in the 1953 session to a high of 80 in 1966, and it averaged 50; that is, 75 percent of the party was on one side of the vote, 25 percent on the other. The Republican's cohesion was only 34 for the same quarter century, 1 point below the Delta legislators' cohesion in the Mississippi House.

The index of group likeness between Republicans and Democrats (hereafter referred to as the IPL, index of party likeness) varied from a high of 88 in 1963 to a low of 53 in 1967, averaging 72 for the period, indicating there was more conflict between Republicans and Democrats in Vermont than there was between Hills and Delta representatives in Mississippi. Of the 937 votes analyzed, a majority of the Democrats voted with the winners on 599 occasions or 64 percent of the time. This

TABLE 7.3

MEASURES OF PARTY VOTING IN THE VERMONT
HOUSE AND SENATE ON COMPETITIVE ROLL CALLS: 1955-1978*

		Measures of Cohesion and Conflict								Democratic Victories			
Years	N		Dem. Cohesion (average)		Rep. Cohesion (average)		Index of Likeness (average)		Majorities in Opposition (percentages)		Type I		Type II	
	S	H	S	H	S	H	S	H	S	H	S	H	S	H
1955	104	20	69	32	35	25	63	78	53	45	16	11	53	60
1957	111	33	67	38	32	22	61	80	44	36	22	27	54	73
1959	74	30	59	52	34	23	67	70	46	57	31	24	66	57
1961	55	33	72	32	29	32	59	84	45	42	27	7	62	59
1963	58	67	66	38	41	30	51	88	67	30	18	35	43	73
1964	15	26	48	60	44	35	67	56	47	77	29	25	67	38
1965	49	54	56	54	45	28	57	63	65	68	41	38	65	55
1966	23	34	82	80	43	31	44	61	65	47	47	33	57	71
1967	33	49	68	78	30	38	58	53	45	65	60	61	81	77
1968	19	65	52	56	29	41	70	63	58	56	45	24	68	59
1969	74	46	72	61	42	52	52	54	71	71	17	25	39	50
1970	98	47	75	54	44	31	51	67	64	64	25	43	52	62
1971	49	50	66	57	44	46	58	56	45	66	10	33	58	56
1972	32	64	64	55	31	39	59	57	56	72	33	33	68	48
1973	47	35	58	53	39	42	72	68	21	51	10	24	78	63
1974	63	57	57	47	32	40	69	68	41	56	19	34	67	67
1975	77	46	42	37	39	32	65	78	57	43	25	55	48	80
1976	81	75	39	33	36	35	75	81	40	39	31	48	52	77
1977	23	32	57	37	36	25	62	79	43	53	50	76	68	87
1978	59	74	58	41	31	36	66	72	53	51	32	47	61	73
Mean	57	47	62	50	37	34	61	69	51	55	29	35	60	64

*For a definition of terms, see Table 7.1

SOURCE: Roll calls compiled by the author from Vermont House and Senate
Journals, 1955-1977. 1978 data provided by Clark Bensen, Vermont
Polidata (South Burlington, Vermont: 1978).

success is attributable to a noncohesive Republican party. Majorities of
the two parties voted on opposite sides of roll calls 55 percent of the time
between 1955 and 1978. When they did, the Democrats won only 35 percent of the contests (see Table 7.3).

In Vermont's thirty-member Senate, the Democrats have been more
cohesive with a mean Rice index figure of 62. The Republicans scored

much lower, only 37, as they did in the House. Competition between the parties did not differ significantly between the two chambers. The majorities of the parties opposed one another on about one-half of the 1,144 competitive votes. Although Senate Democrats found themselves on the winning side of nearly as many roll calls as the House Democrats did, the former managed to carry the vote only 29 percent of the time when party majorities were in opposition because they averaged only 26 percent of the membership. Even with a cohesion of 100, they could muster only 8 of the 30 votes.

Between 1961 and 1979 Democratic cohesion varied in the House of Representatives to form a sweeping bell-shaped curve (see Figure 7.1). During the 1950s their cohesion grew from 29 (1951) to 52 (1959). After a setback in the early 1960s, it began to rise again, and by mid-decade it had reached 65. This means that on the 114 competitive roll calls recorded in the 1967-1968 session, 82 percent of the Democrats would normally be found voting together. In the first half of the 1967-1968 biennium and in the 1966 special session Democratic cohesion reached 78 and 80, respectively (see Table 7.3). During the same period (1951-1968) the IPL fell sharply, demonstrating that increased party warfare was under way. Republican cohesion responded slowly but steadily throughout the 1960s, peaking in the first half of the 1969-1970 session at 52. There seemed to be a clear metamorphosis under way, whereby the Vermont House of Representatives was shedding its old nonpartisan ways and emerging as a new body in which structure based on party discipline was important. Critical to a proper understanding of rural politics is the fact that although Vermont was changing during this period, it was not urbanizing. The most rural state in America was capable of developing and housing legislative partisanship.

The fall away from partisanship in the 1970s, however, was as clear and thorough as the climb toward a more-structured politics had been earlier. After 1967 Democratic cohesion fell steadily until it reached a low of 35 in the 1975-1976 session. Meanwhile the IPL climbed sharply back to the 80-percent level. Republican cohesion, which was never very high, fell less dramatically, but fall it did, until in the first half of the 1977-1978 biennium it registered only 25, its lowest point since 1959. The changes that had seemed to be progressing so inexorably in the 1960s were washed away in the 1970s.

Cohesion of the Democratic delegation in the Senate plunged in the 1970s also. During the sessions of 1971-1972 through 1977-1978, it averaged only 55. For the sessions of 1955 through 1961, their mean score was 67. Except for a high of 82 in the special session of 1966, Democratic cohesion peaked in the 1969-1970 session. After that the

FIGURE 7.1

DEMOCRATS IN THE VERMONT HOUSE, DEMOCRATIC PARTY COHESION,
AND THE DEMOCRATIC-REPUBLICAN INDEX OF GROUP LIKENESS - 937 ROLL CALLS 1951-1978

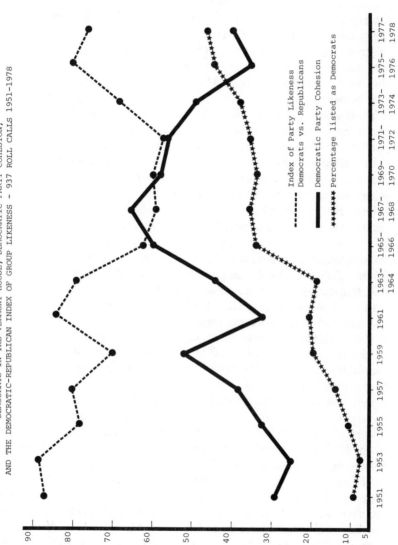

- - - - - - Index of Party Likeness
Democrats vs. Republicans

————— Democratic Party Cohesion

✱✱✱✱✱✱✱ Percentage listed as Democrats

Democrats began to lose cohesiveness, and the low point came in the 1975-1976 session (40). The IPL reacted accordingly, increasing from 1969 through 1975 after a slow, almost imperceptible decline in 1955 through 1969. Republican cohesion was higher in the 1960s than it was in the 1950s or the 1970s, averaging 40 from 1963 through 1969, despite a sharp dip to 30 in the 1967-1968 session. The Democrats started with relatively high cohesion and steadily lost ground during the period. The Republicans started low and ended low. The index of party likeness shows a Senate in the 1970s in which the parties were less dissimilar than ever before.

These changes in partisanship in the Vermont legislature demonstrate the independence of politics from socioeconomic factors and show how politics can change character within a strictly rural environment. Two major events occurred simultaneously with the coming of a cohesive Democratic minority in Vermont. One was reapportionment (1965), the other was the election of the first Democratic governor in over a century (Philip Hoff in 1962). Yet Figure 7.1 shows that increases in the "togetherness" of Democratic lawmakers preceded both. It is also clear that although control of the executive may be a necessary cause for minority-party cohesion, it is not a sufficient cause. Another Democrat, Thomas Salmon, was elected governor in 1972. But during his stay in office, Democratic cohesion averaged only 41, about the same as in the two sessions immediately preceding Hoff, when Republicans held the governorship, and reapportionment was yet to come.

Two events suggest that the presence of Hoff as governor was critical. In the first place, it was Hoff who called the special session of the legislature in 1964 to deal with his new executive program, which had been formulated but not introduced in the 1963 regular session. Democratic cohesion increased by 58 percent between 1963 and 1964, the largest single percentage increase of Democratic cohesion in the modern history of the state. Second, during the final half of the 1977-1978 biennium, Hoff announced his intention not to run for reelection in 1968. Democratic cohesion fell drastically and never recovered.

The Hoff years in Vermont support the breakthrough party theory, which holds that innovation comes in political systems when long-established majority parties fall to upstart minority parties.[38] Reapportionment was helpful (it reduced the size of the House and increased the number of Democrats), but it was not causal. Hoff was. At the height of his power, the legislature took on the markings of the so-called urban model, the Democratic party was voting at extremely high levels of cohesion, and there was major conflict between the parties. In 1967, however, coalitions were formed in both houses that allowed, for the first time in

Vermont's history, the Democrats to win more votes than the Republicans when the two parties were in opposition.

The Vermont case also demonstrates that the relative size of the legislative contingent is not consistently related to the minority party's cohesion. The Democrats chipped away at the Republican majority in the House of Representatives throughout the period. But when the Democrats finally tipped the numerical balance in their favor and elected a speaker in 1975, the cohesion of the party crashed to its lowest point (35) in fifteen years. Numbers, however, count. In the 1975-1976 session, when the Democrats took over the House, their victories increased from 28 percent of the party opposition roll calls to 51 percent, even though their average cohesion dropped from 49 to 35. They improved that score in the 1977-1978 session to 56 percent. Meanwhile the Republicans holed up in the Senate, where a combination of weak cohesion and a small percentage of seats held Democratic wins to one-third of the contests between the two parties.

Prior to reapportionment, the votes tied to more-intense party conflict (the IPL being 10 points below the yearly average) were most likely to occur on bills involving questions of public morality such as blue laws or gambling, educational issues, and political concerns such as electoral laws. Since that time, taxes, labor, and politics have been the principal sources of party hostility. There has been a tendency in Vermont for the party-conflict votes to occur on a narrower range of issues as time passes. In the sessions held between 1951 and 1963 the top three party-conflict issues accounted for only 41 percent of the total number of roll calls showing intense interparty conflict; between 1973 and 1978 they accounted for 63 percent.

There is also a tendency for single-issue areas to dominate party conflict over single sessions of the legislature. In 1973, for instance, 56 percent of the party-conflict votes occurred on Democratic Governor Tom Salmon's tax program. In 1977 half of the decisive party votes were on an unemployment compensation bill. In the years between 1974 and 1978, labor bills were by far the greatest source of interparty conflict. Thus although party conflict has diminished in the legislature since 1968, it has focused on an issue that has been at the root of party differences in many other American states and the U.S. Congress as well. Put another way, without labor legislation to do battle over, party conflict would have dwindled to almost nothing.

The principal difference between the House and the Senate in Vermont is that in the Senate the parties have begun to do battle on appropriation measures instead of on labor bills. Between 1973 and 1978 less than 5 percent of the intense party votes were on labor legislation while 28 per-

cent were on appropriation bills. Votes on tax legislation are also less
partisan in the Senate. As in the House, Democrats and Republicans are
likely to vote on opposite sides of political issues involving such things as
voting regulations, electoral laws, and apportionment.

Legislative Voting: Urban Versus Rural

Vermont's largest city is tiny as cities go, but the difference between
the outback of the Northeast Kingdom and a district in Burlington in
Chittenden County—with its television station, university, airport, and
traffic congestion—is profound. Even in the very rural states an analysis
of voting behavior based on degrees of ruralism and urbanism will tell us
something about district influences on legislative decision making.

Before reapportionment occurred in 1965, 146 of the 246 representatives came from towns (each town was a district) of under 1,000
population, and there were only 26 who represented towns of over 2,500.
After reapportionment the size of the House was reduced to 150
members, and 107 of them represent districts in which a majority of the
population lives in places of 2,500 or more, and only 14 represent
districts in which a majority of the population lives in places of under
1,000. When the number of representatives was reduced so radically, the
cohesion of the rural members jumped sharply. At the same time the
cohesion of the urban members, which was relatively high before reapportionment, fell. Since 1971, however, the small rural group of 14 to 17
members has lost cohesiveness steadily, so that in the 1977 and 1978 sessions the Rice index of cohesion for the urban and rural members is virtually the same and very low, under 30.

By modifying the urban-rural definition so that the two groups are
more equal in size, it is possible to get a better handle on the question of
district as a cue for voting in a very rural state. To rework the definition,
legislators from districts in which a majority of the population lives in
places of over 10,000 population were typed urban, and legislators
elected from districts in which most of the people live in places of under
2,500 were typed rural. Each of these groups represents about one-third
of the total House membership. The remaining one-third from districts
dominated by places with populations of 2,500 to 10,000 were omitted
from the analysis.

The mean cohesion of the urban group in the six sessions between 1973
and 1978 was 34. Rural cohesion was 29. The majorities of the two
groups opposed each other on only 35 percent of the roll calls, and the
IPL was high, 83. The urban legislators were on the winning side 81 percent of the time on all of the competitive roll calls and broke even
(53-percent wins) when they were opposed by the rural group. These

TABLE 7.4

MEASURES OF RURAL AND URBAN VOTING IN THE
VERMONT LEGISLATURE ON COMPETITIVE ROLL CALLS: 1973-1978*

| | | Measures of Cohesion and Conflict | | | | | | | Urban Victories | | | |
| Years | N | | Urban** Cohesion (average) | | Rural*** Cohesion (average) | | Index of Likeness (average) | | Majorities in Opposition (percentages) | | Type I | | Type II | |
	S	H	S	H	S	H	S	H	S	H	S	H	S	H
1973	47	35	49	38	32	33	81	76	15	53	43	41	91	71
1974	63	57	38	40	30	36	82	77	30	45	53	50	79	77
1975	77	46	29	32	30	26	79	87	51	20	59	50	79	85
1976	81	75	36	29	41	27	75	86	48	31	33	43	67	83
1977	23	32	35	29	31	23	81	87	26	34	16	82	83	84
1978	59	74	37	33	32	26	74	87	47	26	19	53	56	86
Mean	58	53	37	34	33	29	79	83	36	35	37	53	76	81

* For a definition of terms, see Table 7.1.

** Urban = a majority of the district's population living in places of over 10,000.

***Rural = a majority of the district's population living in places of under 2,500.

SOURCE: Roll calls compiled by author from Vermont House and Senate Journals, 1973-1977. 1978 data provided by Clark Bensen, Vermont Polidata (South Burlington, Vermont: 1978).

figures are remarkably close to Mississippi's House of Representatives for a similar time period. Legislators in the Senate were classified as urban if more than half the population of their districts lived in places of over 5,000. All other senators were classified as rural. On all four measures of group cohesion and conflict the Senate appears to be very similar to the House. Urban senators do not seem to win quite as often as urban representatives do, however, since there are relatively fewer of them (see Table 7.4).

In the literature much has been made of an alleged bias against urban places and their representatives on the part of rural lawmakers—a bias that would be corrected by reapportionment. But in Vermont urban-rural conflict in the legislature before reapportionment, although it occurred from time to time, was neither intense nor enduring. When urban legislators voted together in unison prior to reapportionment, they invariably won. On 111 roll calls studied in the Vermont House between the years of 1951 and 1966, the year the first reapportioned legislature met, when the urban members' cohesion was 10 points above the yearly average, they were on the winning side of the issue 84 percent of the time, despite the fact that they held only 10 percent of the seats.[39] Since reapportionment they rarely lose at all when they display any kind of group solidarity.

The issues that spark rural-urban conflict when it does occur form no coherent pattern. In the early period morality questions caused many close votes but few rural-urban divisions. The abortion issue assumes a weak urban-rural coloration, but it is likely to be related to the religious and ideological backgrounds of the legislators and only indirectly related to the spatial nature of their districts. The distribution of school aid money has also taken on a rural-urban hue in recent years as some communities have started to feel the pinch of declining enrollments.

In 1974 the index of group likeness between rural and urban legislators in the House dipped from its session average of 77 to 65 on the following proposal.

> A person who is hunting at any time during the 16 consecutive calendar days commencing 12 days prior to Thanksgiving Day, shall wear an outer garment that is of hunter orange color, has a total surface area of at least 100 square inches and is worn above the waist. This requirement shall not apply to persons hunting for raccoon or migratory fowl.[40]

This kind of rural-urban issue is extremely rare. The vote causing the greatest rural-urban split in that session (an IGL of 45) involved unemployment benefits. Labor legislation generally has provided more urban-rural conflict in the House than any other issue. In the Senate, constitutional amendments, apportionment, and appropriations bills are particular sources of divisions between urban and rural members.

The key to a fuller understanding of rural politics is the question of whether or not a very rural state can sustain party cohesion and conflict in its legislature if district types and party strength are not reinforcing variables. For instance it has been noted that Democratic cohesion in the Vermont Senate is greater than it is in the House. We also know that the smaller cadre of Democrats are usually more urban-bound in the Senate. Is the decline of Democratic cohesion and the increase in Democratic seats in the House coincidental? Perhaps the erosion of cohesion has been caused by the expansion of Democratic seats into rural districts, bringing enough rural-urban conflict into the Democratic party to scuttle the inner strength it had in the mid-1960s when its membership was smaller and more homogeneously urban.

That proposition does not appear to be the case, however. The fifty votes that caused the greatest diversity within the Democratic party between 1973 and 1978 were analyzed in terms of the degree of rural-urban voting within the party. In only three of those votes were rural and urban Democrats significantly aligned on different sides, and even then the associations between size of district and the yes and no responses were very weak. In 1973 the rural-urban split within the Democratic party on a bill relating to granting liquor licenses caused a tau correlation coefficient of .30 (p = .02). But that was an exception. The mean tau for the entire set of votes was only .12, indicating that it was not the expansion of membership into rural areas that caused the demise of Democratic unity in Vermont.

Legislative voting behavior based in part on the rural-urban differences within the parties occurred in Vermont during the Hoff administration, when Vermont's first Democratic governor in a century fashioned a coalition of Democrats and a group of urban Republicans. Rural Republicans formed their own small cluster in the mid-1960s as well. However, these arrangements soon faded. For a brief moment in the state's history, Vermont experienced an embryonic legislative party system with the trappings of the classic model clearly visible. This indicates that an extremely rural contextual framework does not by definition preclude party government. Remember, of course, that an array of supportive conditions were in place: reapportionment as a catalyst of mood, a breakthrough party, and an innovative and a progressive governor. The legislature now looks like once it did, a kaleidoscope of patterns that defy typology. Democratic party cohesion has melted into the political topography of Vermont like frost on an October hillside under the morning sun.

Montana: Party Government in a Rural Setting

Vermont demonstrates that a rural environment can host a competitive balance between political parties both in and out of the legislature. But what would have been a more important discovery, partisan behavior of party members, appeared only briefly under very special circumstances, soon to disappear. Montana is a state in which the ratio of Republicans to Democrats in the legislature has swung in the proximity of perfect equilibrium for a century. Yet Montanan constituencies are chopped up by the wildest country left in the forty-eight adjacent states, where hikers still wear bells around their necks to ward off grizzlies and great stretches of badlands spell separation of people from people. Could a disciplined party system exist in the state capital under such conditions? Is it not reasonable to assume that in this land of radically different environments the character of one's district would bear most heavily on one's policy decisions, party identity notwithstanding?

To discover the answer the responses of the state's 100 representatives and 50 senators were recorded on 3,169 roll call votes between the years of 1961 and 1977. On the average the Senate recorded 133 roll calls with an opposition rate of 20 percent, and the House, 184 over the ten-session period. Thirty-two percent of the Senate's roll calls could be defined as intensely competitive; that is, at least 40 percent of the membership was in disagreement with the majority position. In the House a quarter of the votes met that criterion. Both houses have increased their number of generally competitive roll calls (at least 20 percent in opposition) over the period. The Senate's intensely competitive percentage has remained high, and the lower chamber's has dropped off.

Legislative Voting: Democrats and Republicans

Understanding voting in the Montana legislature is made less difficult by the consistent importance of the political parties. Over the ten sessions studied, Democratic cohesion averaged 52 in the House and 56 in the Senate, meaning that on 3,169 different votes recorded over a sixteen-year period the mean condition was 75 percent of the Democratic party agreeing on the outcome. Republican cohesion was nearly as strong, averaging 48 in the Senate and 47 in the House. The IPL for the period was 61 in the Senate and 57 in the House. An IPL of 60 means that there is a percentage-point gap of 40 between the percentage of the Democrats voting yes and the percentage of the Republicans voting yes. On the average, the parties voted on opposing sides of the issue over half the time (see Table 7.5).

Several points distinguish this record from that of Vermont's. First of all, the legislators in Montana took two times as many roll call votes between 1961 and 1977 than Vermont's legislators did. Many of those votes are of peripheral interest and serve to dilute the party cohesion and IPL percentages. Second, although the Democrats' cohesion in the Senate in Vermont is higher than it is in Montana and the IPL is the same in Montana, those scores are not fashioned from a small homogeneous group of Democrats from larger districts as they are in Vermont. Third, the House in Montana is much more party-oriented than is the House in Vermont. The average IPL in Vermont's House is 69, but in Montana it is only 57. Fourth, in both houses in Montana one finds many near-perfect party votes each session, but in Vermont this was never the case. IPL's below 20 are not uncommon in Montana; they are very, very uncommon in Vermont. Fifth, Vermont's party-conflict scores are heavily biased by the burst of activity during the Hoff administration, and Montana's are

TABLE 7.5

MEASURES OF PARTY AND RURAL AND URBAN VOTING IN THE
MONTANA LEGISLATURE ON COMPETITIVE ROLL CALLS: 1961-1977*

PARTY MEASURES OF COHESION AND CONFLICT

Years	N		Democratic Cohesion (average)		Republican Cohesion (average)		Index of Likeness (average)		Majorities in Opposition (percentages)		DEMOCRATIC VICTORIES Type I		Type II	
	S	H	S	H	S	H	S	H	S	H	S	H	S	H
1961	37	133	44	47	53	59	63	55	41	58	67	14	86	50
1963	75	106	47	47	62	56	54	58	59	62	73	21	83	51
1965	84	170	58	61	54	57	52	45	68	75	70	74	77	81
1967	114	164	62	64	40	43	63	55	48	62	69	45	84	66
1969	89	165	62	63	50	41	55	60	61	50	78	36	84	68
1971	110	266	54	56	50	51	61	56	54	60	63	31	80	59
1973	110	221	56	59	42	38	65	59	39	59	70	76	88	86
1974	204	146	43	56	44	38	69	64	43	51	55	72	73	85
1975	244	243	54	61	48	46	57	54	63	67	63	91	77	94
1977	261	223	44	53	38	42	71	65	46	48	51	73	77	87
Mean	133	184	52	56	48	47	61	57	52	59	66	53	81	73

Years	N		Urban** Cohesion (average)		Rural Cohesion (average)		Index of Likeness (average)		Majorities in Opposition (percentages)		URBAN VICTORIES Type I		Type II	
	S	H	S	H	S	H	S	H	S	H	S	H	S	H
1961	37	133	37	35	33	34	89	89	11	8	25	36	92	92
1963	75	110	31	39	29	36	92	87	12	16	33	65	84	96
1965	84	170	31	38	26	27	88	82	27	36	43	67	80	86
1967	114	164	29	33	37	33	88	79	13	39	40	72	90	86
1969	89	165	31	32	27	27	89	87	9	22	50	64	82	91
1971	110	266	38	31	30	25	86	84	17	31	58	73	92	90
1973	110	221	38	44	40	25	88	85	9	19	40	52	95	86
1974	204	146	32	44	33	31	86	85	18	20	72	52	87	84
1975	244	243	48	48	33	29	73	80	46	23	54	73	77	93
1977	261	223	37	48	33	37	83	74	26	31	66	70	81	88
Mean	133	184	35	39	32	30	86	83	19	24	48	62	86	89

* For a definition of terms, see Table 7.1.

**Senate: 1961-1965, rural districts = 0 percent of the population in places of 2,500 or more, urban = the remainder; 1967-1974, rural = less than 60 percent lives in places of 2,500, urban = the remainder; 1975-1977, rural = less than 50 percent lives in places of 2,500, urban = the remainder.

House: 1961-1965, rural = 0 percent lives in places of over 2,500, urban = over 60 percent lives in places of 2,500; 1967-1974, rural = 0 percent lives in places of 2,500, urban = over 50 percent lives in places of 2,500; 1975-1977, rural = less than 50 percent lives in places of over 4,000, urban = over 50 percent lives in places of over 20,000 population.

SOURCE: Roll calls compiled by the author from Montana House and Senate Journals, 1961-1977.

more consistent over time. Finally, what makes for a more competitive situation in Montana is the fact that both parties have been cohesive, but in Vermont it was the Democrats who were most cohesive and then only for a period in the mid- to late 1960s.

The voting record in Montana reveals a mature and, relative to the record in many other state legislatures around the country, rather important party system. There is a party consciousness at large in the Montana legislature that transcends particular circumstances in either house. On no occasion between 1961 and 1977 did session-to-session fluctuations in Democratic cohesion within the houses vary in different directions. When the Democrats increased their cohesion in one house, it either increased or remained the same in the other and vice versa. Although the Republicans were not as consistent, the general flow of the data over the period is very similar for both houses. Product-moment correlation coefficients between party cohesion in the two houses of the legislature for the ten sessions studied are .83 for the Democrats and .78 for the Republicans.

From the historical perspective, there seems to be a weak and qualified general trend away from party-based voting in the House. The IPL, for instance, reached its two highest points in 1974 and 1977, yet the 1965 and 1967 sessions were the ones most clearly associated with changes in party voting. The data have remained fairly constant since then. In 1965 a sharp increase in Democratic cohesion accompanied a steep rise in the percentage of Democratic seats. In 1967 the Democratic percentage of the seats fell back, but the party's cohesion remained high (64). That same year, the year of the first reapportioned session, saw the Republicans' cohesion drop from 57 to 43. It has never recovered. Similar happenings took place in the Senate, where Democratic cohesion rose from 47 to 58 between 1963 and 1965 and Republican cohesion fell from 54 to 40 between 1965 and 1967.

Overall, the Democrats have controlled the battlefield. In the ten sessions they voted on the winning side of the total list of 1,840 House roll calls 73 percent of the time and 81 percent of the time on the 1,330 Senate roll calls. When the parties were in opposition their percentages were lower — 53 percent for the House and 66 percent for the Senate. A slowly declining percentage of Democrats in the Senate means that their winning MIO percentages fell from 70 in 1961–1965 to 56 for the 1974–1977 sessions. In the House an increasing number of Democrats has improved their winning MIO percentage from 17 percent in 1961–1963 to 82 percent in 1975 and 1977. The correlation between the years in which the sessions were held and Democratic MIO success is .80 in the House, where they gained seats over the period, and − .48 in the Senate, where they lost seats.

The issues that have been associated with party conflict in both chambers have narrowed from a broad array prior to reapportionment to an agenda dominated by taxation and labor issues in the 1967, 1969, and 1971 sessions. Those issues plus national resource and environmental issues were important in the 1973 through 1977 sessions. Labor bills dealing with unemployment compensation and the minimum wage provide a thread of continuity throughout the sixteen-year period; one can always count on labor bills to spur intensely partisan roll call responses. Laws regulating the railroads have also sparked party voting in nearly every session. Political questions such as those dealing with the franchise, legislative structure and performance, and elections also are associated with partisan voting. A close inspection of the issue content of highly competitive roll calls reveals how the rural-urban variable can be overridden by party label. In 1967, for instance, a bill providing for the distribution of liquor taxes to the cities touched two topics that generally switch on rural-urban hostilities, liquor and municipal finances. But on that bill House Democrats were united with a cohesion of 94, and the Republicans voted on the opposite side with a cohesion of 60; legislators from the most urban districts split 44 percent to 56 percent, and legislators from the most rural districts were split 50 percent to 50 percent. A close inspection of the issue content of party votes for which the IPL is 20 points below the yearly average in both houses throughout the period reveals that to an impressive extent the issues that have concerned Montana as a polity over the last twenty years have found expression in partisanship. This is another indication that Montana is unique among the rural states in terms of the role played by parties in the political system.

Legislative Voting: Urban Versus Rural

It is necessary to make a judgment concerning the landscape of rural-urban voting in Montana. The data in Table 7.5 do this in a manner similar to what was done for Vermont and Mississippi. Senators and representatives were classified by size of district, and measures of cohesion of rural and urban delegations, conflict between the two, and the success of the urban group were taken. With district boundaries changing on three different occasions, operational definitions of rural and urban needed to be changed as well to ensure that enough cases existed for proper analysis. In the House, the membership was trichotomized by size of place, and the middle range of legislators was omitted from the analysis. In general it was possible to maintain definitions that are statistically meaningful, intuitively satisfactory, and close to those used for the other states.

What we find is that rural-urban distinctions in Montana are even less important than they are in Vermont and Mississippi. Although the cohesion of rural and urban lawmakers in all three states is very similar, the conflict between the two groups in Montana is lower. The percentage of the time that majorities of the urban and rural delegations voted in opposition (the MIO score) was much lower in Montana. On only 19 percent of the Senate votes and 24 percent of the House votes were urban and rural majorities in opposition. In Mississippi the figures were 33 percent and 43 percent, and in Vermont they were 36 percent and 35 percent. The index of group likeness between the urban and rural legislators was also higher in Montana.

Urban delegations have voted on the winning side in a huge majority of the votes recorded, 86 percent in the Senate and 89 percent in the House. They are also more likely to win than are the rural members when the two groups line up on opposing sides of an issue. Reapportionment, however, seems to have had little direct effect on this process. The Senate, which was more malapportioned than the House, displays the greatest increase in urban success between the 1963 and 1965 sessions, prior to reapportionment. The House showed its best urban gain between 1961 and 1963. Nevertheless, reapportionment did increase the number of urban senators in 1965, and they have done better since that time. The important point seems to be that the rural-urban conflict has always been minimal. When it has increased, as in the 1975 session of the Senate and the 1970 session of the House, the urban delegation's success on MIO roll calls has been above average.

Because rural-urban voting in Montana has been so weak, it has not played an important role in party voting. The parties have not been weakened in any consistent fashion by the fact that their membership has often been fairly evenly split on the rural-urban variable. Even when the analysis is narrowed to treat those specific issues in individual sessions that display weak party voting and have at face value a rural-urban component, the rural-urban factor remains absent. Party has usually survived what must be considered a truly inhospitable environment — a huge, sparsely settled state with a few regionally isolated small cities, a state in which the statehouse membership of both parties is likely to be made up of legislators both from the isolated rural counties and from the larger population centers. In the 1977 session, for instance, the ten roll calls that created the greatest havoc (cohesion was less than 10) for the unity of each party in each house were assessed to determine if the rural-urban split within the parties was responsible for the low cohesion scores. It was not.

In the Senate, where tau coefficients based on the rural-urban split and the voting response were tabulated, the coefficient averaged .18 for the Democrats and .19 for the Republicans. In the House there was somewhat more division within the parties based on the size of district. There the tau averaged .29 for the Democrats and .33 for the Republicans. These coefficients, drawn from optimal circumstances, are weak and are the exception, not the rule. Clearly, an inspection of the entire period reveals that it is the political party and not the spatial nature of the district that counts in Montana, and in the great majority of cases the rural-urban factor melts away when it bumps up against the heat generated by party.

Strict urban-versus-rural voting happens so rarely in the Montana legislature that it produces a number of roll call votes so small that it is nearly impossible to establish generalizations about the issues involved. For instance, in the three Senate sessions of 1961, 1963, and 1965, only three roll calls were held that produced a rural-urban index of group likeness that was 20 points below the yearly average. Thus high likeness scores did not hide occasional excursions into rural-urban conflict as they did in Mississippi. In the 1974, 1975, and 1977 sessions, six votes on outdoor recreation and conservation, four on local-government operations, and three on the Equal Rights Amendment (ERA) were associated with rural-urban conflict.

The House was also somewhat barren of rural-urban conflict over the period, although from time to time singular issues did appear: an urban renewal vote and a vote concerning livestock on the highways in 1969, hunting and fishing licenses in 1963, an abortion issue a decade later, and a bill defining "isolation" of school districts for purposes of dispensing aid in 1971 are examples. But overall, the kinds of questions one would expect to trigger varying responses from legislators representing urban and rural districts simply don't. In the 1963 session of the House, for instance, bills on posting land, using salmon eggs as fish bait, nonresident hunters, and the powers of the Fish and Game Commission encountered no rural-urban conflict. In that same session, a bill dealing with off-street parking in cities produced an IGL of 93 between the most-urban and the most-rural members. At the same time, three votes on alcoholic beverages that would have dropped the IGL figure like buckshot in Mississippi sailed through the Montana legislature with scores of 92, 94, and 88. In 1973 votes on gambling, horse racing, and contraception were unrelated to the urban population of the districts. Finally, although a few votes on environmental and energy questions in recent years show an inkling of linkage to rural-urban factors, there is simply no way to judge that possible linkage at this time.

There is some indication that Waldron's tripartite regional classification may contain clues about the voting behavior of Montana's legislators, especially in the House of Representatives. An analysis of a series of roll calls in the 1977 session reveals that on several occasions when the cohesion of both parties was very low, the cohesion of regional delegations was high. But even in such cases cohesion scores of regional delegations rarely rise as high as 50. Oddly, it is often only the western, diversified region that is strongly cohesive. On two votes to amend the state constitution — one to raise the age of majority to nineteen and the other to establish annual sessions of the legislature — representatives from the region west of the Great Divide reached a cohesion of 68 and 64, respectively. This kind of pattern in the House is very exceptional, however, and in the Senate Waldron's regions had almost no impact at all.

Although party-government purists would hardly applaud the Montanan system, and some observers on the scene do not pay great attention to the role of political parties in legislative policymaking, the fact that party beats out region and rural-urban differences as a unifier in legislative voting is important, especially when compared to other rural states. It attests to the resiliency of party even in environments as seemingly inhospitable as Montana's — which is big, regionalized, and packed with cultural differences. It also demonstrates at least one case in which party competition outside the legislature is fierce, party voting inside the legislature is quite high, and both factors are enwrapped by a rural topography.

Summary

In the absence of party we find in Mississippi a fairly clear model of the stereotyped rural legislature. There is a regional factor (Delta versus Hills), which has decreased in importance in recent times. Rural-urban conflict in Mississippi is more pronounced than in either Montana or Vermont, although it is not as strong as one might expect, given the literature on the subject. Rural-versus-urban voting has been triggered by "morality" legislation for the most part, although that is on the wane. Vermont treats us to a special dynamic; a "morning-glory" party system in the legislature that opened with the coming of the first Democratic governor in a century and closed just as quickly when he left office. The rural-urban variable has added complexity to the panorama of Vermont voting behavior but sheds little causative explanation on events. Party stands above either regional or spatial variables in Montana. Rural-urban differences are not important, and region adds little to our understanding of why Montana's legislators vote the way they do.

The odds that reapportionment may have made a significant change in the way policy is hammered into form in these three rural states are starkly diminished by roll call analysis. In some cases additional numbers of urban legislators meant that in head-to-head competition with rural members the urban delegation was more likely to win. But in other cases increased rural cohesion negated the increased number of urban legislators. Overall, the urban delegations have nearly always been on the winning side of contested roll calls before and after reapportionment. From an empirical search of 8,000 contested roll calls in three states over forty-four years one may, quite literally, count on the fingers of two hands the times rural delegations "ganged up" on their urban colleagues and won. Another nail, if you please, for the reapportionment coffin.

Notes

1. Lee F. Anderson, Meredith W. Watts, Jr., and Allen R. Wilcox, *Legislative Roll Call Analysis* (Evanston, Ill.: Northwestern University Press, 1966), pp. 5–6; Malcolm E. Jewell and Samuel C. Patterson, *The Legislative Process in the United States,* 2d ed. (New York: Random House, 1973), p. 443.

2. George S. Blair, *American Legislatures* (New York: Harper and Row, 1967), pp. 273–275.

3. John H. Fenton and Donald W. Chamberlayne, "The Literature Dealing with the Relationships Between Political Processes, Socio-Economic Conditions, and Public Policies in the American States: A Bibliographical Essay," *Polity* 1 (Spring 1969), pp. 388–394. See also Edward G. Carmines, "The Mediating Influence of State Legislatures on the Linkage Between Interparty Competition and Welfare Policies," *American Political Science Review* 68 (September 1974), pp. 1118–1124; and Edward T. Jennings, Jr., "Competition, Constituencies, and Welfare Policies in American States," *American Political Science Review* 73 (June 1979), pp. 414–429.

4. The most complete is a study of twenty-six state senates by Hugh L. LeBanc, "Voting in State Senates: Party and Constituency Influences," *Midwest Journal of Political Science* 13 (February 1969), pp. 33–57.

5. C. Richard Hofstetter, "Malapportionment and Roll Call Voting in Indiana, 1923–1963: A Computer Simulation," *Journal of Politics* 33 (February 1971), pp. 92–111.

6. John Grumm, "The Kansas Legislature: Republican Coalition," in Samuel C. Patterson, ed., *Midwest Legislative Politics* (Iowa City: Institute of Public Affairs, University of Iowa, 1967), pp. 37–67.

7. Bruce W. Robeck, "Urban-Rural and Regional Voting Patterns in the California Senate Before and After Reapportionment," *Western Political Quarterly* 23 (December 1970), pp. 785–794. See also Bruce W. Robeck, "Legislative Partisanship, Constituency, and Malapportionment: The Case of California," *American Political Science Review* 66 (December 1972), pp. 1246–1255. John R. Owens, Edmond Costatini, and Louis F. Weschler, *California Politics and Parties* (London: MacMillan and Company, 1970).

8. Duane Lockard, "Legislative Politics in Connecticut," *American Political*

Science Review 48 (March 1954), pp. 166–173; Sheldon Goldman, *Roll Call Behavior in the Massachusetts House of Representatives* (Amherst, Mass.: Bureau of Government Research, University of Massachusetts, 1968); Thomas A. Flinn, "The Outline of Ohio Politics," *Western Political Quarterly* 13 (September 1960), pp. 702–721.

9. Ronald D. Hedlund and Charles W. Wiggins, "Legislative Politics in Iowa," in Patterson, *Midwest Legislative Politics,* pp. 7–36.

10. Douglas S. Gatlin, "The Development of a Responsible Party System in the Florida Legislature," in James A. Robinson, ed., *State Legislative Innovation* (New York: Praeger Publishers, 1973), pp. 1–45.

11. Susan Welch and Eric H. Carlson, "The Impact of Party on Voting Behavior in a Nonpartisan Legislature," *American Political Science Review* 67 (September 1973), pp. 866–867. G. Theodore Mitau, *Politics in Minnesota* (Minneapolis: University of Minnesota Press, 1960), pp. 66–68.

12. Jack E. Holmes, *Politics in New Mexico* (Albuquerque: University of New Mexico Press, 1967), pp. 279–281; Roy D. Morey, *The Office of Governor in Arizona* (Tucson: University of Arizona Press, 1965), pp. 25–27.

13. Emil Lee Bernick, *Legislative Voting Behavior and Partisan Cohesion in a One-Party Dominant Legislature* (Norman, Okla: Bureau of Government Research, 1973), p. 10.

14. David A. Leuthold, "The Legislature in Missouri's Political System," in Patterson, *Midwest Legislative Politics,* pp. 67–88.

15. Alan L. Clem, "Roll Call Voting Behavior in the South Dakota Legislature," *Public Affairs* (May 1966), pp. 3–6; JeDon Emenhiser, "Utah's Legislative Politics," in Susanne A. Stroiber, ed., *Legislative Politics in the Rocky Mountain West* (Boulder, Colo.: Bureau of Governmental Research, University of Colorado, 1967), pp. 63–106; James J. Best, "The Impact of Reapportionment on the Washington House of Representatives," in Robinson, *State Legislative Innovation,* pp. 136–182.

16. Jewell and Patterson, *Legislative Process,* 2d ed., p. 447.

17. John C. Wahlke, Heinz Eulau, William Buchanan, and LeRoy C. Ferguson, *The Legislative System: Explorations in Legislative Behavior* (New York: John Wiley and Sons, 1962), p. 425.

18. Thomas Page, "Urban-Rural Division in the Kansas Legislature," in Charles Press and Oliver Williams, eds., *Democracy in the Fifty States* (Chicago: Rand McNally and Company, 1966), pp. 366–376.

19. William C. Havard and Loren P. Beth, *The Politics of Misrepresentation: Rural-Urban Conflict in the Florida Legislature* (Baton Rouge: Louisiana State University Press, 1962); Malcolm B. Parsons, "Quasi-partisan Conflict in a One-Party Legislative System: The Florida Senate, 1947–1961," *American Political Science Review* 56 (September 1962), pp. 605–614.

20. Lee Taylor, *Urban-Rural Problems* (Belmont, Calif.: Dickenson Publishing Company, 1968), p. 81.

21. Wilder W. Crane, Jr., "Do Representatives Represent?" *Journal of Politics* 22 (May 1960), pp. 295–299.

22. Murray C. Havens, *City vs. Farm* (Tuscaloosa: University of Alabama Press, 1957).

23. Samuel C. Patterson, "Dimensions of Voting Behavior in a One-Party State Legislature," *Public Opinion Quarterly* 26 (Summer 1962), pp. 185–200; Samuel A. Kirkpatrick, *The Legislative Process in Oklahoma* (Norman: University of Oklahoma Press, 1978), p. 156.

24. Glen T. Broach, "A Comparative Dimensional Analysis of Partisan and Urban-Rural Voting in State Legislatures," *Journal of Politics* 34 (August 1972), p. 917.

25. Harlan Hahn, *Urban-Rural Conflict* (Beverly Hills, Calif.: Sage Publications, 1971), pp. 141–144; Gordon E. Baker, *Rural vs. Urban Political Power* (Garden City, N.Y.: Doubleday, 1955); Hofstetter, "Malapportionment and Roll Call Voting," p. 98. See also John G. Grumm, "The Systematic Analysis of Blocs in the Study of Legislative Behavior," *Western Political Quarterly* 18 (June 1965), pp. 350–362.

26. William J. Keefe, "The Comparative Study of the Role of Political Parties in State Legislatures," *Western Political Quarterly* 9 (June 1956), pp. 726–742.

27. Frank J. Sorauf, *Party Politics in America,* 3d ed. (Boston: Little, Brown and Company, 1976), p. 358.

28. Thomas R. Dye, *Politics in States and Communities* (Englewood Cliffs, N.J.: Prentice-Hall, 1969), p. 138. See also Judson L. James, *American Political Parties in Transition* (New York: Harper and Row Publishers, 1974), p. 214.

29. Edgar Litt, *The Political Cultures of Massachusetts* (Cambridge, Mass.: MIT Press, 1965), p. 186.

30. Robert W. Becker, Frieda L. Foote, Mathias Lubega, and Stephen V. Monsma, "Correlates of Legislative Voting: The Michigan House of Representatives, 1954–1961," *Midwest Journal of Political Science* 6 (November 1962), pp. 384–396.

31. John H. Fenton, *Midwest Politics* (New York: Holt, Rinehart and Winston, 1966), p. 40.

32. Thomas A. Flinn, "Party Responsibility in the States: Some Causal Factors," *American Political Science Review* 58 (March 1964), pp. 60–71; Daniel M. Ogden, Jr., and Hugh A. Bone, *Washington Politics* (New York: New York University Press, 1960).

33. M. Margaret Conway, "Party Responsibility: Fact or Fiction in American State Legislatures?" in James B. Kessler, ed., *Empirical Studies of Indiana Politics* (Bloomington: Indiana University Press, 1970), pp. 68–72.

34. Marvin Harder and Carolyn Rampey, *The Kansas Legislature* (Lawrence: University Press of Kansas, 1972), pp. 134–138.

35. Mitau, *Politics in Minnesota,* p. 71. See also Edward R. Brandt's precise treatment, "Legislative Voting Behavior in Minnesota," in Millard L. Dieske and Edward R. Brandt, *Perspectives on Minnesota Government and Politics* (Dubuque, Iowa: Kendal/Hunt Publishing Company, 1977), pp. 202–222.

36. V. O. Key, Jr., *Southern Politics in State and Nation* (New York: Alfred A. Knopf, 1949), p. 233.

37. *Mississippi House Journal* (Jackson, Miss., 1966), p. 767.

38. Theodore Lowi, "Toward Functionalism in Political Science: The Case of Innovations in Party Systems," *American Political Science Review* 57 (September 1963), pp. 570–583. See also Charles W. Wiggins, "Party Politics in the Iowa Legislature," *Midwest Journal of Political Science* 11 (February 1967), pp. 86–97.

39. Frank M. Bryan, *Yankee Politics in Rural Vermont* (Hanover, N.H.: University Press of New England, 1974), p. 184.

40. *Journal of the House of the State of Vermont,* Adjourned Session, 1974, p. 143.

A Concluding Essay:
Life Without Cities —
Techno-Politics in Rural America

Two roads diverged in a wood, and I—
I took the one less traveled by,
And that has made all the difference.

— Robert Frost
The Road Not Taken

Using Frost's words to begin this essay may be as pretentious as a March dandelion. I'll risk it — not only because I think the odds that there is at least some wisdom in what follows are only 20 to 80 against me — not bad for a social scientist — but also because the central hypothesis *is* a departure. It may seem outrageous and stick in the craw of many of my urban brothers and sisters, and it is a road less traveled. My claim, simply stated, is that the rural states ought to be given the pole position in the study of political development. To catch the directions of America's future governance, the advice is to cast your gaze behind you to the backbeyond states. For previews of what is to come are most likely to occur there.

At the outset, a pair of admissions: Yes, I have a red-neck's chip on my shoulder, carried with me from my high school graduation (class of 1959, numbering seven) into the halls of academia and glued there by the subtle derisions cast by an urban profession. Although I deny it, the urge to cast it off may have spawned the desire to write this essay and will influence its contents. If so, then consider it a lawyer's brief and beware. Yes, the approach is essentially speculative and parts company with the technical presentation used in the bulk of this volume. I remember a November day without sun when, over a snowless forest floor, I hunted white-tailed deer in strange country. Lee told me to take a compass. I didn't. She waited supper. The heuristic skies of social science are forever cloudy, bereft of a westward setting sun to chalk one's courses by. And what snows have fallen are crisscrossed with confusion. But there is no progress in stillness, and I do not believe, as the crusty old Vermonter is said to have told the wayfaring stranger, "You can't get there from here." It is in hesitant wanderings that the density is cut back and the pathways for the future are marked.

Anyone who has long occupied a professorial role in the social sciences has been confronted by the undergraduate bemoaning the fact that his data did not fall into the predicted patterns and wondering if his grade would suffer as a result. There is, of course, a pat answer. If one's methods and techniques are sound and the hypothesis is reasonable, then negation may be more important than substantiation. When is a hypothesis reasonable? When it is generated by notions that are pretty well accepted in the field or when the logic itself stands on its own. From above this volume resembles a graveyard of broken hypotheses — a battlefield where wounded paradigms lie scattered among the dead ones, and those left standing are few and far between. It is time to bite the bullet, for aside from the descriptive-analytical treatment, I must contend that my essential contribution depends on the saliency of knowing that what was expected to happen did not — or did, but in peculiar ways.

What was expected (and what still is expected by all too many political scientists) is wrapped up in a grand hypothesis that entails a substantive judgment, a qualitative axiom, and a resultant logical dynamic. The judgment is that rural and urban living places house different people, cultures, and value-sets. The axiom is that rural equals backward and urban equals forward. The dynamic is that rural and urban political systems will continually be at each other's throats. As Paul Carter so poignantly put it, "Town and country have been putting each other down, with opposing stereotypes of the country bumpkin and the city slicker since the barefoot prophets of Israel left their flocks and herds in the hills to go down and denounce the sophisticated sins of Jerusalem."[1]

True, massification theorists, including many rural sociologists (directly) and a sprinkling of political scientists (obliquely), have suggested that the master hypothesis has lost its sting. But by far the more striking truth is the degree to which the literature is still shot through with propositions flowing from the old hypothesis. Although they are likely to be more explicit in the popular crust of the literature, they exist everywhere. Moreover, when political scientists do see air in the traditional expectations, the direction the new condition will take is usually accepted as a given, that is, rural areas will *follow* urban areas, will become like them — they will, in short, urbanize. The urban condition is, the thinking goes, a mandatory way station on the road to the political future.[2]

The concept of rural as a place of distinct peoples with distinct political cultures is fraught with difficulty (Chapter 1). In the aggregate (Chapter 2) rural citizens act more progressively on many issues than do citizens of urban states, and the rural-urban conflict is minimal on many important dimensions of the policymaking process (chapters 6 and 7). Moreover, in the central chapters we found again and again that predictions based on the old model simply failed to pan out. The existence of stronger participatory habits in rural Mississippi is an example. One of the major reasons for the weakness of the traditional expectations is the weakness of the "urban equals higher SES linkage," which is an essential component of the majority view. It will be remembered (Chapter 1) that rural people differ from urban people on birthright characteristics much more than on achieved characteristics. Thus in Montana and Vermont we found that rural areas did not correlate negatively with many socioeconomic indicators (Chapters 3, 4, and 5). Even when they did, it was often shown that the SES was not meaningful in ways that many would predict it should be. It was not, for instance, an important seed-bed for the Democratic breakthrough in Vermont.

It would be silly to claim that one can find herein a sure-footed stalking of the traditional view. Yet the cumulative effect can be said to lend the traditional view no credence. Too many contradictions abound. It is from the vacuum created by these very contradictions that the central thesis of these paragraphs of final thinking emerges. Although the book was launched as an exercise in descriptive analysis rather than as an exercise in model building, by following the leads of previous scholars I have been caught up in a longing for pattern and uniformity. But the appearance of a conceptual adhesive was not to be. Instead the face of these rural states is pockmarked with craters, devoid of design. Moreover, political events are becoming less predictable over time. The atoms that make up the matter of politics have heated up, and they are beginning to fly about. In each of the three states we have investigated, a major geographic pattern has melted away: the Delta-Hills dichotomy in Mississippi, the mountain rule in Vermont, and the high line in Montana. At the same time a heavy political yoke has been lifted — Republicanism in Vermont, legalized white supremacy in Mississippi, and the Anaconda Company in Montana. The certitude of friends-and-neighbors politics has weakened. In Mississippi Republicanism is emerging from its SES incubator. In Vermont the northwest enclave of Democratic strength has been universalized. Everywhere one looks, faults are appearing in the political bedrock. In a nutshell, the input processes of the rural political systems, never marked by clear uniformities, are becoming hopelessly unpredictable, free-winging, unstable, and therefore weak. In fact the traditional input processes are becoming neutralized and immobilized, *especially* in rural states. They are sitting ducks for bureaucracies.

Let's nail it down. I argue, not uniquely, that the American political experience is entering a second phase of pluralism, marked by the ascendancy of public and quasi-public actors in the arenas of political give-and-take. The process, in other words, is being subsumed by bureaucracies. Make no normative judgments at this point. Ride along on the premise that there is no conspiratorial working-out of some unseen plan, whether it be "creeping socialism" or "the military-industrial establishment." Chalk it up to the consequences of modernism (more on this momentarily) and our insatiable thirst for egalitarianism, which has, despite good intentions, castrated the great forces that countervail the administrative state and traditional political institutions such as parties. Executives are weak; legislatures are consumed by "the electoral connection."[3] The technological imperative ensures a wider and wider discretionary role for the agencies, and then the pluralist imperative divides and conquers—ensuring decision making at the level of the lowest common denominator. The agencies monopolize the information systems, engage in the blackmail of expertise,[4] and act more and more as lobbyists on their own behalf. Meanwhile, legislatures everywhere have thrown in the towel, tossing their representative function after their rule-making function, asking in law that if the agencies must fashion policy that they at least do it only after having maximized as much as is feasible[5] the input of "the people" or, more accurately, the attentive groups—often other public or quasi-public organizations. Agencies are only too happy to oblige, in form at least, and to strengthen their case by coloring their policies with democratic respectability. Understand, the bureaucracy will become no monolithic powerhouse, no island of stability in a political universe gone haywire. Bureaucracy too will atomize, and the dangerous inability of anyone to steer the American ship of state will continue and accelerate.

Most agree that it was the urban-industrial revolution that set in motion and then sustained the character of American governance through World War II. That character has been changed radically in the last thirty years in ways akin to those outlined above. What is the new causal base? What is the conditioner of governance for the next century as urban industrialism was for the last? Technology. We are living in a "postmodern" world,[6] a world in which technology defines the nature of life and politics. Technology and the technological ethic is the lifeblood of the administrative state. In order to lead in the development of the new administrative technostate, rural areas therefore must possess two qualities. One, they must have stepped across the technocratic threshold and be as fully immersed in the environment of technology as are the urban states. Two, they must possess fewer of the impediments to a smooth transition from the old system to the new than the urban states have. In other words, they must be free of conditions that slow the process down.

Those conditions exist in the urban-industrial states that still contain elements of the old thesis: stronger legislatures, more-professional politicians, and more-powerful governors, viable party systems, complex social structures, heterogeneous economic interests (California is both the most urban and the most agricultural state in the nation), and lumpy population distributions (New York City, Buffalo, and Woodstock in New York State, for instance). These complex societies are difficult to program, and programmed life is basic to the technostate. There are too many interest groups, political machines, ethnic enclaves, and competing urban magnetic centers. Just as those nations most prepared to refight World War I in 1939 were burdened by the hardware of the past while Germany, denied access to the old paraphernalia, leaped into the forefront of mechanized warfare, so too will those states in America with the least political baggage left over from the urban-industrial revolution lead in the movement toward mechanized government.

Mississippi, Montana, and Vermont have all been isolated in one way or another from the mainstream of development in America: Mississippi, by the Civil War and the negatives that followed; Montana, by space itself; Vermont, by an inhospitable topography and a rugged climate. In all three states, a less than optimum economic potential has continually thwarted attempts to urbanize. Those states, and others like them, simply sat out the urban-industrial revolution. I argue that that "sitting out" will facilitate the rise of the technostate in those areas. But if rural states did not urbanize, how is it possible for them to have built the second prerequisite for leadership in political development, a techno-based socioeconomic infrastructure? That question poses difficulties only if urbanism is a precondition for postmodern society. It is not.

Part of the metro-bias that pervades American professional circles is the image of rural America as "backward." I will grant that this view has lost emphasis in recent years, but ruralites are still called upon to establish their credentials first. Condescension is still a prominent feature of the urbanite's demeanor in a rural-urban professional conversation, the chip on my shoulder notwithstanding. Urbanites are still surprised and even amazed at the degree to which rural areas have advanced technologically. Cadres of rural economists, sociologists, and agricultural engineers have been quietly spreading the message for years, and the case need not be made again. But the degree to which the message has penetrated the other culture, the majority, urban culture, leaves much to be desired. Perhaps one of the reasons is that urbanites don't want to believe that rural America has developed, that there is no going home, that the clink and crash of the antique mechanical cash register in the old country store has been replaced by a near-silent, efficient whir while bright orange signals flash the price of coffee. In the milk room of a small, one-family farm on the upper Connecticut River in New England there hangs a cryptic green printout from a computer at Cornell University that lists an array of variables for every cow on the place. Now and then the message "cull" appears on the sheet—a programmed death sentence for "Betsy" or "Ann," no longer family cows but walking milk stations in a highly efficient economic enterprise. And that farm is as "family farm" as is possible. Rural America is "in." Believe it.[7]

Once the communications revolution of the 1950s and 1960s had run its course, techno-based life-styles were substantively in place in rural America. In fact technology is a principal precondition of the resettlement of rural places. People are moving back to the small towns in the backbeyond for many reasons. But once outside their technological cocoon they find the romanticism of the countryside wears very thin, very shortly. They need air conditioners in Mississippi to ward off the heat; televisions in Montana to ward off the loneliness of a huge, ever-present white-blue canopy—the big sky; and garden tractors and bug spray in Vermont to ward off the pain of growing backyard vegetables. It is nice to think about milking one's own Jersey cow. On a hot August afternoon amid the sweat and swirling flies, it is much nicer to think about sipping something cool at poolside.

Not only is nothing about nonmassed population distributions anathema to the growth of technology-based social systems, there is much about rural society that made the technological overlay flow quickly, evenly, and smoothly. I said that the new political structures would have easier sledding where objects of the old structure were scarce. The same is true for economic change. It is precisely because Mississippi was underdeveloped for a century that the level of its modernization today is so advanced. Neal R. Pierce, in discussing the new Mississippi economy, subtitles his work "From Cotton to Computers."[8] Rural America was virginal when, after World War II, the communications logjam was broken, the interstate highways wound their way into the outback, and television antennas cropped up overnight on the rooftops of distant farmhouses. As an example, Interstate 91, which gouged its way through rural Vermont with amazing ease, blasting through massive ridges, and spanning entire valleys (and in some cases villages) with giant steel spans, was stalled for several years because of the urban, industrial complex around the Springfield-Holyoke area in Massachusetts. One remembers traffic backed up for fifty miles as fall-foliage gazers tried to return to the megalopolis from Vermont but were bottlenecked by that urban impediment to the postmodern world. There were few institutionalized monkey wrenches available to be tossed into the machinery of the coming technostate in rural areas.

Another supposed roadblock to the technocratic development of rural America was the ruralite's cussedness. The farmers of upper New England would sit on stumps with shotguns across their knees. Montanan cowboys would stoically refuse to bring in the cattle from the open ranges. In Mississippi, farmers and lumbermen would cling to the old ways. Ruralites were scared of change, confused by modernization, and unwilling and/or unable to understand and accept technological innovation. No such thing. Show me a Vermont dairy farmer that would go back to handmilking, and I'll show you a flatlander who does it for fun. Show me a Montanan who will saddle up a horse when he can take a four-wheel-drive vehicle, and I'll show you a drugstore cowboy. Show me a logger in Mississippi who will give up his skidder for a pair of oxen, and I'll show you a counterculturist. The ruralite's hostility to technology turns out to be a myth. Why? Among other reasons,[9] because rural people by nature subscribe to the technological ethic, the reinforcing-value paradigm that has accompanied the arrival of postmodern society.

This is the ethic of perfection, of efficiency. There is a substantial amount of literature that suggests that the secular god of modern man is method, "the most perfect way."[10] Ends become lost from view. Goals are less important than technique. There arrives a "technology" for everything. "How to" books sell like hotcakes. A published technology (referred to as such) now exists for (believe it or not) the jilted—a how-to-mend-a-broken-heart book. The sensuous man and the sensuous woman are programmed for perfect performance, armed with manuals of technique. Psychologists of sport tell us that professional football's great appeal is not unrelated to its adaptability to television—each play is planned and designed beforehand in the huddle while commentators analyze why the last play worked or did not work. The excitement is in the anticipation of the method and the analysis of the event, not in the act as such. The "pause in the action" becomes the action itself. The armchair-quarterback syndrome is a poignant statement on life in a technological society. A brilliant run innovated after a broken play simply lacks the luster of a well-conceived run, performed with precision, with blocking well-planned and perfectly executed. And the team that is best at this perfection, with the computerized coach and plays "sent in" from some unseen superbrain system lurking on the sidelines, is the one people call "America's football team." Soccer and hockey won't do. Too chaotic, no time (for the watchers) to think. Meanwhile, the five Super Bowls held from 1975 to 1979 made it into the top seven TV shows seen by the American public in the 1970s. (The other two were "Roots" and "Gone With the Wind.")[11] The bible of the new religion of perfection was written as the 1970s began. *Jonathan Livingston Seagull*[12] was the story of a bird in search of perfect flight. It was in the perfection that joy was attained, and having been attained there was another level of perfect flight to be attempted. And so on into infinity. The book was an ode to the one best way, the technique, perfection for the sake of perfection. It outsold every single other book of the decade in the United States and was the only book to lead the bestseller list two years in a row (1972 and 1973).

The ethic of perfection or efficiency is as ingrained in the rural dweller's value-set as it is in that of the urban resident. Perhaps more. "It's not nice to fool mother nature," proclaimed the popular TV ad of the mid-1970s. True enough. Those who are close to nature learn from the most efficient of teachers. Nature is unforgiving, totally rational, blindly fair, *ungodly* efficient. If one depends on an interface with nature for one's economic well-being, one understands very quickly the neutral, and therefore fearsome, penalties for sloppy behavior. Rural people are again and again confronted by this relationship, a one-sided yardstick against which performance is measured. There is no appeal. The tomatoes should have been covered. The weeds should have been pulled off the electric fence. The hay should have been raked. The snow tires should have been put on. And so forth. Feedback from the natural world is much like feedback from a computer. The computer doesn't care if 9,999 out of 10,000 statements are correct, a misspelling is a misspelling, and it heartlessly aborts your job. My oxen don't care how many hours I've spent on the beans. They'll munch away a row in no time, heartlessly. I should have fixed the fence. I was inefficient. To have a fence that works perfectly becomes an obsession. The ethic of efficiency is common to rural America. Ruralites have always delighted in the timesaving device, the interlocking of machines that does a better job, in a word—technology.

Life in rural America is typified by an economic system that is techno-based; that is, its essential characteristic is its interrelatedness. The catch-words are planning, design, interlock, connection, feedback. What about the other half of "socioeconomic"? The current widsom is that rural life still dances to the tune of personalism and informality. Face-to-face relations persist. One's neighbors are also one's friends, close friends. Friendship exists in the context of neighborhood. Reject this view. Other things being equal, these conditions are more likely to occur in the cities than in the countryside. They are density-dependent. Again, the Achilles' heel of the current wisdom is the failure to appreciate technology's impact on rural America. It is critical to remember that Riesman's crowd is lonely because technology cut it loose from interpersonal moorings. It separated work place from living place, neighbor from neighbor, friend from friend. It built commuter trains, highrises, elevators, supermarkets, and subways, taxis, and buses. Technology turned a mass of people broken up into neighborhoods into a mass of people walking past one another in solitude.

Technology has affected rural areas in another way. It has allowed for isolation by physical space. Whereas before one stopped at his first neighbor's house, now one drives to a friend's house twenty miles away. It is no longer necessary that economic and social relations overlap, producing the "deep" friendships of the frontier. The urbanite moving to the country today to establish this kind of interpersonalism will be sad to learn that it has vanished like the haymows, the corncribs, and the milk cans. Technology has, in a word, negated the necessity for close-knit life based on geographic proximity. It has provided the magic carpet to the isolation of space and distance. Rural neighbors no longer need each other. They need technological systems. As technology isolated person from person in the city, it is now isolating person from person in the countryside. It has given new meaning to the concept of space.

To summarize, the argument is that rural states will lead in the development of the modern administrative state because one, they are hobbled less by the older input mechanisms (such as strong party systems) and predictable channels of input behavior, both of which are dysfunctional. Two, they are rich in the causal energy that sustains the administrative state, technology, and have a socioeconomic environment with few impediments to further technocratic development. Three, they are equipped with a healthy and supportive techno-ethic—the search for efficiency and perfection. Four, their people relate to one another in noncommunal fashions. The social fabric of rural life matches the systems mentality of the economic framework.

What is the relationship of technology-based socioeconomic systems and politics? Why should public bureaucracies and technosystems thrive so well together? First of all, the input structures of modern governance are geared historically and theoretically to decentralized decision making, and the bureaucracy is geared to centralism. Granted, decision making within bureaucracies succumbs to the decentralist urge as well. But theoretically, decisions can be made in a hierarchical manner that *seem* to deal with the complexities of technological life,[13] and for the proper operation of democracies, semblance is critical. Bureaucracies can plan, evaluate, test, and coordinate in a manner that legislatures, for instance, cannot.

In the second place, the concept of feedback or cybernetics is as securely latched to the concept of technology as the shell is to a turtle's back. Cybernetics implies management, and management implies bureaucracy. Legislators can decide, but they cannot manage, even though they try with their interim committees and other oversight mechanisms. The results are more mismanagement than management, however. The truth is that a great deal of the bureaucrat's time is spent in preparing action scenarios that will neutralize all forms of extraorganizational input. Bureaucrats operate in spite of the directives laid on them from above or suggested to them from below. The techniques for pretending otherwise in a convincing manner would fill a separate volume. There is no other way to say it. As society becomes more and more complex and its elements more and more interrelated, the operation of the body politic craves day-by-day adjustment, a tinkering with the machinery. Whether they meet annually or biennially, create oodles of watchdog committees or none, legislatures are playing more and more the role of unwilling, deist creators who set the universe in motion and then are seen no more. If legislators have little luck in changing directions or fine-tuning events as they transpire, one wonders not why the public-hearing revolution has been hopelessly usurped. The code is technology. The cipher is management.

Third, and most important, bureaucracies can develop and operate the information systems that are the air ducts of technological society. Peter Drucker has said that knowledge has become the central capital, the cost center, and the crucial resource of the economy.[14] As the elements of life become more interrelated, the people of the democracies, through their representatives at the input stations, turn more of the decisions that affect their lives over to governments that are perceived as the one type of organization that acts at the macro level and that are, however imperfectly, controlled by the people. But to act at the macro level takes macro information, information that is organized, systematized, and, critically, seems neutral. Bureaucracies have it or can get it. Legislators do not, despite the best efforts of the new legislative staff services. Lynton Caldwell drives the point home when he says that a high priority for bureaucracies of the future will be "the transformation of information into useable knowledge. . . . In managing the post-modern society, the role of the public administrator becomes increasingly the management of knowledge."[15]

I accept the truth that "knowledge is power" (although there are those who debate the point) and agree with James Carroll of Syracuse University who has said that public bureaucracies must more and more be involved with "the exercise of influence, judgment and skill to affect who gets to *know* what, when, where, and why."[16]

Rural areas have another reinforcing variable that increases the likelihood that bureaucracies will establish fairly safe fiefdoms for the concoction of public policy—the phenomenon of citizen fatigue. As legislatures have turned over the rule-making function to bureaucracies, they have also, through guilty conscience or democratic inclination (one knows not which), insisted that the bureaucracies "take input" before decisions are made. They have created a quagmire of access points to ensure a free-flowing pipeline between citizen and policy. The civic burden on rural dwellers is awesome. They must pay attention to too many mouse holes; the result is that too many mice run free. The proliferation of SIDs (special improvement districts) of various shapes and sizes, of public hearings held by bureaucracies mandated to hold them, and of new boards, commissions, and panels—most using volunteer personnel and formed in the public interest—and finally the new visibility of electoral politics at all levels have overloaded the circuits of citizenry. Even in a participant culture, in which efficacy is high, there is not enough civic interest to go around. This is especially true in rural areas, where the ratio of participant opportunity to the number of potential participants overwhelms. The result is obvious. Access points go unattended. Government officials bemoan public apathy, and the bureaucracies go about their business heeding only the special interests that always find their way to public hearings.

Two potential caveats to the "ruralism means administrative state" model come to mind. First, if, as is claimed in Chapter 3, rural areas are not bastions of voter apathy (in fact may be wellsprings of participation), why is it that that kind of culture will allow an administrative state to develop? The principal point is that that participation is (with the exception of parts of Montana) not organized participation. A bureaucratic culture may well develop *more* easily under the camouflage of high levels of ballot-box activity that is fired by a participant ethic rather than by organizational interests. A second point is that the model is not inconsistent with high levels of interest-group participation, since the contention is that the bureaucracy, like the legislature before it, will after a time be cut to pieces by the pluralistic imperative. The kind of participation that might pull power back from bureaucracies is disciplined participation in the hands of people with the political or institutional power to use it. As long as participation is in the stratosphere of the general election or is at the bureaucratic doorstep but atomized, the bureaucracies will subsume it.

A second possible caveat reads as follows: Technology does not cause complexity (except to the extent that it lets us understand how complex things really are); it results from man's attempt to rationalize or simplify complexity as it exists. Then why should the technostate be so healthy in an environment that is less complex? On what does technology feed? The answer is that rural states are not *that* simple. There is plenty of complexity to whet the appetite of those people who seek to put it all together. Although the task of programming the fragmented urban state may be overwhelming, the rural states have enough raw material to challenge, but not to discourage. The application of EDP (electronic data processing) systems in rural state governments, for instance, often goes much more smoothly than in the urban states.

Whether or not we are barking up the wrong tree cannot be known in the near future. Nevertheless there are a pair of broad-gauged empirical references that indicate we are not completely off the scent. First, it is one of the axioms of modern life that technologies begin to shape the character of phenomena they are created to serve. Rather than designing technologies to serve our needs, we bend our needs to fit available technologies. It is also an axiom of modern life that technology promotes centralization, for uncentered decision making is intolerable to the technosystem. Instead of finding ways to fit governments in rural America to existing conditions, we will redesign those governments to fit the imperatives of administrative technosystems. The most obvious evidence of this tendency is the movement to bring rural governments "up to size" so that specialization and professionalism are possible and economically feasible. Centralization is the result. Hard-core administrative governance is unthinkable without it. Indeed, it is true that the rural state governments are considerably more centralized than are the urban state governments. Although local control and neighborhood government are thought to be a quality of rural life, precisely the opposite is true. Vermont is vastly more centralized than New Jersey or New York; Montana, substantially more centralized than Colorado; Mississippi, more centralized than Florida, Georgia, or Texas. Vermont, the most rural state in America when the 1970 census was taken, led every state but Alaska on increasing centralization between 1957 and 1969. Although the median state increased 4.2 points on Stephens's composite centralization index (See Chapter 2), Vermont increased 14.3 points. Although in the aggregate the positive relationship between centralism and ruralism is not strong, it does exist, and it shows that the disposition to local control in the urban states has outlasted that in the rural states.[17]

The second, more direct indicator of the tendency for rural states to out-bureaucratize the urban states is the simple statistic, per capita public employees. This factor has been referred to elsewhere as "bureaucratic load." It tells us, for instance, that in Montana in the mid 1970s there were 6.9 public employees for every 100 people in the state while in Connecticut and Rhode Island there were only 5. In Vermont there were 7.1 while across Lake Champlain in New York State there were 6.3. Although Mississippi's bureaucratic load was not great (5.8) at mid decade, only three states exceeded Mississippi's increase over the preceding twenty years. When all fifty states are plugged into the analysis, bureaucratic load and population density in the states correlates at − .46. Under controls for a number of other variables, such as party competition, Democratic strength, policy innovation, and federal aid, the relationship remains negative and moderately strong (− .25). Again, if it were not for the expectation that urbanism is a breeder of bureaucracy, this coefficient would have much less clout. The fact is, however, that the rural states are more centralized and more heavily bureaucratized than are the urban states. On these two measures (which are not unimportant) the rural states are ahead, they *lead* in political development in America.[18]

I am not arguing that life in the postmodern world is incompatible with the notion of democracy as it is generally understood. But I am arguing that the traditional input structures we set forth in the past to make democratic principles operational are not, in their present form, synchronized with reality. Whether or not to repair them may depend on the success of the current moves to democratize bureaucracy. The point is that the rural states are the places where these dilemmas are best investigated because they are where the movement toward the new technocracy is most advanced. The ascendant condition is one in which the traditional input mechanisms have been rendered impotent. The legislature is hamstrung by dual forces − an obsession with constituency and the urge to pass on complexities to experts. Meanwhile the bureaucracy maintains the appearance of order by attempting to implement decisions set in place by itself. These are themselves lowest-common-denominator reactions to a myriad of interests, including the "people" (through public hearings), the legislature, and an ever-growing swarm of special-interest groups. The rural states, unfettered by the habits of the past but steeped in the potion of the future, will be the first to display the dimensions of the new condition, however unpleasant that prospect may seem to those people who cling to the old norms.

Notes

1. Paul Carter, *The Twenties* (New York: Thomas Y. Crowell Company, 1968), p. 73.

2. Nels Anderson and K. Ishwaran, *Urban Sociology* (New York: Asia Publishing House, 1965), pp. 6-7.

3. David Mayhew, *Congress: The Electoral Connection* (New Haven: Yale University Press, 1974).

4. Paul Goldstone, *The Collapse of Liberal Empire* (New Haven: Yale University Press, 1977), pp. 51-53.

5. Daniel P. Moynihan, *Maximum Feasible Misunderstanding* (New York: Free Press, 1969).

6. Lynton Caldwell, "Managing the Transition to Post Modern Society," *Public Administration Review* 35 (November/December 1975), pp. 567-571.

7. Although I disagree with his use of the term "urbanization" when I think he means "technocratization," Lee Taylor's work is supportive: Lee Taylor, *Urban-Rural Problems* (Belmont, Calif.: Dickenson Publishing Company, 1968), pp. vii-viii.

8. Neal R. Pierce, *The Deep South States of America* (New York: W. W. Norton and Company, 1974), p. 207.

9. Frank M. Bryan, *Yankee Politics in Rural Vermont* (Hanover, N.H.: University Press of New England, 1974), pp. 241-245.

10. Jacques Ellul, *The Technological Society* (New York: Random House, 1964). See also Friedrich Juenger, *The Failure of Technology* (Hinsdale, Ill.: Henry Regnery, 1949); Victor C. Firkiss, *Technological Man: The Myth and the Reality* (New York: New York Times Company and Braziller, Inc., 1969); and Milford A. Sibley, *Technology and Utopian Thought* (Minneapolis, Minn.: Burgess Publishing Company, 1971).

11. David Gergen, "Collector's Item," *Public Opinion* 3 (December/January 1980), pp. 18, 43.

12. Richard Bach, *Jonathan Livingston Seagull* (New York: MacMillan, 1970).

13. The question of whether or not public bureaucracy, which is "antithetical" to pluralism, can withstand the urge to pluralize is very much open. See Nicholas Henry, "Bureaucracy, Technology, and Knowledge Management," *Public Administration Review* 35 (November/December 1975), pp. 572-578.

14. For a series of articles on this subject, see James D. Carroll and Nicholas Henry, eds., "Symposium of Knowledge Management," *Public Administration Review* 35 (November/December 1975), pp. 567-602.

15. Caldwell, "Managing the Transition to Post Modern Society," pp. 570-571.

16. James D. Carroll, "Service, Knowledge, and Choice: The Future as Post-Industrial Administration," *Public Administration Review* 35 (November/December 1975), pp. 578-581.

17. G. Ross Stephens, "State Centralization and the Erosion of Local Autonomy," *Journal of Politics* 36 (February 1974), pp. 44-76.

18. David H. Rosenbloom and Frank M. Bryan, "The Size of Public Bureaucracies: An Exploratory Analysis," (Paper presented at the Annual Meeting of the Midwest Political Science Association, Chicago, 1979).

Bibliographical Remarks

This book was designed to describe and analyze various components of the political process in rural America. In doing so three conceptually unique types of literature were consulted: (1) literature on general rural-urban differences, for which we owe a great debt to our brethren in sociology; (2) literature dealing with the hypothesis that served to focus the descriptive analytical treatment of specific political processes and patterns; (3) literature of a more general nature on governance in the three rural states used as case environments — Mississippi, Montana, and Vermont. Studies on the effect of rural-urban residence patterns on a sense of community satisfaction fit in the first category. Treatments of the relationships between ruralism and political breakthrough are an example of the second type, and V. O. Key's *Southern Politics in State and Nation* (see below), which has a chapter on Mississippi, is an example of the third. There is also some literature that is better discussed separately, although it might be squeezed into one of the three molds with varying degrees of difficulty.

A thorough listing of all relevant material would fill a book in itself, and moreover, this volume is heavily footnoted by chapter. What follows, therefore, is a selective listing with related commentary on some of the major works that have guided my research. I have also attempted to bring order to the process by emphasizing those sources that are particularly relevant to the spatial variable in the political process. Thus, from the huge array of works on civic participation, those I have found most useful in describing the rural-urban influence on participation are most likely to appear here. The reader may consult footnotes in the relevant chapters for a more complete listing.

Literature on Rural-Urban Differences

Scholarship on rural-urban differences has followed several pathways. There is, first, a shelf of works that concentrates on determining if rural-urban distinctions are associated with different types of population, social structure, attitudes, and behavior. The findings are mixed. Duvall and Motz find, for instance, that social adjustment of urban and rural adolescent girls is similar. Evelyn M. Duvall and Annabelle B. Motz, "Are County Girls so Different?" *Rural Sociology* 10 (September 1945), pp. 263–274. Polansky is "impressed by the extent to which phenomena in our rural mountains parallel those reported by urban sociologists and social psychologists. Norman A. Polansky, "Powerlessness Among Rural Appalachian Youth," *Rural Sociology* 34 (June 1969), pp. 219–222. Others find rural-urban differences insignificant or diminishing. Michael F. Nolan and John F. Galliher, "Rural Sociological Research and Social Policy: Hard Data, Hard Times," *Rural Sociology* 38 (September 1973), pp. 491–499. Some find ruralism is important only in combination with other variables. J. Lynn England, W. Eugene Gibbons, and Barry L. Johnson, "The Impact of a Rural Environment on Values," *Rural Sociology* 44 (Spring 1979), p. 119–136. But Keyes indicates that there is an association between varying levels of urbanism and social institutions found in the community. Fenton Keyes, "The Correlation of Social Phenomena with Community Size," *Social Forces* 36 (May 1958), pp. 311–315.

Other studies find differences based on the rural-urban distinctions. Fertility, overall value structure, expenditure patterns of older people, personality adjustment, intelligence, attitudes toward civil rights, occupational aspirations, community satisfaction, marriage and divorce, and concern for the environment have all been shown to vary with the size of place of residence. See J. E. Veevers, "Rural-Urban Variation in the Incidence of Childlessness," *Rural Sociology* 36 (December 1971), pp. 547–553; John B. Stephenson, "Is Everyone Going Modern? A Critique and a Suggestion for Measuring Modernism," *American Journal of Sociology* 74 (November 1968), pp. 265–275; Sidney Goldstein, "Urban and Rural Differentials in Consumer Patterns of the Aged, 1960–61," *Rural Sociology* 31 (September 1966), pp. 333–345; A. O. Haller and Carole Ellis Wolff, "Personality Orientations of Farm, Village, and Urban Boys," *Rural Sociology* 27 (March 1962), pp. 275–293; Wilma B. Sanders, R. Traus Osborne, and J. E. Greene, "Intelligence and Academic Performance of College Students of Urban, Rural, and Mixed Backgrounds," *Journal of Educational Research* 49 (November 1955), pp. 185–193; Hart M. Nelson and Raytha L. Yokely, "Civil Rights Attitudes of Rural and Urban Presbyterians," *Rural Sociology* 35 (June 1970), pp. 161–174; Lee Taylor and Gordon Bultena, "Occupational Aspirations and Indecisiveness of Students in an Urban and Rural Consolidated High School," *Southwestern Sociological Proceedings* (1962), pp. 85–94. See also Lee Taylor, *Urban-Rural Problems* (Belmont, Calif.: Dickenson Publishing Co., 1968), p. 34; Michael K. Miller and Kelly W. Crader, "Rural-Urban Differences in Two Dimensions of Community Satisfaction," *Rural Sociology* 44 (Fall 1979), pp. 489–504; Karen Woodrow, Donald W. Hastings, and Edward J. Tu, "Rural-Urban Patterns of Marriage, Divorce, and Mortality: Tennessee, 1970," *Rural Sociology* 43 (Spring 1978), pp. 70–84; Kenneth R. Tremblay, Jr., and Riley E. Dunlap, "Rural-Urban Residence and Concern with Environmental Quality: A Replication and Extension," *Rural Sociology* 43 (Fall 1978), pp. 474–491.

The view that rural-urban differences are real but that they don't matter much is popular. Richard Dewey, "The Rural-Urban Continuum: Real but Relatively Unimportant," *American Journal of Sociology* 66 (July 1960), pp. 60–66; Fern K. Willits and Robert C. Bealer, "The Utility of Residence for Differentiating Social Conservation [sic; Conservatism] in Rural Youth," *Rural Sociology* 28 (March 1963), pp. 70–80; T. E. Lasswell, "Social Class and Size of Community," *American Journal of Sociology* 64 (March 1959), pp. 505–508.

Finally, there is a series of studies that seeks to explore the causal chain between the differences in life-style characteristics that accompany variations in size of place of residence and behavioral patterns. Lee G. Burchinal, "Differences in Educational and Occupational Aspirations of Farm, Small-Town, and City Boys," *Rural Sociology* 26 (June 1961), pp. 107–121. Orientations toward the environment, support of George Wallace in the South, use of health care facilities, attitudes toward pesticides, and personality traits are some of the variables that have been associated with size of place of residence but have lost their linkage to ruralism when other factors such as income, birth order, education, age, and occupation have been controlled. Frederick H. Buttel and William L. Flinn, "The Structure of Support for the Environmental Movement, 1968–1970," *Rural Sociology* 39 (Spring 1974), pp. 56–69; Harold G. Grasmick, "Rural Culture and the Wallace Movement in the South," *Rural Sociology* 39 (Winter 1974), pp. 454–470; Bert L. Ellenbogen and George D. Lowe, "Health Care 'Styles' in Rural and Urban Areas," *Rural Sociology* 33 (September 1968), pp. 300–312; Rodolfo N. Salcedo, Hadley Read, James F. Evans, and Ana C. Kong, "Rural-Urban Perspectives of the Pesticide Industry," *Rural Sociology* 36 (December 1971), pp. 554–562; Ivan F. Nye, "Adolescent-Parent Adjustment: Rurality as a Variable," *Rural Sociology* 15 (December 1950), pp. 334–339.

The studies on rural-urban differences fall into three time slots. The first was the period generally prior to World War II when the majority view was that there were unimportant differences. Two examples of this view are C. P. Loomis and J. A. Beagle, *Rural Social Systems* (New York: Prentice-Hall, 1950); and Pitirim A. Sorokin and Carle C. Zimmerman, *Principles of Rural-Urban Sociology* (New York: Holt, Rinehart and Winston, 1929).

The second time period was the 1950s and the early 1960s when a revisionist school appeared. Two of the early revisionist-school studies were Irving A. Spaulding, "Serendipity and the Rural-Urban Continuum," *Rural Sociology* 16 (March 1951), pp. 29–36, and Howard W. Beers, "Rural-Urban Differences: Some Evidence from Public Opinion Polls," *Rural Sociology* 18 (December 1953), pp. 1–11. By the mid-1960s several more studies had appeared, which in varying ways question the utility of using size of place as a variable in the social sciences. Some of these are Charles M. Bonjean and Robert L. Lineberry, "Size of Place Analysis: Another Reconsideration," *Western Political Quarterly* 24 (December 1971), pp. 713–718; Kenneth E. Boulding, "The Death of the City: A Frightened Look at Post Civilization," in Oscar Handlin and John Burchard, eds., *The Historian and the City* (Cambridge: MIT Press and Harvard University Press, 1963); Lee G. Burchinal, Glenn R. Hawkins, and Bruce Gardner, "Adjustment Characteristics of Rural and Urban Children," *American Sociological Review* 22 (February 1957), pp. 81–87; Otis Dudley Duncan, "Community Size and the Rural-Urban Continuum," in Paul Hatt and Albert J. Reiss, Jr., eds., *Cities and Society* (Glencoe, Ill.: Free Press, 1956); Robert S. Friedman, "The Urban-Rural Conflict Revisited," *Western Political Quarterly* 14 (June 1961), pp. 481–495; Glenn V. Fuguitt, "The City and Countryside," *Rural Sociology* 28 (September 1963), pp. 246–261; and Herbert Kotter, "Changes in Urban-Rural Relationships in Industrialized Society," *International Journal of Comparative Sociology* 4 (December 1963), pp. 121–129.

The third time slot is the current period in which the view that differences do matter has become important again. Examples include Leo F. Schnore, "The Rural-Urban Variable: An Urbanite's Perspective," *Rural Sociology* 31 (June 1966), pp. 131–143; and George D. Lowe and Charles W. Peek, "Location and Lifestyle: The Comparative Explanatory Ability of Urbanism and Rurality," *Rural Sociology* 39 (Fall 1974), pp. 392–420. During this period, rural-urban differences have been found to be associated with general satisfaction, happiness, and fear among the elderly; personal adjustment among children; and a sense of community satisfaction. Lawrence M. Hynson, Jr., "Rural-Urban Differences in Satisfaction Among the Elderly," *Rural Sociology* 40 (Spring 1975), pp. 64–66; Hart M. Nelson and Stuart E. Storey, "Personality Adjustment of Rural and Urban Youth: The Formation of a Rural Disadvantaged Subculture," *Rural Sociology* 34 (March 1969), pp. 43–55; and Ronald L. Johnson and Edward Knop, "Rural-Urban Differentials in Community Satisfaction," *Rural Sociology* 35 (December 1970), pp. 544–548.

Ruralism And Politics

Ruralism and Political Participation

A central question relates to rural-urban differences in political activity and the interplay of SES forces on these differences. Studies that analyze the SES component in the rural context are Robert E. Agger and Vincent Ostrom, "Political Participation in a Small Community," in Samuel J. Eldersveld and Morris Janovitz, eds., *Political Behavior* (Glencoe, Ill.: Free Press, 1956), pp. 138–148, and Phillip Althoff and Samuel C. Patterson, "Political Activism in a Rural County," *Midwest Journal of Political Science* 10 (February 1966), pp. 39–51. Within neighborhoods Huckfeldt finds that a high-status ecology promotes more participation among high-status persons. R. Robert Huckfeldt, "Political Participation and the Neighborhood Social Context," *American Journal of Political Science* 23 (August 1979), pp. 579–592.

Cross-polity studies are divided on the impact of urbanism on voter turnout and participation. Some of those studies that score urbanites as more involved are Phillips Cutwright, "National Political Development: Its Measurement and Social Correlates," in Nelson W. Polsby et al., *Politics and Social Life* (Boston: Houghton Mifflin Co., 1963), pp. 569–581; Karl W. Deutsch, "Social Mobilization and Political Development," *American Political Science Review* 55 (September 1961), pp. 493–514; Daniel Lerner, *The Passing of Traditional Society* (Glencoe, Ill.: Free Press, 1958); Seymour Martin Lipset, *Political Man: The Social Basis of Politics* (Garden City, N.Y.: Doubleday, 1960); Samuel P. Huntington, *Political Order in Changing Societies* (New Haven: Yale University Press, 1968).

Those studies that question the notion that rural areas are seedbeds for apathy and/or urbanism increases participation are Wayne A. Cornelius, Jr., "Urbanization as an Agent in Latin American Political Instability: The Case of Mexico," *American Political Science Review* 63 (September 1969), p. 833–857; Mark Kesselman, "French Local Politics: A Statistical Examination of Grass Roots Consensus," *American Political Science Review* 60 (December 1966), pp. 963–973; Bradley M. Richardson, "Urbanization and Political Participation: The Case of Japan," *American*

Political Science Review 67 (June 1973), pp. 433–452; Sidney Tarrow, "The Urban-Rural Cleavage in Political Involvement: The Case of France," *American Political Science Review* 65 (June 1971), pp. 341–357; Jae-On Kim and B. C. Koh, "Electoral Behavior and Social Development in South Korea: An Aggregate Data Analysis of Presidential Elections," *Journal of Politics* 34 (August 1972), pp. 825–859. Two of the more explicit denials of the relationship are Alex Inkeles, "Participant Citizenship in Six Developing Countries," *American Political Science Review* 63 (December 1969), pp. 1120–1141; and Norman H. Nie, G. Bingham Powell, Jr., and Kenneth Prewitt, "Social Structure and Political Participation: Developmental Relationships, II," *American Political Science Review* 63 (September 1969), pp. 808–832.

Studies that question the urban-participation linkage in the United States are Gerald W. Johnson, "Research Note on Political Correlates of Voter Participation: A Deviant Case Analysis," *American Political Science Review* 65 (September 1971), pp. 768–775. Johnson's correlation between urbanism and participation registers consistent, negative coefficients for West Virginia counties. Alan D. Monroe, "Urbanism and Voter Turnout: A Note on Some Unexpected Findings," *American Journal of Political Science* 21 (February 1977), pp. 71–78; Warren E. Stickle, "Ruralite and Farmer in Indiana; Independent, Sporadic Voter, Country Bumpkin?" *Agricultural History* 48 (October 1974), pp. 543–570. The two essential books published in the 1970s are Lester W. Milbrath and M. L. Goel, *Political Participation,* 2d ed. (Chicago: Rand McNally, 1977), and Sidney Verba and Norman H. Nie, *Participation in America: Political Democracy and Social Equality* (New York: Harper and Row, 1972). An excellent new volume has appeared as this book goes to print. Using survey research tools Wolfinger and Rosenstone comment on the center-periphery model, which has special relevance for rural politics, as follows. "These findings lead us to think that there are limits to theories of turnout that emphasize 'center-periphery' differences." Raymond E. Wolfinger and Steven J. Rosenstone, *Who Votes?* (New Haven: Yale University Press, 1980), p. 30.

Ruralism and Party Competition

The question in studying ruralism and party competition is one of locating the optimal environment for political competition. Many argue that a critical antecedent variable is missing in rural areas, that of socioeconomic diversity. Thomas R. Dye, *Politics in States and Communities,* 3d ed. (Englewood Cliffs, N.J.: Prentice-Hall, 1977); Heinz Eulau, "The Ecological Basis of Party Systems: The Case of Ohio," *Midwest Journal of Political Science* 1 (August 1957), pp. 125–135; Malcolm E. Jewell, *Legislative Representation in the Contemporary*

South (Durham, N.C.: Duke University Press, 1967); and Duane Lockard, *New England State Politics* (Princeton: Princeton University Press, 1959). Lee Sigeleman summarizes much of the modernization literature in cross-polity analysis in *Modernization and the Political System: A Critique and Preliminary Empirical Analysis* (Beverly Hills, Calif.: Sage Publications, 1971); see also John L. Sullivan, "Political Correlates of Social, Economic, and Religious Diversity in the American States," *Journal of Politics* 35 (February 1973), pp. 70–84. Others believe that party competition may exist or emerge in the absence of socioeconomic diversity. Ira Sharkansky, "Economic Development, Representative Mechanisms, Administrative Professionalism, and Public Policies: A Comparative Analysis of Within-State Distributions of Economic and Political Traits," *Journal of Politics* 33 (February 1971), pp. 112–132.

For developmental analysis, see David R. Cameron, "Toward a Theory of Political Mobilization," *Journal of Politics* 36 (February 1974), pp. 138–171; and Everett Carll Ladd, Jr., *American Political Parties* (New York: W. W. Norton, 1970). Additional sources are Leon Epstein, "Size of Place and the Division of the Two-Party Vote in Wisconsin," *Western Political Quarterly* 9 (March 1956), pp. 138–150; David Gold and John R. Schmidhauser, "Urbanization and Party Competition: The Case of Iowa," *Midwest Journal of Political Science* 4 (February 1960), pp. 62–75; and Phillips Cutwright, "Urbanism and Competitive Party Politics," *Journal of Politics* 25 (May 1963), pp. 552–564. The study with the widest data base is Charles M. Bornjean and Robert L. Lineberry, "The Urbanization-Party Competition Hypothesis: A Comparison of All United States Counties," *Journal of Politics* 32 (May 1970), pp. 305–321. Finally two articles that provide excellent biographical material are Philip Coulter and Glen Gordon, "Urbanization and Party Competition," *Western Political Quarterly* 21 (June 1968), pp. 274–288; and Billy J. Franklin, "Urbanization and Party Competition: A Note on Shifting Conceptualization and a Report on Further Data," *Social Forces* 49 (June 1971), 544–549.

The Reapportionment Revolution

There is no better litmus test for the meaning of ruralism as it impacts on the political process than to measure the effect of the reapportionment wave triggered by *Baker* v. *Carr*. There were a great many articles in journals of opinion establishing the essential hypothesis that an unfair ratio of rural legislators meant trouble for the cities. Among the articles are J. Anthony Lukas, "Barnyard Government in Maryland," *Reporter* 26 (April 1962), pp. 31–34, and also in Glendon Schubert, ed., *Reapportionment* (New York: Charles Scribner and Sons, 1965), pp. 55–58;

Helen Hill Miller, "The City Vote and the Rural Monopoly," *Atlantic Monthly* 210 (October 1962), pp. 61–65; Richard L. Neuberger, "Our Rotten Borough Legislatures," *Survey* 86 (February 1950), p. 54; Richard Lee Strout, "The Next Election Is Already Rigged," *Harper's* (November 1959), pp. 35–40; "Baker vs. Carr" (editorial), *Commonweal* 52 (April 13, 1962), pp. 52–53; "Justice for Metropolis" (editorial), *America* 101 (July 18, 1959), pp. 522–523; "People vs. Pigs," *Newsweek* 58 (July 24, 1961), p. 25; "Unrepresentatives" (editorial), *New Republic* (January 29, 1962), pp. 3–5; Editorial, *Atlantic Monthly* 208 (December 1961), p. 4.

A series of studies in the 1960s that compared the policy outputs of malapportioned and well-apportioned states generally disagreed with the popular wisdom. See David Brady and Douglas Edmonds, "One Man, One Vote—So What?" *Trans-Action* 4 (March 1967), pp. 41–46; Thomas R. Dye, "Malapportionment and Public Policy in the States," *Journal of Politics* 27 (August 1965), pp. 586–601; Robert E. Firestine, "The Impact of Reapportionment Upon Local Government Aid Receipts Within Large Metropolitan Areas," *Social Science Quarterly* 54 (September 1973), pp. 394–402; Richard I. Hofferbert, "The Relation Between Public Policy and Some Structural and Environmental Variables in the American States," *American Political Science Review* 60 (March 1966), pp. 73–82; Herbert Jacob, "The Consequences of Malapportionment: A Note of Caution," *Social Forces* 43 (December 1964), pp. 256–261; John P. White and Norman C. Thomas, "Urban and Rural Representation and State Legislative Apportionment," *Western Political Quarterly* 17 (December 1964), pp. 724–741; A. Spencer Hill, "The Reapportionment Decisions: A Return to Dogma?" *Journal of Politics* 31 (February 1969), pp. 186–213; William de Rubertis, "How Apportionment with Selected Demographic Variables Relates to Policy Orientation," *Western Political Quarterly* 22 (December 1969), pp. 904–920; George W. Carey, "A Comparison of Rural and Urban State Legislators in Iowa and Indiana," in James B. Kessler, ed., *Empirical Studies of Indiana Politics* (Bloomington: Indiana University Press, 1970).

Earlier, amid the din of an urban nation crying for reform, several scholars had sounded dissonant tones on the importance of reapportionment. See for example John B. McConaughy, "Certain Personality Factors of State Legislators in South Carolina," *American Political Science Review* 44 (June 1950), pp. 897–902; Murray C. Havens, *City vs. Farm* (Tuscaloosa: University of Alabama Press, 1957); David R. Derge, "Metropolitan and Outstate Alignments in Illinois and Missouri Legislative Delegations," *American Political Science Review* 52 (December 1958), pp. 1051–1065; Robert J. Pitchell, "Reapportionment as a Control of Voting in California," *Western Political Quarterly* 14

(March 1961), pp. 214–215; Robert S. Friedman, "The Reapportionment Myth," *National Civic Review* 49 (April 1960), pp. 184–188; Daniel P. Moynihan, "The Question of the States," *Commonweal* 77 (October 12, 1962), pp. 65–68; Duane Lockard, *The Politics of State and Local Government* (New York: Macmillan Company, 1963), p. 319. See also "No Miraculous Cure," *National Civic Review* 54 (October 1965), p. 464, and Alfred de Grazia, "Righting the Wrongs of Representation," *State Government* 38 (Spring 1965), pp. 113–117.

One of the unabashed supporters of rural overrepresentation was Noel Perrin, "In Defense of Country Votes," *Yale Review* 52 (Autumn 1962), pp. 16–24. Other sources that analyze a single component of the importance of reapportionment are Robert S. Erikson, "The Partisan Impact of State Legislative Reapportionment," *Midwest Journal of Political Science* 15 (February 1971), pp. 57–71; H. George Frederickson and Yong Hyo Cho, "Legislative Apportionment and Fiscal Policy in the American States," *Western Political Quarterly* 27 (March 1974) pp. 5–37; Charles Press, "One Man–One Vote and the Farmer," *Farmer Policy Forum* 17 (1964-65), pp. 9–14. In an ambitious and valuable volume there is an attempt to assess the effect of reapportionment in the West—Eleanore Bushnell, ed., *Impact of Reapportionment on the Thirteen Western States* (Salt Lake City: University of Utah Press, 1970). Other studies focus on individual states. Examples are James J. Best, "The Impact of Reapportionment on the Washington House of Representatives," in James A. Robinson, ed., *State Legislative Innovation* (New York: Praeger Publishers, 1973), pp. 136–182; Alan L. Clem, "Distorted Democracy: Malapportionment in the South Dakota Government," *Public Affairs* (November 1964); Clarice McD. Davis, "State Legislative Malapportionment and Roll-Call Voting in Texas," *Public Affairs Comment* 11 (May 1965), pp. 1–4; and Allan Dines, "A Reapportioned State," *National Civic Review* 55 (February 1966), p. 7. Dines studied Colorado, where reapportionment is said to have "created an atmosphere for action." Other examples include Karl H. Dixon, "Reapportionment and Reform: The Florida Example," *National Civic Review* 62 (November 1973), p. 548; William C. Havard and Loren P. Beth, *The Politics of Misrepresentation: Rural-Urban Conflict in the Florida Legislature* (Baton Rouge: Louisiana State University Press, 1962); Richard Lehne, *Reapportionment of the New York Legislature: Impact and Issues* (New York: National Municipal League, 1972); Bruce W. Robeck, "Legislative Partisanship, Constituency, and Malapportionment: The Case of California," *American Political Science Review* 66 (December 1972), pp. 1246–1255; and Ira Sharkansky, "Reapportionment and Roll Call Voting: The Case of the Georgia Legislature," *Social Science Quarterly* 51 (June 1970), pp. 129–137.

There are several early general works and editions of readings and articles that are very helpful, including Gordon E. Baker, *Rural vs. Urban Political Power* (Garden City, N.Y.: Doubleday, 1955), and Malcolm E. Jewell, *The Politics of Reapportionment* (New York: Atherton Press, 1962). These works were followed by Gordon Baker, *The Reapportionment Revolution* (New York: Random House, 1965), and Glendon Schubert, ed., *Reapportionment* (New York: Charles Scribner and Sons, 1965). As new apportionment plans were set in place, analysis cautiously began. See Calvin B. T. Lee, *One Man One Vote* (New York: Charles Scribner and Sons, 1967); Marjorie G. Fribourg, *The Reapportionment Crises* (New York: Public Affairs Committee, 1967); Howard D. Hamilton, ed., *Reapportioning Legislatures* (Columbus, Ohio: Charles E. Merrill Books, 1966); Robert B. McKay, *Reapportionment Reappraised* (New York: Century Fund, 1968); L. Papayanopoulas, ed., *Democratic Representation and Apportionment* (New York: New York Academy of Science, 1973); and Nelson W. Polsby, ed., *Reapportionment in the 1970's* (Berkeley: University of California Press, 1971). See also A. Spencer Hill, "The Reapportionment Decisions: A Return to Dogma?" *Journal of Politics* 31 (February 1969), pp. 186–213; and Yong Hyo Cho and H. George Frederickson, "The Effects of Reapportionment: Subtle, Selective, Limited," *National Civic Review* 63 (July 1974), pp. 357–362. For an excellent treatment of the reapportionment discussions and their impact on political systems, see Ward Y. Elliott, *The Rise of Guardian Democracy* (Cambridge, Mass.: Harvard University Press, 1974). See also Nathan Glazer, "Towards an Imperial Judiciary?" *Public Interest* (Fall 1975), pp. 120–121. A recent, thorough study of the effects of reapportionment on a comparative state basis is Timothy G. O'Rourke, *The Impact of Reapportionment* (New Brunswick, N.J.: Transaction Books, 1980).

Other Sources on Ruralism

The definitional properties of ruralism and the "rural-urban continuum" have been long debated. The following works are helpful: Robert C. Bealer, Fern K. Willits, and William P. Kuvlesky, "The Meaning of 'Rurality' in American Society: Some Implications and Alternative Definitions," *Rural Sociology* 30 (September 1965), pp. 255–266; William W. Falk and Thomas K. Pinhey, "Making Sense of the Concept Rural and Doing Rural Sociology: An Interpretive Perspective," *Rural Sociology* 43 (Winter 1978), pp. 547–558; Fern K. Willits and Robert C. Bealer, "An Evaluation of a Composite Definition of Rurality," *Rural Sociology* 32 (June 1967), pp. 165–177; and Louis Wirth, "Urbanism as a Way of Life," *American Journal of Sociology* 44 (July 1938), pp. 1–24.

On the problem of the interface of rural and urban in the postmodern period the following sources have been most helpful: Theodore R. Anderson and Jane Collier, "Metropolitan Dominance and the Rural Hinterland," *Rural Sociology* 21 (June 1956), pp. 152–157; Kenneth E. Boulding, "The Death of a City: A Frightened Look at Post-Civilization," in Oscar Handlin and John Burchard, eds., *The Historian and the City* (Cambridge, Mass.: MIT Press and Harvard University Press, 1963); William Christian, Jr., and William Braden, "Rural Migration and the Gravity Model," *Rural Sociology* 31 (March 1966), pp. 73–80; Robert L. Carroll and Raymond H. Wheeler, "Metropolitan Influence on the Rural-Non Farm Population," *Rural Sociology* 31 (March 1966), pp. 64–73; Glenn V. Fuguitt, "The City and Countryside," *Rural Sociology* 28 (September 1963), pp. 246–261; Glenn V. Fuguitt, "County Seat Status as a Factor in Small Town Growth and Decline," *Social Forces* 44 (December 1965), pp. 245–251; Lee Taylor and Arthur R. Jones, Jr., *Rural Life and Urbanized Society* (New York: Oxford University Press, 1964); Arthur J. Vidich and Joseph Bensman, *Small Town in Mass Society,* rev. ed. (Princeton: Princeton University Press, 1968); W. Keith Warner, "Rural Society in a Post-Industrial Age," *Rural Sociology* 39 (Fall 1974), pp. 306–318; Larry R. Whiting, ed., *Communities Left Behind: Alternatives for Development* (Ames: Iowa State University Press, 1974); Larry R. Whiting, ed., *Rural Industrialization: Problems and Potentials* (Ames: Iowa State University Press, 1974).

For an excellent selection of readings on the linkage between the agricultural subsystem and modern society, see "Farming in an Urban Society," in Louis H. Douglas, ed., *Agrarianism in American History* (Lexington, Mass.: D. C. Heath and Company, 1969). An early article that deals with a similar subject is William L. Colvert, "The Technological Revolution in Agriculture, 1910–1955," *Agricultural History* 30 (January 1956), pp. 18–27. For a general comment on some of the forces shaping rural politics in the current period, with an emphasis on reapportionment, see David Knoke and Constance Henry, "Political Structure of Rural America," *Annals* 429 (January 1977), pp. 51–62. See also the readings in Suzanne Fremon and Morrow Wilson (eds.), *Rural America* (New York: H. W. Wilson Co., 1976).

The Three States

Montana

There are several excellent overviews of Montana's politics in the modern period. Among these is Neal R. Peirce, *The Mountain States of*

America (New York: W. W. Norton, 1972). The title for his chapter on
Montana is taken from Joseph Kinsey Howard's history, *Montana:
High, Wide, and Handsome* (New Haven: Yale University Press, 1959).
But Pierce adds, poignantly, the adjective "remote." Other overviews in-
clude Thomas Payne, "Montana: Politics Under the Copper Dome," in
Frank H. Jonas, ed., *Politics in the American West* (Salt Lake City:
University of Utah Press, 1969); Ellis Waldron, "Montana," in Eleanore
Bushnell, ed., *Impact of Reapportionment on the Thirteen Western
States* (Salt Lake City: University of Utah Press, 1970); and Ellis
Waldron, "Montana," in JeDon Emenhiser, *Rocky Mountain Urban
Politics* (Logan: Utah State University Press, 1971). See also the last
chapter of Michael P. Malone and Richard B. Roeder, *Montana: A
History of Two Centuries* (Seattle: University of Washington Press,
1976). For an overview of legislative politics, see Susanne A. Stoiber,
ed., *Legislative Politics in the Rocky Mountain West* (Boulder, Colo.:
Bureau of Government Research, University of Colorado, 1967). A more
dated chapter on Montana is Newton Carl Abbott, "Montana: Political
Enigma of the Northern Rockies," in Thomas C. Connelly, *Rocky
Mountain Politics* (Albuquerque: University of New Mexico Press,
1959).

A series of articles published in the *Western Political Quarterly* dealing
with elections in Montana is most useful. Jules A. Karlen analyzes the
elections of 1948 and 1952, Thomas Payne contributes an article dealing
with elections from 1954 to 1968, and an article for 1970 is written by
Brad E. Hansworth. For the 1978 election see Richard L. Hains, Lauren
S. McKinsey, and Jerry W. Calvert, "Montana," in B. Oliver Walter,
ed., *Politics in the West: The 1978 Elections* (Laramie, Wyo.: Institute
for Policy Research, University of Wyoming, 1979), pp. 75-89. The articles appear in the odd-numbered years. Much of what we know about
Montana's politics we owe to Ellis Waldron, who published extensively
during the period in state and regional publications such as the *Montana
Business Quarterly,* the *Montana Law Review,* and *Montana Public Affairs.* The last is published by the Bureau of Government Research at the
University of Montana at Missoula and is the best outlet available for
scholarship on Montana politics. Jerry Calvert at Montana State University in Bozeman has penned several valuable articles on Montana's
politics, especially legislative politics. See Jerry W. Calvert, "The Social
and Ideological Bases of Support for Environmental Legislation: An Examination of Public Attitudes and Legislative Action," *Western Political
Quarterly* 32 (September 1979), pp. 327-337, and "Revolving Doors:
Volunteerism in State Legislatures," *State Government* 52 (Autumn
1979), pp. 174-182. By far the best source book on Montana

politics is Ellis Waldron and Paul B. Wilson, *Atlas of Montana Elections 1889-1976* (Missoula: University of Montana Press, 1978). This volume contains socioeconomic data, election results for statewide offices by county, referenda votes, and state legislative results. It also includes maps, tables, and an excellent index and may well be the best document of its kind in existence for any state.

Mississippi

For the state of Mississippi there are substantially more articles published in academic journals than for Montana and Vermont. It is also helpful that many studies have been published on the South as a region that give, in varying degrees of importance, insight into Mississippi. To begin, however, there is still no way to beat V. O. Key's chapter on Mississippi. See V. O. Key, Jr., *Southern Politics in State and Nation* (New York: Alfred A. Knopf, 1949). For a more contemporary analysis see Neal R. Pierce, *The Deep South States of America* (New York: W. W. Norton, 1974); Numan V. Bartley and Hugh D. Graham, *Southern Politics and the Second Reconstruction* (Baltimore, Md.: Johns Hopkins University Press, 1975); and Jack Bass and Walter De Vries, *The Transformation of Southern Politics* (New York: Basic Books, 1976). In the latter work, see especially the chapter on Mississippi "Out of the Past." A third important chapter on Mississippi is Charles W. Fortenberry and F. Glenn Abney, "Mississippi, Unreconstructed and Unredeemed," in William C. Havard, ed., *The Changing Politics of the South* (Baton Rouge: Louisiana State University Press, 1972). For a focus on the legislators see Charles W. Fortenberry and Edward H. Hobbs, "The Mississippi Legislature," in Alex B. Lacy, Jr., ed., *Power in American State Legislatures* (New Orleans: Tulane University, 1967). A source for several aspects of Mississippi's politics is David M. Landry and Joseph B. Parker, eds., *Mississippi Government and Politics in Transition* (Dubuque, Iowa: Kendall/Hunt Publishing Company, 1976).

Among the regional studies that I have found useful are E. C. Barksdale, "The Power Structure and Southern Gubernatorial Conservatism," in Harold M. Hollingsworth, ed., *Essays on Recent Southern Politics* (Austin: University of Texas Press, 1970); Monroe Lee Billington, *The Political South in the 20th Century* (New York: Charles Scribner and Sons, 1975); Earl Black, "Southern Governors and Political Change: Campaign Stances on Racial Segregation and Economic Development, 1950-69," *Journal of Politics* 33 (August 1971), pp. 703-734; Bruce A. Campbell, "Patterns of Change in the Partisan Loyalties of Native Southerners: 1952-1972," *Journal of Politics* 39 (August 1977), pp. 730-763; David Campbell and Joe R. Feagin, "Black

Politics in the South: A Descriptive Analysis," *Journal of Politics* 37 (February 1975), pp. 129–162; Bradley C. Canon, "Factionalism in the South: A Test of Theory and a Revisitation of V. O. Key," *American Journal of Political Science* 22 (November 1978), pp. 833–848; Carol Cassel, "Change in Electoral Participation in the South," *Journal of Politics* 41 (August 1979), 907–917; Bernard Cosman, *Five States for Goldwater* (University: University of Alabama Press, 1966); Bernard Cosman, "Presidential Republicanism in the South, 1960," *Journal of Politics* 24 (May 1962), pp. 303–322; Lester M. Salamon, "Leadership and Modernization: The Emerging Black Political Elite in the American South," *Journal of Politics* 35 (August 1973), pp. 615–646; Louis M. Seagull, *Southern Republicanism* (New York: John Wiley and Sons, 1975)—a thorough and valuable empirical contribution; Allen P. Sandles, ed., *Changes in the Contemporary South* (Durham, N.C.: Duke University Press, 1963); Donald S. Strong, "Further Reflections on Southern Politics," *Journal of Politics* 33 (May 1971), pp. 239–256; and George Brown Tindall, *The Disruption of the Solid South* (Athens: University of Georgia Press, 1972).

We are fortunate to have several good articles on Mississippi politics published in the journals, especially the *Journal of Politics*. This kind of material is not available in any quantity for Vermont and Montana. Among the pieces I found particularly useful are F. Glenn Abney, "Factors Relating to Negro Voter Turnout in Mississippi," *Journal of Politics* 36 (November 1974), pp. 1057–1063; Sam Kernell, "Comment: A Reevaluation of Black Voting in Mississippi," *American Political Science Review* 67 (December 1973), pp. 1307–1318; John R. Skates, Jr., "World War II as a Watershed in Mississippi History," *Journal of Mississippi History* 37 (May 1975); Lester M. Salamon, "Mississippi Post Mortem: The 1971 Elections," *New South* 27 (Winter 1972), pp. 43–47; Lester M. Salamon and Stephen Van Evera, "Fear, Apathy, and Discrimination: A Test of Three Explanations of Political Participation," *American Political Science Review* 67 (December 1973), pp. 1288–1306; Raymond Tatalovich, "Friends and Neighbors Voting: Mississippi, 1943–1973," *Journal of Politics* 37 (August 1975), pp. 807–814; and William F. Winter, "New Directions in Politics, 1948–1956," *Journal of Mississippi History* 37 (May 1975).

There are several other sources of a more general nature that are strongly recommended for information on Mississippi. Loewen and Sallis's controversial history, although written as a textbook for high school audiences, is excellent—James W. Loewen and Charles Sallis, eds., *Mississippi Conflict and Change* (New York: Pantheon Books, 1974). Other sources include Albert D. Kirwan, *Revolt of the Rednecks:*

Mississippi Politics, 1876–1925 (Lexington: University of Kentucky Press, 1951), and Robert Sherill, *Gothic Politics in the Deep South* (New York: Grossman Publishers, 1968). Two continuing publications that help in understanding Mississippi politics are *Mississippi's Business* (University of Mississippi, Bureau of Business and Economic Research) and the quarterly, *Public Administration Survey* (University of Mississippi, Bureau of Government Research). The Mississippi Research and Development Center of Jackson is an excellent source for up-to-date material. The center publishes, for instance, a *Handbook of Selected Data for Mississippi,* which is very good. The *Mississippi Official and Statistical Register,* compiled and published by the secretary of state in Jackson, is one of the better "blue books" in the country. Of the three states examined in this volume, the public record is the most available and easy to use in Mississippi.

Vermont

Published material on Vermont is scarce. The best treatment of Vermont politics through the 1950s is Duane Lockard, *New England State Politics* (Princeton: Princeton University Press, 1959), but see also Joseph Schlesinger, *How They Became Governor: A Study of Comparative State Politics, 1870–1950* (East Lansing, Mich.: Government Research Bureau, Michigan State University, 1957). Schlesinger's use of Vermont as an example of a particular type of recruitment pattern sheds considerable light on Vermont politics. Other more current sources are George Goodwin, Jr., and Victoria Schuck, eds., *Party Politics in the New England States* (Durham, N.H.: New England Center for Continuing Education, 1968); David R. Mayhew, *Two Party Competition in the New England States* (Amherst, Mass.: Bureau of Government Research, University of Massachusetts, 1967); Frank M. Bryan, "Who Is Legislating?" *National Civic Review* 56 (December 1967), pp. 627–633, 644; Frank M. Bryan, "The Metamorphosis of a Rural Legislature," *Polity* 1 (Winter 1968), pp. 191–211; Frank M. Bryan, "Reducing the Time Lock in the Vermont Constitution: An Analysis of the 1974 Referendum," *Vermont History* 44 (Winter 1976), pp. 38–47; Frank M. Bryan, "Does the Town Meeting Offer an Option for Urban America?" *National Civic Review* 67 (December 1978), pp. 523–527; William J. Smith, "My Poetic Career in Vermont Politics," *Harper's Magazine* 228 (January 1964), pp. 54–62; Robert V. Daniels, Robert H. Daniels, and Helen L. Daniels, "The Vermont Constitutional Referendum of 1969: An Analysis," *Vermont History* 38 (Spring 1970), pp. 152–156; Lyman Jay Gould and Samuel B. Hand, "The Geography of Political Recruitment in Vermont: A View from the Mountains," in Reginald L. Cook, ed., *Growth and Development of Government in Vermont,* Vermont Academy of Arts and Sciences, Occasional Paper no. 5 (Waitsfield, Vt., 1970). The last paper is the best source for Vermont's important "mountain rule." In the 1970s three additional sources appeared. The first, Frank Smallwood, *Free and Independent* (Brattleboro, Vt.: Stephen Greene Press, 1976), is a first-person accounting of how legislative politics in Vermont works. It is also good political science. The other two are Neal R. Peirce, *The New England States* (New York: W. W. Norton, 1976), and Frank M. Bryan, *Yankee Politics in Rural Vermont* (Hanover, N.H.: University Press of New England, 1974).

Political data may be obtained from the *Vermont Legislative and State Manual* and the biennial election statistical reports, *Primary and General Elections,* both published by the secretary of state's office. A valuable source of topographical information and socioeconomic data (broken down by town) is Harold A. Meeks, *The Geographic Regions of Vermont: A Study in Maps,* Geographical Publications at Dartmouth, no. 10 (Hanover, N.H.: Dartmouth College, 1975). Unfortunately Vermont has no bureau of governmental research or public affairs to publish current research like that found in Mississippi's *Public Administration Survey* or *Montana Public Affairs.* Vermont does have an excellent journal of the state's history (*Vermont History*), however, published quarterly that includes contemporary articles on poliitics from time to time.

Index